# My Effin' Life

*Also by Geddy Lee*

GEDDY LEE'S BIG BEAUTIFUL
BOOK OF BASS

# My Effin' Life

# GEDDY LEE

*with Daniel Richler*

HARPER
*An Imprint of HarperCollinsPublishers*

HarperCollins books may be purchased for educational, business,
or sales promotional use. For information, please email the
Special Markets Department at SPsales@harpercollins.com.

FIRST EDITION

*Designed by Headcase Design*
*Layout by Lynne Yeamans*
*Photographic credits on page 510*

Library of Congress Cataloguing-in-Publication Data has been applied for.

ISBN 978-0-06-315941-9

23 24 25 26 27  LBC  6 5 4 3 2

*For my family*
*past, present and future*
*with heaps of love*

*We're only immortal*
*for a limited time*

— NEIL PEART

*As a comic in all seriousness...*

— EUGENE LEVY,
AS *BOBBY BITTMAN*

# PROLOGUE

---

YOU PROBABLY KNOW ME AS GEDDY LEE, BUT my birthname was Gershon Eliezer Weinrib, after my maternal grandfather who was murdered in the Holocaust. As per tradition, my mom, her sister and her brother all named their first-born male children in his honour; my two cousins and I, all of us born within a couple of years of one another, were given that same first name, Gershon.

In the old country my family spoke both Yiddish and Polish, the former being the language they used at home and whenever they didn't want the Poles to understand what they were saying. So my family all had both Yiddish and Polish names, too. Mom, for example, was known as both Manya and Malka. On most of the official documents I've found, their Yiddish names were used but sometimes spelled unrecognizably, as they would have been pronounced by some bureaucrat in the Polish or German government—or, after the Second World War, the International Refugee Organization.

As was the case with my grandfather, whom I've seen referred to as Gershon, Gierszon, Garshon *and* Garszon, identification for the émigrés was never a simple matter. My father's name, for example, had its own set of complications. His full Yiddish name was Moshe Meir ben Aharon Ha Levi, yet in an old passport that I recently discovered, it's spelled out as Moszek Wajnryb and its anglicized

*Ready for work with my toolkit in one hand, hammer
in the other, and of course, to protect my brain, what every
workman needs: a tiny sombrero.*

translation, Morris Weinrib. I'd never even heard the name Moszek before; my mom and our family usually called him Monyek, Moishe or simply Morris.

After eleven days at sea, on December 20, 1948, the ship carrying my parents from Germany docked in Halifax, Canada. They barely spoke any English as they walked down that ramp, so when they registered with customs and immigration, the official came up with anglicized approximations of their names, beginning with the same first letter.[*] Thus Manya became "Mary" and Moishe became "Morris," and in turn when their children were born, they gave us each a Jewish name and its English equivalent: in my case, Gershon and "Gary."

My middle name is Eliezer, but from kindergarten through the end of public school, I answered at roll call to "Gary *Lorne* Weinrib." Confused? I was too! When I turned sixteen and was preparing to apply for a driver's licence and a Canadian Federation of Musicians card, I asked my mother for a copy of my birth certificate, which she duly requested from the government. When it arrived, I opened the envelope and found myself listed as Gary *Lee* Weinrib. WTF?

"Mom," I said, "what's going on here? It says my middle name is Lee, not Lorne!"

She looked away, thought about it for a moment and said with a sheepish laugh, "*Oy, takeh*. Yah. I tink maybe you *vere* Lee . . . Your cousin, *he* was Lorne. I forgot . . ."

Huh? You forgot? I'm not sure which freaked me out more: my sudden loss of identity or the fact that my own mother couldn't remember my effin' name.

I recently discovered that my cousin Gary Rubinstein *was* in fact the actual recipient of the middle name Lorne. The best explanation I have

---

[*] Other new arrivals, meanwhile, were arbitrarily assigned English names. An oft-told fable about a young Jewish boy arriving at Ellis Island in New York has an immigration official asking him his name. The fearful child responds in Yiddish, *Shoin fargesn*, which means "I've already forgotten." And the official writes down . . . Sean Ferguson.

for the mix-up is that, since Mom would have been speaking English for only a few years by the time I was born, the anglicized take on Eliezer was for her just an afterthought. And after she and her siblings made a group decision to name all their first-born male children after my grandfather, she misremembered which middle name they'd agreed on for me.

But wait . . . There's more.

My mom usually called me Garshon at home, saving Gary for when we were out in public. Then one day in my early teens, I was hanging out in front of our house with my pal Burd when she called me indoors for supper.

"Hey," Burd said. "If your name is Gary, how come your mom calls you *Geddy?*"

Mrs. Morris Weinrib
invites you to worship with her
at Sabbath Morning Services
when her son
Gary Lorne
will be called to the reading of the Torah
in honour of his Bar-Mitzvah
בר מצוה
on Saturday, August the sixth
nineteen hundred and sixty-six
at nine o'clock
Beth Emeth Bais Yehuda Synagogue
100 Elder Street
Downsview, Ontario

*My bar mitzvah invitation, and proof that my mother did not know my name.*

"She doesn't," I said. "Her accent only makes it *sound* like that."

He laughed and said, "Well, I'm gonna start callin' you *Geddy* too!" And that was that.

When I turned pro, the musicians' union application form asked for "professional, stage or band name" and I thought, *How cool*. Perhaps I should be ashamed of this, but in my desperation to assimilate into a less ethnic world, I didn't think "Weinrib" sounded very rock and roll. Lennon, Plant, Clapton, Moon and Hendrix—now, *those* were effin' rock star names. (In an attempt at self-justification, I asked myself if Robert Allen Zimmerman had had similar fears before he became Bob Dylan.) So I combined my nickname and rediscovered middle name to create a professional moniker for myself and legitimize my new aspiring identity.

A few years later I took that even further and changed my first name legally to Geddy. By then, even my siblings were calling me Geddy or Ged, so it was all good. To people who asked, I'd explain that it was like in *Leave It to Beaver*, where the kid's real name was Theodore but everyone, even his parents, called him "The Beaver."

At any rate, as you can see, I had two identities right from birth: "Gershon Eliezer" and "Gary Lorne."

And now "Geddy Lee" made three . . .

# CHAPTER 1

OU MAY NATURALLY ASSUME THAT I
grew up in a house rich in music, that my desire to play must
have grown out of musical influences all around me. But
music was in little evidence in my childhood home. The
radio was always on in the car, but I don't recall Dad ever speaking
about music, or mentioning any artists he liked, or even humming
along as we drove. I just thought music didn't register with him.

It wasn't until many years after his death, when I was playing a
show in Detroit and reconnected with the family of his only surviving
brother, Sam, living in the suburbs of the Motor City, that my aunt
Charlotte let slip some startling information.

"It's so nice zat you have become a musician," she said casually.

"After all, so was your father." As my brain reeled, she continued, "Oh, yes, back in za old country, he played za balalaika, I zink. Parties, bar mitzvahs, weddings and so on."

All I could muster was a "*Really?*" It seemed so out of character with the man I thought I'd known that I wasn't ready to believe what she was saying. Was he really a "player"? If so, music must have thrilled him in his early life and . . . oh man, what questions I would have loved to ask him. But foremost in my mind was why my mother had never mentioned it. Seeing as I was a professional musician by that time, you'd think it would have been a pretty vital tidbit to share with me, no? I was more perplexed than angry, and immediately after getting home from that leg of the tour I asked her to verify the story and give me an explanation.

Visibly embarrassed, she proceeded to relay this to me . . . For a while after their liberation my parents lived in Germany at the Displaced Persons camp at Bergen-Belsen, formerly the officers' quarters of the concentration camp where my mom, her mother and her sister had been incarcerated for the final months of the Second World War. (Obviously this is a *much* bigger story, and one that I will be telling you.) They then moved into an apartment in a nearby town, trying to put their lives back together as so many survivors were, and finally committed to emigrating to Canada. As they were readying for departure, my dad declared that he was packing his balalaika, but my mom refused to allow him to "*schlep dat feedel*" across the ocean with them. She regarded the instrument as superfluous, his musical endeavours an indulgence they could ill afford as they forged a new life in a new land. This, she now told me, was a decision she'd long regretted. It was a heartfelt and meaningful confession, and for me a revelation as to my own inherent musical aptitude. I guess I came by it honestly! It's in my effin' genes! Yet, sadly, it also goes a long way to explain my father's silence on all things musical and so many other joys of life. Looking back all those years later, I had to wonder if I'd missed any signs of his musical soul. Perhaps the decision to buy a piano so my sister, Susie, could take lessons was his way of planting a musical seed and, as such, connecting with his buried past. But I will never know.

I was six or so when my parents bought that piano—primarily for Susie, who was two years older than me. Apparently, they thought this was what well-raised Canadian schoolchildren did. A piano teacher was hired, and as Susie did battle with the keyboard, I'd quietly listen to the lesson from the next room or hiding under the table. She came to play well enough to participate in a school recital but didn't stick with it. After I'd enjoyed some success in music, by contrast, my mom liked to relate how, once the teacher had left, I would hop on the piano stool and, by ear, pick out the melodies Susie had been learning— "*pre*fectly," as she insisted. Like any big fish tale, this story was most definitely enhanced over time. I do recall tinkling the ivories after Susie's lessons, but I can assure you I was no Glenn Gould.

IN THE EARLIEST memory I have of my father, the three-year-old me is at the picture window of our Shaw Street home in downtown Toronto, waiting for him to return from work. The winter light of day is fading into dusk—always a melancholy time for me, even now—and I can hear the tinny fanfare of *The Mickey Mouse Club* on television in the background. I watch him coming down our street from the street-car stop at the corner, up the walkway and into the house with a tight smile and a weary *Ich bin shoyn aheym!*—"I'm home, already!" He brushes by me on his way to the kitchen, goes straight to a high-up cupboard and takes out a bottle of Canadian Club rye whiskey. He pours himself a snort, knocks it back, then smacks his lips and makes a sound I always remember with a smile of my own, "Ahh . . ." It was only after he'd had his schnapps* that he felt rid of the day's grime and could pick me up and give me a kiss, playfully scratching my face with his five o'clock stubble. (I can smell the liquor on his breath as I type these words.) Then he puts me down and goes on to do the same to Susie, and finally hugs and kisses our mom.

This handsome man with dark European looks came to Canada in 1948 with the proverbial ten dollars in his pocket and the love of his life on his arm. Moishe and Manya stepped foot on their new homeland as Morris and Mary—anglicized personae for an anglicized world—seeking a fresh start in a dominion unscarred by war and genocide. Morris already had family here: a sister, Rose (Ruchla), who had left Poland for Toronto before the war. For someone who had lost both of his parents, five siblings and countless other family members, all murdered by the Nazis, reuniting with her was the urgent and natural thing to do. Soon after their arrival, the remainder of my mother's family chose to join her and

---

\* I never heard an adult call whiskey "whiskey." What I did hear was *bronfen*, which when I grew up I imagined was a piss take on Bronfman, the Moldovan-Jewish-Canadian family whose bootlegging operation in the Roaring Twenties gave rise to the more respectable Seagram Company. However, it turns out that *bronfen* was originally a Yiddish word for spirits, booze and even moonshine. According to Daniel Okrent, author of *Last Call: The Rise and Fall of Prohibition*, "It was almost fated that the Bronfman family would make its fortune from alcoholic beverages."

Morris in their great Canadian adventure: her sister, Ida; brother, Harold; and their spouses, but most important, her mother, another Rose and the heroine of the Rubinstein tribe, as I will show you in time.

My dad was a loving father, but strict. He had an explosive temper, but it took a lot to trigger it. I pause here, because it seems unfair to mention any of the few bad moments in my short life with him; unfair because the fact that he survived the war, the fact that he made it to the blessed shores of Canada at all, is a miracle. Suffice it to say that I was pretty accomplished at provoking him, and as with most parents of his generation, if any of us kids did something really wrong, well, we'd get an ass-whooping.

We knew that he and Mom cared deeply for each other. They argued sometimes, but hey, that was life in a Jewish home. What seems like shouting to gentiles (or "white people," as we sometimes referred to them) was just a regular conversation around our dinner table. When the whole family got together for the High Holidays . . . my god, it was a shouting match! But the love my parents had for each other won out

*The greenhorns enjoying a typical summer weekend on Toronto Island. My mom is second from the left; my dad, with his dashing pencil moustache, is in the middle.*

over any argument, and they were demonstrative about it. I remember when I was about eight years old, Dad must have been feeling amorous. We were watching TV when he surreptitiously raised his arms above his head to get my mom's attention and made a scratching motion with one hand in the opposite palm. I didn't know what that meant until the kids at school told me it was a signal for sex. Wow, *really?* Ew!

Both our parents worked hard. Motivated to build a new life and raise a family, they held down factory jobs on Spadina Avenue, the hub of Toronto's *shmatte* industry, which, like many greenhorns when they first landed, they referred to simply as "on Spadina." Once my mom had Susie, and me two years later, she stopped work and it was up to my dad to hustle a living and pay the bills. It helped that they also received reparations from the German government, but we were a decidedly working-class family without much spare cash or time for the pursuit of frivolous hobbies like music. With no money for hotels or fancy holidays, we did like many immigrants still do in Toronto: on Sundays we picnicked with my family and cousins on Toronto Island or in High Park. The men would sit on a blanket playing cards and laughing, and I always could hear my dad's voice louder than the others'. They drank Red Cap Ale and Carling Black Label; if you're a Canadian, you'll remember those stubby little bottles. (*I* remember sneaking away once to taste a Black Label, but to me at that age it was just god-awful.)

At one point Dad was hired by a distant cousin to work in his "shoddy mill."[*] He rose in the ranks to a position of some authority, but one day came home ranting that he'd been unfairly treated by his own cousin and in a rage had quit his job. It didn't take him long to bounce back, though. He found a partner and proudly started a business of his own, Lakeview Felt. I remember going there with him and wandering around the wide-boarded floors in awe of the machines and the odors of wool and oil. But that, too, came crashing down when, at the first sign

---

[*] "Shoddy" was inferior material spun from waste woolen cloth and used as stuffing for inexpensive furniture.

of struggle, the partner panicked and made a quick deal behind his back with his former boss. After that betrayal Dad was unemployed for a lengthy period. I remember him being around the house and down in the dumps while he looked for opportunities. Then he decided he no longer wanted to worry about partners or factory life at all and started looking for a small retail business instead. He eventually found a little variety store called Times Square Discount in the burgeoning town of Newmarket, Ontario. That was a pretty bold move on his part, since he'd never worked in retail before, but he ran it well, the locals liked him a lot and there was even an article in the local newspaper reporting on him as a boon to the community.

After the war and throughout my childhood, Toronto's immigrant population was bent on moving north. My mother used to say the Jews were the first, and when they went even farther out the Italians would move in and so on, like hand-me-down neighbourhoods. It was an exodus

*In every early picture I have of me, I look like a total doofus. Either my pants are up to my tits or my corduroys have checkered cuffs, and with that haircut I can imagine people saying, "Oh, the poor boy. Where did they get him from?"*

from Toronto's crowded, grimy downtown, where they had little choice but to live and work when they'd first arrived. The charm of a home with older bones was lost on them. This was the New World, after all; they wanted a New World house with a new kitchen, a two-car garage with a backyard and space between the houses on either side, as different as they could get from the crowded, battered buildings they'd left behind in Europe. Our first house had been a rental on Crawford Street, in what's now known as Little Portugal, which is where my sister, Susie, was born; when I came along we moved to another, one block over, on Shaw Street. By the time I was five they had scraped enough money together to actually buy a house, and that investment took them north to 53 Vinci Crescent, a small bungalow in the North Toronto suburb of Downsview.

Situated on the crescent, we were blessed with a large triangular slice of property and a rare bower of plum and apple and cherry trees in the backyard, a blissful Garden of Eden that transcended our humdrum location. I'd play there with my friends and, towards the end of summer, pick off the ripest fruit. The blackberries were pretty sweet, though the plums were never as ready to pluck as my parents insisted they were. Maybe it was wishful thinking on their part, but most likely they were relishing the fact that, after all they had survived during the war, here they were now in their own home, growing their own fruit, which, ripe or not, tasted of . . . well, freedom. And to this day I, too, have a taste for plums that are a little hard and tart.


**FRUIT TREES ASIDE**, what were these suburbs like? In a word, bland. In two words: mind-numbingly bland. The architecture was unimaginative and repetitive, practically but not aesthetically built, with garages jutting out in front of the houses—the inescapable message being that cars were more important than the people who lived there. The neighbourhoods were virtually treeless, the backyards big but mostly empty except for the occasional swing set, with metal or wooden fences so low you could stick your nose into your neighbours' business. Ironically, many years later when my son, Julian, was the same age and we'd take him to the suburbs to visit my mom, he never wanted to leave. He'd ask, "How come we can't live in the suburbs like Bubbe does? It's so clean and beautiful." Yikes! One child's ceiling is another one's floor, I guess.

To my parents, of course, the burbs must have seemed like heaven, a safe place where their kids were free to play in the streets or ride off on their bikes pretty much anywhere, but the reality was that having survived the war, they had other things on their mind, like building a new life. Today every minute of a child's day is monitored, but in those days there was neither the time nor the inclination for helicoptering. As children themselves under bombardment, they'd have routinely been sent on hazardous missions such as dashing out for loaves of bread; now they'd look up from their work benches only if they heard we'd gotten into serious trouble—and they didn't know the half of what we got up to. I remember one time we rode our bikes over to my new school, when we saw some older boys climbing up a drainpipe to retrieve a load of tennis balls that other kids had lost up there. We climbed up after them—or at least I did, for when I looked around, I realized my pals had decided against it and split. I scrambled about the rooftop and collected as many balls as I could while they shimmied back down. Only then did I fully realize how high up I was, how much scarier it would be to descend than it had been to climb. I tried to slide down a drainpipe but slipped and landed flat on my back with the wind knocked right out of me, gasping up at the vast blue dome of suburban sky. I eventually limped home with my bike and my swag, snuck past my mom, who was preparing dinner, and got into the tub to soak my aching body. I was sore for days. Did anyone notice? Nope, but hey, that was a kid's life back then.

At Faywood Public School I was something of a loner, a quiet kid who rarely got into trouble. I did my schoolwork in my usual unnoticeable and less-than-stellar manner, with no particular passion for any particular subject. My report cards consistently featured comments to the effect of "If he would only apply himself, he could do very well," or "Gary has a tendency to daydream in class." I remember thinking, *What does "apply himself" even mean?* I was a classic underachiever, neither bad enough to fail nor good enough to excel. It's a common mistake to assume that when a kid (or an adult for that matter) is quiet, he must be some sort of deep thinker. In my case I'm afraid it was simply that I didn't have much to say. Not all still waters run deep.

In grade five, I sang in the school choir—that was one thing I can say I really did enjoy. (It will come as no surprise to you that I was a soprano.) I attended practices for the Leonard Bernstein musical *On the Town* as an alternate, meaning I'd only get to perform if someone fell ill. The night of the play, I was sort of dopily wandering around the school looking for where the alternates got to hang out and must have looked lost. A teacher I had previously seen in the schoolyard and pegged for someone pretty mean came up to me and asked what I was up to. I shrugged kinda pathetically. He said, "Follow me!" and took me up to a little room where the spotlights were operated. "How would you like to help out?" he said, and for the two-night run I swung those big scorching Klieg lights to and fro across the stage. It was total magic up there, way more fun than singing in the choir. To see the production from that perspective was surreal, and I loved being part of the crew. My first taste of show business, thanks to a kind man who made me feel useful and valued. Thank you, Mr. Geggie.

Oh, before I continue, here's a piece of trivia from my public school days: there was a boy in my class named Rick Moranis. Yes, *the* Rick Moranis of *Ghostbusters* and *Little Shop of Horrors* fame. We weren't close friends or anything but were in the same class every year from kindergarten right through to grade six. In 1981, by which time he'd become successful as one of the McKenzie Brothers in the "Great White North" sketches on *SCTV*, he asked me to sing the lead on a song called "Take Off!" for their comedy album, *The Great White North*. That would be my first entry into the Top 20 and the biggest hit single of my career!*

Around grade four or five, nerd that I was, I started collecting stamps. My starter collection was a beat-up old album my father gave me. For years, I was under the impression that it had been his own, but I

(BELOW) *"Ten bucks is ten bucks, eh?" So began my life in comedy . . .* (BOTTOM) *My grade five class under the fine tutelage of my distant cousin Mrs. Burns . . . Spot the nerd (me, who else?) but better still, try and spot Rick Moranis.*

---

* The song made #16 on *Billboard*'s US singles chart. Rush's most successful single in the United States (released the following year) was "New World Man," at only #21.

don't remember him ever showing any interest in philately, and knowing what I know now about his life in the aftermath of the war in Europe, I suspect that he either acquired it on the black market there or, most likely, it had been given to him in Canada and he passed it on to me. Anyway, there was a kid in my class I'd go to hobby shops with, whenever I could afford it, to buy stamps from far-off countries. While Canadian stamps looked dull to me, featuring nothing but variations on Queen Elizabeth's profile, I was transported by colourful designs from mysterious and exotic sources like "République du Togo" and "Magyar Posta." I embraced stamps as a way of seeing the world from my bedroom (or my desk during exceptionally boring math classes), and considering my obsessive, almost addictive nature, I think of them now as a gateway drug of sorts. Those stamps were, you could say, my first art collection.

JUST BEFORE I started grade six in the spring of 1964, Mom and Dad, with three young kids under the roof now (my brother, Allan, was born in 1960) and facing a daily hour-long commute, decided to look for somewhere to live closer to the store. We searched even farther north, to the very edge of the city, and found a brand-spanking-new house on Torresdale Avenue in the brand-spanking-new suburb of Willowdale, which was even more suburban than Downsview; newer but starker and soulless. Viewed from above, you would have seen a town planner's map of some ideal future suburb, the trees mere saplings, with houses like some Lego construction and little plastic people on the grid-like streets. It was the very edge of town, like in Pete Seeger's song "Little Boxes," where "they all get put in boxes, and they all come out the same." All we'd do as teens was dream of moving downtown where everything was happening, where the hippies were, where the musicians hung out. The farther you got from the epicenter of cool, the less cool you felt, and where we were, you couldn't be more disconnected from cool.

The mention of "Willow Dale" and "the River Dawn"[*] in "The Necromancer," the song Rush would one day write for *Caress of Steel*, was a jokey reference to that bland suburbia we were all trying to get away from—Pleasantville, if you like. And eight years later, with "Subdivisions," we were trying to express more seriously the same dead-end feelings of isolation and almost painful yearning. Apparently that song rang true for a *lot* of people—including guys like the documentary filmmaker Michael Moore, who's said he believes it has "actually saved lives." I'm not sure I'd go that far, but it has definitely resonated powerfully with a great many individuals who, listening to it in their identical housing units on the great suburban matrix, at least realized they were not so alone.

Willowdale was more a tile in a mosaic than the idealized Canadian melting pot of cultural influences. I hesitate to use the word "ghetto," considering the *real* ghetto conditions my parents barely survived in Poland, but our neighbourhood was made up mainly of Jewish families, across the tracks from the older farm community beyond the city limits— the main east-west thoroughfare of Steeles Avenue. Not all of those folks were pleased to see a burgeoning Jewish community on their patch; antisemitism was still rife in those days, handed down to a fresh new generation of hate-mongering teenagers. The farm boys and other locals were on the lookout for young ethnics like me to terrorize.

I was a particularly easy target: shy to begin with and self-conscious about my outstanding nose. I'd already been razzed about it from time to time, but the abuse was worse now, and growing my hair long, as I started to at around twelve in my earliest emulation of my rock and roll heroes, further stoked the ire of those goons. The neighbourhood was too new to have a junior high, so we were bussed to the nearest one, R. J. Lang Elementary and Middle School, about fifteen minutes' drive away. On arrival every day, we "Jews from Bathurst Village" had to briskly walk the gauntlet across the yard to the main entrance; if you broke into an actual

---

[*]   The actual river that runs through Willowdale is the Don.

run, you were asking to be chased. Sometimes the waiting kids would stand there unnervingly silent, watching our every move; other times they taunted us, jeering, "Dirty *Jews*," pushing and shoving until fights broke out—even between the girls. Not exactly the way the world looks at us nice polite Canadians, eh?

I wouldn't rush to call it antisemitism, necessarily; more than anything it was a territorial war. These jerks trolling the streets and hallways for Jews to torment beat on *anyone* who didn't fit into their worldview. They really weren't all that discerning. But come to think of it, as the Chosen Fucking People we *did* get singled out for special treatment. Okay, yeah, I've changed my mind. It *was* antisemitism.

One time in the hallway, as I was bending over to retrieve something from my locker, I was shoved from behind and rammed right into it with my head and ears stuck inside, and humiliatingly had to be helped back to my feet. Another time after school, I was standing with a friend at a bus stop smoking a cigarette (yeah, lots of us smoked at twelve back then; if you could puff on an Export "A" without coughing your head off—which I could not—you were a real man) and when I threw the finished butt away, a couple of farm boys strode up and pushed me hard, and one menacingly said, "*Hey*. I didn't like the way you threw that away."

"Uh, okay. Sorry. *Sorry*," I said, holding my breath until they'd walked away. I escaped a beating that time, but on it went. More often than not we'd be greeted when we got home by knuckleheads waiting on their bikes at the bus stop to harass us, whooping and hollering, all the way to our doorsteps. We learned to run pretty damn fast, I can tell you. We never told our parents, partly because we didn't want to admit our fear even to ourselves, but we also knew that our experience couldn't compare to what they had been through during the war. Even now they had enough to worry about, and we didn't want them to see us as the weak and frightened students we really were. The consequence, however, was that nothing was ever done to protect us. In those days I was a big fan of DC comics, especially *Superman* and *Green Lantern*, and I remember wishing, *If only I had the power to become invisible, then I could walk amongst these assholes without being so afraid.*

Working-class immigrants like our parents were hard-pressed to simply put food on our plates. We kids knew no different and for the most part didn't care, but there were times when it stung. Not knowing how to skate, for instance, was an instantly alienating offence for a Canadian boy and certainly didn't help a little *pischer* like me to assimilate. I was bought a pair of skates but was otherwise left to learn on my own and spent many a freezing cold Sunday afternoon shaking off frozen fingers and toes as I dragged myself around the ice on my ankles. Needless to say, I would never be anyone's first pick for games of shinny—if I made the cut at all.

Baseball, meanwhile, was in my bones—long before music started to seriously divert my attention. There was no major-league Toronto team then, but on weekend afternoons I'd watch the New York Yankees on

*Requiem for Maple Leaf Stadium: packing up one of my memories.*

TV, beamed in from stations in Buffalo, with stars like Mickey Mantle, Whitey Ford, Yogi Berra and Roger Maris, as well as their rivals, the Detroit Tigers, of whom I was a big fan, and I remember hopping on the bus and streetcar with my pals for the trip downtown to watch the Maple Leafs, Toronto's Triple-A International League team. I must have been just ten or eleven and can't recall the presence of an adult with us at all, so those memories feel like my earliest independent moments. Maple Leaf Stadium, at the south end of Bathurst Street near the lake shore, was a typical minor-league ballpark of the period, with high bleachers, metal box seats and wooden benches wrapping around from foul pole to foul pole and behind the infield. In truth, by the time I was old enough to go, it had become dingy and rundown and the games were sparsely attended; it was demolished not long afterwards, in 1968, after the team had left town to play as an unaffiliated club, grooming players for various major-league clubs. Nonetheless, photos of the old ballyard, with banner ads along its walls at the back like READ THE STAR FIRST FOR SPORTS, EXPORT and STONEY'S BREAD COMPANY, spark nostalgia in me. Those balmy days were among the happiest of my childhood.

I spent countless hours on our driveway pretending to be a pitcher, throwing a rubber ball as hard as I could against the wall of our house. I'd say to myself, "I can throw harder . . . *yeah*," with a feeling that I always had a faster throw in me—even if I didn't. When I was eleven, I summoned the nerve to try out for my neighborhood baseball team, but I didn't make it and was crushed. Licking my wounds, I played out the rest of my sports career in the school playground—much of that time bent over baseball cards, of which we were fervent collectors. We considered them precious but flung them around in a game called Close-ies, competing to get closest to the schoolyard wall, and Lean-sies, where you'd lean one card against the wall and take turns trying to knock it down with a well-judged flip of another, creasing the corners in the process. Oh my *god*, how it hurts to think that today those cards, in perfect condition, could be worth hundreds of thousands if not millions of dollars . . .

My dad was not much of a baseball fan, but I do remember watching *Hockey Night in Canada* with him—not too often, for it would be past my bedtime. I'd sneak out of my room and crawl under the furniture to watch without him knowing, or at least that's what I thought, until he'd calmly say, "Gary, go to bed now." Busted! But my favourite memory of him and sports was watching him watching the wrestling. OMG, he would get so effin' excited. Seaman Art Thomas, Sweet Daddy Siki, Haystacks Calhoun, Lord Athol Layton . . . man, he loved the shtick. I don't think he cared whether it was real or fake at all. He was so *into* it that he'd mimic the wrestlers' holds—so much so that one time he wrestled himself right off the couch and bang onto the floor.

Summers were lazy and hazy, my siblings and me hanging out on the streets with all the other unsupervised kids. On Saturdays from breakfast to lunch, I'd be rooted to the carpet in front of our faux-wood-panelled RCA Victor,[*] mesmerized by *The Bowery Boys*, then *The Three Stooges*, and rounding out the morning with an array of horse operas featuring those singing cowboys Roy Rogers and Gene Autry, or more "authentic" westerns starring John Wayne or Randolph Scott. Dang, I loved them all . . . still do! Basically, I was left alone to watch as much TV as I wanted.

But TV wasn't only for goofing off. It brought the world into our living room on Vinci Crescent, from the Cuban Missile Crisis to the assassination of presidents to—on February 9, 1964—the Beatles on their first appearance on *The Ed Sullivan Show*, and suddenly there was my sister kneeling on the floor in front of the television, crying and reaching for the TV screen as if she might touch the Fab Four and have one of them all to herself. I remember laughing to myself and thinking, *What is* wrong *with her?* but seeing the impact that rock and roll had on her made a definite impression on me. Needless to say, our parents were singularly *un*impressed, but rock and roll music had entered our home and, as my mom would say, "De rest is history."

---

[*] To my wife's chagrin it still sits in the basement beside the TV set that was the model for the cover of *Power Windows*—my failed attempt at collecting vintage televisions.

Little by little this nerdy Jewish kid with immigrant parents was assimilating, blending in and meeting new friends as best I could, going to new schools and hearing about new bands on an almost daily basis. North York may not have been the beating heart of the Swinging Sixties, but we sure wanted to be a part of it. We were buying records now. The British Invasion had begun—not just the Beatles, but the Kinks, the Stones and Donovan, and our young minds were opening up to fresh ideas about clothes and style. I grew my hair longer, letting the bangs drop over my forehead to cover my eyes.[*]

Then, on the night of October 8, 1965, my father died in his sleep, and the music stopped cold.

**HE'D COME DOWN** with the flu. He was supposed to stay home with me, as I had it too, but while Mom was readying for work he heard his carpool buddies honk the horn outside, grabbed his jacket and ran out to jump in with them. Mom was furious because she was then forced to take the bus to the store in Newmarket, and when she got there gave him an earful and sent him home. I remember being in bed, semi-delirious with the fever and hearing him return. I remember him asking me how I was. And I remember him heading off to his bedroom. That was the last time I saw him alive.

I awoke to screams. Struggling to rub the sleep from my eyes, I saw Mom in her nightclothes crying hysterically, then running out into the street yelling for help. Pandemonium. Soon our neighbours filled the house, the police were called, firemen were stomping indoors and slipping heavily on the stairs. My sister and I sat side by side in silence on the edge of our parents' bed, staring, stunned beyond comprehension, at Dad's lifeless body, there where he ordinarily slept—a chilling sight I

---

[*]   Years later when I told Neil Peart about this, he said he'd had the same kind of bangs, which he referred to as the "Flick Snowstorm." The reason? You were constantly flicking your head to see through your bangs, and if you had dandruff . . . ? You get the idea.

shall never, ever forget. In time we were hustled out of the room and I was put back to bed, still feverish, while Susie was taken to a neighbour's house for the duration of the madness. I don't even know where my little brother was or who was taking care of him, but I imagine it was my grandmother or Mom's sister, Aunt Ida.

I fell into a fever dream. Some hours later I was roused from sleep by my uncles and told to get dressed. Everything was still manic. People were arguing.

"He should put on a suit!"

"No, look at him, *der kint chot a feveh!*"

"But he needs to look nice, it's his father's funeral!"

This went on all the way down the steps to the black sedan waiting at the front door. In the back seat on the way to the cemetery I was lost in a world of my own. When we arrived at the grave site I was told to wait in the car. It was dusk and raining. I looked through the window at the huddle of mourners around my father's open grave, women sobbing and comforting one another, a cohort of men in dark coats, led by the rabbi, all *shokelling*, swaying on the spot as they prayed. Then two men, maybe my uncles, started arguing again as they opened the car door.

"He should come out and say the Kaddish!"

"No, the child is sick, and it's raining! It will be forgiven if he doesn't say it!"

Someone slammed the door back shut and told the driver to take me home. I looked back through the black rain as that terrible, somber crowd faded from view.

Morris Weinrib passed away at the age of forty-five. I was twelve. Outwardly, he'd survived the horrors of the Holocaust seemingly unscathed, but his heart was damaged by six years of slave labour in the camps. I believe he'd suffered not just physically but spiritually too—by which I really mean that he lost his *religiosity*—if he had any in the first place. After the experience of the camps, he only put that on for my mother's sake. But you know, here I'm just guessing, because he never shared such thoughts with me. He never told me what was in his heart. He never told me about his anger towards the German people or the Nazis or any of that. He never talked about the war at all, not that I remember. He was always more reticent about the war than my mom was, and about pretty much everything else too.

I do, however, have one concrete reason to believe that he'd only been pretend-religious . . . When I was about ten, I accompanied him and Mom to Eaton's and Simpson's, two big department stores across from each other at Yonge and Queen in downtown Toronto. As Mom pulled us towards the women's wear department, Dad said he'd go for a coffee and a smoke instead (he smoked Export "A"; I remember distinctly because I thought their green package with the Scots lass in her tasselled tam was cool). Bored stiff hanging around with Mom, I slipped away after him, but when I got to the lower-level cafeteria, I had to stop short on the stairs. There he was at a table, on his own, with his coffee and cigarette . . . eating *bacon and eggs*. My eyes nearly popped out of my head. My own dad eating *traif*. Then, as I watched him from afar, a sly grin spread across my face. Not only did I love the fact that I had busted him, but a heretical idea was planted in my brain that all these religious rules were bullshit. It was like getting a hall pass, a Get Out of Jail Free card, and I knew that one day I was gonna use it!

In the end, how I imagine him is assembled from just a smattering of observations, my own and those of others: quiet until spoken to, more physical than verbal, except at parties when he was the life of the party, always the jokester. Everyone in our resettled family adored him. I have photos of him at parties in which you can see he's wasted; his eyes are a little less bright than everyone else's, so I suspect he enjoyed a drink or two. He'd kid with the other children as much as with me. He'd think nothing of slinging my cousin Gary up onto his shoulders and horsing around with him. If somebody farted or if *he* farted, he would turn to us and go, "Did you *see* it?"

He could be hard-headed—you wouldn't want to get on the wrong side of him—but he was funny, upbeat, hard-working, proud, fully filling the shoes of the New World Man. He had *joie de vivre*. He was able to push aside whatever demons walked around with him. Maybe he wanted to live a good and happy life but was simply mugged by a bad heart—a condition that would be fixed today just like *that*.

These are the memories I have of him, the slide show in my head. Among the last snapshots, clear as day, is one from when I was eleven or twelve: him standing on the porch of our house on Torresdale, giving me a serious look. I had my bike with me and was chit-chatting with a couple of girls. He called me over and said bluntly, "Don't talk to girls. You're too young." Now, although I did have a bit of a crush on one who lived down the street, I was just a little *schmeckel*! I had no idea what I was doing. So I guess he saw a twinkle in my young eyes and felt compelled to give me some fatherly advice and a wag of the finger. But soon he was gone, and that was the full extent of the birds and the bees that I ever got from him. (My mother never, ever went there, so like most kids of my generation, that was something I'd have to figure out for myself.)

In the end, while I can still picture his expressions both funny and stern, I'm sorry to say that I can barely remember a single conversation we shared. There wasn't a lot of time to have one.

# CHAPTER 2

VERYTHING IN MY LIFE CAME TO A STAND-
still. My mother's grief knew no bounds. She was devastated,
and although life did carry on, she never fully recovered in her
heart. (Over the years, every visit she ever made to his grave site
left her as inconsolable as the day he died.) Our household became a dis-
combobulated mass of neighbours, relatives and religious elders coming
and going without cease. In the old country before the war, my mother's
side of the family had been Orthodox Jews, which required them—and
especially me as the eldest male child—to observe strict rules for grieving.
These stages of mourning affected me profoundly and, I believe, set the
stage for my life to come. For, let me tell you, we Jews know how to effin'
grieve. We are *awesome* at it, as if misery were second nature to us.

Immediately after burial, we sit shiva for about seven days, usually at the home of the bereaved. We cover up all mirrors as a reminder that this is not about us but the one who has passed away. We sit on low chairs or remove the pillows and cushions from the sofas. (I've never been able to determine the exact reason for that; I assume it's to ensure we are uncomfortable and reminded that loss is painful.) For seven days, we're supposed to not leave the house except on Shabbat to synagogue. We don't work, shave or cut our hair. We don't bathe other than for essential hygiene, don't wear cosmetics, leather shoes or new clothing. No festivities are permitted, nor sexual relations (as if!), nor even any study that gives you pleasure.

After the shiva there's a thirty-day period of mourning called *sheloshim*, an easing back into semi-normal life, but as the eldest son it was also my duty to say Kaddish, the prayer for the dead, three times a day—for eleven months and a day. This I did without fail. During such a period, you may partake in celebrations only so long as there is no music, so when I had my bar mitzvah the following summer, it was devoid of music and dancing. (Thankfully, you are not forbidden to accept envelopes of money from relatives!)[*]

As part of a regular Jewish upbringing, most kids in my 'hood went to *cheder* (Hebrew school) either full time or, like me, after school between four and six a couple of days a week and on Sunday, but I *hated* it. I found it pointless in the world I wanted to live in. Hebrew was a language that struck me as existing only in dusty books and scrolls, and I found it hypocritical that the teachers didn't seem to care if we understood the actual words—that reciting them phonetically at the bar mitzvah ceremony was good enough. They were brutal in meting out corporal punishment, throwing chalk at you for the slightest infraction—not an environment, in my humble opinion, in which to

---

[*] About six months after your loved one is buried, the gravestone is unveiled, and you're told that your grief should now turn to remembrance. I find that a rather beautiful concept and a fine example of age-old rabbinical wisdom.

---

build a trusting and devoted rapport. The moment my dad passed away and there was no longer any male authority figure in the house to enforce my attendance, I resolved to quit.

Needless to say, my mom was disappointed in me, even crestfallen. My aunts and uncles berated me for my newfound acts of independence or, as they saw it, defiance: not just quitting *cheder*, but growing my hair longer and hanging around with *goyische* friends. One day, even as my family and I were visiting my father's grave site, they started in on me. I remember one uncle saying, "You're killing your mother! You rebel, you *delinquent*." I was to obey without argument, and when I wouldn't they ganged up on me. Not a single adult relative asked me how I was dealing with *my* loss. Other than the occasional aunt who might swipe the bangs out of my face and say, "You poor boy. Be a good son and cut your hair," not one so much as asked me, "Are you okay?" I never fully forgave them, and have never, *ever* forgotten the way that one prick of an uncle crossed the line, while I was standing *in front of my own father's grave*. Fact is, to this day I have a long fucking memory for people who treat me badly.

My mother's pain and bereavement sucked the air out of every room in the house. Please don't get me wrong: I felt deeply for her being left with the loss of the love of her life and three children to protect, a mortgage and a business to run. But it took me years to forgive my uncles and aunts for their indifference to me at that fragile time; indeed, part of me never has. I know they were grieving my dad's loss too, trying to be supportive of my mom while labouring to rebuild their own families and keep alive traditions that had been pummelled by the horrors of war. They would never recover entirely from the Holocaust. But I was only twelve and my life, too, had changed in the blink of an eye, and it felt to me all too readily accepted that I—and my sister and little brother—were simply collateral damage, that we would have to learn to look out for ourselves.

Enter Max Guttman, a kind, generous and pious man in his early fifties with a thick Hungarian accent, who as it happened was also grieving his recently deceased parents. He volunteered to pick me up every morning and afternoon and accompany me to the Beth Emeth Bais Yehuda Synagogue, where he taught me how to behave in *shul* and how to say all the prayers and sing their mournful melodies. (A musical influence of a very different kind!) He showed me consideration and treated me as a young adult learning to cope with new responsibilities. He also helped me prepare for my own bar mitzvah in that same year of grieving: "Today I am a man" and all that.

After a time, I believe that Max started to see himself as a surrogate father figure. I think he liked me but, like a lot of religious people, was mainly trying to do what was right for the community and, specifically, for my mother. But I wasn't having it. I'd been growing my hair almost with a vengeance, and one day he took it upon himself to intercede.* On the way home from morning services he said, "Let me take you to my barber. You don't have to cut it short. Let's just clean it up a bit." Perhaps my mother had asked him to, I don't know. She'd certainly been bugging me about it as much as every other adult I knew, including the school principal, Mr. Church (perfect name, eh?)—a royal pain in the ass, a regular tyrant who made us stand nose to the wall for an hour or more if he caught us in the halls with our shirts not tucked into our trousers or if we dared to grow our hair long enough to touch the back of our collar. It seems almost quaint now, but Mr. Church, Max, my uncles, all of them saw hair as the beginning of rebellion and wanted to crush it, quite literally nip it in the bud before it became a real problem. So, I sat in the barber's chair but informed the man as sternly as I could that I only wanted a *trim*. He said okay, but then I caught Max's reflection in the mirror, his hand making a motion to cut it *all* off. I freaked, jumped up and stormed away in outrage, shouting at him that he was a liar and reminding him that he was *not* my father. After that outburst, he backed off and our relationship

---

* I say "with a vengeance," but that still only meant bangs and a little over the ears; it wouldn't reach my eyebrows, let alone my stomach, for years.

suffered, which was a shame, because I did feel some kindness and gratitude towards him for what he was doing for Mom, the time he took to help instruct me and never laying guilt on me as viciously as my uncles did.

I have to hand it to him, Max was creative. He asked a cantor he knew to make a recording of the Torah portions I was supposed to learn for my bar mitzvah. My first gig, I guess! A cantor, in case you don't know, is the vocalizing counterpart to a rabbi, the one who sings the psalms and prayers during the service—a much cooler job than rabbi if you ask me. So I memorized all the Hebrew words, the traditional melodies and the vocal nuances off this recording, and on the day I was called to the Torah I managed to recite the entire program

*In every home with a bar mitzvah boy, there sits in a place of honour a photo portrait memorializing the day he became a man. But my mother was so ashamed of my long hair that she refused to allow a photo to be taken. Instead, she commissioned this painting of an idealized me with shorter, tidier hair. It hung proudly on her wall, perpetuating that Great Lie for almost sixty years.*

by heart, sort of *pretending* to read it. I saw Mom smiling proudly through her tears in the front row, and my relatives were now saying, "Oy, such a lovely voice. You should be a *cantor.*" I nodded my head and gratefully took their envelopes of bar mitzvah money while thinking to myself, *Yeah, right. But sorry, folks. I'm done with all of that.*

My mother may have been crying tears of joy that day, but there was no real exploring faith with her or anyone else in my family. It was all dogmatic and unintellectual. There was nothing to discuss. They simply did as they'd been taught. How dare I even question it? There was one direction only: doing what Jews were expected to do and behaving how Jews were expected to behave. Children in the Old World were to be seen and not heard. Anything more was disrespectful and a reason to be punished with the stick of shame. (My mother in particular knew how to wield that stick—with precision!) Of course, in time I realized that faith for them was a way of keeping the dead alive, a tribute to them, an assertion that they had not perished in vain. And in more practical terms, these survivors were committed to rebuilding the Jewish population. For the vast majority of observant Jews, the mantra was and remains "Get married, have lots of kids and keep them faithful to the religion." Thus, it's not just a matter of the past but the future too. So, yes, in time, I did come to understand that that's what drove them, but I still could not bring myself to feel the same way. Please understand, I love being a Jew and I'm super-proud of all that "my" people have accomplished in so many aspects of life—especially in the face of persistent prejudice, hatred and outright murder—but I consider myself a devout *cultural* Jew: I love the history, the humour and even some of the food! But a belief in God and organized religion? Not for me. A line from Woody Allen's *Love and Death* sums up my feelings well: "If it turns out that there is a God . . . the worst you can say about him is that basically he's an underachiever."

The fact that all three of Mom's children would eventually marry out of the faith was, in her mind, a heartbreaking failure of her own parenting skills. Even after I'd become an adult, she tried to guilt me back into synagogue: she'd say that by not being observant I was committing a sin against God and betraying my family and all those who'd died in the war. (Jews are really, *really* good at guilt, no?) But it was to no avail. I had prayed for the last time. Surprisingly, once the penny dropped that we were not going to change, *she* did too. It's a testament to her innate intelligence and maturity that she'd learn to accept and even embrace people for who they are. She'd grow fiercely devoted to her daughters-in-law and adored them unquestioningly till the day she died. I find that hugely admirable for someone of her age and with her past, and wonder if I would have had the strength to change as she did.

My sister also struggled mightily after Dad died. She was the first-born, his little girl, and clearly had enjoyed a deeper relationship with him than I; she was fourteen when he passed, already in the throes of adolescence, and his death hit her that much more viscerally. She tried to escape the household at every opportunity, lashing out and staying out worryingly late. As the "man of the house" (as everyone loved to remind me) I had to stand up for Mom, which led to more fights. I, too, was itching to escape, particularly after my synagogue duties were over. I was percolating beneath the surface, starting to reject adults at every turn, and as soon as my eleven months of mourning were over, I spent less time at home and sought out a new breed of friends.

In 1966 I started at Fisherville Junior High in North York, just walking distance from our house. It was also there that Susie started hanging out with some tough guys—"Greasers," we called them. At R. J. Lang throughout my year of woe, I'd continued to be one of the school's most popular punching bags, but in the first semester at this new place, as I was walking home and one of these kids grabbed me by the lapels, winding up to make my life even more of a misery, another kid said, "Hey, leave him alone. That's Susie's little brother." *Whew*. Big sister to the rescue!

And *then*, when I made friends with a guy I shared a couple of classes with, a good-natured guy with a cheeky grin named Steve Shutt, the harassment petered out altogether. How come? Well, Shutty was a rising hockey star, even in grade seven. He was revered, super-cool, and just by association with him my kosher bacon was saved. If you're a hockey fan, you know he went on to become a perennial All Star for the Montreal Canadiens, part of the devastating offensive line alongside Guy Lafleur and Jacques Lemaire, scoring a career 424 goals, and in 1993 was elected to the hockey Hall of Fame. He was a year older than me, so we had only a few mutual friends, but we dug the same music and would soon both develop an interest in the bass guitar. He was growing his hair then too, and in the sixties, man, those with long hair bonded instantly. (He'd grow it out every summer, cutting it all off again without hesitation as soon as the hockey season began; he knew his priorities.) I'm not sure if Steve was actually aware of being my saviour. We never spoke of it. But our friendship did allow me to walk amongst the bullies with impunity.

By now, I wouldn't be surprised if you were hoping for the juicy rock and roll bits, i.e., the story of Rush, to begin. I *will* tell you all about it, but I'm afraid that first a few more heavies are in order. In the next chapter I'm going to relate my parents' experience of the war. After all, if it wasn't for what happened to them then, I wouldn't be here to tell you *my* tale now and I wouldn't be the person who I am. A lot of what loomed over me as a boy went into forging my own personality, my value system—the good things and the bad. But most important, I feel both duty-bound and honoured to tell you *their* story. For *their* sake. If you find it half as harrowing to read as I did writing it, you may be tempted to skip right along. If you do, I won't blame you and I'll see you in chapter four, but I've included it in this book because I feel we're living in an era that seems to have forgotten what can and will happen when fascism rears its head. I think we all need reminding of it in the face of those who either deny the past or never knew about it in the first place.

# CHAPTER 3

HEN WE WERE CHILDREN MY MOM would tell us about her experiences in the war, and when our uncles and aunts were over, talk would sometimes turn to theirs as well. It made me angry to hear what they'd seen and suffered at the hands of the Nazis, and when I went up to bed my rage would boil over into waking dreams. Lying in my darkened room, I'd wish that Hitler would magically appear in front of me so I could vanquish him myself with brute force — with my bare hands, punching and strangling him (in a way that Quentin Tarantino would approve of). For me those stories cast deep doubt on the existence of a higher power — certainly one with an ounce of compassion — and on the very point of religion. After my dad died, I

*I took this photo in 1995 of the infamous gates at Auschwitz, just one of the horrific camps in which my parents were incarcerated during the Holocaust.*

was like, *Hey, God, what have you done for me lately?* I was amazed that my mother came out of such a horror show still believing.

The story that follows is sewn together from bits and pieces my mother and other family members have shared with my siblings and me over the years, as well as some independently published survivors' accounts and books I discovered while doing my research. As is typical of many eyewitness accounts of events that took place so many years ago, particularly ones recalling events as traumatic as these, some details were hard to pin down, and we must bear in mind—as Christopher R. Browning writes in the introduction to his superbly well-researched book: *Remembering Survival: Inside a Nazi Slave-Labor Camp*—that "these were childhood memories refracted through the horrible experiences that followed."[*] Furthermore, all the family members who survived the war—including my mother, who kept on trucking until she was almost ninety-six—have now passed on.

Thanks to the dedication of various diligent Jewish and other Holocaust memorial organizations, many interrelated accounts have been recorded in print and on video for posterity. Astonishingly, as I have found, some of these accounts are from survivors who not only came from my mother's hometown but who suffered the same grueling experiences as she and her family did in exactly the same places. This has given me the opportunity to cross-reference the occasional divergent memories. I strongly believe that the stories I relate to you now are not only true but capture the essence and spirit of what my mother and father lived through as teenagers—the awful and the good.

There is, sadly, a paucity of information about my father's side of the family. As I said earlier, he never discussed the war with us, maybe partly because he knew our mom would and did. As a result, there is

---

[*]   A key theme in Browning's book is the fallible nature of shared memory. Indeed, he felt compelled to write it after seeing Walter Becker, the brutal Gestapo officer in charge of the liquidation of Wierzbnick, escape conviction; the defense lawyers were able to poke holes through the testimonies of survivors who were now elderly and whose memories had become confused over time.

little here from his own lips or, for that matter, from his siblings'. He left this world in 1965, and I've gleaned little about him from the remainder of his side of the family since. What I do have, I hope I have right.

So yes, there is a bias towards my mom's version of events for the simple reason that she was more willing than he to share their experiences with us. She would talk in detail about all that she and her family had endured, how time and time again *her* mother had saved her life. My mother spoke as if telling these stories to her kids was the most natural thing in the world. I can tell you that it wasn't. Today such parental behavior might be considered irresponsible, even unthinkable, yet it seemed somehow okay at the time, and I don't regret hearing any of it. In her mind, sharing with her children this six-year nightmare was not just a way of passing her own history along to us, but a way that we could help the world "never forget." What's more, bizarre as it sounds, it was probably healthy for her to talk about this stuff, even to her kids. Who else was she going to tell, a therapist? That was not an option for people of her generation. Had I suggested such a thing, her answer would surely have been "Vot, I should pay money to tell this to a *stranger?*"

## LOVE AND HELL
### SLAVE #A14254[*]

**MY MOTHER WAS** born in Warsaw, Poland, in July 1925. Her Canadian passport says Starachowice, but we believe that to be incorrect;

---

[*] All prisoners in Nazi camps had numbers tattooed on their arms, but it was a particular indignity for Jews because it's prohibited in the Torah: "You shall not make gashes in your flesh for the dead, or incise any marks on yourselves: I am the Lord." When my mother talked about the war, she would often point to her forearm to bring her tale to life. She, my aunts and my uncles all had tattoos. In a sign of more modern times, a kind of identity reclamation, I suppose, both my kids would choose to get tattoos, which we always hid from her—even when Julian inked a Star of David on his arm. But by then, I don't think it would have mattered to her anyway. What really mattered was that she loved her grandchildren and they loved her. As for me, I'd never stick needles in my arm. I've noticed how addictive they are. After Jules had a couple, to break the trance he was in I asked him to agree to a moratorium for a year. Two weeks later he put a stud through his lip, but at least it wasn't permanent!

she and her siblings always insisted they were born and lived in Warsaw until she was five years old. Moreover, her mother, Ruchla (aka Ruzia or Rose), was born and raised in Warsaw, in the Wielka Wola district, and was living with her family and working as a successful dressmaker when she met and married my grandfather Gershon (Gerzson) Eliezer Rubinstajn.[*]

Born in Wierzbnik in October 1900, Gershon was a butcher by trade. He and Rose had three children, the eldest being my mom, Malka (Manya or Mary), followed by her younger sister a year later, Ida (Yita), and lastly brother Herszek (Herschel). They lived in the part of the city that in 1943 would be the site of the Warsaw Uprising, but they were long gone by the time that violent liquidation occurred. Gershon had been having trouble finding work, so after a consultation with their rabbi (to whom pious Jews usually went for advice of a serious nature), and despite his wife doing very well as a clothing designer, they decided in 1930 to move the family 160 kilometers south to Starachowice-Wierzbnik, where the Rubinsteins lived and worked as a close-knit clan, and he joined his mother and two of his brothers in their thriving butcher business. They found a good and stable home there, living at number 6 Kolejowa, a small house across from the train tracks, and quickly resumed life as a middle-class, highly observant Eastern European Jewish family. (I was surprised to hear from my mother that she had learned to speak Yiddish only upon their arrival there; as residents of the bigger, more sophisticated city of Warsaw they mostly spoke Polish, even to one another.) My grandfather, a generous man, soon became a respected community leader, head of a local *shtiebel*,[**] who would often bring needy strangers home for dinner on the Sabbath.

Starachowice was separated into two distinct sections by the Kamienna, a tributary of the Vistula, Poland's largest and longest river. It was a small but growing industrial city of mines and steel works, whose

---

[*]  The original Polish family name, later germanized to Rubinstein.
[**]  "Home synagogue," a modest chapel set up in people's homes.

factories produced guns for the Polish army before the war, whereas Wierzbnik was more like a *shtetl* made up mostly of wooden houses, and where 90 percent of the Jewish population lived. That little river dividing the city has been described as a symbol of regional antisemitism, separating the Jews from the rest of the Poles; even before the Nazis arrived, the munitions factory of Starachowice was already off-limits to Jewish employment. Another survivor from their town, my cousin Zecharia Grynbaum (Zachary Greenbaum), wrote in his own auto-biography, "The Jews and gentiles lived together peaceably enough, but the hatred was always there, burning underneath." In fact, my uncle Harold recalled that as the war got closer the Poles of Starachowice grew less afraid to show their true colours, standing in front of Jewish shops discouraging people from doing business with "dirty" Jews.

In 1938 rumblings of a German invasion were starting to spread, yet my family, along with many others, did not give these whispers much credence. Like most of their fellow townspeople they were caught woefully unprepared for the fall day on which the German armed forces bombed and marched their way right into their life and tore it to pieces.

On the afternoon of Friday, September 1, 1939, my mother and her first cousin and close friend Miriam, both fourteen years old, were sent as usual to the Starachowice side of the river to buy some bread for the Sabbath. They were expected to return home before dark but were still on the road when the bombs began to drop. Polish soldiers were shout-ing and scrambling as they leaped into the trenches built in anticipation of such an attack—though notoriously there was little resistance—and my mom and her cousin were forced to hide in one of those ditches. The fighting went on for more than a day as they cowered there. At daybreak when the city finally fell quiet, they crawled out from amongst the many dead or injured Polish soldiers and started walking back to Wierzbnik.

Along the way they heard stories from people about two young Jewish girls who'd been killed in the raid. They entered their part of town to find the streets deserted. As my mother describes it, "We were like the only two people walking in the whole wide world." They went from house to house, seeking their families, finally opening one door to find their fathers, Gershon and his brother Josek (Yankel), saying Kaddish for their missing daughters. Being Orthodox Jews, women were not allowed to pray in the same room as men, so when the girls entered the house their fathers grabbed them and pressed them close beneath their *tallitim* (prayer shawls) until the prayer was over, then took them to show their wives and sisters that the girls were still alive.

Within ten days the occupation began. As one resident, Yitzhak Edison-Erlichsohn, described: "The entire market was filled with Nazi soldiers. The following day the persecution and torture of Jews began; kidnapping them for work, frightful beatings, robbery of Jewish possessions, and the laughter and ridicule of our neighbours of a thousand years—the Poles."

The country was now under the strict control of the German General Government, led by the SS chief, Heinrich Himmler, who in 1942 would be tasked with carrying out the Nazi "Final Solution." Under his command the important factories of Starachowice legally became the Braunschweig Steel Works Corporation, owned and operated by Reichswerke Hermann Göring.

New rules for the Jews were quickly established and violently enforced. In an ominous message to the Jewish citizenry of Wierzbnik, shortly after the Yom Kippur holiday was concluded the central synagogue of their community was burned to the ground. Schools were now off-limits to Jews; curfews were imposed, and a ghetto was being delineated to further limit their movements. Public degradation of Jews became the norm. The German word for Jew, "Jude," was painted on all Jewish shop windows, and it became mandatory for Jews in public to wear a yellow badge in the shape of the Star of David, either as armbands or sewn onto their clothing.

Standard operating procedure for the Nazis during an occupation was to go house to house, removing at gunpoint all adult Jewish males (or other undesirables) deemed a potential threat to their command. They would either march them to a secluded location and murder them en masse or transport them by train to prison, the gas chambers at Treblinka or some other destination where they would meet the same terrible end. This was my grandfather Gershon's brutal fate.

My mother used to tell us with guilt and regret that before the Germans arrived her father had an idea to run away to the Soviet Union, but she was so distraught at any talk of him leaving the family that he abandoned the idea and stayed on, only to meet his doom. It's a pain she had to bear her entire life.

The SS came to their door in the winter of 1940, in the middle of the night. They ordered Gershon out of bed with a "Get up, dirty Jew, you're coming with us." When my grandmother dared ask why, she was smacked in the face. Gershon, only forty years old, was the first male of the town to be arrested in this manner. He was marched off amidst the chaos and the crying and protestations of his family. My mom ran after them. She caught up and took hold of her father's arm, refusing to let go until the soldiers beat her into submission, leaving her unconscious in the snow. Her mother found her there a few hours later.

Later that day a local policeman who'd been one of Gershon's friends informed Rose that those arrested were to be transported by train to the town of Radom that same evening. My mom and one of her male cousins slipped out of the house and went to the station, where they found the men lined up and shackled and waiting for the train. My mom left her cousin watching from a safe distance to try and alert her father to her presence. She got much too close and tripped, falling at his feet. While Gershon quietly pleaded with her to run away before it was too late, a German soldier came up and stabbed at her hand with his bayonet, piercing the skin on her thumb (when we were kids, she used to show us the scar) and yelling at her to get out of there.

As her cousin hustled her away, she looked back at her father, never to see him again.

As daily conditions worsened, Rose fought to learn of her husband's fate, eventually discovering that he was still alive and sitting in a jail cell at Radom. According to prison records, he had been arrested on January 14, 1942, charged with the "distribution of illegal meat" and sentenced to one year and three months. (Starvation was a real problem in the ghettos. The German-allotted per-person ration was just 100 grams of bread per day, so the smuggling in of food was a matter of survival. Being a butcher, Gershon was able to set up a system with friends outside the ghetto, giving him access to a few cows in a shed to help provide for the community. *That* was his heinous crime.)

Records also show that in March 1942, Rose and an attorney were able to secure permits to see her husband. My mom's family were mostly blonde and didn't share many typically Jewish facial features (unlike me!), and as such Rose could pass for a Pole and slip out of the ghetto simply by removing her yellow Star of David.

Despite his having already served five months in jail, Gershon's sentence only officially began on May 29, 1942, and was set to end over a year later, but an addition and stamp on the prison documents indicate that on August 18, 1942, he was deported, likely to Treblinka, where he met his death. I've racked my brain trying to understand why the Germans and the Polish police under their command would have undertaken such a circuitous procedure to eliminate him when so many others were shot on the spot for, say, dawdling. The only answer I have is that in the early days of the Final Solution, my grandfather must have been considered a man of some stature in Wierzbnik, such that the authorities felt the need for a "legitimate" paper trail of crime and punishment. As we know from extensive war records, the Nazis had honed not only a system of arresting and killing Jews but a routine of keeping files to document it too. Talk about the banality of evil.

*My grandfather's arrest warrant, his punishment decree and sentencing and his deportation order—in essence, his death sentence.*

The family had no choice but to try to carry on without their patriarch. Similar to Jews in cities and towns all across Poland, they were now living under armed patrol in a small and highly crowded area of their town, dubbed the Ghetto of Wierzbnik. There were more than 3,500 local Jews and about a thousand others from elsewhere, all living in a few dark and narrow laneways. My family was marginally better off, as their house was on the edge of the ghetto and they got to remain in their home, albeit jammed in there with many others. Brutal treatment, sudden shootings and public hangings had by now become commonplace. As they tried to adjust to a life of fear, my blonde mom would remove her star and go with her friend Oscar to purchase scraps of food from unsuspecting shop owners in the city.

In the early days of the war, an organization was created by the Germans called the Judenrat, a committee of Jews acting as an administration agency between the Germans and the Jewish population of each ghetto. Of course, by the very nature of its creation, their powers were limited, but the Judenrat of Wierzbnik interceded as much as it could, either by stealthily arranging bribes to improve conditions for some or obtaining work cards for others. For corrupt German officers, providing work permits had become a booming black-market business. The Judenrat was instrumental in persuading its overseers that it would benefit the war machine if it constructed work camps to house the *Arbeitsjuden*, or "Work Jews," close to the steel works, brick works and munitions factory. The Judenrat gambled that, if successful, this plan would stave off the transport of Jews to even more deadly places such as Treblinka.

In the fall of 1942, in accordance with the Nazis' Final Solution policy, Jewish ghettos across Poland began to be liquidated in a process the Germans called an Aktion: the SS would gather the Jews in a central location, and those who were deemed too young, too small or too old to work would either be executed on the spot or transported to one of the death camps. As news spread and fear grew, some residents contemplated escape to the forests while others, like my family, were in denial, taking an attitude of "it won't happen here," mistakenly thinking that due to the importance of Starachowice's munitions and steel manufacturing they would somehow be spared.

In the early dawn of October 27, 1942, an Aktion came to the Wierzbnik ghetto. People were roused from their houses by the SS shouting, "Jews out! Out!" and ordered to gather in the *rynek*, or market square. They were told to leave their possessions behind, but some had already hidden valuables in their clothing or prepared backpacks while others grabbed things that were most easily carried. Panic ensued as gunshots rang through the night, many from inside the houses of those either too slow to leave or too slow to walk. In the terrible chaos of that Aktion, any random movement interpreted by the soldiers as resistance meant instant death. My cousin Chuna Grynbaum (Henry Greenbaum) once described how on that morning his uncle, dressed and praying in their home, was murdered right there on the spot.

Another survivor, and the head of the Wierzbnik Judenrat, Simcha Mincberg, describes that nightmarish experience in these words[*]: "This bloody day, 27.10.1942 was carved into my memory as a dark, bitter day, a day of cruelty and murder . . . humiliated, tortured Jews flowed out, their feet buckling under them and their faces stricken, men, women and children all headed to the place of gathering. A little while later, the entire town square was filled by nearly 5,000 Jews, locals and refugees alike.

"The place was surrounded by bloodthirsty brutes, led by Becker (*Police Chief*) who was brandishing a pistol. Dozens of Jews, men and women, were killed on that accursed day, and their names are carved in this Yizkor book . . . Of those who lived, some were considered capable of working and were ordered to the labour camp in the forest called 'Strzelnica.' The rest, the majority of our people, were led toward the train station, where they were loaded on the death cars on their way to annihilation."

---

[*]  *Wierzbnik-Starachowitz; a memorial book (Wierzbnik, Poland)*. Translation of *Sefer Wierzbnik-Starachowice*. Edited by Mark Schutzman (Tel Aviv, 1973).

From seven in the morning until past noon they stood in rows of five waiting to be chosen for the first of a series of "selections" that day. Those with work cards were chosen first and sent to line up at the far side of the *rynek*, and then those who looked strong and old enough— usually twelve or older—were pulled out to join the workers' line. After selection they were marched or forced to run to the Strzelnica labour camp. All the remaining Jews deemed unfit, meaning the elderly, the very young and the infirm, were put in a line on the other side of the square and transported by train to the gas chambers of Treblinka.

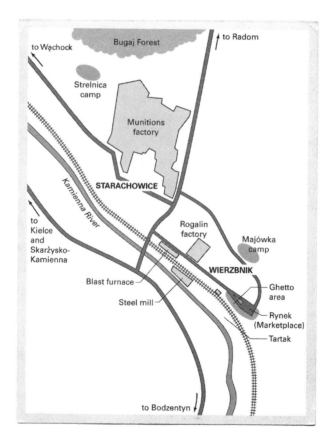

*Wierzbnik-Starachowice: ghetto, factories and labor camps.*
*My mother's house was at the edge of the ghetto by the railroad tracks.*

The same policeman who'd known my grandfather risked his life again to intercede on my family's behalf. He obtained work cards for them that assigned them to slave labour—even my uncle Herschel, who was barely of age but tall was given a card and jostled into the work line. I prefer to believe that this man acted out of friendship rather than taking a bribe, but regardless, he certainly helped save my family that day. This would be just the first of many such excruciating selections that they would have to endure in the camps over the next three years.

According to Christopher Browning's book, in Wierzbnik alone the Germans sent approximately 1,600 Jews—1,200 men and 400 women—to these slave labour camps and deported nearly 4,000 to Treblinka. As he explains, the fact that more than 25 percent of these people were not killed immediately was remarkably atypical for the SS in this region; the deportation rate during these liquidations was usually around 90 to 95 percent. It's hard to know if this was intentional or an accident of fate. Was it due to their proximity to the factories and the pressing need for more slave labour? Was it the number of bribes taken in exchange for work cards? Browning posits that the Judenrat was able to bribe and manipulate the German soldiers and management into thinking that it was in their best interests to keep the Jews alive and exploit them. Whatever the explanation, in the history of the Holocaust in Poland, the number of Jews from my mother's particular area who survived is highly anomalous.

Three camps were built in the Starachowice area. The workers' line was divided into two groups. One went to a smaller camp nearby known as Tartak, which was based on an already existing sawmill and lumberyard; the other prisoners were sent to the Strzelnica on the other side of the sprawling munitions factory producing casings for shells and grenades. My mom, Herschel and their mother, Rose, along with her aunt Rachu and my mom's cousin Miriam and her two sisters, were processed and then moved on to a third camp, Majowka, which was closer to the steel works, the blast furnace and the Rogalin brick factory, while my mom's sister, Yita, and her uncle Yankel remained at Strzelnica.

Some towns such as Ostrowiec (that included the tiny suburb of Gozdzielin, where my father's family lived), had already been liquidated in October of that year. He was one of 110 young, strong males spared death and sent to join the workforce in the nearby Starachowice camps. This is most likely how my father came to meet my mother . . .

Upon their arrival, on penalty of death, the prisoners were ordered to give up all their valuables and other possessions. This was a wrenching decision, as most of them knew how valuable bribery would be in the camp. My mom's uncle Yankel, for instance, was put in charge of the kitchens due to some well-placed bribes, although he was still searched and, when money was found on his person, beaten within an inch of his life. The fact that he was so big and strong was the only thing that saved him that day, but that beating left an unforgettable impression on the other inmates.

My mother was assigned to make bricks at Rogalin, not far from the blast furnace where my dad had been assigned to work, while her siblings toiled in the munitions factory and my grandmother Rose delivered food to the Germans, taking parcels of food to the barracks and officers' residences.

These teenagers had no choice but to adapt quickly to life as slave labourers in disgusting conditions. The camps were hastily built and woefully lacking in any acceptable hygiene. Soon Majowka, and especially Strzelnica, became foul places to live, infested with lice and outbreaks of typhus; on top of the numerous illnesses, a reign of terror and murder was conducted by the Bergen-Belsen camp's sadistic security chief, Ralf Alois "Willi" Althoff. How sadistic? Well, my uncle Herschel recalled that at least once a week Althoff would select a number of Jews just to make them run in a wide circle while he randomly shot them down like it was a game of target practice. Over a three-month period in late 1942 he conducted so many mass killings and raids on the sick that the work force was decimated, and Jews from other regions had to be brought in to keep up productivity.[*]

By late summer 1943, Strzelnica was deemed so unsanitary that it was abandoned. Yankel and my aunt Yita joined the rest of their families at Majowka. Life in these places was like walking a deadly tightrope. Inmates might be shot at the whim of any soldier or beaten with a rubber club by a Kapo.[**] After the war, Miriam said of this treatment, "If they didn't like you, or even if they didn't like a look in your eyes, they just shot you, like you were no more than a chicken."

Despite the risks, bribery was an essential method of improving one's chances for survival in all these camps, and inmates smuggled in Polish zlotys or whatever else they could hide. The wealthier ones brought in jewels and money (usually US dollars acquired on the black market) often sewn into the lining of their clothes, behind buttons or cached in scooped-out loaves of bread. Compared to most concentration camps, the ones near Starachowice were in uniquely close proximity to the inmates' former homes, and there are accounts of some who relied upon their few loyal Polish friends on the outside to help smuggle in whatever hidden valuables they had left behind.

SOMETIMES MY MOTHER would go to Uncle Yankel, who was very fond of her, and get extra potatoes from him. But word of that spread, causing resentment in the barracks. Fearful that her husband would be shot if the authorities found out, her aunt Rachu asked her to stop.

Mom and her friends met other adolescents on the work brigades. She tells a story from her time at Majowka of loading cargo with some men, when a young Polish boy offered her some bread. Mistrustful of

---

[*]   After he was removed from command in March 1943, Althoff disappeared, living out the rest of his life under an assumed name. He was never investigated nor brought to justice.
[**]   Jewish inmates who worked for the SS as police, supervisors, block elders or camp administrators in return for preferential treatment. The Kapo system was an integral part of Nazi "divide and control" protocols.

him, she refused to accept it, but after that he continued to look out for her. It was at this time that she also noticed a strong older boy working a crane that carried hot iron back and forth. He continually caught her eye, and she assumed that such a strong guy must be a Pole and couldn't possibly be Jewish. *(Hey, wait a minute!)* Little did she realize that this strongman was also keeping a close eye on her, and one day he appeared with the Polish boy to ask why she wouldn't accept the gift. My mother was shocked to discover that not only was this fellow Jewish, but *he* was the one behind the offers of bread. Many years later she admitted to us that at first she'd been quite intimidated by him. After all, he was five years older, muscular and rather good-looking. But a romance was budding, even in this brutal place.

His name, of course, was Moczek (Moishe) Wajnryb, aka my dad. He'd been born and lived in a small village called Gozdzielin, about thirty kilometers down the road from Wierzbnik. His father was Ahron

(Left to right) *My dad with three of his four brothers: Icek (I think), Pinkwas and Shloima. Only he and Shloima survived.*

Wajnryb; his mother, Chaja Sura Wajnryb, née Cytrinbaum. By all accounts, theirs was the only Jewish family in Gozdzielin, and it suffered a terrible toll in the war: along with both parents, my dad lost three brothers and two sisters to the Germans. Only his brother Shloima (Sam or Szlama) survived the camps, while his sister Rose, as I mentioned earlier, avoided the Holocaust entirely by emigrating to Canada.

Moishe continued to do what he could to improve my mom's lot in these cruel surroundings. Hoping to secure her a less arduous job, he bribed one of the higher-ups with some gold he'd hidden in his shoe. She was subsequently given work spraying down the hot iron with a hose, and whenever possible he would try to see her at work. On one of these encounters he revealed to her that he carried her photo, which had been given to him by her brother, Herschel. He was clearly crushing for her in a big way.

During their time at Majowka both my parents were involved in an escape attempt. A boy Mom knew named Alter told her that some inmates were going to make a break and asked her to join them. He came for her on the night, but Rose refused to let her go. A tug-of-war ensued and my mom fell and twisted her ankle. Unable to walk, she could only watch as Alter and several others, including my dad's brother Shloima, leaped the fence. Dad himself was supposed to go with them, but when he saw that she wasn't with them he hesitated, and in that moment shooting broke out. He was able to slip back to his barracks while some of the others, Alter included, were killed and still others injured badly. Uncle Shloima was one of the few who made it out and was able to hide successfully for a good part of the war in a Polish farmhouse. The wounded, meanwhile, were dragged back to camp and, as a deterrent, left to bleed to death for the whole camp to see.

Their flirtation continued throughout their incarceration. It's hard to believe that under such horrific circumstances anyone could be thinking romantically, but one has to think of their age and the resilience of youth, and the need to believe in something other than imminent death. And in what I guess must pass as survivor humour, for years Dad would jokingly remind Mom of the time she saved his life by twisting her ankle.

As summer approached, the Majowka and Tartak camps were closed. My family and the other surviving prisoners found themselves moved to a newly built camp on the grounds of the munitions factory. Tensions had been rising over the spring as other survivors from Lublin arrived, bringing with them stories of what they had seen and heard along the way: confirmation of the rumours of gas chambers at Majdanek and Treblinka. I can only guess at the impact this news must have had on them. As it became clearer that their time in Starachowice was soon to end, many tried to escape but were shot dead as they clambered over the fences.

Then, on the sweltering evening of July 28, 1944, the surviving Jews, including my mother, her family, my cousins and my father, were jammed and locked inside cattle cars with just two small windows to make the 140-mile journey to the Auschwitz-Birkenau concentration camp. The cars were grossly overfilled, especially the first one, which carried between 120 and 150 men, among them Uncle Yankel.

They had to endure a torturous thirty-six-hour ride without water, and as they struggled for air skirmishes erupted. By the time that first car pulled into the station at Birkenau just before dawn on Sunday, July 30, as many as thirty had died in that car alone, including Yankel. After the war my cousin Chuna Grynbaum, who was also there, said, "They stuck us in there like sardines. That's when the commotion started, fighting during the day, everyone trying to get some fresh air from that little window, everybody pushing one another and getting angry." Whether they died from suffocation and dehydration or at one another's hands can scarcely be imagined.

Between 1940 and 1945 the Auschwitz-Birkenau compound comprised more than forty death camps and sub-camps. It's hard for anyone with a rational mind and a fully functional heart to fathom a mindset that could devise and construct a place dedicated to the sole purpose of the extermination of human beings, and on such a mind-boggling scale. Of course, Nazis did not view Jews, Gypsies or other "deviants" as human beings at all.

The train car carrying my family pulled into Birkenau, past the main gates of Auschwitz where, in wrought iron high above the entrance, were the cynically perverted words *Arbeit Macht Frei* ("Work will set you free").* As the people were hauled out of these train cars and down the ramp the chaos immediately escalated to an even more nightmarish level.

My mother described this moment many times to us. "When we first arrived, we heard screams and shots, and we couldn't breathe from the smoke. The guards were shouting, 'Go right! Go left!' My mother and sister went to the right, but I went to the left. My mother jumped out of the line, even though she could have been killed on the spot, and dragged me back in with her and Yita and told us, 'If we go, we all three go *together*.'" **

They would soon be separated into different camps by sex, which meant my mom and dad would not have access to each other for long. According to camp records of the new arrivals, 1,298 women and 409 men were taken to be tattooed that day, each with their own number on their arm.

My mother was now officially Slave #A14254. From then on, the Nazis would address prisoners only by their numbers, never by their names, in order to dehumanize them even further.

---

* There's no room in my book to go into the twisted history of this phrase (but do look it up!). Suffice it to say that it is featured on the gates of at least four Nazi death camps—not just Auschwitz, as is popularly imagined.
** The eyewitness survivor accounts of the arrival of this trainload of Jews from Starachowice are strangely and distinctly of two minds about the timing of this first selection, and whether or not it took place immediately upon arrival in Auschwitz or in the days following. My family members have consistently described this happening on disembarkation, but it is possible that this is an example of a communal or shared memory; in *Remembering Survival*, Browning sifts through numerous survivor interviews and camp records, and presents compelling reasoning as to why he believes that to be the case. Either way, there is no doubt that these excruciating selections did indeed take place, and more than once, during their incarceration in Auschwitz.

After that they were herded over to be washed. There was a tremendous fear that instead of water coming out of the shower heads, it would be Zyklon B gas, for the prisoners were by now well aware of the *other* kind of "showers." My grandmother peeked around back and, seeing people were exiting from the other side of the shower room, concluded they were safe. Then, after they'd cleaned themselves, they were taken to have their heads shaved and were given striped prison uniforms and wooden shoes without socks.

Considering everything she had endured to this point, it was the loss of my mother's "beautiful blonde" hair that was a tipping point for her. It was the injury to her teenage pride that broke her, and she became hysterical. She screamed through her tears, "I don't *want* to be liberated!"

"My dear daughter," her mother reassured her, "you have a head, and you're going to have hair, so much hair you will have to go to the hairdresser once again. You can't have it today, but it will come."

My mom used to tell us, "In the camps, your grandmother always knew how to talk to me and calm me. She was my saviour."

They would be quarantined in the "Gypsy Camp" for a time, before being assigned to barracks elsewhere in this vast complex. As they walked towards it on that first day, with the smell of death literally hanging in the air, they would have to endure one more punishing indignity. Playing on loudspeakers was a jolly German folk song called "Arbeit macht dein Leben süß," which translates as "work makes your life sweet." Every morning, for the duration of their imprisonment in this extermination camp, this music would accompany them as they trudged off to do their slave labour.

As far as hygiene was concerned, inmates actually found conditions in Auschwitz a considerable improvement over the squalor they'd been living in at the Starachowice camps, yet the quality and quantity of food was another story entirely. For some, including my family, the ease of bribery in Majowka and the presence of Uncle

Yankel in the kitchens meant more food had been available to them and, as a result, most of them were less malnourished than other new arrivals from Hungary and elsewhere, which lent a slightly better prospect of survival.

My aunt Yita described the meager rations in Auschwitz. "We would be woken at six a.m. and have roll call at six thirty. Breakfast would be only water, then we would be taken to work. For lunch they would give us a piece of bread so thin you could see through it, and for dinner some soup made from water and vegetables, like you would give to a horse." However, my family also told stories of the occasional willing Polish kitchen worker who, for a few dollars, would smuggle out morsels of food for them.

One of the sweeter moments in Auschwitz was the time my mother received a pair of shoes, courtesy of my dad. He had bribed one of the guards to procure a pair, then tried to pass them to a woman who often walked by the fence between the male and female camps. He asked her, "Do you know a Manya Rubinstein?" and when she said she thought she did, he asked her to take them to her. The woman refused, thinking it too dangerous, but he persisted, suggesting, "How about only one at a time?" to which she said okay. She hid the shoe, took it to my mom, and a few weeks later brought the other one. My mother was amazed. Not only was it a message that Moishe was still alive, but that he was thinking of *her*. But soon they would all be transferred again, and it would be quite some time before either would know the fate of the other.

The plumes of smoke coming from the ovens were an almost daily reminder of how thin the line was now between life and death. During their four months in Auschwitz-Birkenau, they lived in constant fear of the next terrifying selection. These would come without warning, and every time it was the same awful ritual of being gathered together and stepping forward one by one to be divided into two lines: one meant work, the other took them to the showers—which meant, of course, the end of the road. The designations of these lines changed daily, so prisoners would never know if this would be their last day on earth or not. My grandmother ensured that she and her daughters were always in the same line, and luck broke their way every single time.

Among the many threats and indignities they suffered at the hands of the Nazis in Auschwitz, and one that almost killed my mom and her sister, was the taking of blood. Josef Mengele, known to history as the Angel of Death, was the SS chief medical officer in charge of selections. I have seen video testimonials of survivors describing him as a dark-haired, good-looking man, standing calmly in the midst of all the tumult of arriving prisoners, wearing white gloves and personally pointing at which sad souls were to go directly into the line for the gas chambers.

He also performed medical experiments at Auschwitz and was obsessed with experimenting on twins. Even though Mom was a year older than Yita, they looked very much alike. Mom told us, "Mengele thought we were twins, and I would say no, no, we are not twins! Still, they took our blood time and time again."

My aunt confirms this story. "We gave so much blood, every second day, for over a month or so. After, they would say you could go now, but when we got up, we would faint to the ground. We were so very weak, yet we would still have to go to work somehow."

At one point my mother, beyond caring anymore, defiantly said to her captors, "Why do you need my blood? I'm a *Jew*, you know. It's *Jewish* blood!"

The response was simply "It matches the soldiers' blood."

So much for pure Aryan blood. My aunt also tells of when she was at the end of *her* rope, and said to Mengele himself, "I just can't do it anymore."

He turned to her and replied coldly, "What do *you* need blood for? *We* need it." The inference was clear.

The Auschwitz-Birkenau complex was liberated on January 27, 1945, but when the Soviets arrived that day they found the camp silent and largely abandoned. The thousands of inmates who remained, hiding in the warehouses, had simply been left to die. But where had all the others gone?

By late 1944 the Germans could already see that the Soviets were close, and panic broke out amongst the Nazi brain trust. As they attempted to hastily destroy evidence of what had been happening there, Jews and other surviving prisoners were hurriedly transported by train out of Poland to camps inside Germany. Auschwitz was not the only camp to be suddenly evacuated; the same was happening all across the Reich as the Allies closed in on them. Jam-packed trains crisscrossed Germany in a desperate attempt by the crumbling Nazi regime to stave off the inevitable. And if trains were not available, the wretched were force-marched westward by foot towards Germany or distant train depots, sometimes for miles; it is estimated that these marches took the lives of more than 15,000 sick and emaciated prisoners. My mom believed that my dad had to endure one of these death marches. Her brother, Herschel, barely survived one that saw 3,400 people trudge from the Buchenwald camp to Munich for four long weeks, and by the time they were liberated in 1945, only 142 were left alive.

According to my aunt, they had a Kapo in their barracks, a Czechoslovakian woman who could be strict but also had a soft spot for mothers struggling to protect their children. She apparently sensed that unless they were moved, they would not survive Mengele's obsession with them. Yita says, "She couldn't stand to watch us suffer so badly when we came back from giving blood." As it happened, a train arrived to transport them to the Bergen-Belsen concentration camp in Germany, and despite some risk to herself this Kapo made sure my family did not miss it.

Just as my mother was returning to the barracks from a work detail, the Kapo said to Yita, "Go outside and stand in the square and wave at your sister so she can come to you." As Yita tried to do so a German guard grabbed her viciously by the neck, but she managed to break free and scramble onto the train with my mom. It is somewhat heartening to know that in that hellhole the occasional shred of decency was possible. Thankfully, it would not be the last time they would experience some kindly intervention.

In October 1944, my mother, grandmother and Aunt Yita arrived at Bergen-Belsen in Lower Saxony, Germany. Established as a prisoner-of-war camp the year before, it was hastily converted into three smaller camps as the war went on and the demand for space grew: the POW camp (*Kriegsgefangenenlager*), the Residence camp (*Aufenthaltslager*) and the Prisoners' camp (*Häftlingslager*). With the daily arrival of thousands of Jews and others from all over Europe, all three facilities were quickly overwhelmed.

Auschwitz had been purposefully designed as a systematic and efficient killing machine; Belsen was anything but. It was a place where these hapless people were basically left to die. The conditions were atrocious beyond measure. One Hungarian survivor, Alice Lok Cahana, also a teen at the time, said of it simply, "Bergen-Belsen was Hell. It was Hell . . . day and night."

When my mother first arrived winter was fast approaching. It was already cold and raining, and they were forced to live in tents until more barracks were built. After long torrential nights, they would wake up in pools of water and surrounded by those who had perished during the night. They had little food, existing mostly on a kind of watery cabbage soup. (In Canada my mother used to say the smell of cabbage alone made her ill.) Disease and starvation were rife. Tens of thousands died under those conditions, and by the end of the war the Germans no longer even bothered to bury the bodies piling up all over the camp. Mom told us once, "By that time we were like zombies. We would live and even sleep amongst the dead, sometimes for three days before anyone would take them away. Then they would just pile them up outside. We were numb, like we had no feelings left." These were almost unbearable stories for us to hear as children, but my mom wanted to emphasize what a miracle it was that she had survived.

She did in fact contract a serious case of typhus while she was in Belsen and was taken to the so-called hospital, which was nothing more than another barracks. As was the case in all of the camps, soldiers would come into these places at night, take the sick out and shoot them—if you couldn't work you were of no use. My grandmother had befriended a German nurse who volunteered to give her a heads-up as to which nights the soldiers were meant to come, and together they would push my mother out the window and take her back to the barracks or hide her in the latrine. The next morning during roll call my grandmother would hold her up as best she could, hiding her face so they couldn't tell how sick she was, and then conceal her under the straw in the barracks until it was dark. Then she would return her to the hospital, which was of course now empty of patients. Mom's illness was so serious that this back-and-forth went on for more than a month.

Unbeknownst to my mother as she was fighting for her life, Aunt Yita had been singled out by one of the German "commanders" (as I've learned, survivors seem to refer to any German of rank as a commander) to select six people for a special job. Among others Yita picked her cousins. At first they were upset with her, afraid of what horrible task they were in for, but they were taken to a room and told to separate and repair clothing that had belonged to the dead, to repurpose it for the living. Compared to the strenuous and often gruesome detail forced on most of the prisoners, it was a strangely sane and gentle piece of work. They did as they were told and were even allowed to choose some clothing for themselves, and at the end of the first day, this commander brought them food, including warm soup made from rice and milk to share with their families.

Yita remained in that job for weeks, scarcely believing her good fortune, and eventually discovered that the *Kommandant* was acting out of a desire to secretly do some good. When she asked him why he was helping them he said, "I have a daughter your age, and you remind me of her." When he saw Yita crying one day and asked her what was wrong, and she answered, "My sister is very sick with typhus, and I'm afraid she won't live," he actually slipped her some antibiotics. It's very likely that this one act of kindness saved my mother's life. In fact, Mom used to tell us about being awoken by a pinprick, opening her eyes and seeing the nurse standing over her with a smile on her face. Yita never knew the commander's name; prisoners were not permitted to address any German personally, only by rank or "sir." Shortly after their liberation, this rare man capable of decency shot himself rather than face justice for what he, willingly or not, had been a part of.

At long last, on April 15, 1945, the 63rd Anti-Tank Regiment and the 11th Armoured Division of the British Army entered the gates of Bergen-Belsen to free the approximately 60,000 prisoners still barely hanging on to their lives. My mom described the scene to us: "I was working in a woodshed piling wood. We were all starving or sick, and I noticed out one window that the Germans were standing with both hands up. I even joked to the others about it. 'Look!' I said. 'Now they're saluting Hitler with *both* hands.' We worked thirty minutes beyond our liberation because we didn't realize the British had arrived. When we were told to come out, and that we were free, we could not believe it. We were in shock. We had assumed there was no one left alive to save us, otherwise why had they not come sooner?"[*]

---

[*] When I told this story to Neil Peart in the early eighties, he and I wondered how far from hope one would have to fall to believe the only explanation for their continued incarceration was that no one else in the world was left alive to save them. This conversation led to the writing of our song "Red Sector A."

Yita's experience was quite different from my mother's: "When the British arrived, they lifted me onto the first tank. As I showed them around the camp, I was so happy, it was the greatest day of my life!"

My mother continued, "When we came out of the woodshed the British were so stunned to see us, they couldn't take it. They were just sitting down and, you know, crying. They couldn't believe the horror of it. And yet we were used to it."

I recently watched some heart-rending video footage of the scenes my mother is talking about. It brought me to tears, not for the first time whilst writing this account. The British soldiers *were* clearly devastated, many of them weeping and being physically sick from what they had found. They forced the now-arrested Germans to move the hundreds of bodies tossed in piles around the camp from trucks to the mass graves, while the now-liberated prisoners shouted and cursed at them in a Babel of languages.

"But the soldiers were also making some mistakes," Mom said. "They would put the Nazis in the trucks but forget to search them—some would have a gun hidden and start shooting innocent people. So even though the war was over, some prisoners died *after* they were liberated.

"The British couldn't do enough for us. They gave us food, whatever they had, candies or whatever, which my mother forbade us to eat. She would take it all and every day give us just a little bit, which was so wise because we weren't used to that kind of food. Many others got sick from it, and without enough medication to help them recover, some even died. So up until the very end my mother kept on saving us."[*]

Honestly, I cannot for a moment imagine where they found the strength and courage to carry on. Many survivors, like my own family,

---

[*] Tragically, of the approximately 40,000 prisoners who died at Belsen between the years of 1943 and 1945 (including its most famous inmates, Anne Frank and her sister, Margot), more than 13,000 prisoners were too ill to recover and died after they were liberated.

desperately held on to their faith to get them through; shockingly to me, their belief in God had persisted throughout those six years of carnage; others relied on their own defiance as a survival-of-the-fittest mentality; and others, well, they simply tried not to succumb for as long as they possibly could. My cousin Zecharia described his liberation this way: "By some miracle I survived. God makes miracles, but this was not a miracle from God. I am a religious man, but I don't know where God was then."

Throughout my life, whenever I've thought back on my parents' horror-filled experiences, I've felt immeasurable admiration for their strength and enormous sadness for what they endured. I also get why so many *children* of survivors struggle. It sounds absurd that a child of a survivor should suffer guilt for something they had absolutely nothing to do with, but it's a real thing. I understand that living in the shadow of so much suffering can cause deeply stressful if irrational emotions, and that some people are never able to shake them off. To find happiness in my life I've done my best to reconcile those feelings through therapy, through self-examination, through acceptance. The healthiest way to deal with them, in my experience, is to talk about them—so I'm thankful to my mother for having told us her stories at the dinner table; they were proof that the human spirit can overcome terrible adversity without ever forgetting those who sacrificed *everything* to make happiness possible for me and the ones I love.

As I mentioned earlier, details of my father's survival after Auschwitz are very sketchy, but I believe he was transferred or marched out around the same time my mom was sent to Belsen. For a long time, I imagined that he'd found himself in the prototype of the death camps, Dachau, on the outskirts of Munich, and my sister recently found a piece of paper amongst my mother's things that not only bears this out but lists *all* the camps he had been incarcerated in until his ultimate liberation on May 5, 1945, an unbelievable seven in total, making his survival even more miraculous: Starachowice, Auschwitz,

Flossenburg, Landsberg (aka Kaufering, one of eleven sub-camps that comprised the Dachau concentration camp), Buchenwald, Leipzig and Mauthausen. He never talked about how he survived. I have to assume it was down to his physical strength and his ability to keep working, but his body paid a terrible price, for after the war he was diagnosed with serious heart damage, which cost him his life when he was only forty-five.

We do know that sometime after his liberation from Dachau in May that spring, he ended up in Feldafing Displaced Persons Camp, twenty miles southwest of Munich in the American Zone, where, amazingly, he ran into my mom's brother, Herschel. Every day after that reunion, they would check the bulletin boards where the names of survivors across Germany and beyond were posted, in hopes of finding

*This note in my mother's handwriting lists the places of*
*Dad's incarceration. By "dead March" she means "death march."*

any scrap of news of their families. This was where my dad first learned that only he and his brother Shloima had survived. Then one day, there in black and white, he saw the names Manya, Ida and Ruchla Rubenstein. Unbelievably, all were alive and living in Bergen-Belsen. *Halle-fucking-lujah!*

Initially, they planned to make the nearly six-hundred-kilometer journey to Belsen together, but Herschel needed to gather his things from where he was staying in Munich, and by the time he returned to Feldafing my dad, impatient and desperate to be reunited with my mom, had left without him. They travelled separately by foot and on open train cars with numerous other survivors in search of the remnants of their lives.

Meanwhile, my mother and her family were recovering in the Displaced Persons Camp at Bergen-Belsen—basically the soldiers' and officers' quarters beside the camp. Here they were still required to line up for food, mostly soup in these early post-liberation days. During that time a policeman named Leon took a liking to my mom. He'd pay her special attention and even bring her extra soup, and when he saw that she was sharing a room with another family, he arranged for her, Ida and their mom to settle in one of their own. Clearly, he had *intentions*. When my mother told him she had a boyfriend, even if she didn't know whether or not he'd survived, he replied, "Well, if he's no longer alive, then I will be your friend."

Whenever she stepped out with him, she always brought along a cousin as a chaperone. One day they went to a party with some people from the area around Leon's hometown of Ostrowiec—an area that included my father's, Gozdzielin. At that party a person told Leon he had a letter for someone named Manya Rubinstein and was instructed to give it to her in person only. After some back-and-forth, my mom grabbed the letter from him and ran off saying, "I know her, I'll give it to her!" (In the rampant paranoia of the time, people didn't like announcing who they were. Survivors all suffered from different kinds of post-traumatic stress disorder—and some of them kept strange habits to the day they died.

My mother, for example, could never abide an unlocked door, even if we were playing right outside it, because she feared the Germans might come marching in. She always used to say, "It could happen again!")

She grabbed the letter and, not knowing whether it contained good news or bad, ran off to read it in private. Then she screamed and ran home to share the incredible news but was so hysterical that my grandmother had to slap her to snap her out of it. Finally she got the words out: "Herschel and Moishe are alive and coming to us!"

Some days later an opera was being performed on the grounds of the Displaced Persons Camp. As my mom approached with Yita, she saw someone in the crowd she thought she recognized. She asked Yita to call his name, which she did, but he didn't answer. They continued on until they came to a small stream, which they had to jump over to get to the opera. She paused and asked her cousin to wait a moment. "Something was pushing me to go and see who those people were. I was hoping so much that it was him. So I got close and called out loud, 'Moishe?' and he turned to me. It *was* him."

Though my mom knew Herschel was also alive and on his way, when four days later she looked out the second-story window of her barracks, the sheer disbelief of seeing him too in the flesh made her weak at the knees. She leaned so far out the window that my grandmother had to grab hold of her to keep her from falling.

On November 21, 1946, my mother and father were married in the Officers' Mess Hall at Bergen-Belsen. What had been a roomful of coldblooded and ruthless persecutors was now a room filled with love, family and the promise of a new future together.

## LIFE AFTER THE WAR

**AFTER THEY WERE** married, they lived together at the Displaced Persons Camp. Postwar Germany and Poland were then suffering, bombed-out places, divided into different sectors and controlled by the British, American or Soviet military police. Inevitably, there was lawlessness everywhere as devastated people tried to feed themselves and pick up the pieces of their war-torn lives. During this time, my dad, who'd gone into the camp with nothing and come out with ten bucks, tried to earn money selling jewelry with a friend and dabbling in the black market with his brother, but that meant frequent hitchhikes across Germany, and his absences were nerve-racking for my mom. Then he was arrested and thrown in jail in Celle, near Bergen-Belsen, and of course my mother was desperate to get him out. As luck had it, when she got to the jailhouse, all the officers had run off to deal with some big protest going on in another part of town, leaving no one

(LEFT) *Mom and Dad posing post-wedding in front of their home in the barracks of the Bergen-Belsen Displaced Persons Camp.* (RIGHT) *Can you imagine a wedding in such an effin' location? Somehow my grandmother managed to scrounge up enough material to make my mom a beautiful wedding dress.*

standing guard. Arresting black marketeers was a daily occurrence in that period, and he wasn't a murderer or a hardened criminal, so security was lax, and she managed to set him free.

This time my mother said, "Enough!" and he left the black market. They were then so afraid the police would come and take him back to jail that when they were told of an available apartment in Wörth an der Donau, near Regensburg, 450 kilometers away, they jumped at the chance. It meant leaving her mother and the rest of her family behind, but the farther away they could get from that jail in Celle the better. Of course, the police never came. In all the chaos of those times, there were much bigger fish to fry.

My parents were bitter at how readily they had been betrayed by the Poles, and fearful of how they might be greeted should they return. Nonetheless, they resolved to go back to Poland to find what remained of their homes and possessions—and most important, glean whatever information they could about missing family members. They hitchhiked with a group of people—although the sunny-sounding word "hitch-hiked" belies how dangerous a journey it was across such a smouldering, desperate postwar landscape. Soon after reaching Poland, they'd begun to realize that the wounds of betrayal by their former Polish neighbours were still fresh. Returning survivors were often met with anger and resistance from locals who claimed that they had been given or had purchased their former homes—even though some houses still had the original owners' possessions in them. In the end, the trip was too confrontational and painful. They gave up and turned their backs on their former homeland, vowing never to speak the Polish language again.

The one thing of significance my mother was able to retrieve was a single photo of her father in a Polish Army uniform from the First World War. It remains the only photo she or any members of her family possess of him. Wherever we lived when I was a child, I saw it in a place of prominence, and it was on display in her home to the day she died.

(TOP LEFT) *Life in post-war Germany: I don't know the exact circumstances of this photo, nor who the people are aside from my mom and dad (on the right at the back), but it seems to me they are standing in a burial ground. Their grim demeanor and the pine boxes at their feet tell us all we need to know.* (TOP RIGHT) *My uncle Herschel Rubenstein and an unidentified cousin (back row), Aunt Yita Rubenstein, my mother (middle row); and the camp rabbi Dr. Tvi Helfgott (in front), my cousin who performed the marriage ceremony for my parents.* (BOTTOM) *The only surviving photo of my grandfather, Gershon Eliezer Rubinstajn.*

With the help of my dad's sister Rose, who had been living in Canada since before the war, my parents eventually decided to emigrate. They had to wait two more years, but finally got their official travel documents, and on a snowy Christmas Eve in 1948 they arrived in Toronto, Ontario. They would begin their new life in this foreign land as Mary and Morris Weinrib.

## POSTSCRIPT

IN 1995 MY mother received a letter from the organization of her hometown, the Wierzbniker Society. It was an invitation for her and her family to attend the official ceremonies celebrating the fiftieth anniversary of the liberation of Bergen-Belsen. Many towns in Poland had one of these societies, set up to help their former citizens, and especially survivors of the Holocaust. The Toronto chapter is remarkable in that it has the largest single community of survivors from that region.

So one day my phone rings and Mom's on the line. Rather coyly she says, "So, I got a letter from the Wierzbniker Society. Their main office, in New York City."

"Oh yeah?" I reply. Silence on the other end. "*And?*"

"Vell, dey are havink a ceremony in Germany at Bergen-Belsen and dey are inviting some survivors to go."

"Really?" I say. "Is this something that interests you?"

"Vell . . ." she says. "*Maybe* I could go . . ."

I started laughing and said, "Oh, you *could* go? Mom, are you asking me to reach out to them? You sound like you *want* to go."

She answered in her typical passive-aggressive way, "Vell, if *you* want to go, I'll go?"

Again I laughed. "Okay, Mom, how about I phone them and arrange a family trip. Susie and Allan and me, we'll all go with you, what do you say?"

"Okay . . ." she said. "It's a good idea. All right, ve'll go."

Well played, Mrs. Weinrib, well played.

The plan was to fly with her to Germany for the ceremony at Bergen-Belsen and make a trip to Poland afterwards. We'd spend a couple of days researching her roots in Warsaw, then drive south, stopping off in her hometown of Starachowice en route to the Auschwitz-Birkenau concentration camp. We'd end our trip in nearby Kraków.

My mom was surprisingly keen to return, but nervous too, and I thought it was courageous of her to undertake the trip at all. My brother and I agreed to share video and audio recording responsibilities, reckoning it a fine opportunity to interview her about her past and record her memories for posterity—as well as interview any other willing survivors or military personnel we encountered along the way.

We arrived at Celle, the nearest town to Bergen-Belsen. That night we attended a ceremony in the Schlosstheater. There we met several other survivors with their families, and a British soldier named Frank Chapman, who, along with his wife, had come there from their home in North Yorkshire. Frank had been part of the initial tank force entering the camp on that extraordinary day in April 1945. He was a

(LEFT) *My mother at the entrance to the camp* (RIGHT) *and with one of her saviours, Mr. Frank Chapman, still haunted by the horror the British Army came upon that day in April 1945.*

gentle man, thrilled to see my mother and the others as he told stories about the gruesome jobs his brigade had been tasked with on their arrival at Belsen. His wife told me that he still had nightmares of those days, and she hoped that the trip would be healing for him as much as for the people he had liberated. I can tell you that his face lit up when my mother took his hands in hers and thanked him for saving her life, and I truly hope his experience helped to ease his troubled soul.

The next morning we joined a busload of survivors and their families and were taken to visit the camp for the commemoration ceremonies, which would include a speech by Chancellor Helmut Kohl.

When I say camp, I really mean memorial site, since back in 1945 the British and German authorities had decided it should be razed to the ground. Fifty years later there was little left but mounds of mass graves and memorial plaques. At the time of liberation, the reason—or more to the point, the *excuse*—they gave for its immediate destruction was that there was too much disease, typhus mostly; it was for the protection of all that the place be burned to the ground. Typhus had indeed been a real threat to the inmates of the camp—my mother

(LEFT) *The mass graves of Bergen-Belsen then, and* (RIGHT) *fifty years later.*
*As difficult as you may find looking at the photo from 1945, it is typical*
*of the images burned into the childhood memories of my siblings and me*
*and makes clear why the gentle Mr. Chapman—whose main job it was to*
*operate the bulldozers—was so troubled for the rest of his life.*

barely survived it—but it was more complicated than that. The real reason was likely political. At the war's end, Germany's government (such as it was) was pressuring the Allies not to allow such a foul reminder of what had transpired on their own soil to be left standing, especially within spitting distance of the local populace.

The barracks and officers' quarters were still standing, however, and as we had lunch at one of the long tables in the large mess hall, my mother made a stunning announcement. As if she were in the middle of a thought she said, "Yes, I think that this is the room I was married in . . . Yes, after the war we lived in zat building over there, and ven your father finally found us, soon we got married . . . Right *here*, in *this* room. Uncle Helfgott performed the ceremony and arranged for all of the British soldiers to leave the building during it."* My siblings and I went silent as we took in what she'd just said. Here we were, in the very room where my parents had been married forty-nine years before, as we sat eating our rubber chicken.

As the luncheon continued, a woman about my mother's age leaned in and asked her name. It turned out that not only had they lived together in the same barracks, but they'd slept in the *same bunk*. They'd had two-tier bunks, my mother up top and her below, sleeping nine in each—in three rows, head-to-toe. As our cousin Miriam once described, "If one person turned over, you *all* had to turn over. Can you imagine sleeping crowded like that, so close together on bare wood with just a little straw? Like herrings!" (Miriam's two-year-old sister and grandmother had both been killed by the SS on the day of the Aktion, while, incredibly, she'd spend almost the entirety of the war with her two sisters and mother in the same barracks alongside my mother, my aunt and my grandmother. Miraculously, they all survived *three* different concentration and death camps together.)

It was a solemn day listening to the speeches and wandering around

---

* Hermann Helfgott (aka Dr. Zvi Asaria), the chief rabbi of the British-occupied zone in Germany, was actually a cousin, the son of my mother's grandmother's brother (try saying *that* five times quickly!), but they called him "uncle" out of respect.

the large mounds of grass—the final resting place of innumerable murdered men, women and children. We were deeply affected, but it was time to move on to another and possibly more emotional destination: Manya Rubinstein's Poland.

The following day we arrived in Warsaw and were picked up by a friendly driver who spoke very bad English. My mother started speaking to him, fluently, in the language she had avoided for close to fifty years. (She and Dad often spoke Yiddish at home, so we understood that one; they'd only revert to Polish when they wanted to talk privately or when my grandmother swore at us for behaving badly.) This was when I first noticed a change come over her.

In Germany, she'd seemed a little frail and subdued, weighed down by the moment, obviously, and my siblings and I had made all the travel and logistical decisions for the trip. We were guiding *her*. But in Poland she came to life. Even that first day, walking through the Old Town market square, we could see how excited she was to be there as the memories of her childhood flooded back (even though the entire town square was a replica of the original, which had been completely destroyed during the war). Although on one level she was anxious, the overall effect on her was positive, and in some ways she became the strong one; she was now the one dealing with the locals, announcing us to the hotel clerk, ordering in the restaurants and giving our driver directions—while we reverted to being the children.

She was a bit disoriented when we first arrived in Starachowice. It had been fifty years, after all, and the architecture and layout of the town had of course changed. But she soon found her footing, instructing the driver to follow the train tracks to what used to be Wierzbnik. In a matter of minutes, we were parked in front of her old home, which was not only still standing but, incredibly, looked to her as it had the last time she'd seen it. She pointed out her bedroom window, and my brother and I got out to take pictures and shoot some video. But as soon as we did, she started yelling.

"Get back in the car, it's not safe! Someone could shoot you!"

If her reaction sounds extreme, you should remember that when she'd last been there Europe was ravaged and smouldering, as survivors faced the reality that they'd become citizens without a country. In June 1945 alone as many as eleven Jews were murdered by local Poles in the Starachowice area when they tried to reclaim their property. Their betrayal by the Polish people would never be forgotten. Nor would the locals care to be reminded of it yet again. This trip was a first for us, but many other Jews had returned in search of their lost past before us, which some of the older Poles regarded as snooping around. In the short time we were there, though we did receive kindnesses, our mere presence provoked more than one incident of drunken people coming up to us, even at memorials, spouting words of hate for we Jews. It's no wonder so many survivors gave up and turned their backs on their homeland for good.

We did not linger in Starachowice but continued south towards Kraków and our next destination, Auschwitz-Birkenau. It was a journey,

(LEFT) *Look at this modest, seemingly innocuous house in Wierzbnik, my mother's childhood home. Can you imagine huddling with your family there when, in the middle of the night, SS soldiers barge in to drag your father away?* (RIGHT) *Kraków town square. So I say to this local, "You mean to tell me, just an hour's drive from Auschwitz and no one knew what was happening? Yeah, right."*

(TOP LEFT) *The road to Auschwitz-Birkenau. The sheer scale of the grounds shocked me.*
(TOP RIGHT) *The gatehouse, through which the jam-packed train carrying my family arrived at the selection platform.* (MIDDLE LEFT) *What remains of one of the gas chambers.*
(BOTTOM LEFT) *The prisoner barracks in the women's section of the camp that my mother called home for three months before being shipped on to Bergen-Belsen.* (BOTTOM RIGHT) *Inside the barracks, where they slept nine to a bunk "like herrings."*

I can tell you, that filled us with dread. We did our best to keep the spirits high for Mom's sake, but by the time we arrived the atmosphere was intense.

As we walked through those gates beneath the infamous *Arbeit Macht Frei* we all got chills. My mother looked down to the ground a lot, her eyes welling up. She tried to get her bearings, but the installations there were a nightmare of disorientation: display cabinets filled with massive quantities of eyeglasses, prosthetic limbs, suitcases and other belongings, and photographs with images that one can never unsee. We followed the train tracks and saw the purpose-built ramp next to it, where all the arrivals had endured their first selection. Then we made our way to the barracks zone, where my mother tried to recall which hut she'd lived in for those four months in 1944. Finally, we wandered down to the bombed-out gas chambers and the still-standing ovens. A school group from Israel walked solemnly ahead of us.

All things considered, Mom held up pretty well. We slowly made our way back to the car and drove off towards Kraków—none too soon, I might add. I was in dire need of a stiff drink, as I'm sure my siblings were (and as you likely are right now). Kraków is a beautiful, ancient and surprisingly hip town, full of college kids, and strolling its mediaeval streets and hearing music throb from its clubs and underground caverns was a balm to the soul. In my mind I raised a toast:

"*L'chaim!* To life!"

But I must give the last words of this account to my mother. As we stood beside her on the grounds of the concentration camp at Bergen-Belsen, listening to Chancellor Helmut Kohl speak, she said to the three of us, "As I listen to these speeches, I realize, maybe for the first time, that it was I who have actually won the war. I am still here, standing on German soil with my three children, and the Nazis are dead and gone. I only wish that my sister and my brother would have come here with us for this event, it would have done them good!"

After fifty years, she had triumphed. Talk about closure.

# CHAPTER 4

*The earliest known photo of me playing guitar: summer of*
*'66 on a visit to Detroit, wowing my cousins with "For Your Love"*
*(and my brand new Beatle boots). Cool enough for ya?*

EFORE I LOST MY DAD, I WAS PAINFULLY
aware of being a nerdy kid and very much a loner. You'd
reasonably reckon my year of mourning and the isolation
that came with it would only escalate my angst and make
the chances of busting out of that loner persona tougher, but if there is
one thing you can say about Jewish rules for grieving, it's that they're
nothing if not practical. I had done my duty, and although I was now a
thirteen-year-old going through wildly mixed emotions, I was formally
encouraged to return to the land of the living. My mom knew that I

had been a good enough boy by continuing to say Kaddish thrice a day without too much complaint, and she allowed me to circulate with friends and get back into some kind of groove. By June 1966, with school done for the year, I was still saddened beyond measure by my loss but champing at the bit to enter teenage society.

Can you imagine how alienating that dark and solemn year had been for a twelve-year-old boy who'd only just developed a taste for rock and roll? In my year of mourning no music was allowed at home (not even studying it). I did occasionally hear songs in shops or in someone's car, and the radio was also always on in the background at the variety store Mom was now running alone, but when I emerged, I was still a fish out of water. I knew nearly none of the current hits, had lost touch with my favourite bands and was woefully out of step with my classmates and my friends. I was embarrassed and desperate to catch up.

That year of frustration had lit a fire under my ass. I became obsessed with buying records, mostly singles, spending everything I earned from working at the store: Roy Orbison's "Oh, Pretty Woman," the Yardbirds' classic "For Your Love," Billy Joe Royal's "Down in the Boondocks," and the Hollies' "Pay You Back with Interest," off their *Stop! Stop! Stop!* album, was an early fave. Mom had started selling records, meanwhile, mainly older releases she'd bought at wholesale discount, but I'd occasionally find a Motown or pop nugget in the bin (since before my voice broke, I'd always been drawn to Aretha Franklin and the Supremes' voices; I liked their range and would imagine them in my head) and I remember being mesmerized by the cover of *Are You Experienced* with its fisheye-lens shot of Hendrix, Redding and Mitchell surrounded by luscious gold and that fabulous, psychedelic purple font. I'd go down to a friend's house at the bottom of my street to put my copy of the Beach Boys, *Surfer Girl* on the platter: songs like "Little Deuce Coupe" and "In My Room" were my favourites, the latter mostly because it was to that one, in that basement, that I first slow danced and kissed a girl.

My next-door neighbour Terry Kurtzer told me he was selling his acoustic guitar. It had palm trees painted on either side of the sound hole, which were kinda goofy, but to me the idea of owning an actual guitar was beyond cool. I begged Mom for the money to buy it, and surprisingly she relented—if with a furrowed brow. I wish I could recall what made me think I could learn to play, but all I know is that I *really* wanted it. Once I started fiddling and plunking, I was ecstatic to find that I could reproduce the first few notes of "Oh, Pretty Woman." I pushed on to learn some chords and could soon play part of "For Your Love" by ear (don't be too impressed; it basically has only four chords!). After that I fell into it full tilt.

My first band was made up of a few neighbourhood kids. We rehearsed in my friend's apartment bedroom with no amps to speak of. I played my acoustic until the mother of the bassist decided she didn't want him hanging out with the rest of us degenerates. No one wanted to take up the bass, so we drew straws and I "won." Actually, that was fine by me—it had fewer strings, for a start, and I hadn't advanced very far with six—but alas, I didn't own one. I went to my mom again and wore her down to front me money that I promised to work off in the store.

For the thirty-five dollars she loaned me, I bought a black solid-body Japanese-made Canora electric bass. I hadn't learned to do much on my acoustic but strum a few chords and had never tried soloing, but took to this instrument quickly, obsessed with singling out the bass parts on any song I happened to hear. I started to woodshed big time, buying more records and listening over and over, determined to be the best player I could. I had to know *all* the bands, the coolest and most obscure songs, and connect with all the other kids who could play. Aside from music being the only thing that turned me on, it was the quickest route to acceptance by my peers, not to mention the best way to get noticed by girls in grades seven and eight. I took it all *very* seriously. Actually, before I started writing this memoir, I hadn't really realized just how seriously I took it, or how quickly I shed my nerdy skin that year.*

By then Shutty and I were hanging out regularly and going to concerts, mostly at North York Centennial Arena or the local YMHA. We saw some terrific bands, like the Kensington Market; the Paupers, whose drummer Skip Prokop would later cofound Lighthouse, and whose bassist Denny Gerrard we both held in awe; and Mandala, a blue-eyed soul group featuring the singer George Olliver and the Toronto guitarist Domenic Troiano, who had some success in Canada with a single called "Opportunity." Troiano was a local legend with his twangy, funky Telecaster sound. Every city's young musicians need someone local to look up to, and in a city without many homegrown guitar heroes he stood out by a mile as an originator and champion of funk-rock guitar. His reputation spread beyond Canada when he took Joe Walsh's place in the James Gang on their underrated *Straight Shooter* album, and joined the Guess Who after that.

My friends and I, "weekend hippies," used to take the bus downtown to Yorkville Village to walk amongst the *real* ones. At the time it was Toronto's answer to San Francisco's Haight-Ashbury, with a raft of clubs and coffeehouses like the Riverboat, the Gaslight, the Mynah Bird, the Penny Farthing and the Uppercrust, where we'd nurse a baguette and a pot of tea for as long as we could get away with, looking groovy and hoping to catch a glimpse of one of our local heroes.

The dad of one of my pals opened a restaurant in a laneway off Yorkville called the Cabbage Roll, where my pal and I got jobs washing

---

* Skin itself can be a measure of your seriousness as a guitarist: in those early days, pressing down on the bass's fat strings wore my fingertips down so badly that some days I could barely play—and that would get worse once I learned that John Entwistle and Chris Squire used round-wounds and acquired some for myself. I tried bandaging my fingertips, but that muted the sound; I tried that fake skin stuff, Nu Skin, to no avail. In the end, there was nothing for it but to play through the pain until the nerves were deadened and the skin grew a tough shell, with grooves where the strings went. Then, diving back into intensive rehearsals after a layoff, I'd find the carapace had softened and would have to suffer the process all over again. Only after many years of abuse would my fingers become permanently insensitive—and I could stick pins in the tips for a manly party trick.

dishes. On breaks we'd smoke cigarettes in the back alley, trying to fit in with the hippies—a much older crowd, but we didn't care. A rock club called the Flick shared the same basement area as the restaurant, and I remember sneaking in the back door one afternoon to look at the gear that a band called the Stitch in Tyme had set up on a low stage.* I stood there in awe of the amplification equipment that glimmered and glowed in the semi-dark, thinking, That's *what I want to do* . . . The stuff of dreams!

*Denny Gerrard of the Paupers (seen here at the Monterey Pop Festival in 1967) was my first bass hero. After Steve and I saw him play, we both decided to take up the bass. I persisted with that four-stringed piece of wood; he stuck with hockey sticks. Good calls!*

---

\* They were a psychedelic cover band who had a national hit with the Beatles' "Got to Get You into My Life." More pub quiz trivia: they'd originally called themselves the Golden Earing, but had to switch when they learned of the existence of a Dutch band, the Golden Earrings—who themselves would change their name when they dropped "the" in 1967 and the "s" in 1969!

IT'S TRUE, IS it not, that out of chaos sometimes comes order? It can focus the mind. For in retrospect I can see that bass had always been, you might say, in my blood and bones. Listening to the radio in the car on the way to work with my parents, it was usually the bass line in songs, often Motown ones like "In the Midnight Hour" and "My Girl," that drove a song for me. (I also used to drum on the dashboard. The tinny car radio gave you the crispness of the snare, while beating your hands on the dashboard provided the extra bottom that AM could not. So many kids did that, I'm sure, that some of the drums you'd hear on records in the sixties and seventies were a subconscious re-creation of that sound. Listen to the snare sounds that Bill Szymczyk used to get when he produced those Eagles records and tell me he wasn't channeling that same memory!)

Mom, meanwhile, was discovering herself to be a strong and highly capable businesswoman. In spite of the load she was carrying, she made the store such a going concern that she soon bought the old Canadian Tire building a few doors down, occupying half of it while renting out the other half. Gotta give it to her, she had the survivor spirit, smart and unafraid to take chances, but of course it weighed heavily on her that I was more and more interested in rock music than in school. The irony of my unknowingly following in my father's musical footsteps cannot have been lost on her.

I was burying myself in music, mimicking the artists I loved, dreaming of nothing but being in a band and escaping the grief-stricken place that our home had become. I began listening seriously to a lot of San Francisco–based bands like the Grateful Dead and Jefferson Airplane—to Phil Lesh and especially Jack Casady, whose tone and inventiveness blew me away: I loved the audacious tendency he had of building his own melodies within a song, with just enough taste to temper that audacity. I liked players like Paul Samwell-Smith of the Yardbirds, but they sometimes seemed much of a muchness to me with their bottomy sound and their reluctance to step boldly outside of the rhythm section. Paul McCartney was the best of the bunch—his notes bounced more melodically and inventively, just as the early Motown bass players like James Jamerson had—but it wasn't until I heard Casady and Jack Bruce of Cream that I got a different sense of the role a bass could play, assuming a bolder, darker, more authoritative sound, commanding attention the way a lead guitar was expected to, but in the subspace of the audio spectrum. From then on I would always gravitate towards players like Casady, Bruce, John Entwistle and Chris Squire, training my ear to hear that sound, fine tune it and somehow make it my own.

I soon went from that bedroom band to another along with my drummer friend Burd—the same guy who had dubbed me "Geddy." Sparked by his hyperactive imagination, we gave ourselves several far-out, imitatively psychedelic band names, including the Dusty Coconuts, the Aqua-Lined Dimension of the Mind and the Blueberry Hyena Underwater. What do you expect? It was the sixties, man! This was during a phase of burning incense and even "meditating" to our records. We were suburban wannabe freaks, fans of Frank Zappa and open to oddities like the Fugs and Sky Saxon and the Seeds. I loved harder rock, but Fugs songs like "C.I.A. Man" and "Kill for Peace" struck me as daring, relevant and funny. (Listen to the lyrics of "Wide, Wide River" with them singing "river of shit" in three-part harmony!) Those guys could surprise you with their melodic skill on songs like "Morning, Morning," but how could a teenager not love a band that swears on their albums and protests "the Man"? Think of the times, when even Canadians were affected by the anti-war movement in post-Kennedy America. Draft dodgers were coming north and settling incognito all across the country, and we teens wanted to identify, letting our freak flags fly even if we didn't altogether "grok the fullness" of the situation. (Burd and I were such big Fugs fans that in October of 1968 we went to see them at Massey Hall in Toronto. Tuli Kupferberg stuck around after the show to chat with a few of us in the front row. I had stars in my eyes talking to a real rock star, if a fairly obscure and unlikely one. He gave up so much time to answer our questions that the rest of the band left without him, and Burd and I had to help him hail a cab out on the street. His generous nature and my first-ever brush with fame left a lasting impression on me.)

For months Shutty, one of the first gentile friends I made outside of my suburban Jewish "ghetto," had been insisting I meet a certain blond kid he knew—someone I'd already noticed around the school flashing his cherubic smile, his short blond hair brushed over to one side and wearing a white-and-purple paisley shirt that was all the rage at the time. Shutty couldn't say this guy's Serbian last name, calling him "Zivonovich." In fact, of all our friends, only I seemed to be able to pronounce it correctly: Alexandar Živojinović . . .

*Grade nine shop class. Mr. Wilson (whom we dubbed "Fuzzby" after the multitude of hairs tufting out of his nostrils) would announce, "Gather round the metal lathe, please," as Alex and I stifled our laughter.*

Alex was well-liked at school, despite presenting as a bit of a teacher's pet. You know the type: front of the class, sitting bolt upright with a grin on his face. But after we finally met in that same class, the proverbial trouble began. We'd sit together in the last row and goof off, provoking each other, cracking each other up and obsessively sharing our love of hard, blues-based rock music when we ought to have been paying attention. The way Alex describes us is like being a "little island" unto ourselves—not unfriendly towards the other kids, just not as interested in hanging around with them any longer.[*]

There wasn't enough time in the day to talk about bands, players, technique and musical styles: John Mayall and the Bluesbreakers, the Who, Ten Years After . . . During recess and lunch hour, Burd and I would recite entire Mothers of Invention songs by heart. ("Brown shoes don't make it / Quit school, why fake it?") Amongst the other budding young players in our schoolyard, it was mainly about speed, always arguing about which guitarist or bassist was fastest up and down the neck.

"Jimmy Page is the fastest, man!"

"No way, man. Alvin Lee is way, *way* faster!"

"But what about Mick Taylor on 'Driving Sideways'? His parts are amazing!"

Alex would come over after school to jam and spin records, and it was around that time we both became mad for Cream. Jack Bruce, Eric Clapton and Ginger Baker set the bar for us, with *Fresh Cream* just about glued to my turntable as we tried to figure out "Sleepy Time Time," "Rollin' and Tumblin'" and "Spoonful." (In the not-too-distant future these songs would become staples of early Rush sets.) We were becoming tight pals, choosing our classes together, picking the ones we thought would be easy, like, er . . . typing, and one time even signed

---

[*]   I should mention that writing this book has given me an opportunity to reminisce with Alex, compare notes and verify the accuracy of my recollections. He has an incredibly specific memory for things I've long forgotten—and vice versa. In many ways our neural pathways operate in a complementary fashion. But that's for my science program next week!

each other's name to our exam sheets. Despite our budding bromance, meanwhile, we were still playing with other people; Alex and his friend John Rutsey had first been in a band called the Projection, and then formed a trio with a singer and bassist named Jeff Jones . . . It was John's older brother who suggested they call *that* band "Rush."

One day we got it into our heads to paint our instruments in a terrible imitation of Clapton's psychedelic Gibson SG. We applied little dots of some gummy fluorescent green material to the headstocks, "BLUES" in fluorescent orange all the way from the bridge to the treble pickup, and in a style not even *close* to that of the Fool, I managed a rather shitty cartoon of myself.* What I'd pay to see *that* thing again.

Then one day Alex (the self-styled "Supreme Pothead of the Universe") told me excitedly that he had some marijuana.

"Wow," I said. "That's illegal, isn't it?"

"Well, yeah, but it's cool," he reassured me. "Let's go to the schoolyard and smoke up."

We sat by the portables,** and I smoked my first joint—the first of several thousand for me, but about a zillion for him. I got so effin' high I felt like I was walking on the moon. Then in a panic I remembered I had a rehearsal at Burd's house. Alex and I walked over together, but when we got there it was obvious I was in no shape to play. Burd on the other hand was straight as an arrow and, despite having a wild imagination, not in the least interested in smoking weed. He was livid and threatened to tell my mom. We split, but I felt too paranoid to go home. Alex said, "Don't worry, we'll go to the gas station and get a bottle of Coca-Cola. Coke brings you down, man, you'll be fine." Alex the scientist to the rescue—except, of course, it was useless. The best I could do was sneak into the house, straight to my room, close the door, listen to music and wait it out.

---

* Formed by Simon Posthuma and Marijke Koger, the Fool was an art collective most famous for decorating John Lennon's Rolls Royce and the Beatles' Apple store.
** Temporary wooden classrooms outside the main school building.

It may come as no surprise to you that at that time Alex was often in trouble with his parents, once even running away from home and living in one of the neighbourhood parks. "I was very emotional," he told me. "I was rebellious without a cause, just normal teenage stuff, I guess, but I'd snap quickly, like, 'You can't tell me what to do! Fuck you, I'm *outta* here.' I'd sleep in a park for a day and then come back home and go, 'Hi! What's to eat?'"

He'd come to my back door so I could sneak him some food, mostly blueberry buns that my mother always kept in the house for the children to snack on. When he tired of sleeping outdoors, I suggested he climb the TV antenna into my sister's room, where I'd be waiting for him. Then we slipped into my room and he crashed on the floor. Of course, we both slept in and awoke to my mother freaking out about the blond girl asleep beneath a blanket by my bed. When she realized that it was him, she was only a little relieved. After peppering him with questions she called his mother, Mellie, and that was the start of ongoing communication between the moms regarding what could be done about their wayward boys. Oy, what in the world would ever become of us?

My basement band was still impatient to do a real show. We got up enough nerve to set up an audition for a Battle of the Bands at Fisherville Jr. High. Burd's parents helped us cart our gear to the school and set up in a classroom. Two teachers appeared and sat in front of us as we launched into our first number. We were doing all right and had almost finished when Burd, a major Who freak, decided to pull a Keith Moon. Drums and cymbals rolled and crashed around the classroom as the teachers sat aghast and our guitarist and I stood stock still, embarrassed as hell. Seeing our crestfallen expressions, they told us we could still play—but only if we found a different drummer. So that's what we did.

I can't recall the name of the drummer who sat in for Burd, but I distinctly recall the gig. We rented two small matching white Ace

Tone amplifiers and set them up on either side of the drum kit on the cafeteria stage. We played something by the Blues Project with Al Kooper and the great guitarist Mike Bloomfield slipped into Marianne Faithfull's "As Tears Go By" and finished to a nice round of applause. After the show Susie told me how proud she was and, typical of my overly emotional sister, said this with tears in her eyes. That memory still puts a smile on my face.

My friendship with Burd started to fizzle out after that episode, which was too bad because he really did turn me on to a lot of different bands, which helped me reintegrate with the other kids after my Year of Woe.* I was now connecting with new players around my 'hood, trying to get a fresh band together. Up until then I'd availed myself of friends' equipment at rehearsals but had no amp of my own. At home I figured out that if I rested the bout of my bass on the dresser it would reverberate through the furniture, but that wasn't loud enough to play along with a record; I then tried jerry-rigging my stereo, which worked okay, but I couldn't play my bass and a record at the same time. Finally, after scrimping and saving all year at Mom's store, I was psyched and flush enough to buy a Traynor Bass Master Amp with a twin 15-inch speaker cabinet that I'd been drooling over in the window of Long & McQuade, the coolest music store in the city. I used to go there just to salivate over their Fender and Rickenbacker basses and a grand array of guitars and amplifiers, but on a blizzardy day that winter, Burd and I took the bus downtown to take the plunge.

Only after I'd paid and they brought it out boxed and ready to go did we realize just how big and heavy the stack was. Holy crap, now we'd have to lug it to the bus stop, take the bus back to the northern suburbs and somehow get it through the blowing snow to my house.

---

* Burd's real name was Steven Fruitman. Years later I discovered that his love for music had not diminished at all. He had become and is to this day a DJ who takes pride in promoting Canadian music, primarily folk, and hosting his own classic vinyl radio show on the smallish college station CIUT-FM in Toronto.

Luckily it was *so* effin' cold that the ground was solid ice and we could slide it the final stretch in its protective cardboard. Home at last, I unboxed and plugged it in. It looked gigantic and out of place between my dresser drawers and my single bed, and as the tubes heated up it gave off that awesome new amp smell. I couldn't turn it up as loud as I wanted, but I'll never forget how, as I tentatively played through it, that first rumble caused the furniture to throb. The red glow of the pilot light lit up my room all night long as if a UFO had landed in my bedroom, but I was too excited to turn it off. I was ecstatic. My own pro-model amp. The best day ever.

Shortly thereafter I was introduced to a guitarist named Peter Daniels, who asked me to join a band he was putting together to play a bar mitzvah party. Peter loved the music of the Grass Roots, as did I—"Midnight Confessions" and "Let's Live for Today" were in my Top 100.* Also in that band was a solid drummer named Sammy Roher, who'd been a friend since I was five on Vinci Crescent (and who I think replaced Burd after that Battle of the Bands debacle). We played some cover band staples of that period such as Sam and Dave's "Hold On, I'm Comin'" and Wilson Pickett's "In the Midnight Hour." Not only was it a blast, but it could well have been my first paying gig.

Quite recently I was thumbing through Instagram, and a photograph I'd never seen before from that very gig popped up on my feed, posted on a fan site. I couldn't believe my eyes. It's one of only two photos that exist of me playing in that early pre-Rush period. You can see my bright and shiny new Traynor amp in the background, and a bass I owned for only a short time: a white Hagstrom HBII with the Futurama control panel. Now, this might not be big news for most people, but it is for me, as I recently published a book showcasing more than 250 of my basses but never found a trace of that particular

---

* I didn't know at the time that Kenny Fukomoto was one of the rare bass players who also sang lead. Nor did I know until recently that Creed Bratton, who appears as himself in the American version of *The Office*, was singer and guitarist in one of the Grass Roots' iterations!

relic. This pic brought back a few fading sparks of memory, but I still can't remember where I got the bass or where it went; it's possible that I soon traded it in for my first Fender Precision. Anyway, I posted the photo on my own Instagram page and—hello, Internet! —the sister of Anthony the bar mitzvah boy reached out to me. She very kindly sent me a more complete version, as well as another with her in front of the band while we played.

Then, on the morning of September 13, 1968, Alex rang. I assumed he wanted to borrow my Traynor, but instead he said, "Ged, we have a problem. Jeff can't make the gig tonight. Can you fill in for him?" I told him I didn't know their set, but he assured me we could load in early and rehearse until I was comfortable. So off I went.

We set up in the basement of St. Theodore's of Canterbury in Willowdale, which once a week acted as a drop-in centre for neighbourhood teens called the Coff-In. There was no stage, just an empty

*Smirk. And so it begins...*

room with us at one end. We didn't even have a mic stand, so we improvised, using an old floor lamp with the only mic we had taped to it. I had seen the band's drummer, John Rutsey, around, but I didn't really know the guy, and rehearsals started a bit awkwardly. We didn't have time to learn more than seven or eight songs that day and would have to play some of them twice to fill the time, but luckily I already knew a few: the Jimi Hendrix Experience's "Fire" and "Foxy Lady"; a Yardbirds song, "Shapes of Things"; a John Mayall number; and we ended with a long jam on the Cream version of Willie Dixon's classic "Spoonful," which for quite a while afterwards would be a signature song at our shows.

Playing this kind of music in a trio really gave a bass player a ton of latitude to stretch out and wander all over the neck, or at least as far up the neck as my skill level would allow. So I was super happy about that. There weren't many people in attendance that night, but the organizers asked us to return the following week. We split up the night's take, around six dollars each, and John suggested we celebrate by going to Pancer's Deli on Bathurst Street. "They have awesome chips and gravy," he said, and thus began our first ritual, the "after-show hang"; whenever we played the Coff-In we'd end the night at Pancer's. The next day Alex phoned me and asked if I'd consider joining the band on a permanent basis, which I did without hesitation. We'd go on to play the Coff-In regularly through to the middle of January 1969, building our very first following.

# CHAPTER 5

 LEX, JOHN AND I REHEARSED IN MY BASE-
ment, my little brother, Allan, sitting on the hallway steps
flicking the lights on and off in time to the music, all of
which drove my grandmother to distraction. She'd yell epi-
thets at us in Polish, calling my *goyische* bandmates "little Hitlers" and
banging on pots in protest.* One time I saw a knife zing out of the
kitchen, scooting along the floor until it came to rest point-first on the
floor at our feet, which the guys thought was pretty exciting. John used

---

* The only Polish I ever heard my grandmother utter was when she was mad at us—and
even then, apparently, just a stream of swear words in Polish (the very language that after the
war she'd vowed to never speak again) often mixed with Yiddish: "*Cholera psiakrew! Bootska
medla!*" If I asked my mother what it meant, she'd be too embarrassed to explain, so I never
did find out exactly, but I sure got their gist.

to call her "Crazy Head," which inspired us to write a jokey song by the same name. Poor woman, she must have been thinking, *I survived the war for this* mishegas?

With Motown on the radio all the time, funk had a major influence on us; just as we dug British guitar gods appropriating the blues—Eric Clapton playing Robert Johnson, Jimmy Page copping Otis Rush, anything John Mayall did—we were into blue-eyed soul and funk-rock too. The Rhinoceros instrumental "Apricot Brandy" was a must-learn song for us, with its infectious guitar and bass riff.* We played as a trio for a while—which I loved—but as our musical tastes expanded John pushed us to inject more musicality and ever-greater diversity into our sound. Around the start of 1969, we brought in a friend of Alex's named Lindy Young to play guitar and electric piano and to sing. Having a piano allowed us to play songs like Procol Harum's "Kaleidoscope," and his strong rhythm guitar playing took some pressure off Alex so he could express himself better as a soloist without having to worry about filling in the sound. All in all, the addition made us a better and more polished band. Lindy also had a great singing voice, but deeper and more rockabilly than mine, and we blended quite well together, him providing backup vocals or taking the lead on certain songs.

I liked singing and wasn't insecure about it. At that point, I wasn't yet screaming like "the damned howling in Hades" (as my reputation would later have it); I was singing Cream and blues songs in a sort of tenor/soprano or, if you prefer, a soprano/castrato style. I was a fan of guys with a higher range like Steve Marriott in the Small Faces and Humble Pie. (Humble Pie's *Performance: Rockin' the Fillmore* would be a hugely influential record to me and most of my peers; you can hear

---

* This American band featured two Canadians, singer John Finley and keyboardist Michael Fonfara, later of the Downchild Blues Band, and was thus somewhat homegrown. (Canucks, accustomed to being ignored on the world stage, are exquisitely sensitive to provenance!) For years later on, Alex, Neil and I would break into "Apricot Brandy" during soundchecks. Call us proggers if you like, but we were always asking ourselves, "Can hard rock *funk*?" Of course, we'd never compare ourselves to Parliament/Funkadelic or any of the real masters of the funk universe, but nor did we want to be just another, er, average white band.

the influence of "I Don't Need No Doctor" on my early singing.) We weren't so much a product of American blues, as American blues that had been shipped to England, amplified, rock-a-fied and sent back across the water to me sitting in Toronto waiting for my life to begin. I would often later be compared to Robert Plant, and while he certainly pushed me into the higher registers, I do think a comparison with Marriott would be more accurate. He had a soulful voice with a strong vibrato but he *rocked*.

Soon Jon Anderson's mellifluous singing would affect me too. He had a high range but his voice wasn't scratchy or abrasive; it was beautiful, soulful and emotive, not unlike a schoolboy chorister. Another singer who impressed me was Roger Hodgson on the early Supertramp records, and I liked both Paul Simon and Joni Mitchell a lot. (Through the years, there were of course many others. I was a huge fan of Björk later on in life. No one would think to make the connection, but there are certain words I sing in Rush in a very Björk-like manner.) I wasn't aiming for raspiness; I just responded intuitively to the music we wrote. Where my voice went was out of necessity, relating to what we were writing and the key we were writing it in. (We weren't very savvy about keys, either. If the key we wrote a song in felt right, I'd just have to make do. What we came to learn was that in certain lower registers, my voice had no power, but when I booted it up an octave, *there* was the power!)

Watching the movie *Coda* recently, I was struck by the scene in which the choir teacher tries to bring out his student's inner frustrations, coaxing her to sing from the gut (she's the only hearing member of a deaf family). Even if it's an ugly sound, he says, it will feel good. Turn your angst into power! And it dawned on me that my earliest vocal style may also have been rooted in my childhood, listening to the stories of what my parents had endured in the camps, suffering all that bullying and alienation, so that when I did begin to sing it did come rushing out as a screaming banshee. I was releasing all those suppressed emotions just by stepping up to the mic and screaming "*Ooh* yeah!"

Of course, then I had to learn how to actually sing . . .

Lindy also had a basement where we could rehearse—and where his redhead sister, Nancy, had a room. I'd met her once before about a year earlier, when she'd invited Alex (who was already friends with her and Lindy) to hang out at her friend Kathy's apartment, and he'd asked me to join him. I rather shyly agreed, and the four of us bunched up on the sofa, creeped out and giggling as we watched Vincent Price on TV in *The Fly*. ("Help me! Help me!") It was all very innocent, but to a teenager without a steady girlfriend, tantalizing too. I had made out with a couple of girls, but I ached to be properly in love. Now, a year later, here I was at band practice, sneaking peeks at Nancy whenever she walked bewitchingly back and forth between her bedroom and the bathroom in her leotard. I would ogle her like she was on a catwalk as

*Babes, bell bottoms and the Beatles: Kathy and Nancy groovin' in Nancy's basement apartment, 1969. (We would likely have been making noise rehearsing in the next room.)*

we worked on music and she shook her head, plugging her ears, making it amply clear that the noise was driving her crazy. She'd run up the stairs scowling and yelling until she was out the door, but none of it bothered me at all, as I was silently crushing on her . . . and in due course I would discover the feeling was, in fact, mutual.

ALEX AND JOHN decided to bring on board a manager, a guy named Ray Danniels I'd seen around at various shows on the Yorkville strip and hanging around the coffeehouses. He was clean shaven with blond shoulder-length hair that he was always playing with at the back of his head—and that he used to iron to keep straight. He'd left his home in Waterdown, Ontario, and, something of a hustler, earned his money however he could. He tried singing in a band, but that didn't work out, so he set his sights on managing instead. When I first met him, he had his phone and his papers on the floor, which was basically his desk. His first agency was called Universal Sound, after which he formed the Music Shoppe, which in 1973 became SRO. He was ambitious, clever and a born salesman. Clearly, he saw something he liked in the band. But it wasn't me.

So, one afternoon as I'm walking to rehearsals, I see Lindy coming towards me across the field on the way to his house, and I ask him where he's going.

"Oh, hey, Ged," he says, looking at the ground. "Uh, listen . . . Rehearsal is cancelled and, uh, well, the band is breaking up."

Back home I got hold of the other guys, but they were weird and aloof on the phone. It seemed that Rush *had* disbanded, though I suspected I wasn't being told the whole story. I tried not to dwell on it and started calling around to other musicians I knew, trying to get something else going, but then in May, I heard that Alex, John and Lindy had reformed as Hadrian (after the Roman emperor) with a new bass player named Joe. It was all a ruse. I'd been out-and-out lied to!

Ray had offered to manage them but made it clear he didn't think I was right for the band. It's important to say, however, that it turns out it wasn't his idea in the first place. I've been informed some *fifty years later* that it was Rutsey's. Just recently I asked Alex about that time — something I'd always wondered about but never really brought up. (Maybe I was afraid of the answer, I dunno.) He sheepishly responded that back then he was the kind of guy who just went along with things, and that the decision to replace me was driven by John, who was keen to reinvent the image of the band and wanted someone hipper . . . whatever that meant. "I didn't want to get on John's bad side," he told me. "You *know* how he had a very strong personality. He made all the decisions. As for Ray, he was just being opportunistic." In my place they brought in a friend of John's named Joe Perna, a good-looking chap whose playing, it would turn out, was not up to snuff.

*Hadrian on the steps of Yorkview Public School in 1969:* (CLOCKWISE FROM TOP LEFT) *manager Ray Danniels (with freshly ironed hair), Lindy Young, Joe Perna, John Rutsey and Alex. How'd that work out for ya?*

Whoever's idea it was, the way they all went about it was deceitful and frankly chickenshit, and I was shocked and hurt. Still, I didn't want to sit around and feel sorry for myself, so I said to myself, *Fuck them*, and resolved to start a band of my own. I've always pictured myself as a mousy kid, blowing with the wind and following the crowd, but the mysteries revealed when going back in time to write this book are, well, revelatory! I couldn't have been entirely a will-o'-the-wisp or I would not have had the chutzpah to keep on keeping on. Clearly, music meant everything to me, and despite my supposed lack of confidence I instinctively knew that I had to take control of my own destiny, if only hoping that success would be a kind of revenge.

Like everyone, I suppose, I realize that over time I've forgotten or blocked out a lot of things. Even typing out the name Hadrian just now set a sort of fugue in motion. First my brain took me to the hike my wife and I took a few years ago from Bowness-on-Solway to Wallsend—along Hadrian's Wall—when, trudging beside her, this memory suddenly presented itself: Hadrian was playing its debut gig at a local church, Willowdale United, and I'd been curious to hear the band. I'd gone to the show, but to do that I had to give up a pair of tickets for another, at Maple Leaf Gardens the same night. No big deal, really, it was only . . . *the Jimi Hendrix Experience.*[*] Doh! What an idiot. I'd reckoned I could always catch them next time they came to town, but Jimi died sixteen months later. Going to that Hadrian show was a mistake on another level too. It was no fun watching my former bandmates. They had a decent, fairly enthusiastic crowd, but their playing was sloppy. They didn't really click, and Joe looked lost and struggling. Honestly, I took little pleasure in witnessing their mediocrity.

Meanwhile, I'd started a band of my own with Sammy Roher and Xavier "Sam" Dangle, whose speedy, nimble playing was inspired by

---

[*] Even that Gardens show (on May 3, 1969) nearly didn't take place: Jimi was arrested for possession of drugs that day at Toronto International Airport and released only just in time to hit the stage at ten.

Alvin Lee. We called ourselves the Ogilvie Blues Band. It was a goofy name, but its very goofiness made us laugh. We played songs by John Mayall, Paul Butterfield and Ten Years After and even wrote a couple of our own and got pretty good in short order (we were just a blues band, but pretty decent mimics at our young age), booking several gigs around southern Ontario throughout the late spring and early summer of '69.

One time, about an hour before going onstage at a small club in Ancaster, bright spark that I was, I decided to drop some LSD. Launching into our set, I did my damnedest not to let myself trip—mind over surreal matter. No matter how weird the audience appeared or the band sounded to me at that moment, I *had* to ignore it, staring with all my might at the fingerboard of my bass and desperately trying to sing the right words in the right order. How we got through the gig I'll never know, but luckily, it was blues not prog—so ya know, a lot of latitude there—and no one said anything untoward about the show, so I assumed with enormous relief that we had pulled it off. I wonder if Dock Ellis went through the same thing the day he pitched his no-hitter on acid. Maybe he enjoyed the ride, but I certainly did not. All I got out of it was a massive headache and a majorly important lesson: mixing psychedelics and playing, especially in front of people, is a pretty stupid idea.

Then I heard that Lindy had lost interest in Hadrian, bowing out right before their second gig. I always liked Lindy. He was a sweet guy who I knew had never felt good being tasked with the lie about the band breaking up. He was a really good musician, embarrassed about carrying on with someone who clearly couldn't play very well and frustrated by how disorganized this new band had become. I contacted him and asked if he would come to rehearsal to check out *my* new band. We jammed well and he agreed to join us for the long term, which felt good after what had gone down. By then Ray Danniels had started his company Universal Sound, hoping to book gigs for Hadrian and (the balls of the man!) us. He found our quirky name problematic, however, and asked for something easier to pronounce. So about the time Lindy joined we changed it to Judd; I never cared for it, it was hardly more alluring, but if more work came our way, what the heck.

Quite often I'd run into Alex and John hanging around Ray's "office" — the apartment he shared with our friend and very first roadie, Ian Grandy. As for Alex and John, despite my being dumped by them, we were still friendly, mostly just hanging around and getting high. I refer to that period as the "Summer of Acid," as we were so bored and restless between gigs that we'd invariably end up smoking dope or dropping a tab, then raiding Ray's fridge and eating whatever we found in it. He would come home and start freaking out: "Who ate my salami? Who ate my *salami?*" while we fell about laughing.

Those acid trips, by the way, were the almost inevitable rite of passage for the era, but I rarely enjoyed them. I usually ended up feeling paranoid and decidedly unhappy. Coming home quite evidently out of it, I'd have to deke around my mother as she demanded, "Vats de matter vit your eyes?" I'd just cop to drinking a beer and then scurry up the stairs. Not until I slipped into bed, put my headphones on and listened to CHUM-FM* could I relax and drift away before falling asleep. It wasn't about the music per se, but an island of tranquil hallucinations as opposed to the extreme anxiety I'd suffer while tripping out in public with people's faces melting all around me and my heart beating in my ears, every little sound surreally amplified, and me convinced that *everyone* knew I was on an illegal high.

One time when my mother heard me coming home, she wanted to talk to me about the problems she was having with my sister. It was one of the hardest things I've ever had to do: listen to this poor woman who'd lost her husband, whose teenage daughter was out at all hours and who wanted some comfort from her eldest son — who she didn't

---

* Those were the fledgling days of free-form radio on CHUM-FM in Toronto. In 1968's "Summer of Love" the famed New York DJ Murray the K helped kick off a progressive rock format, leading a brigade of young local radio personalities that included my school mate Rick Moranis.

realize *was tripping on acid*. I remember sitting on the edge of the bed, nodding my head and thinking, *Hold it together, hold it together, hold it together*. I'm looking at the hairpins in her hair, and they're *coming alive*. When she finally left, what an incredible relief it was to get under the sheets and enjoy my trip.

One of the reasons I stopped doing drugs in my twenties was because dropping acid and smoking pot brought out my insecurities. Being high interfered with my personality: straight, I could be funnier, quicker-witted and respond the way I wanted to respond, to question everything around me; but if I was high in company, I'd usually go quiet. Or just turn into Woody Allen and keep on jabbering and joking, like when he talks about getting high and trying to take his pants off over his head.

I'd like to claim that I was "high enough on life, man," but the truth is that all the way through my teens into adulthood, and even as a very young child, I used to have moments of sudden, extreme aware-ness of my own existence that would freak me out: acute and unpre-dictable episodes during which everything around me felt hyperreal. I guess now we would call this "existential angst," but at the time I had no words to explain it; only that I spent too much time alone inside my own head. As a child I couldn't interpret those moments for what they were: me struggling to grasp the concept of the metaphysical. It wasn't until many years later that I read something by Ayn Rand and realized that having these episodes was not so unusual.

*Existence is the perceptually self-evident fact at the base of all other knowledge, i.e., that "existence exists." To be is to be something, existence is identity. To be is to be an entity of a specific nature made of specific attributes.*[*]

Um, in essence she was arguing that you can get on with your life only once you've accepted that existence exists. Pretty heady stuff, eh? A fancy explanation for navel gazing, perhaps, but I found it reassuring.

---

[*]   Rand, Ayn (1996) [1961]. *For the New Intellectual: The Philosophy of Ayn Rand*. New York: Signet. ISBN 0-451-16308-7.

BACK ROW: G. Waud,
Walterhouse, P. Wasserman,
Weinberg, G. Weinrib, S. Dankevy,
Wong, B. Wilkinson. THIRD RO
E. Williamson, T. Wilson, S. Weisbe
S. Dawe, H. Vlahakis, E. Wright,
Weagle. SECOND ROW: A. Walla
W. Wise, H. Wilson, J. Wilson, I
White, D. Wiltkinson, Mrs. Blan
FIRST ROW: H. Weiner, D. War
P. Wilton, E. Weiss, P. Kelly,
Walton, D. Waisglass.

(TOP) *Outtake from our first set of official publicity photos, c.1970.*
(BOTTOM) *Made it to grade ten, whoopee. Who's got the acid?*

I still have those moments. They're far less frequent, and they don't freak me out as they used to, but the feeling is like an old, uneasy friend. If I stop myself right now in mid-sentence and look around this room, the feeling takes me over: I've time-warped outside of the conversation as if my own personal camera has pulled back on the scene, is scoping me and my life, freezing me in the moment . . .

WHERE WAS I? Oh, right: Hadrian was failing to get much work, if any. "I took my new girlfriend, Charlene, to a gig at St. Timothy's or something," Alex now tells me, "and I remember how horrible it was. It was so *flailing*. Nobody could play. Bob Vopni, our new singer and second guitar player, sat there saying stupid things—reading aloud, I remember, with his glasses and a light on, like, 'The fool on the hill . . .' in a self-important voice, and I was like, oh my god, no! What is going on here? After that gig the band just fell apart."

In the fall of '69, Rutsey called to ask me back—feeling shame and remorse, apparently. He knew he'd fucked up and that it was now up to him to make amends. "As was so often the case with Rutsey," Alex says, "after a month or six weeks, he'd suddenly flip. And you're his best friend all of a sudden!"

The reason I didn't bear a grudge for long was that I really missed playing with Alex, and still thought that Rush was a more exciting alternative to the band I'd started. I saw the potential for something heavier and more original, and the practical thinker in me was willing to drop resentments. Whatever blow to the ego I may have sustained was behind me, and I won't deny that there's something sweet to savour in your ex-bandmates admitting they made a mistake and confessing they need you more than you need them. In the end, the whole painful experience made the sixteen-year-old me more confident, not to mention more skeptical, which, let's be frank, is not a bad thing to have in your toolkit—especially, as will be amply illustrated later on, when it comes to dealings in the music business.

Alex and I were no longer actually classmates, as he'd moved farther east and was now at a different school. I started hanging out at Newtonbrook Secondary with a guy named Oscar, a guitarist with an honest musical pedigree—he was a son of the great Canadian jazz pianist Oscar Peterson. What bonded us at first was not music but a mutual love of *Monty Python's Flying Circus*, whose skits we knew by heart, but soon it was all about music. I had never met anyone as passionate as he was, and we became inseparable.

In Oscar I found a fellow traveller in the progressive vein, and his musical interests had a strong catalytic effect on my own. When we entered the age of concept albums and rock operas we'd obsess over Yes, Genesis, ELP, King Crimson, Jethro Tull, Van der Graaf Generator, as well as folkier acts like the Strawbs, Amazing Blondel, Paul Simon and Joni Mitchell. Albums by the Who and Cream were top of the pile for both of us, but the prog had a powerful impact on me not just as a player, but as a musical dreamer and hopeful writer of rock songs.

I caught a bunch of classic acts with Oscar, including Pink Floyd on the *Dark Side of the Moon* tour, Jethro Tull for *Thick as a Brick* (another album we had memorized), and he and I lined up with Alex all night outside Maple Leaf Gardens for Yes tickets—the only time I've ever done that for a band—freezing our asses off in the late October air, taking turns fetching coffee, people around us pitching tents on the sidewalk and partying till dawn. It was worth the wait, too, as we got second-row tickets. Oscar and I also caught Genesis's first Toronto show, opening for Lou Reed at Massey Hall (one of those mismatches booked without regard for fans' tribal allegiances). Genesis arrived late and without most of their highly touted light show, but the bare-bones set was still so powerful, so mesmerizing that by the time Reed started his laid-back set, a lot of people were already drifting to the exits— ourselves amongst them.

We also loved to get high together. I don't know what the fuck we were thinking, but one time we even dropped acid at school. We were in class when I started tripping, and all I could think was, *Shit, I have to get out of here*, which we both did as soon as the bell rang. We'd often bunk school and go to one of our houses, fry up some Spam, listen to music and jam together.

Whether our meeting was sheer social accident or due to us both being racial outcasts, we were instantly drawn to each other. We both felt like outsiders; just as he was the first Black person I'd ever known, I was often acutely aware of being the first Jew many of my friends had encountered. He was also, in a sense, fatherless like me. His dad, whom he admired enormously and who by then had divorced his mom, was constantly on the road. I remember hanging around on his birthday, waiting for Oscar Sr. to phone. The phone call never came. Oscar just laughed, and we celebrated anyway, but his disappointment was palpable. It hit me hard; I couldn't imagine a father forgetting such a thing. But he had a devilish sense of humour, and his way of dealing with difficult matters was to laugh at the most inappropriate times. (He laughed all the way through *The Exorcist*, for instance, while I was so terrified, I slept with the light on that night. He thought it was an effin' comedy; in hindsight, perhaps it was.)

MEANWHILE, RUSH WAS heavying up its sound. And what happened in 1969 to bring this on?

At the corner of Toronto's Yonge Street and Davenport Road stood a venerable old building most of us had strolled past many times on our way to nearby Yorkville Village without taking much notice. It had been built as a Masonic Temple, but by 1969 that edifice of secrecy had become the coolest rock and roll club and venue in town, the Rock Pile. In February John had been one of the few attendees of a show there by an unknown band called Led Zeppelin. At that time the main draw was their guitarist, the ex-Yardbirds' Jimmy Page, but Rutsey had been especially blown away by the drummer, John Bonham, whose style and tone were uniquely solid and powerful without ever seeming too busy. He couldn't stop raving, so as soon as their first album was released we ran to our local Sam the Record Man, only to find that word was spreading fast and it was already out of stock. When the re-order finally came in, we grabbed one, headed home and laid it on my turntable. I can still remember the three of us sitting there on the bed in utter awe, listening to the heaviosity of "Good Times Bad Times," the fire of "Communication Breakdown" and oh, that drum sound! Plant's extreme vocal range and Jimmy's guitar histrionics put this band way over the mark, and for me John Paul Jones's emotionally moving bass lines welded perfectly to the drum parts, grounding the band and creating a rhythm section for a new age of rock. The Who were full of abandon, rockin' hard and melodically brilliant; Jimi was musical voodoo and flamboyance incarnate; Cream was a showcase of bluesy virtuosity; but this? This was heavy, man. Zep had reforged the blues in an explosive and very English style that would speak to our generation of players like no other. For us there was Rock before Zep came along, and there was Rock *after*. This was our new paradigm.[*]

We tried to learn a couple of their songs, but they were beyond us at that stage; even when we got the notes close to right, the sound was wrong. (Zep would only work its way into our set list when Rush was playing the bars, with "Living Loving Maid" from *Led Zeppelin II*.) Regardless, Zeppelin challenged the way we felt about our own sound: if it wasn't *heavy* now, it felt just plain wimpy.

As 1969 wound down, the band went through a period of inactivity— by which I mean *zero* gigs. We felt ignored by Ray, who was pouring all of Universal Sound's energies into other, more commercial bands; we

---

[*] In the 1980s a Boston academic would comment that Zeppelin had lent the poignancy of Mississippi Delta blues all the subtlety of thermonuclear rape. But hey, you can't please all the people all the time.

were not an "easy sell," because we insisted on inserting a lot of original material into our sets. I'm not saying we were accomplished songwriters, but we resisted playing songs that had made other bands famous. We reckoned that for us to get anywhere we'd have to write our own.

One weekend, I was at a family gathering talking to my cousin Manny (married to my father's niece). I liked him; he was only in his thirties, a gentle sort with unkempt curly hair and a bright smile who had always been kind to me, especially after my dad passed away. He was also the only adult I knew who smoked pot, which made him the hippest member of my clan, for sure. He asked me about my band, and when I told him that we felt we were spinning our wheels, he said he knew someone who might help us out. A short while later, he came to one of our practices at Lindy's house with a friend of his named Vince. They sat on the basement steps listening to us play, nodding their heads—not bothered at all, apparently, by the intense volume. Afterwards, Vince said he liked us and, if we were interested, could be our manager. Now that I think of it, we didn't even ask him if he had any experience, just stupidly sort of assuming that he did. Well, we were

*Note the early spelling of my name. Eventually I'd*
*add another "D" to make it more, uh . . . sophisticated.*

desperate, and I did trust Manny. We decided at a band meeting that we had nothing to lose.

By this time, Lindy had rejoined Rush, but his taste in rock couldn't compete with our burgeoning desire to be the next Zep. He was more into Procol Harum and some of the bluesier guys; he had a more varied sensibility than we did. He liked folk rock and a lot of things that demanded a four-piece ensemble. In short, it was our first encounter with the time-honoured root cause of countless bands' breakups: "musical differences." Shortly after the audition with Manny and Vince, he decided to leave the band for good, and we returned to the trio of John, Alex and me. Meanwhile, when Zeppelin returned for two shows at the Rock Pile that August and I had no money for a ticket, I went down to Church Street and pawned the typewriter my grandmother had bought me for my birthday. I felt super guilty about that, but that typewriter stood no more of a chance than Lindy had.

Vince said we now needed proper publicity material and set up our first real photo shoot—at what we expected to be an actual photo studio but which turned out to be just some guy's office, all bare walls and empty space. Still, it was as close to a professional situation as we'd ever experienced; before that, we'd simply have friends take snapshots of us outdoors, in parks or anywhere else we thought was a backdrop— and where lights weren't required.

At the makeshift studio, Vince stood at the back suggesting poses. The photographer had wrapped us in a blanket so that just our heads stuck out (was he thinking of Pink Floyd's publicity shot from the year before, of the band shrouded in a pink sheet?), and just as he was about to take a shot, Vince said:

"Guys, make stoned eyes. Look like you're stoned!"

*Is this guy for real?* I mean, how do you make "stoned" eyes? Then he directed Alex to stretch his hands out in front of his face, eyes peering between his fingers at the camera. Whatever psychedelic effect the guy was after, when we saw the shots a couple of days later, we just laughed at how goofy Alex looked.

He asked us to rendezvous with him at a second-story club on Yonge Street to meet the owner, a guy he knew named Marvin. We were at first excited by the possibility of an actual gig and said okay, but when we walked upstairs we were greeted by signs advertising a strip club called Starvin' Marvin's Burlesque Palace. Vince introduced us to this chubby bearded dude, who sized us up and asked us questions about our songs, and it was immediately clear that Vince had been grooming us to be the house band there, playing sets between the strippers.

We said nothing and left the club pretty downcast, indignation rising with every step we took away from the place. Every instinct in my body told me this was wrong. Finally, the guys looked at me and said, "Ged, this is fucked up. No way we're doing this. You gotta call Manny and get us out."

*An ad in* Toronto Life, *August 1971. RUFKM? Nothing against working girls, you understand, but this scheme was singularly fucked up.*

Manny was put off at first, but really had no choice. After all, we were cousins. He said he'd take care of it, and that was that. We never spoke of it afterwards, nor did I ever see Vince the hairdresser again, but "Make stoned eyes" lived on forever in the Rush lexicon, never failing to crack Alex and me up, especially in the middle of future photo sessions.

Shortly after that, someone asked if we would be interested in playing a bar mitzvah—but unlike the basement party I'd played at Anthony's when I was fifteen, this was a big and proper dinner in a rented hall with stage, lighting and all. By then we were playing more high schools and had accumulated a little more gear but were still not gigging a ton and would take (almost) any gig that came along. We set up on the day, and everything seemed to be going just fine . . . until we cranked it up and started to play. The kids were diggin' it, but within moments the older guests, especially the ladies with their bouffant hairdos and flounced dresses, were running for the exits with their ears covered, yelling, "Make it stop! Make it stop!" The bar mitzvah boy's father stood in front of the stage waving his hands and shouted, "I'll pay you, but you can't play anymore. That's it, show's over!" Kinda stunned, we had no choice but to tear our gear down, even as several of those bubbes continued to complain, "Oy, *givalt*. This you call *music?*" I can still picture the poor boy watching us pack up and looking forlorn. Sorry, kid. Didn't mean to wreck your big day.

MEANWHILE, I HAD come to a crossroads with my education. In 1968 I'd started grade ten at Newtonbrook Secondary School, but just a year and a half later was really not into staying the course. The only thing that stopped me from quitting was knowing my mother would be heartbroken.

The looming decision was tearing me apart. All I thought about was music, listening to records and learning songs, working on my chops and trying to write my own material. At that point we were playing high school concerts and dances. Yeah, you heard me right: dances. I know it's hard to imagine, but we most certainly did play Sadie Hawkins dances, where the girls picked the guys to dance with under a twirling mirrored disco ball, and Halloween dances with everyone in costume. To come clean, people rarely actually danced to our music at these events . . . and we weren't even playing in 7/8 yet.

One time we were booked to play a high school near Magnetawan, Ontario, about three hundred kilometers from Toronto. We set off at the end of our school day but underestimated the travel time. We got there late, were greeted by the attendees standing out in front of the gymnasium with their arms crossed and had to load in to a chorus of jeering. The audience watched our set from the back of the room. I remember thinking as we played, *Weird, don't they know we don't bite?* Maybe they were intimidated by our volume or maybe they really hated our sound, but either way, though they did eventually warm up a bit, the gig was not a smashing success—and a message to me about priorities.

We didn't have much gear—two amps, a guitar, a bass and a drum kit. To get to neighbourhood gigs we'd beg one of our parents to make a couple of round trips with instruments poking out of every orifice of the vehicle, but as we were taken farther and farther afield, we started leaning on the few friends we had with licences and access to a car or van. There was Gary "Doc" Cooper, a neighbour of Alex and John's with a car of his own who'd drive us so long as we paid the gas; Larry "Label" Back was another, and a guy named Ron who had an actual VW van. For several years they helped us hump the equipment, rent a U-Haul or what have you. I can still picture myself crouching for hours atop an amplifier in the back, painfully pretzelled but happy that we were *on the road.*

However late we'd get back to town, it became a routine of ours to grab a bite at a 24-hour diner called Fran's, where I'd automatically order the open-faced roast beef sandwich—a very ordinary-sounding memory that conjures up the feeling for me of camaraderie and cheating life just a bit. We ought to have been in school being groomed to become proper citizens but were pursuing our dream instead. Maybe that's why for Rush's entire career, having a drink alone with Alex and Neil after almost every show would be so important; it was a nightly reminder that we'd *gotten away with it.*

Inevitably, as my attendance dwindled and my already mediocre marks took a deeper nosedive, I was called in to see a guidance counsellor, a Mr. Woodhouse, who you could say was my first therapist. He wanted to know it all, my history, my goals and why I was struggling. After a few sessions he asked me if I smoked cigarettes, which I did (back then pretty much every kid I knew smoked). He locked the door and we lit up. It impressed the hell out of me that he was less concerned about breaking school rules than winning my trust. Sometimes we'd drive over to a nearby deli or coffee shop to smoke and talk and drink coffee. He was the first adult male since my father passed away who treated me as an equal. Clearly his primary goal was to keep me in school, but I sensed that he also wanted me to learn to make decisions for myself.

Once he grasped my dilemma, he suggested a compromise: I would be allowed to build a class schedule that would have me done by around one or two p.m. and get me on the road in time for gigs just about anywhere in the province. I chose theatre arts, screen arts and graphic arts, plus English, history and phys. ed. (if they'd had any more subjects that ended in "arts" I would have taken those instead). He pointed out that my post-secondary education options would be almost non-existent if I dropped both math and science, but since I had no intention of going to university anyway, I didn't care. This schedule, I hoped, would keep me in school long enough for Mom to become resigned to me becoming a full-time musician.

It didn't work out too well. I was now able to make our gigs on time but was still getting home so late that rising bleary-eyed for an

8:45 class was nigh on impossible, and after a couple of months I was back at the crossroads. Never had Robert Johnson's words "Believe I'm sinkin' down" meant so much to me. I knew how much anguish I'd be causing my mother, but I *had* to leave. Naturally Mr. Woodhouse was disappointed, but he promised to help explain my decision to her, and when he did just that a few days later, sure enough, she broke down in tears. I felt *terrible* but was undeterred and cleared out my locker. I was now a musician all right, but also a high school dropout, barely eking out a few bucks a week. I was scared but resolute. I had to conjure a proper living now from nothing but a dream and a band (one that had already kicked me out once), if for no other reason than to justify what I was putting my mother through. When I got home, she wouldn't talk to me. It's a standard quip to say that Jewish parents want you to become a doctor or a lawyer, but she really thought I was *insane*. The music and the culture were utterly alien to her. She figured it was a one-way road to drug addiction, at best the equivalent of running away to join the circus.

Thinking back on that critical juncture in my life, I'm struck by what a different person I'd become from the one I'd been as a little kid. For years I'd been chronically indecisive, a procrastinator, vague and aimless, possessed of few opinions. Neither parents nor teachers had ever really encouraged me to make up my own mind about anything. I was sheltered. I was a blank page. Mom and Dad simply told me to do what I was told, and I obeyed. The only helpful thing my mother ever said to me in that regard was after she'd been watching me play with a bunch of kids on my street and saw that anything they did, *I* did. That's when she pulled me aside and said, "Garshon. Be a leader, not a follower." Even though she'd never taught me in my early life *how* to be a leader—on the contrary, in fact—she apparently expected me to be one. I have to imagine that her memories of the war—with an entire race of people following one another into the gas chambers—had taught her this in the hardest of all possible ways.

That phrase in her voice would reverberate in my brain throughout my life. As I grew, I made conscious efforts to formulate opinions, to educate myself so that I could participate in conversation and examine my own feelings about any given subject. I expended a *lot* of internal energy trying to grow myself in such a way that allowed me to actually *have* interests; to absorb things; to react to things and then analyse those reactions—in the end, to form opinions, which after all is what makes a person a personality. And one result of developing a personality was that I became more decisive. Still, it's funny: she gave me the right advice, but as I *did* start to become a leader, not a follower, and my decisions went against her ethos—leaving school, joining a band— really it was "Be a leader, don't be a follower—so long as you agree with me"! After I quit school, between us it was—for want of a better term—cold war.

But boy, was Mr. Woodhouse ever what one could hope for in a counsellor. After all the success I'd later enjoy, I sometimes wondered if he was aware of just how profound an influence he'd had on my life. More than once I've thought of looking him up but got cold feet. Is it ever too late to say thank you?

# CHAPTER 6

ALEX WAS REGULARLY HITCHHIKING downtown in those days to see a girl who happened to be roommates with Lindy's sister, Nancy, and one evening I accompanied him to a party at their apartment. Alex and I used to stoke up before parties with an alcoholic blend he called Panther Piss, a diabolical mix of rye whiskey, vodka and kosher wine (or in his case *slivovitz*, a foul Yugoslavian plum brandy), siphoned off in what we hoped were imperceptible amounts from each and every bottle in our parents' booze cupboards, but on this occasion we took so much time mixing our brew, then travelling downtown, fueling up in a local park and getting lost, that by the time we arrived it was way past dark.

We knocked on the door, the sounds of Procol Harum within, but when we entered there was no party—just Alex's girlfriend, Beverly, and Nancy Young looking fine with her long red hair and a sly grin. Yes, I had been set up. Alex disappeared with Bev pretty fast, while I shyly watched Nancy pour me a glass of cheap rosé. And, well, nature took its course as we kissed to the orchestral tidal waves of "Nights in White Satin"—a moment captured for posterity by Beverly lurking around the corner with her camera. Did I notice? Uh, nope, I didn't even stop to breathe. *TMI*, you may be thinking, but how many folks can boast a relationship of fifty-plus years and still have a photo of their very first kiss?

Now, you may be wondering why such a hot redhead was attracted to this quiet, odd-looking eighteen-year-old Jew. Well, first of all, there was actually a tremendous physical attraction, but we also knew each other as friends before we hooked up and already *liked* each other. I was painfully introspective, while she could talk a blue streak, had zero fear in social environments and was funny, all of which was good for me to be around. It was sometimes hard when she'd be chatting everybody up in the room, but it also helped me come out of my shell. As for how she saw

*It's in the kiss.*

me, well, I was a shy, long-haired, brooding character, which I hear some women find attractive! But seriously: when I did open my mouth, I regularly made her laugh, which she loved. Alone, we were very caring towards each other. We'd found each other as willingly orphaned, if you will, from our own families; mine was at odds with my musical ambitions, while hers made her unhappy for a variety of reasons (which are her private business, of course; suffice it to say that she demonstrated an independent and determined spirit by hitchhiking across Canada with a boyfriend when she was barely sixteen). I respected her as an individual with strong ideas and, long before she started her own design firm named Zapata, a strong creative streak was in evidence. She was one of the few people in my life back then who never questioned my absurd dreams of rock and roll success. We made a nest in each other's arms. We gave each other understanding and, as best we could, unconditional romance. We gave each other the confidence to strike out on our own.

It wasn't long before we were going steady. I'd hitchhike downtown as often as I could to meet her at a grocery store in Rosedale where she worked—a handy convenience, as I had little or no money and could

*Rehearsing for my future.*

count on her for cigarettes and yoghurt. How romantic is that! We'd go for walks past the neighbourhood's stately houses, joking that one day we'd live in such a place. One afternoon we stopped in front of a grand old pile that was more castle than family residence, where Tchaikovsky's *1812 Overture* was blasting through wide-open windows above a set of arched wooden garage doors. Naturally, I had to ham it up for my new girlfriend, conducting the orchestra long enough for her to snap a photo—a photo that's like an image in a crystal ball, for not only would that overture be a life-changer for Rush and me, but Nancy and I would eventually live in that very neighbourhood for more than forty years.

TORONTONIANS LOVE THEIR "cottage country," a land of many lakes a hundred and fifty kilometers north of the Big Smoke. They call their houses there "cottages," but while some are unwinterized cabins, others are proper mansions; we had zero money, not even the wherewithal to stay at a motel, and had to use campsites around Ontario's provincial parks. Whenever we had no gigs Alex, Nancy, our friends and I would pool together a tent, a stove and a cooler to go camp and play guitars and sing and drink too much in the great outdoors.

One time, as we were driving tent pegs into the ground, Alex kicked over a bees' nest and out swarmed a cloud of them, really pissed off. We freaked and ran in all directions. I got a couple of stings—I had to pick a yellow jacket off my ass, in fact—but then I heard an almighty boom. I ran toward the sound and saw the front end of Alex's Mustang raised up and wrapped around a tree, steam coming out of the hood and the front wheels spinning. We feared the worst but soon found him down at the waterside with blood running from his mouth. He'd tried to flee the bees, intending to drive to the lake and dive in, but they flew through the open window after him, angrily swirling around inside until he lost control. Now he was in shock, babbling over and over, "Hahaha, isn't that great? My dad is gonna *kill* me. My dad is gonna *kill* me."

He got to a hospital where they bandaged him up, swollen from dozens of bee stings, but the worst of it was that his bottom teeth had been sheared right off on impact with the steering wheel, and he was going to need major dental work. What a catastrophe. The car, he said, wasn't even properly insured. We lay in our tent that night, smoking joints to ease the pain, high as kites and singing songs from *Led Zeppelin III*, as together we imitated the drone that kicks off "Celebration Day." In the end, the echoing of our voices in the forest, Alex's misshapen mouth and the absurdity of it all had us in fits of demented laughter. What else could we do?

Looking to pick up a little extra cash in the summer of 1971, we played an insurance company's Canada Day picnic—just the two of us on acoustic guitars with a few crowd pleasers like "As Tears Go By" and Zep's "Babe I'm Gonna Leave You." For two hours we played the same songs over and over again, becoming sloppier and sloppier as they plied us with beer. No one noticed, however, because the suits were way ahead of us. These respectable-looking business sorts, politely mingling with their colleagues, lost all inhibition as mild flirting turned into an out-and-out grab fest, with the men literally chasing the women through the woods—one of them an older, heavyset boge* wearing nothing but his boxer shorts. *Ooh! Ugh! Al, avert your eyes!*

As juveniles, we weren't yet allowed to work the bars but lucked out that year when we turned eighteen, just as Ontario lowered the drinking age from twenty-one. A peculiar holdover in those days were traditional beer halls, or "Men's Rooms." They were exactly that, for men only; taverns and licenced restaurants were the only drinking

---

* Not to be confused with "bogue," an acanthopterygian fish, "boge" was an essential word in the Rush lexicon—a leftover from my friendship with Burd, who used to refer to his parents as "The Boges." We adopted it to represent any person of any age who acted old, straight and grumpy before their time. Thus you could be a boge at fifty or at eighteen; it was a state of mind and to be avoided. (Yes, there was and still is a Rush lexicon, just as most bands have their inside jokes and codes to speak surreptitiously in the company of others. I would share more of them with you, but that would be a breach of trust and a *drurken* idea, i.e., an idea to be avoided.)

*Between the summers of '71 and '72, gigs were scarce. So when we weren't doing odd jobs like playing for drunken boges, we went camping. It was cheap and cheerful! Note our first Rush T-shirts, with RUSH - ENERGIZED ROCK on them. We paid for them ourselves—just enough for the band, our girlfriends and our pals (including Oscar, seen here holding the bow saw).*

establishments in Ontario that welcomed both sexes. The day the drinking age law changed, the first thing we did to flaunt our legal right to drink was go into one of those fluorescent-lit and rather depressing places. They were bland as hell and reeked of cleaning solvent, with small round café tables on greyish linoleum floors that sat up to four dour-looking men getting to the serious business of draining their after-work allotment of piss-thin draft. Waiters sold you beer by the glass but would cursorily try to upsell you a jug. It was strictly quantity over quality. Thankfully, these vibeless places were a dying breed. The province's sudden younger clientele forced a tectonic shift in the industry, many Men's Rooms were turned into rock bars for both sexes, and for us those new rock bars were the right place at the right time.

Now it was time to turn pro and join the musicians' union. We felt it would legitimize our ambitions; it was a way of proving not only to others but to *ourselves* that we were serious. Alex put an end to his days of having to spell out his long and foreign name, choosing a direct translation from Serbian to English: "Živojinović" literally means "son of life," and so he became "Alex Lifeson." With my own new alias, I was seizing the chance to shed the skin of that sad little boy I'd been for too long. My life had always felt unimportant in the shadow of all that my parents endured in the camps, and even more so when Mom struggled as a grieving widow. After the turmoil of my father's passing, this was a chance to reinvent myself and stand out in the crowd.

As I'd entered adolescence, particularly after my father's passing, there's no question that I withdrew. The atmosphere at home drained away a lot of my energy, and I clearly recall how subdued I was in the company of adults and new friends at school. The teens are an awkward phase for everyone, of course, but my dad died just as we'd moved into an alien suburb rife with antisemitism, and when I came out of my year of mourning, my shyness was reinforced by the shame of being fatherless and being pitied for that loss. I felt gawky, self-conscious, out of touch and hypersensitive to the idea that, thanks to my big old schnozz,

I looked not just Jewish but *too* Jewish. Whatever self-confidence I'd ever had was replaced by fear, and I went through the motions of adolescence with my head bowed. Trying to blend in with my mostly gentile social scene and driven by the idea that I needed to be a "better" person, I suppressed my Jewishness, hiding behind my lengthening curtain of hair and striving for a cool attitude. If I looked hip, I thought, then I must *be* hip, right? And since I was already alienated anyway, why not double down by raising up my freak flag?

But I also wanted to be part of the conversation. To speak out and speak well. And to do that, I knew I needed to get smarter. I worked at that seriously, through music first; fortunately I had an aptitude for it, and woodshedding on my instrument let my fingers do the talking. I also versed myself obsessively in bands and their albums, well-known and obscure, and was soon able to join the schoolyard arguments over which musicians were cool and which were not. I then turned my attention to cinema, which won me some respect from my peers, but it still was not enough. I felt shut out of discussions around books, so I started to read—fantasy fiction at first (thank you, marijuana! Thank

*Et voilà! Gary Weinrib and Alexandar Živojinović have metamorphosized into Geddy Lee and Alex Lifeson!*

*My effin' life with Rush yet to begin, here are the earliest shots of me "onstage," moonlighting at a kid called Anthony's bar mitzvah party. At bottom is my old friend Sammy Roher on drums and, up front and center, Anthony's little sister Susie.*

*Our very first band pictures, likely taken by our friend Doc Cooper in the fall of '69, on the construction site behind Rutsey's apartment building, south of Bayview Avenue.*

*Halloween hijinks. Our first two weeks away from home, and the circumstances were miserable, full of bikers who kept unplugging our speakers when we weren't looking. Needless to say, we found ways to amuse ourselves—on and offstage. In the seated group shot (left to right): our two-man crew, newbie Liam Birt and our original roadie, the stalwart Ian Grandy; yours truly; and John. Meanwhile: "Amazing Kabuki?" We were there for two whole weeks, for fuck's sakes. Change the sign, already!*

*What can I say? This is what comes of smoking too much dirt weed, kids.*

(ABOVE) *John Rutsey and Alex had been pals first, starting a band called the Projection. His dad, Howard, was a well-respected crime reporter for the* Toronto Telegram *who died, as mine had, when John was barely a teen. You'd think that might have lent us some commonality, but we never shared our feelings.* (LEFT) *Oscar, Santa, Rutsey, me (and Ian Grandy out of frame on the left).* (BELOW) *1973: the only known colour photo of Rush at the Gasworks.*

*Glam, bam, thank you, Ma'am! Just the other day I found my old platform shoes downstairs, and here they are. I've often claimed that we neither understood nor cared about our image, but that's not true for this period. I used to ask Nancy for help, and being a fashion student, she loved digging up cool vintage pieces for the stage (which made her complicit in any and all of my fashion crimes). I even learned how to apply studs and shiny sequined bobbles to the pockets of my jeans, painted my nails black and wore a shiny star on my cheek. After John left the band, the importance of glitter gradually fell away. We had bigger fish to fry—like playing well—and that's where our focus remained . . . until the infamous Kimono Years.*

# *RUSH*

(TOP) *1972, Green Park, UK. Nancy snapped this pic of me in my civvies on our first-ever trip across the pond, while taking a break from the grooviness of London Town: the Kings Road in Chelsea, the Marquee Club in Soho, even the ubiquitous Wimpy Bar. It was all so effin' cool, a real eye-opener that stoked in both of us a desire to seek more from life. So, as soon as got home, despite having had such a great time, we, er . . . broke up!* (BOTTOM) *Two wild and crazy guys pretending that their manager's car belongs to them. (Why? Because soon will be de foxes!)*

you, Mr. Tolkien!)—building a vocabulary with which to express myself more succinctly.

But most important, I realized that if I didn't understand something, I had better damn well start asking questions. That was a huge hurdle because I then risked being looked down upon for admitting ignorance, but to my surprise, my queries were usually welcomed (at least until later when my incessant quizzing started driving recording engineers batty). Here's a valuable tip for you, something key that I learned about people: they love to share their opinions.

Even as an adult today, my shyness will occasionally threaten to drag me down, but being the crusty old pro that I am, I can usually swat it aside. One such moment was in 2017, when I walked into the rehearsal hall to practice "Roundabout" with Yes before their induction into the Rock and Roll Hall of Fame. At first, I stood there in awe, looking around at these older versions of my childhood heroes—musicians who were *surely* more experienced than me—and I needed a moment to gather myself. All it took was a warm hug from Steve Howe to help me enter the fray, but that brief hesitation was a reminder that regardless of my physical age, I can still revert to that little kid from the Willowdale suburbs.

FOR MOST OF its forty-plus years of touring life, Rush would essentially be a big-venue band that eschewed the bars, but the clubs that formed in the wake of those dying Men's Rooms were the break we really needed, a shot at self-sufficiency, a chance to work nightly instead of just on weekends, and an opportunity to play to an older if inebriated audience. However, we soon hit roadblocks as we discovered how resistant these venues were to a band that dared to think of itself as having concert potential. It was normal then to be contracted to do four forty-minute sets, plus one fifteen-minute set to close the night, and then there were the hateful Saturday matinees. I'd never been a fan of getting up earlier than I had to, especially after playing late into the night, but to get my voice ready for a mid-afternoon show was torture. And not only were Ontario bars unused to bands as loud as we were, they didn't dig bands playing their own—that is, unknown—material. To get hired we had to submit a sample set list, and when Rush did, we were quickly put straight: add some hits from the radio or at least some cover songs or you won't get hired. And when we did manage to get some gigs in the hotel bars outside of Toronto, the waitresses complained they couldn't hear the beer orders.

From the outset, I wrote some entire songs on my own, such as "In the Mood" (which would eventually appear on our first record); for others John would come up with a cool title, and Alex and I would work out the music as we waited for his lyrics to follow. (Interesting, isn't it, that both drummers in Rush wrote the lion's share of our lyrics?) Working side by side, we'd often develop vocal melodies before we had lyrics, because John rarely delivered them promptly. Paul McCartney famously talks about having no words for the melody of what would become "Yesterday"; for days he walked around humming to himself, "Scrambled eggs / Oh my baby how I love your legs" until finally the right ones came to him. But we'd go *onstage* without the lyrics ready. I'd just go up there and make them up on the fly. That's a stupid and scary thing to do, but I got really good at it in time, learning to form patterns that suggested words; what jazz people call "scat" would morph into lines, and the lines become a lyric. Scatting allowed me to work out the phrasing in advance, adding a breath here or taking a word away there, so that when the lyrics finally did come along I had the right articulation and rhythm.

Thing is, while our originals were naïve and crude at that stage, we knew that no one ever soared to the top playing cover songs (except Joe Cocker with his raspy soulful voice and so much charisma that you were happy to hear him sing the telephone directory). So, we compromised—always an ugly word for us even back then—by peppering our set lists with songs by impressive big-name artists, but only their deep cuts. That way we could have our cake and eat it too. We added songs like the

Rolling Stones' version of the Buddy Holly classic "Not Fade Away," Procol Harum's "Simple Sister," Cream's "Spoonful," Led Zeppelin's "Living Loving Maid" and eventually David Bowie's "Suffragette City" (that one became a super popular bar song for us), all of which we'd reshape to make our own. For example, we played a fifteen-minute version of Junior Walker and the All Stars' "Road Runner," just jamming the hell out of it with an Echoplex-heavy solo courtesy of Alex. It worked, and we started getting booked a *lot.*

In the early seventies, the Toronto circuit basically consisted of the Abbey Road Pub, upstairs from George's Spaghetti House on Queen Street, and the Gasworks and the Piccadilly Tube, both on Yonge. Those were the days before moshpits and body surfing, so the only time I ever had *that* kind of interaction with the audience was when I got drunk on my birthday and fell into the crowd and they very kindly pushed me back up onto the stage. There was also the Meet Market (renamed the Colonial Underground in punk's heyday) with a seriously rambunctious crowd—Alex had just had a wisdom tooth removed before one gig there, so out of it due to the painkillers that he had to play sitting down on a chair, his mouth swollen and bleeding, the upside being that he had a front-row seat for a fight that broke out in front of him *right as we were playing* "You Can't Fight It"! Then there was an oddball show at the Queen Street Mental Health Centre,[*] with patients dancing/convulsing in every imaginable way, and me discreetly mumbling the line "They got some crazy little women there / And I'm gonna get me one" for a rocked-up cover of Wilbert Harrison's "Kansas City" we were playing at the time. We laughed about it for years after, but truthfully it was sad and disturbing. I can only hope that to them it felt like a party.

---

[*]   Opened in 1850 as the Provincial Lunatic Asylum, it became the Asylum for the Insane in 1871, and by the 1990s, after attitudes towards mental health had evolved, the Centre for Addiction and Mental Health. But our parents always referred to it simply as the 999—as in, "You vill do what I say or I send you to . . ."

While never taking our growing Toronto following for granted, Ray would often send us gigging around Ontario, way out of town. He booked us in some pretty obscure places (for us, anyway), sometimes for a week or two at a time. The Russell Hotel in Smiths Falls was one memorably shabby party place. Then there was the unforgettable two-week stand at Finnigan's in the Thunder Bay Motor Hotel in, you got it, Thunder Bay, where our deluxe accommodation consisted of two big rooms with cots scattered about, and zero heating. I remember sleeping with a blow dryer under the covers and having to turn it on every hour to warm myself up. Then on waking we'd have a shot of rye whiskey just to get the blood circulating. The owner was a real dick who wouldn't advance us any money; being broke, we couldn't go out for so much as a 99-cent burger and had to take all our meals on credit in the hotel, running up a food bill that in the end would come off our pay. His only kindness was just before the final Saturday matinee (attendance, two to three drunk patrons), when he sprang for a couple of jugs of draft beer, which of course we annihilated before the set—half of which Alex and I ended playing horizontal. It hardly mattered to the crowd, such as it was. I recall one regular yelling, "Neil Young was born here! Neil Young was born here! Neil Young was born here!" Okay, dude, thanks for letting us know . . . again.

On the bright side, enduring years of cat calls and slurred requests for "Smoke on the Water" did build character and gave us a thicker skin. As official working musicians now, we simply took it in our stride and would end our bar days in July 1974 headlining upstairs at the Colonial Tavern, the venerable jazz club where greats like Cannonball Adderley and Thelonious Monk had once played; it was the only place any of our parents came to see us, as you could book a table upstairs overlooking the stage and enjoy dinner while we pummelled you from below.

Now, this whole business of writing a memoir is a dicey proposition, especially when one is over the age of, *ahem*, sixty-nine. (Yikes, did I just

*In addition to the bars, we still did high schools that had us crawling all around Ontario (and all over the stage). The first shot (TOP) inspired the "devolved" stage set for the encore finale of the R40 Tour in 2015.*

(ABOVE) *December 21, 1970, at A.Y. Jackson School. One of many gigs before we were allowed to play the bars.* (BELOW) *Vices of the road.*

say that out loud?) I, for one, am filled with self-doubt and recrimination when the old hard drive fails to bring up a file on demand. Some memories are solid as a rock—usually moments of triumph or failure, turning points, instances of sadness or loss—but others are . . . a blank. This is troubling. You'd think that the life I led, especially between '68 and '72, was so new and exciting that the memories would be indelibly imprinted on the little grey cells, yet to my dismay there are tracts of time and even relationships that have blown away like so many fallen leaves.

Why? Why so many lost gigs? I suppose that some were simply not of much consequence, while others are simply too painful to recall. I can barely remember a thing, for instance, about the hiring of the guitarist Mitch Bossi, the gigs he played with Rush or even my relationship with him. Why not?

Bringing him on board was John's idea, as they were friends. He started with us in the late fall of 1971, maybe early spring of '72. He was a sweet guy and a decent rhythm player; I remember that much. He lent us a fatter sound; as Lindy had before him, his parts gave Alex more freedom to solo, and he definitely looked cool onstage with his groovy shag haircut. As we became more successful on the bar circuit, John himself was getting more and more into fab threads and had cut his hair into a cool layered Mod vibe. Maybe that's a reason John wanted Mitch in? To some degree they were brothers in fashion. Alex and I weren't so concerned about the band's visual appeal, but I guess we went with the flow. After a few months, however, we decided he wasn't working out. Alex recalls that as Mitch was opening his guitar case one day, John broke the news to him. Mitch simply closed the case, picked it up and walked out without a word.

Beyond that, all I've had in my mind's eye for years were images of Mitch sitting in a parking lot with us, and another occasion at a shoeshine stand. But rummaging through the old files, I find that both of these "moments" are in fact publicity shots from the period. In the grand scheme of things, I'm sorry to say, our connection was tenuous at best.

AT HOME, DESPITE giving me the silent treatment for leaving school, Mom had more or less resigned herself to the fact that I wasn't changing my mind. She helped with the occasional handout of cash and paid for my driving lessons, and I even inherited her old car, a beat-up Pontiac Grand Parisian that I used to drive to gigs in places like Oshawa. She was a powerhouse, I have to say: whilst almost single-handedly raising my ten-year-old brother, she'd built up the store in Newmarket enough to consider expansion. She was struggling, however, to come to terms with my sister, Susie, who'd married outside of the faith (and given birth to my nephew Robbie), and I knew she'd find the idea of me following suit very hard to swallow. I had left religion behind me after Dad died, so Nancy being a gentile was never an issue for me at all, but this was not the life Mom had imagined for herself after surviving the war! Unless things became serious—like *marriage* serious—there was little to gain from adding to her woes, and although I was technically still living at home I was out and about so much that it felt just as easy to keep a little truth like my relationship with Nancy from her.

*The only performance photo I have with*
*Mitch Bossi (at the Abbey Road Pub, I believe) . . .*

Did I say "marriage serious?" In reality, things were becoming strained between Nancy and me. It's a big enough ask for anyone, let alone someone as fiercely independent as she, to hook up with a musician, but the extra pressure we'd created for ourselves by keeping our relationship a secret made it increasingly tough to be on the same page. It was looking more and more like we needed to flap our wings a bit, and one day she suggested we break up. I was shocked and hurt at first, arguing that we could work it out, but she was determined to move on. Then I thought, maybe the timing wasn't so bad. She wanted to get out and have fun, while I was more preoccupied with the band and writing music. Alex had also just become single and bought himself a 1963 MG—a "piece of crap," in his words, the hood tied down with a clothes hanger—which we could make good use of in a quest to be swingin' bachelors, and I took her rejection even more in my stride. (That car really was a piece of crap: driving to a show in Newmarket, the hood came loose and flew up smack into the windscreen, blinding and scaring the hell out of us. Probably from the shock of it, we ended up on the side of the road helpless with laughter.)

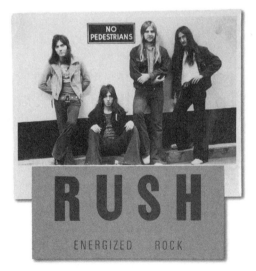

*. . . and one of the only publicity shots with him (seated).*

BETWEEN THE ABBEY Road, the Gasworks and a repurposed old tavern called Larry's Hideaway, Rush solidified its local following, and those places became showcases for record company execs to check us out. The owners and managers at the Abbey Road particularly liked us; we gigged there so often that we felt like the house band. We'd hang with the staff after closing, sharing stories and playing drinking games into the wee hours, before staggering outside and weaving our way home.

WE WERE DESPERATE to make a record and snag an opening slot on some major band's concert tour, but our brand of "Energized Rock," as our stickers and T-shirts proudly proclaimed, was at first rejected by *every single record company* in Canada. Fortunately, when you're young you're also arrogant: if somebody casts aspersions at you, you just think they're being a dick. You justify any bad reviews by saying, "Well, that guy doesn't know what he's talking about." So we were disappointed by the rejections—and the rejections after that, and after that—but not broken. We understood that we were not commercial. They were looking for hit singles, and we were not a hit single band. We had a crude sound, and we knew it. And we liked it.

It probably wasn't just our lack of commercial viability. Record companies in Canada at the time were mostly branch offices without much autonomy when it came to signing acts, the head office usually in Europe or the States. Canadians like us would start to break through in America only after a touring circuit had been established there. Without the precious airplay from a hit single, we'd have to sell our music directly to fans on the ground—the whole word-of-mouth thing. The door would open for us only with the rise of AOR, or "Album Oriented Rock," as it was known in the industry, played on FM stations where a grassroots following could request our kind of music.

By then Ray Danniels had partnered up with Vic Wilson, an industry veteran (and sax player for, among others, the Downchild Blues Band), to create SRO Management. It was a larger company with more employees and a roster of acts including Max Webster, Fear, a Beatles cover band called Liverpool and another novelty act called The British Are Coming!, which covered all the British Invasion bands of the sixties. SRO made no bones about it: those two were blatantly commercial groups that were in a sense paying for us. But eventually, Ray and Vic resolved to break the impasse for Rush, and they did this with a two-pronged attack.

First, we needed an album, and since we were having zero luck with the labels, they'd have to start their own. A few ambitious, independent thinkers in Canada had already tried their hands at this. The inimitable Bernie Finkelstein was one: his True North Records, which released music by folk-driven talent like Bruce Cockburn and Murray McLauchlan—whom he also managed—were an inspiration. But while

*Part one of the SRO master plan begins with a celebration of our signing to Ray and Vic's new label, Moon Records.* (BACK ROW, LEFT TO RIGHT) *Vic Wilson; Ray; S. Maley, SRO; me; engineer of our first record, David Stock; J. McDonald* (FRONT ROW) *Alex and John.*

it was easy enough to start an indie record label, actually making money from it would be more difficult.

Second, with a record to release, SRO would establish itself as a show promoter. In that capacity it could slot us in as an opening act for whichever big-name bands were brought in from abroad and connect with booking agents from all around the world. With any luck, this ambitious plan would lead to a cross-country tour, a wider (and more sober?) audience than the ones we were facing off against in the bars and ultimately a record deal in the USA and beyond.

Recording our own songs was a potentially expensive proposition. (We had only ever recorded once before—just a few songs[*] at a demo studio called Sound Horn at the back of a parking garage beneath the notorious Rochdale College building.[**]) No manager or band wants to spend their own money if they can help it—no record company, either; as we would discover later, that's what advances are for—which meant booking session time in a small studio in the middle of the night when the rates were very low. We were playing five sets a night at the Gasworks at the time, so we had to load out at one in the morning after our last set and take our gear to Eastern Sound Studios on Yorkville Avenue, record our songs through the night, clear out before their first morning session, go home, get some sleep, then bring the gear back to the Gasworks and do it all again. Thankfully, we pulled it off in only two sessions.

Eastern Sound's Studio B was a small eight-track studio. Alex recalls that on the first night he stumbled into Studio A by mistake, where an advertising session was going on. Some dour-looking guy turned around, looked down his nose and gave a *harrumph*. Alex muttered back, "Stupid boge," and closed the door. For me, walking into that place that night was to enter an Aladdin's cave, an awe-inspiring world of wonders. It

---

[*]  Engineered by Billy Bryans, later the drummer and cofounder of the Parachute Club.
[**]  Rochdale had been built to accommodate students in an experimental free-form education environment, but descended into chaos with squatters, bikers and drug dealers roaming the corridors. It was closed in 1975.

*Here we are in our finery, playing at the venerable Gasworks. Deep in the throes of glam, we'd change into our sequins and studs in a tiny dressing area situated beneath a restroom, which more than once leaked through the ceiling, forcing us to go onstage redolent of urine.*

**Before / after**

① Well I've been seeing the comin
of something new today,
~~something~~ ~~new~~ ~~and~~ ~~something~~ ~~blue~~
Sometimes ~~a little~~ faded but
never washed away.
— Now your finally listeni
to what I have to say
— well the time is right
it is today.
— yeah —

② Well you ~~aren't~~ ~~listen~~ listeni
I'm ~~you~~ ~~not~~ talking, we aint
gettin no where ~~all~~ ~~through~~ ~~to~~ ~~you~~
I KEEP TRYIN TO GET THROUGH TO YOU
All ~~you~~ ~~do~~ ~~is~~ STARE
— Don't you see that I need you
~~want~~ ~~to~~ ~~you~~ try to underst
— I don't want to be ~~ya~~
baby I want to be your

---

~~FINDING BACK~~
FINDING MY WAY

BEEN GONE SOLONG,
LOST COUNT OF THE YEARS
SANG SOME SAD SONGS
CRIED SOME BAD TEARS,
~~but~~ ~~I'm comin~~ ~~ooh!~~ ~~ooh!~~
~~I'm comin~~ ~~ooh!~~ ~~ooh!~~ ~~ooh!~~
BUT I'M FINDIN MY WAY BACK HOME

BEEN THROUGH HARD TIMES
AND BEEN THROUGH SOME GOOD,
LEARNED ~~TWICE~~ FROM MY CRIMES
AS MUCH AS ANY MAN COULD

BUT I'M FINDIN MY WAY BACK HOME,
CAUSE I'VE HAD IT FOR NOW LIVIN
ON THE ROAD

---

I'VE SEEN
~~_____~~ YOU STANDING THERE,
WITH YOUR finger IN THE air,
EVERYTHING WE DO,
YOU WANT TO LEAVE IT UP TO YOU.

WHO DO YOU THINK YOU ARE
YOU THINK YOU ARE A STAR,
TRYING TO RUN THE TOWN,
ALWAYS TRYING TO PUT US DOWN.

CHORUS YOU THINK THAT YOU'RE RIGHT
YOU THINK YOU'RE out of sight
TELL ME SOMETING MISTER
WHY YOU HAVE TO MAKE US SO
UPTIGHT.

WELL YOU SAY YOU'VE BEEN TRYING,
YOU KNOW THAT YOU'RE lying,
I THINK YOU NEED SOME cooling
WHO DO YOU THINK YOU fooling NOW

WELL YOU BETTER START CHANGING,
YOUR LIFE NEEDS rearranging ~~———~~
WE'D BETTER DO SOME ~~BAD~~ TALKIN,
OR YOU'D BETTER DO SOME WALKIN,
NOW
CHORUS

---

| | Min. | Sec. | |
|---|---|---|---|
| FEEL SO GOOD | 4 | 10 | |
| TALK | 3 | 43 | |
| NEED SOME LOVE | 3 | 07 | ~~Lovelight~~ |
| LOVE LIGHT | 4:25 | 10:20 | 5.55 |
| IN THE MOOD | 3 | 35 | |
| CHILD REBORN | 2 | 37 | |
| MIKES IDEA | 5 | 32 | |
| RUN WILLIE RUN | 2 | 05 | |
| NUMBER I | 3 | 04 | |
| ~~MARGERITE~~ | 3 | 45 | |
| TAKE A FRIEND | 5 | 15 | |
| ~~WORKING MAN~~ WHAT YA DOIN | 9 | 08 | |
| | 4 | 13 | |
| GARDEN ROAD | 3 | 10 | |
| SLAUGHTER HOUSE | 3 | 43 | |
| SING GUITAR | 6 | 48 | |
| CAN'T FIGHT IT | 7 | 14 | |
| 3:55 | | | |
| 5:55 | | | |

---

(TOP AND RIGHT) *Lyric sheets I wrote on the spot in-studio for "Before and After"
and "What You're Doing" (and "Finding My Way" before the Terry Brown sessions).*
(BOTTOM LEFT) *Figuring out what to record: John's reckoning of all our songs.*

didn't matter that it was tiny and equipped only with an eight-track recorder; it might just as well have been the cockpit of a supersonic jet, with its smell of electronics, the studio baffles and knobs, dials and gauges that seemed to go on forever. When you closed the thick, heavy door of the vocal booth you were enveloped in a vacuum silence—my god, like saying goodbye to the rest of the world.

Like anyone making their first record in an utterly foreign environment, we had no idea what we were doing. A studio is a dead-sounding space in which you have to rely on the engineer to capture the way you sound live and at your best—or at least the way you *think* you sound— and what's coming back off the speakers is not that. Not having an audience feeding back to you or the sound of your amplifiers buzzing in a live room, creating excitement, is no small thing. An isolation chamber is unforgiving. Playing live, you may think you're in tune, but even if you're not, the moment's gone in an instant, never to remind you how you actually sucked; in the studio you're laying it down for the rest of your life. At a gig you start out stiff, but as you warm up and your muscles loosen, you start to gel and you hit a groove; in the studio you're playing the same song over and over again, and all your focus is on the mistakes instead of the vibe and the fluidity of the overall performance.

This was a huge and daunting adjustment for us. We asked a million questions of the producer our management had hired, David Stock, a British guy living in Toronto and working with Vic and Ray as their in-house engineer/producer. He seemed like a good fellow, and we buckled down, eyes wide open and trusting.

As a rhythm section John and I had a lot to learn, but because we'd been playing long sets back-to-back nightly for weeks, we had our parts down pat. Likewise with Alex on both rhythm and lead guitars, double tracking for the first time. It was all pretty magical, and at first as we played ourselves back while turned up to 11 on the studio speaker system, we thought the tracks sounded awesome . . . if not quite awesome enough. Naturally we wanted to reproduce the energy, power and heaviosity of our live shows, and when we said with the full authority and technical know-how of a band that had never been in a studio before, "David, can you make the guitar sound . . . ya know . . . a little *heavier?*" he answered, "Don't worry, lads. It'll all be fixed in the mix."

Of course we nodded and said, "Okay." In time we'd learn that those are the *exact* words no musician should *ever* have to hear.

We laid down all the bed tracks on the first night, including those for "Working Man," a number we'd written with a heavy riff and a lengthy jam in the middle with the express aim of proving ourselves the fastest guns in Willowdale, and at our management's insistence a cover of the Stones' "Not Fade Away" that also did well for us in the bars. On the second night, I was excited and nervous because it was time to record the vocals. Though I was tired from singing all night at the Gasworks, my vocal cords were young and resilient, and I felt up for the challenge.

As I mentioned earlier, while waiting for John to come up with actual lyrics, I used to make up substitute words on the fly to tide us over, and after several performances those substitutes would sometimes form a pattern. Thank goodness for that practice, because on night two in the studio, John was nowhere to be found. We waited, hoping he'd turn up, but he never did. We then received a message from him. I don't recall verbatim, but it was basically "I wasn't happy with them, so I tore them up."

I was stunned.

He never really explained himself to Alex or me, either that night or later on, and in retrospect I don't think he understood his own actions. He never apologized because he was not an apologetic guy to begin with. He always kept so much to himself. A while later, it was clear that he was embarrassed for what he'd done, but mainly because it was a failure of his own personality on display for us to see. And indeed, what Alex and I understood that night, as clear as day, was that he'd been defeated by his own demons.

John was a moody guy. He was highly intelligent with a great sense of humour but cynical too. He could light up a room with a clever quip just as quickly as bum you out with a glare. He could make you feel you were his best pal or wither you with a sarcastic remark. He was a difficult guy in the dressing room. Some days you'd come in and he'd be happy, and when he was happy, everyone was happy. But other days you'd come in and he was pissy, and if you said the wrong thing to him, he would just snap a retort at you, dress you down in a sentence. Contrast this with after Neil joined the band: you could count on one hand the number of snarky comments that we threw at one another over forty years. If we wanted to make a point, we'd do it with humour, not from a place of nastiness. Alex will say that insecurity made John take things out on the very people who cared for him the most, and that he was angry about his health issues, as if he felt he'd been ripped off for a good life. He suffered from Type 1 diabetes, which we suspect had been alienating for him as a boy (and with us he still had to inject himself with insulin every day), but whatever the root causes, John's moods could be wearying.

Even before we entered the studio, it was becoming hard for us to work together. While Alex and I improved and became more adventurous as players, messing around with odd time signatures that echoed our love of Yes and Genesis, John was more into Free, Bad Company, the Rolling Stones and the Small Faces—bands that played straight ahead driving rock and, crucially, *looked* hip. Fifty years on, it feels unfair and a little unkind to guess at the causes of his inner conflict— there was so much we didn't know; we were teenagers entering our twenties, each with our own shit to sort out—but this much I can say: while he genuinely dug music and being in a band, showing up to gigs in ever more glam and glittery stage clothes, he seemed to simultaneously suffer from a fear of success. As our gigs improved his health deteriorated and his struggles increased. Alex and I were loath to replace him, but with the puzzling and ill-timed episode of the missing lyrics, the writing was on the wall.

But first, on the clock in the studio, I was in a serious pickle. I asked David to give me a couple of hours while Alex worked on his guitar parts, and I sat down to complete the words for the songs we had on tape, one by one, based on my onstage improvisations. Reluctantly, I was now the band's lyricist. We were shocked by John's no-show, but that night, once I finally started singing, I found it an effin' blast. I even learned the basics of double-tracking my voice—essentially singing along with a track I'd just completed to make the voice sound broader—then overdubbing harmonies to my own lead vocal parts. There was so much to learn!

Once I was done, Alex finished his solos and then it was mixing time—another first for us and another wake-up call. On the third night, while we did our gig at the Gasworks, David mixed the entire record. An *entire album* in two hours? After the show we sat down in the studio to listen, and our hearts sank. (Talking about it recently, Alex and I both uttered the same word at once: "crestfallen.") Song after song, the sound was *dinky*: the drums lacked power, the vocals sounded thin and the vocal echo effects were wrong, wrong, wrong. And *cheesy*, especially on "Not Fade Away." David either didn't get it or, to be more charitable, had been unable to capture our sound in the time allowed. Whichever it was, we did not sound heavy in any way, shape or form.

Even today it's painful for me to listen to "You Can't Fight It." Even to say it sounds cool as a *relic* is a generous description. It takes me right back to the disappointment I felt in that studio the night it was first mixed. I was thinking, *What is this? We've been neutered!* Since the late sixties, playing high school dances, then the bars and now the occasional small arena, we'd become so accustomed to how big our live sound felt onstage that when we heard that first playback, it was shocking how starkly it missed the elements that gave us power and size. It didn't sound like us at all.

Fuming, we went to Ray and Vic. They promised to find someone to rescue the album, but insisted on putting out two single sides to help promote our gigs. What could we say? We didn't feel we had much choice in the matter.

# CHAPTER 7

I N SEPTEMBER '73, MOON RECORDS RELEASED David's mixes of "Not Fade Away" b/w* "You Can't Fight It." Around five hundred copies of that lousy production were pressed, and it remains our weak first record. There was no way we would stand for a full album to be released sounding like that, not with our name on it, but as we pondered what to do with the remainder of the sad thing, we were now at least a bona fide recording act—"Moon Recording Artists, Rush," the press releases said—and we had gigs to play.

In October, Ray and Vic began to make good on their promise of using their clout as promoters to further our career. They slotted us in as the opening act for the New York Dolls, a sensation at the time

---

* "Backed with," in the biz.

with their androgynous glam-punk vibe. A theatre gig was a legit step up from the bar circuit. I have vivid memories of that night and some of the band and crew with their thick *Noo Yawk* accents, but I would prefer to share a description of the show that Alex later wrote for an article in the *West End Phoenix* newspaper:

*The venue for the gig was the Victory Theatre, built in 1921 and home to burlesque in Toronto until it closed in 1975. We were honoured to have worked the same stage as strip artistes Knackers Knock, Ineda Man and Cupcakes Cassidy, whose PR photos still graced the grimy, grey walls of the lounge. The dressing rooms were more Tower of London than chic and gaiety.*

*The Victory, in its waning days, was faded. Whatever charm it had in 1922 or 1962 had long disappeared and it had become just another dark and dusty haunted building, its plumbing rusty and sweating, its aroma musty and dank. The single lightbulbs in the hallways and dressing rooms created the perfect setting for a horror film. But the catering was good!*

*That night, the stripping, or at least our stripping—we changed in and out of our stage clothes—commenced before the first set, then again after the first set, then all over again before the second set, followed by one more at the end of set two. From the first note the audience was spellbound by our performance and couldn't wait till the last one. Between those notes, they made useful suggestions regarding solo sex acts, our moms and turning off our amps.*

*Rush was doing well financially at this time, so I only had to hitchhike halfway home. I had my guitar with me and walked for 10 minutes in the cooling evening before a couple picked me up. I squeezed into the back and thanked them for stopping. They were pleasant enough and smart, so I figured they were college students. As we got to know each other more intimately, I asked what they had been up to lately.*

"We were at the Dolls show at the Victory and it was great except for the horrible opening act," said the cheerful young man driving. "Yeah," said his charmingly cherubic girlfriend, "I wanted to chop that goddamn singer's head off . . ." and it was here that she turned to face me in the back, "with a dull piece of razor wire." Then she turned away and didn't feel like talking anymore. Me neither.

At the next light, I quietly jumped out the window and commenced the short 35-kilometre walk home in the soft drizzling October rain. Don't hitchhike, kids.

**"THERE'S A RUSH ON THE MOON"**

MOON RECORDS and RUSH are making a simultaneous debut.

RUSH is a three man generator of energized ROCK.

Alex Lifeson, Lead Guitar and vocals; Geddy Lee, Bass and Lead Singer; and John Rutsy, Drums; are the talent that gives you a RUSH for your money.

Dedicated to making Music that compels the Audience to 'Move It and Shake It' the Band has been entertaining in clubs all over Ontario and particularly in Toronto for the past five years.

MOON RECORDS is the conception of Vic Wilson and Ray Danniels who are well known for their association with companies like Concept, Music Shoppe International and S.R.O. Productions Ltd. and the Toronto music scene at large.

"NOT FADE AWAY"

moon RECORDS

"CAN'T FIGHT IT"

(MN-OOIX)

Distributed by London Records

*Our first-ever press release. Grammatical errors and hyperbole. Even John's last name is spelled wrong. Still, it was a coming-out party of sorts.*

*Who does your
nails, Ged?*

A few weeks later Vic suggested we meet with an expat British engineer/producer friend of his named Terry Brown, who owned and operated a studio called Toronto Sound in the eastern end of the suburbs. He didn't seem very interested at the start, but agreed to try to save the day. He listened to the record and said he understood the problems: the drum sound was feeble (out of phase, in fact), the guitars lacked weight, things that should have sounded big sounded small. By then we'd written some new songs, "Finding My Way," "Need Some Love" and "Here Again" (for which Alex wrote the lyrics), and after Terry came to a bar gig to hear us play live, he recommended we substitute them for a couple of the old ones. So we said bye-bye to "Not Fade Away" and "You Can't Fight It," and they remain the only orphaned songs from those sessions.

In November we went into his studio and worked around the clock over three days until we had the version of the album as it exists today. It was such an effin' relief for us, I can't begin to tell you. *Everything* sounded so much better. If we'd had deeper pockets—or more accurately, if SRO had increased the recording budget—we'd have re-recorded *all* the original bed tracks. Still, from the opening chords of "Finding My Way" we felt well represented, with the bonus that in Terry we had found a mentor and a kindred spirit—someone who was well schooled and had good taste in heavy rock sound, who knew how to make drums and guitars kick ass and was fun to work with to boot.

One of the first things Terry taught us was not to worry if one of Alex's guitars sounded slightly out of tune when he was double tracking. "No, no, leave it," he'd say. "It makes the guitar sound wider, *bigger*." It became a bit of a studio joke whenever a guitar sounded out of tune to say, "It'll sound bigger now, right?" It was essentially the same as a chorusing effect: when you put your guitar through a chorus pedal, you're using a tight delay that is slightly out of tune, which has the effect of making your sound wider in the stereo spectrum. That's true for double-tracked vocals as well. If you track something too precisely, it doesn't sound double-tracked anymore; if it's too precise it can even be in phase with itself and will actually sound narrower. Ideally you want to sound almost like two separate people singing.[*]

Multi-tracking was a fun new toy for us, but also a double-edged sword. In the studio you can pile on as many instruments as you like, but then when you go to play that song live and the solo kicks in, where is the rhythm guitar? There *is* no rhythm guitar! In the years to come, as the rhythm section in a trio, Neil and I would have to compensate by playing busier parts, which is kind of how our style developed the way it did (good excuse for playing too many notes, eh?). I'd also conjure up a bottom end *and* trebly tone that helped take up the space of the missing rhythm guitar.

As I've said, it can be painful to hear our records again, but I would say *some* of them stand up quite nicely. For example, I've been surprised by how well *Fly by Night* was recorded, and I really am feeling renewed respect for all the work we did with Terry, because in the early days he was both producing and engineering, and he was a damn good engineer. (Still is: as I write, he's actually mixing some live tracks from 1981 for us.) So maximum kudos to him for saving our skins, even if on listening to the first album again after all these years, much of it *still* sounds innocuous to me.

Of all the songs from that first record, most notable to me is "Working Man." It's always been one of my favourite songs to play. It has special poignancy because it's the only song from the John Rutsey era that we kept in our live repertoire for most of our forty years, often playing it as our show closer. I wrote its final lyrics on the eve of recording it, inspired by observations made whilst playing all those shitty bars around Ontario, watching working men pounding back their beers after work, guys on the dole spending their checks on as much as they possibly could before going home. In one sense I was singing about anyone, really, who worked hard, anyone who eked out a living without

---

[*] Part of Sting's signature sound with the Police was all those loosely double-tracked vocals. He sounded like a bunch of Stings. A *hive* of Stings?

much to look forward to. The song is about wanting more from life than just that. By comparison to these guys', my job didn't feel difficult. There I was, trying to make *my* living up on a two-foot-high stage in a room that smelled of stale and rancid draft, but I didn't get up at seven and go to work at nine. Playing in a band was a dream. (I'm reminded of how when a ball game starts, the umpire calls out, "Play ball!" not "Work ball!") From the first time I sat in a beer hall as a newly christened eighteen-year-old and looked around me at those men wondering what their lives must be like, I told myself, *There has just got to be more.* You have to demand more from life.*

We started to actually get a wee bit of airplay, here and there, late at night—"Working Man" on WMMS south of the border, and both "In the Mood" and "Finding My Way" in Canada. I remember hearing "Finding My Way" on the radio for the first time, and that was really, *really* exciting. It was an almost out-of-body experience to hear this record you yourself had made suddenly coming out of the same speakers all the *real* records came out of—and not just your speakers but other people's too across the land! Then our families and friends started bombarding CHUM-FM with requests, and word began to spread . . . I don't remember the first time, meanwhile, that I found our record in a store, though I do remember finding that the colour was never printed the same, but in various pinkish hues, some yellowy, some darker red, which you could say was just the start of a lifetime's frustrating pursuit of *getting it right.* (Note to self: ask for final approval on everything!) Still, it was awesome to see copies in stores—and of course, whenever you did, you'd move them to the front of the bin.

A couple of nights later my mother and her new husband, Max, came down to see us at the Colonial Tavern. Yes, she had remarried. And yes, that was weird. Max Rubenstein was a distant cousin from the old country who happened to live just a couple of blocks from us,

---

* Not only was it the first song that broke through for us in America, it was also the very *last* that Rush would ever play—at the LA Forum, August 1, 2015.

had two kids of his own and lost his wife to cancer. He and Mom agreed that a marriage was in the best interest of his young daughter and my younger brother, Allan. It was Old World thinking for sure, but there's no question he helped smooth over her troubles with me and my sister, bringing some normalcy to the household.

At the same time, with the gradual rise in stature that airplay conferred, my mother began to look kindlier on my chosen profession. And after we played a rousing show at Laura Secord Secondary School in St. Catharines that was televised on *Canadian Bandstand*, broadcast from CKCO in Kitchener,* if anyone asked what her son did for a living, she could say with no small measure of *naches*,** "Oh, yes—he's an *entertainer*. And he's on the *television*." I don't think she ever listened to our music in the early days, but later on she had Q107 on around the clock and *loved* it when we came on. She'd report religiously on who was getting more airplay, especially if it was another Toronto band, and became a mini expert on Toronto talent. She'd report to me and become quite upset, threatening to call up Ray Danniels and say, "You need to get them on the radio more!" She also stuck posters up in the window of her store and even gave the album away to kids who didn't have the money.

The story I will only briefly tell you now is well documented in the annals of Rush online and elsewhere: Bob Roper, a friend of ours who worked at A&M Records at the time, started sending copies of our LP to radio program directors across Canada and the States, and Donna Halper at WMMS in Cleveland liked the record a lot too. She played several songs from it but found that "Working Man" especially resonated with her listeners. As a matter of fact, the phones lit up, as they say, and Rush became one of the station's most requested albums

---

* It's a curiosity I urge you to look up on YouTube if you haven't already seen it—if for no other reason than to clock the earliest video documentation of my first Fender bass (before it was carved into a dune buggy sky-blue teardrop shape), my groovy ear pendant and Alex's necklace, Rutsey addressing the listless teenage audience from behind his drum kit and the spectacle of the emcee in his natty plaid suit.

** In Yiddish to *shep naches* means to take pride or pleasure.

despite it being available in American record stores only as an import.

The phones started ringing at SRO too. This time it was the record companies, and Ray and Vic dove into negotiations. Now, here's what I was told at the time: right as they were close to a deal with Casablanca Records (who had just signed KISS), they got a call from the head of national radio promotion at Mercury Records in Chicago, Cliff Burnstein. He begged them to wait for a day or so, since it was the weekend and no one was in the office in Chicago but himself, saying he was mad for the record, knew about the radio response and that Mercury had recently had major success with another Canadian band, Bachman-Turner Overdrive. Wisely, Ray said he'd wait. Two days later Mercury made us what Ray told us was a better offer than Casablanca had, and we signed a long-term deal with the label. In Cliff we had a true believer who made all the difference in the world, and I'm happy to say we've remained good friends to this day. Meeting over that record changed the fortunes of both of our lives, as Cliff here testifies:

*Late June 1974. Monday morning. My job is "National Album Promotion." Arrive at work at Mercury in Chicago just before 9am.*

*Our champions and saviours, Cliff Burnstein* (LEFT) *and Donna Halper* (RIGHT).

*The assistant to Mercury President comes by my office with a copy of Rush on the Moon label. She says to listen to it immediately and recommend "sign or pass" ASAP.*

*Why me? It's not my job. Irwin's in LA, the head of A+R is out of the office. Seems like I'm the only one there that might have an ear for this kind of music.*

*The album comes with a note that says it was sent by a booking agent at ATI. The band is Canadian, but the album is hot in Cleveland. Claims 6000 have been sold there.*

*I'm perplexed. I've read in* Creem *about a Canadian band called Mahogany Rush with an "amazing" guitarist. Could there be two Canadian Rush bands?*

*I put the record on. Blown away by "Finding My Way." Makes me a little nervous. I've only worked at Mercury for one year straight out of grad school, and I don't want the boss to think that I get excited about anything put in front of me.*

*That's around the time that Donna Halper, the WMMS (Cleveland) music director gets into the office. I'm going to see if she confirms this report of import sales. I'm skeptical.*

*Donna says that WMMS is playing the album, and, it's true, the record is a hot seller as an import. She says, wait till I hear "Working Man," that will blow me away.*

*I get off the phone and put on side two. Sure enough, "Working Man" is a tour de force. The publicity department hear the music coming from my office and invite themselves in. Comparisons to Cream, Zeppelin, and Sabbath are made.*

*Feeling more confident now, I relay the message that I think Mercury should sign the band.*

*That was probably the most eventful day of my career. It would set the stage for my future in the music business.*[*]

---

[*]  Cliff Burnstein would later establish Q Prime with Peter Mensch, managing Metallica, Red Hot Chili Peppers, Smashing Pumpkins, Madonna, Cage the Elephant . . . I could go on. And on. Pretty effin' good track record.

---

At the time, as I understood it, the whole eleventh-hour show-down between Mercury and Casablanca was the kind of wheeler-dealer drama that's the stuff of movies. In actual fact, Casablanca had taken a pass on us, and Mercury only came along in the nick of time. Alex and John and I were fed the same hype that Ray was whipping up to get a better deal out of Mercury. That was very much Ray's style. He loved leverage; if there wasn't any, he'd invent some! That's what a master dealmaker does—and Ray has always been a master dealmaker.

No, in reality, as the Casablanca record exec named Larry Harris has since confessed, there was no bidding war. In his book, *And Party Every Day: The Inside Story of Casablanca Records*, he writes,

*A booking-agent-turned-manager at ATI wanted to give us first dibs on an act he was representing: a Canadian trio hailing from Toronto. The club where the performance was happening was a dark, dingy place called the Colonial Tavern, which had a thread-bare sound system that couldn't come close to keeping up with the band. I could appreciate the fact that the trio gave the high-energy type of performance. Their downfall in my eyes was their look. They were ugly. I would have taken a flier on them, but there wasn't enough money in the Casablanca coffers to afford a ham sandwich and I decided not to make an offer. As the years went on, the wrongness of my choice just grew and grew. Even now I cringe just looking at these words: The band I chose not to sign was Rush.*

# CHAPTER 8

**R**USH **WAS RELEASED BY MOON RECORDS** on March 1, 1974, and by Mercury for international distribution the first week of August. Mercury's was the same version as the Canadian one apart from our logo on the cover being strangely (or just sloppily) changed from a kind of Fiesta Red to a pinkish hue—but hey, we could live with that! In May we played a festival in East Lansing, Michigan, featuring the New York Dolls and several bands on SRO's roster including the Beatles cover band, Liverpool. What I'll always savour about that gig is not the excitement of America per se, or even playing for Americans; I'd been to America before and grew up watching it on TV. This was the first time I'd crossed the border to work there as a *working musician.*

In June a gig was arranged to meet the buzz in Cleveland that Donna Halper had sparked; thanks to all the airplay we were getting on WMMS, we were added as special guests to a bill headed up by ZZ Top, with a band from Hungary called Locomotiv GT opening the show. Man, we were in awe of the whole experience. Donna showed us around, proud to have almost single-handedly broken us and treating us with a kindness we'd never received before. She took us downtown, although Cleveland was a sprawling place without a truly vibrant downtown—life there happened mainly in the suburbs[*]—but we went to some music stores and walked the streets and drove past the Allen Theatre, where we'd be playing that night. When we hit the stage the crowd's response was infinitely more demonstrative than what we'd known in Canada. They just blew us away. They knew our songs—especially, of course, "Working Man"—and called us back for an encore, but the show was running late, so our night was over. Still, a great experience and a taste of what was to come.

Behind the scenes, meanwhile, drama was building. Even after our success on Cleveland radio, John still seemed at odds. Our little taste of stateside touring life had excited Alex and me but not him. His commitment felt increasingly half-hearted. We knew that something had to change sooner than later. By that time, we'd done some gigs with our SRO label mates Max Webster, who had a terrific drummer named Paul Kersey. Vic spoke with Paul about jumping ship and joining us, but following some thoughtful consideration and a brief flip-flop, he opted to stick with Max. For us, meanwhile, there was no turning back. In a meeting at SRO, John agreed it would be best for all if he left the band, and that was that. His last show with us would be opening

---

[*] We'd play there many times over the years. On one of our earlier returns, Alex partied with a rhythm and blues band called the Electric Sparks who were friends of our road manager Howard, and they all got really high together. This one African American chick was looking at Alex, both of them wasted, and said, "Man, y'all have a deep mouth." He was like, Huh? WTF is a "deep mouth"? God, we were white. But it stuck and became another catchphrase to forever taunt Lerxst with!

for some American up-and-comer called KISS at Centennial Hall in London, Ontario, on July 25, 1974.

It's long been rumoured that Rutsey left the band partly due to his diabetes, but that's not the whole story. Yes, he must have wondered if he could hack a long tour on the road because he had to take insulin every day, but the bigger issue was musical differences. To give just one example, Alex and I had written a piece in 7/8 time that would eventually be part of "Anthem," which John had no interest in playing. As I've said before, Alex and I were becoming more and more influenced by prog bands, while John was listening to simple, direct rock and roll; we were into Bill Bruford of King Crimson, while one of his favourite drummers was Simon Kirke of Free and Bad Company. Maybe at some point in his life he feared for his health, but the main thing that had been building for a long, long time was that he wasn't happy playing what we wanted to play.

*Allen Theatre, Cleveland. June 28, 1974.*

He became increasingly distant during this period, hanging out more and more with his own set of friends, many of whom were strangers to Alex and me. And I never had a conversation with him about his departure. We barely stayed in touch. The only time he and the band would be together in the same room again was in 1976, when he and Neil were seated at the same table at my wedding! That would of course be a pretty big year for Rush, and I can only guess what was going through his head at the time. I don't know what regrets—if any—he ever had.

JUST AT THE moment of John's departure, we were booked at a big gig in the States, to support Uriah Heep at the Pittsburgh Civic Arena . . . but wait. Like that great line from one of Rush's all-time top bus movies, *High Anxiety*, "Hey, Norton . . . Missin' somethin'?" John left the band in July, and here we were talking about starting an

*John's last gig.*

American tour on August 14? We needed a drummer! We had *work* to do! We cancelled all our pending Canadian gigs, drummers were contacted to audition, and we packed into a rehearsal hall in Pickering, just east of Toronto. I believe the historic date was July 28.

Neither Alex nor I had ever been to an audition before, let alone held one of our own, so it was awkward as hell. I remember nothing of the first candidate, I'm afraid, but I know the next guy was Gerry Fielding, a good steady player we knew and liked, and that two others were scheduled. After Gerry left, a Ford Pinto pulled up to the loading dock and out popped this lanky, goofy-lookin' guy with short hair and no shirt and his drums in garbage bags—a Rogers drum kit, I believe, with twin 18-inch bass drums, the smallest kick drums I'd ever seen; when he sat on the throne behind them he looked like an effin' giant. I remember him carefully checking their positioning, then the rest of the kit, then starting to play triplets, which with those teensy bass drums sounded like *machine gun fire*. Those were eye-popping triplets! A grin spread from one of my ears to the other, and as we ran through some songs that grin never left my face. Man, he was *so* good, and *so* powerful. I suggested we jam on the same piece I've mentioned that John wasn't into, and he nailed it. I mean *nailed* it. I didn't need to hear anyone else.

His name, of course, was Neil Ellwood Peart.

There was no effin' way I was letting him escape. After his audition we lay down on the floor and gabbed away about a variety of things—*The Lord of the Rings*, *Monty Python*, stage wear and more—excited to find we had so much in common with him, and even more that he could play double bass drum triplets in 7/4 time! Alex was quiet, however, upset with me because we'd agreed beforehand not to select anyone before hearing each and every candidate, and there I was acting like Neil had already got the job. Later, I had to apologize and agree to hear the others. It was all such a role reversal for us; Alex is usually the one who wears his heart on his sleeve, while I'm generally the methodical decision maker. But I couldn't contain myself. Here was the drummer of our dreams.

Just before he left, I overheard Neil talking with one of our crew over a smoke by the mixing console in the hallway. He asked Neil why he'd want to join our band, to which Neil replied, "I really like the raw materials." For me that comment revealed not so much a respect for our musicianship as for his own ambitions. I could have taken offence, but I actually liked that he was thinking big—not just about taking a gig but being a part of something that could be molded out of *raw material*.

So anyway, the next drummer arrives and quietly sets up his drums. He'd made out drum charts to all the songs on our album. He played along correctly and, I'm sorry to say, tamely. Following Neil the poor guy didn't stand a chance, and even Alex was winking at me; he, too, knew we already had our man. We called Neil that night, and he came in the next day to officially join the band. I turned twenty-one that day. *What a birthday present.*

Three trios had greatly affected the overall sound of early Rush: Cream, Led Zeppelin and the Who.[*] Our first single, "Working Man," with its long jam, had been inspired in particular by "Spoonful," a song we covered from the start. The twelve-bar blues configuration, with that all-too-familiar walking bass line, was in effect my first "busy" bass pattern, but I pushed beyond it over time because I was always worried about us sounding empty, and once Neil joined the band I had a partner in crime, another guy who liked to be busy. He liked to follow me just as much as I liked to follow him, both of us thinking, *Who follows who now?* It was immediately clear to me that our interplay was going to be a blast. The hyperactive rhythm section was born!

We went into rehearsals straightaway, and also revelled in what was like walking through Door #1 on *The Price Is Right*. Mercury Records had signed us to a five-year deal, with Rush expected to deliver two

---

[*]   I know that strictly speaking the last two weren't trios, but with vocalists who played harmonica once in a while, their musical architecture was that of a trio.

albums a year over that term, and with that contract came our first-ever advance, so we raced down to Long & McQuade to stock up on gear for our tour. I had been eyeing a Jetglo Rickenbacker 4001, the closest I could get to the one played by my hero of the moment, Yes's Chris Squire (famously, his was a white 1964 4001S, but you knew that already because you read my *other* book, right?). Alex bought a 1974 Tobacco Sunburst Les Paul Deluxe, while Neil got himself a stunning silver Slingerland kit with some big-ass 22-inch bass drums; not bad after being in a band for a week. It was a dream come true for all of us, but let's pause for a quick reality check: that's right, I said two albums a *year*. And that advance I mentioned, short for "advance on royalties," was only a loan against *future earnings*—so yeah, it felt like we were spending their money when in fact it was our own.

Imagine what those first few weeks must have been like for Neil. Several years earlier he'd left the comforts of home and, high on expectation, moved to the UK in search of success. He'd hooked up with

*This photo was taken within three weeks of Neil joining the band. We were virtual strangers thrown together on the road, sharing long car rides, short stays in motel rooms and twenty-six-minute gigs. Yes, there was pressure, but was he in over his head? Hell, no. All three of us were happy as clams.*

some excellent players, but over a period of eighteen months suffered a string of disappointments and ended up managing a souvenir shop on Carnaby Street—faced with the choice, as he wrote in his book *Traveling Music*, "between playing good music and starving, or making a poor living playing bad music." He'd then returned to St. Catharines resigned to playing weekend bar gigs, his days spent selling farm equipment parts at Dalziel Equipment Ltd. beside his dad, Glen Peart, the owner of the store. Suddenly, a white Corvette pulls up with life-changing intent. A couple of guys get out, one of them a burly, bearded guy with a record in his hand who introduces himself as Vic Wilson, co-manager of Rush. He tells Neil he's heard terrific things about him, that the band has a worldwide record deal on the table with a tour of the USA ready to go, but no drummer. Neil is understandably doubtful. He says he has to take it all in before agreeing to audition. Thankfully for us (and the world of air drummers) he puts his hesitations aside and agrees to come out to play. A matter of only weeks later, having taken his pick of any drum kit he wants, he's fully armed and dangerous, warming up for Uriah Heep and Manfred Mann's Earth Band at the Civic Arena in Pittsburgh, USA. Talk about a whirlwind.

EARLIER IN THE summer of '74, with Mercury coming in, all of a sudden Vic and Ray had put a lot of pressure on us to sign a publishing deal with their Core Publishing Co. John was sick at home, so Alex and I attended a big meeting without him at Vic's house. Their lawyer was a skilled negotiator while ours . . . Hey, wait a minute—we didn't *have* one! We were literally on our own.* It was very typical for bands to give up their publishing rights in those days, but I was instinctively

---

* Our only potential lawyer was a distant relation to Alex by marriage, but on meeting him the first time, our accountant gave us a look as if to say, "Who the fuck is *this* guy?" Apparently he later got himself into so much trouble that he took off to South America before the authorities could investigate him, and was never seen again.

skeptical and kept insisting to Alex that we *not* sign everything away. With them dangling the promise of a record deal and a big US tour in front of us, however, he was all too ready to give up the ghost, and after he gave in, I was left on my own to stop the onslaught. It was a terrible position to be put in, and one that I've needled Alex about many, many times over the years. When I did so again just recently, he summed up the tension of the moment perfectly: "I mainly remember they were feeding their St. Bernard all of this fuckin' *beefsteak*. We were sitting in the living room and Vic's wife was making up this big dog bowl of piled-up meat and I was thinking how *I* would love to eat such a beautiful steak, if I could only afford it. How easy it was for them to just take advantage of us!"

My guts churned over the decision. *ERROR! ERROR!* was flashing in my brain. But I didn't yet have the confidence, legal advice or leverage to push back, so I, too, caved in and signed. And afterwards even their *lawyer* said, "I can't believe how you guys trust these people so much." Doh!

Ray and Vic might argue that you can't blame them for what they demanded. Back then the Canadian music industry made for slim pickings. There were only four significant sources of revenue: record sales, radio play, ticket sales and publishing. Other Canadian artists, like Neil Young, Anne Murray and Gordon Lightfoot, had hit singles and filled medium-to-large venues, as did BTO, April Wine and the Guess Who, but there were few big arena-touring rock bands, no Zeps or Creams or even Van der Graaf Generators; however much we aspired to it, we did not yet fill that bill. Rush fell into a musical black hole. Our songs weren't radio-friendly either, and while our managers made a commission from our gigs, earnings from bar and high schools and the occasional soft seater were never going to line anyone's pockets with gold. So they had to chase other streams.

One potentially significant source of moolah that remained was publishing—so much so that if you were a singer-songwriter who wrote catchy tunes that *other* artists might want to record, you could do well by signing with one of the bigger music publishing houses before even approaching a record label yourself. Publishing rights raked in money generated by airplay and, if the song connected with the public, record sales. The publishing pie was sliced down the middle: half to the artist and half to the publisher.

Now, pop versions of Rush music would not be appearing anytime soon on radio stations, or in elevators or dentists' offices, but our songs might conceivably be a valuable investment for the future. If one day we did achieve some measure of success, whoever owned the rights would be rewarded for having had the foresight to sign such a rookie band. If not, well, no great loss—it'd be written off as a tranche of their own kind of hedge fund. In that spirit, Ray and Vic had founded Core Publishing, and were now seeking the publisher's share of our music. (The artist's share was paid directly to whoever wrote the song, so that was not up for discussion.)

This was long before artists like us woke up to the realization that we could just as easily start our own publishing houses. Those types of naïve errors (or moments of exploitation, depending on your perspective) were the norm rather than the exception, though. Quite simply, we saw giving up our rights as the price of passage into the larger world of rock and roll that we were desperate to enter, and to which very few other Canadian bands of our ilk had access.

I was learning, though. We'd eventually retain a corporate tax lawyer rather than a typical music business one—a good guy, a good thinker—and when we entered into a long and protracted renegotiation with SRO, we got pretty tough. That wouldn't happen immediately, of course. It was only after the success of *2112* that we knew we held the big stick. By then I was also getting advice from other management people who were friends as to what was fair. I was doing my homework. I'd become wise to the way Ray deployed the classic divide-and-conquer, calling each band member up, schmoozing each of us in turn, telling us what we wanted to hear, and I persuaded the guys that from then on, I would quarterback the renegotiations. I said, "Ray's gonna call you, but don't say *a word.*" This time around I was ready to push to the nth degree, and although it took a little time, we ended up improving our deal dramatically.

THROUGH OUR STATESIDE booking agency, ATI, we now acquired our first tour manager, an affable and hilarious character by the name of Howard Ungerleider. He was originally given the job to report back everything that was going on with us to his superior there, but he soon became an incredibly loyal asset to us. He was a master at intentionally mangling words to comic effect—out of his mouth, for example, Winnipeg became Whip an Egg, or he'd add the sound "hern" to random proper nouns, hence New Haven became New Havehern, Lock Haven became Lockhavehern, etc. Thus, he came to be known as Herns, and his manglings "hernsitudes." He was also an unparalleled storyteller who loved an audience and never let the facts stand in the way of a ripping yarn. He'd worked with Savoy Brown and Brian Auger, and picked up a helluva lot about lighting along the way. At the start, like any tour manager, Herns was responsible for booking hotels, doing the advance work—i.e., calling the promoter to review our rider and gig details, booking rental cars—and the settlement after every show and so on. A fairly straightforward routine for an opening act, you might say. Just don't leave our fee on the hood of a car, which was exactly what he did after one of our very first shows in the USA. (Thankfully we noticed it there before driving away.)

Before Howard joined, we had a two-man crew: Ian Grandy, who had been with us since Day One and before we could even afford to pay him, was our loyal everyman; then in late '71, Liam Birt came on, only seventeen and a year under the drinking age, so we had to sneak him into our bar gigs. He was our stout defender and friend and, like Herns,

*Rush's three-man crew in 1974 (clockwise): Howard in full "Herns costume," which he always wore in hotels; a very young Liam "Leaf" Birt testing his wings and Ian Grandy setting up the mixing gear.*

(LEFT) *This is the big time: three cases of beer, two bottles of Blue Nun, one mickey of Southern Comfort and another of Jack. Par-tay!* (RIGHT) *Chillin' with Neil at the motel.*

in our employ until the very last gig in 2015; if I ever tour again, I expect both Howard and Liam to be right there on the road with me.

In those early days, we knew none of the rules. We were a small-time regional band attempting to step onto a big international stage and making shit up as we went along. We didn't even know what per diems were! We had zero luxuries in the dressing room and travelled by rental car for years until we started earning a bit more money as headliners. That, incidentally, is when a tour manager's job becomes a fine art: checking which expenses claimed by promoters are legit and which are not. In 1974, that was Howard's main responsibility, but years later, when he followed his true calling to become our full-time lighting director, the job fell to Liam—who, let me tell you, was one feisty Scotsman. Rising to the occasion as tour manager, Liam got to the bottom of every effin' receipt. I mean, he even demanded them of *us*. He wouldn't let fifteen cents go unaccounted for and would nail any promoter or employee to the floor until they coughed it up. That was a beautiful thing to watch in action.

For the big stateside gig on August 14, 1974, with Uriah Heep and Manfred Mann's Earth Band, Ian and Liam drove our gear across the border in a leased truck while we flew into town with Howard. It wasn't long before we got our first lesson in American Aggressiveness 101: as we pulled out of the airport another car cut us off and our taxi driver yelled out the window, "You cocksucker, I oughta slit your throat!" Whoa. It was like, Easy, guy, you've got some nice Canadian boys on board, eh?

We were in complete awe of everything. It was the first time we'd flown into the USA, which felt more professional than any other arrival to a gig we'd ever experienced, and it was new and exciting to be working in a town we'd only heard of from movies and television shows and documentaries—all those multisyllables uttered on newscasts, "Pittsburgh, Pennsylvania"! The venue was a massive round structure, the largest we'd ever played, and before the show I went walking around the entire periphery to see *everything*. It didn't feel real to me. It was magic, like a waking dream. I wasn't sure I even belonged there. What's more, an empty venue has its own special vibe; it's always exciting to arrive for soundcheck as the event is still being assembled. After forty years, of course, you're somewhat inured to it, but we were as green as could be. We didn't even have road cases yet; we were still carrying cables in plastic milk crates, just embarrassingly bush league.* Then I ran into Uriah Heep's Ken Hensley and Gary Thain as they were climbing out of their limo, looking very much the rock stars du jour—in all their experience and glory, a rock and roll success story in the flesh. *That's* where I wanted to be. For them it was the wrap of their successful Wonderworld tour, while for us it was only the beginning. Needless to say, we were eyes wide open, eager to learn and drinking everything in. They were all super-friendly, but today when I look at this picture of me posing

*"Not this bleedin' guy again!" Me with Manfred Mann's Earth Band at the Charleston Civic Center, August 17, 1974.*

---

* Liam remembers us then graduating with pride to steamer trunks and smaller suitcase-style cases made of a high-density cardboard.

with them and see myself being full of myself, I wonder if they weren't secretly going, "Crikey, what a greenhorn."

The day raced by and before I knew it, we were on in ten. This being Neil's first gig with us after only two weeks of rehearsal, we were *very* nervous. Herns had advised us to request a modest dressing room rider with a deli tray, Heineken beer and Blue Nun wine, but I asked for a bottle of Southern Comfort because I'd read that rock stars drank that stuff, and when time was called I took a big swig of it. It went straight to my head, and when we hit the stage I was so tipsy I thought I'd fall right off.

Whatever condition you're in, it's a huge adjustment from being in a club with people right in front of you to realizing you're just a little speck trying to reach an audience in the bleachers. Now there's an enormous gap between you and them; you're *much* higher up, there's a photographer's pit and a barricade, and beyond that it's just faces that blend away into a kind of surreal oneness. Paradoxically, though, the stage becomes a kind of sanctuary where you get down to work with your buddies without too much awareness of whether you're projecting into the mass or not, and with no time to take it all in we gave it everything we had. People were only just arriving and looking for their seats as Alex's opening chords to "Finding My Way" smacked around the mostly empty, cavernous concrete building. We blazed through our twenty-six-minute set to a polite smattering of applause and . . . that was it! Over before it started. That was tough. When you're an opening act, you play that short half-hour for people who mostly haven't heard of you and are judging the fuck out of you. There's no instant love. You work really hard, playing as fast as you can, concentrating like mad on making an impression: the first song goes by, then you're into the second one and just as your fingers are warming up and you're starting to sweat and get a groove on it's "Thank you! Good night!" Over time, of course, you get used to it and learn to savour those precious twenty-six minutes as best you can, but when we left the stage in

*Welcome to the Big Apple! Central Park outtakes by David Gahr (and when a random kid walked by, David put him in the shot. Where is he today?).*

Pittsburgh it was like, *What just happened?* Still, with our first gig under our belts, we ran triumphantly back to the dressing room to get high and drink the rest of our "free" booze, then ventured back out to watch the other bands play. Halfway through Heep's set the retractable roof of the arena opened and that soulless concrete cathedral filled with soft, warm summer night air. It was pure magic.

The record company told us that we needed a proper promo shot pronto, and arranged for us to meet up on a day off in New York with the preeminent photographer David Gahr. His was an unenviable assignment. Far from us unknown Canucks having any sort of image, Neil didn't even own stage clothes; for the occasion he borrowed a blue velvet jacket of mine with embroidered flowers on it, while Alex (to whom David referred constantly as "Eric") wore a frilly shirt and jeans, and I — ahead of John Travolta by three years, I'll remind you — wore a white suit. He marched us into Central Park and parked us in front of a few of his favourite spots, where we stiffly stood. He tried everything in the book to loosen us up, including, "Okay, smile . . . you *cocksuckers*," which got us laughing just long enough to capture something acceptable in front of one of the park's many archways.

I used to tease my hair. In pictures of me from the early seventies you can see how thick it was, but the ones on this tour sometimes reveal how thin it was actually getting on top, and how I had to comb it over to cover up a widening bare spot. After just a few weeks on the road, I contracted an ailment called alopecia areata, and I seriously feared that I might lose *all* my hair. The treatments were regular shots of cortisone injected directly into the bald areas. *Yowie, mama!* I was also given a topical steroidal ointment, which Alex would apply for me. Now, that's a pal. Yeah, man, I was all jacked up on roids, which, *ahem*, explains my manly physique.[*]

---

[*]   No one really knows the cause of alopecia, but my doctors suggested it was the stress of the tour. Maybe. I mean, I didn't feel overly stressed, just excited! (You may think you now know the inspiration behind our song "I Think I'm Going Bald," but you will have to wait for that.)

Things came at us fast and furious for the remainder of 1974, as we zigzagged anywhere either management or agent could snag us an opening spot—usually as a last-minute add-on to a tour already in progress. We even appeared on a corny daytime TV show for teens called *Barry Richards Rock and Soul.* Just imagine: the fast-talking emcee introduces a series of pop groups, the kids dance, out of nowhere there's this heavy metal trio and then they move on to Martha and the Vandellas. Just weird! On camera Barry Richards asked me, "Hey, what's it been like playing with Uriah Heep?"

I said, "It's been great."

And that was it.

We zipped back to Pittsburgh to open for Blue Öyster Cult at the Stanley Theatre, only to find the venue's A/C on the fritz, the lineup delayed and disrupted and our set cut down to two songs—basically, "Hello, Pittsburgh!" followed by "Thank you! Good night!" In the fall we headed south to open for Rare Earth, T. Rex, KISS and, ill-advisedly, Sha Na Na. Yes, that's right, our agent idiotically added us to a show of theirs in Baltimore where their fun-loving, brilliantine-quiffed, rock-and-rolling Fonzie lookalike fans so little appreciated having to sit through our brand of hard rock that they roundly booed us off the stage.

*The first three shows ever with Neil Peart on drums.*
*Nice to see our name in the paper, eh? (If you can find it.)*

In St. Louis a few days later we opened for the Climax Blues Band and the Italian prog rockers PFM (Premiata Forneria Marconi) at the Ambassador Theatre, and were slated to do our first-ever important radio interview at the powerful radio station KSHE, but our after-show party got out of hand when someone distributed some mescaline (or was it STP?), keeping us up all night laughing at ridiculous things. I was still tripping the next morning when Herns called up to say that everyone else had crashed, but he and I had to leave for the station in twenty minutes. Thank god he was with me. My response to almost every question I was asked was prefaced by a "thoughtful" pause, before blurting out a suitable answer that Herns had whispered in my ear. When we got back to the hotel the guys assured me I'd done just fine. Thanks, liars!

Rock Star Lesson #1: Do NOT drop psychedelics before an interview.

We were set to headline at the Agora Ballroom in Cleveland the following night. We smoked a few joints en route as per usual, and Alex and I jammed on acoustic guitars in the back seat, coming up with what would eventually be "Making Memories"—an almost fatally apt title, considering what happened next. We were strumming away when one of us noticed a sign that read MEMPHIS 120 MILES. I said, "Uh, Herns . . . Is Memphis on the way to Cleveland?" In a panic he pulled into a truck stop and, sure enough, we'd been heading south and were now ten hours by car from where we were supposed to be. Howard plugged a small fortune into a phone booth (remember, no cell phones or Google Maps in those days) and booked us a flight to Cleveland from Evansville, Indiana, about 140 miles away. As we hightailed it down a network of ever-smaller highways and roads it started to rain and, passing through some town just in the middle of a flash flood, we found ourselves driving in deep, deep water. We slowed to a crawl, pulling at last into the Evansville airport, just in time to watch our flight take off. Undeterred, Neil jumped behind the wheel and drove us through the night, arriving so late at the Travelodge in Cleveland that they had cancelled our reservations. They deployed some cots for us in a conference room, and I will never forget how hard Neil crashed, flat on his back, asleep within seconds. To say that nothing could have woken him is an understatement.

After Cleveland we had an afternoon set at the Minnesota State Fair, then raced back east the next day to Asbury Park, New Jersey, then played two quick shows over the border in Canada. We were still making next to nothing, living off a weekly stipend of a hundred bucks or so from a combination of our meager earnings and tour support. Driving being our only cost-effective means of travel, we learned how to sleep on our luggage in the back of our rental station wagon, piling in like college students in a phone booth, chowing down along the way at some IHOP or Howard Johnson's. Good to be young and resilient, but even better if you have a supply of pot to tide you over on the interstate! We'd get high, sleep on the bags or smush ourselves into a corner, and

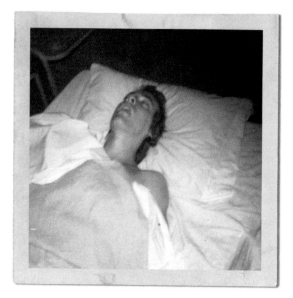

*To sleep . . . perchance to sleep.*

*Warming up for*
*Nazareth at*
*the University of*
*Western Ontario,*
*October 23, 1974.*

when we'd wake up we'd have crease marks crisscrossing our faces. The times we crashed in our clothes at a Holiday Inn, we were grateful just to have a bed.

In Evansville, incidentally, we opened for KISS with Billy Preston as the special guest. The night before, we'd stayed at the same hotel, and were up to our usual shenanigans when Preston, hearing the music from down the hall, knocked on our door and asked if he could join in. We thought, *Wow, cool! The legendary "Fifth Beatle" wants to hang with us?* We had a riot drinking and jamming with him and ended the night with a rousing rendition of "O Canada." The next day, when Billy arrived backstage surrounded by his entourage, we waved and called out his name. And he blanked us completely. We looked at one another puzzled. He didn't have a problem drinking all our booze . . .

Rock Star Lesson #2: Famous people can be dicks.*

---

* Herns called people who did that "blankers," and liars "bluffers." Those Hernsitudes made their way into "Best I Can": *Blankers and boasters / All the bluffers and posers / I'm not into that scene . . .*

# CHAPTER 9

I N THE SPACE OF TWO YEARS, NANCY AND I had lived the entire life cycle of your average romance: we'd gone to London on holiday together, returned home only to break up and see other people (she became something of a disco queen at the time), then tentatively started talking on the phone once more. The clincher was when her mum was away and she invited me over. I guess I'd been fending off the flu or something, because that evening I fell into quite a fever. She took care of me for a couple of days and nights, and through that feverish flux we reconnected and fell for each other all over again.

Nancy was working in a law office where she was learning how, among other things, to deflect lascivious advances from the older lawyers while seriously pondering a return to fashion school, when we moved into an apartment above a Chinese restaurant, enduring Top 40 hits all night through the floorboards whenever the owners forgot to turn off the radio before locking up. Actually, you could say it was mainly my record collection that moved in, because more often than not I'd be on the road. We'd write to each other often and make sure of a weekly phone call, but being so far apart for so long was new and difficult for both of us—mainly for her, I should say, as I was the one having adventures while she was at the office being chased around the desks. It wasn't just the long absences; with a work-obsessed nature like mine, you can get so used to thinking as a solo act, so to speak, that when you're finally together it takes some serious recalibration to think and act as a couple again. Given how shockingly high the failure rate is for relationships with musicians, I was fortunate that she was so independent, but it would still all come to a head some years later . . .

I remember talking to Pete Way, the funny and affable bassist of UFO, about the difficulty of touring and keeping a relationship together. (He was on his second marriage at the time.) A true rock and roller, Pete *loved* being on the road, but his second wife was not so amenable. On the eve of one US tour he was so afraid of telling her he had to fly out of England again that he left the house on the pretence of running some errands, then phoned her from the train station. "Sorry, love, I just found out I have to, y'know, be on tour with the boys. Call you when I get there! Love ya! Bye!" (He was such a good storyteller that I'm not sure if that really happened, but I suspect it did; he'd be married six times before he departed this world.)

**SINCE BY NOW** Rush was starting to be reviewed in the music and mainstream press, this is probably a good moment to acknowledge one of the more controversial aspects of Rush's sound: my *voice*. (Oh, *must* we?) John Griffin wrote in the *Montreal Gazette* that I sounded like "a guinea pig with an amphetamine habit"; in *Circus*, Dan Nooger said, "If Lee's voice were any higher and raspier, his audience would consist exclusively of dogs and extra-terrestrials." (In 1979, perhaps kindlier, John Rockwell would comment in *The New York Times*, "Mr. Lee sings in a spare but unusual way—a brittle and androgynous tenor.") I didn't realize at the time that I was—what did one critic call it? "Shout-screaming" or something. When I listen back, it sounds to me like I'm talking in a really high voice and throwing a little melody in. But a lot of it is not melodic. It's *controlled* screaming developed to cut through the density of the band in its earliest form.

My voice had to cut through our heavy rock barrage, and as that whole blues-based rock attitude became more complicated—or "sophisticated" or "pretentious," depending on the descriptor you prefer—its bluesy-ness stood out even more, because suddenly the context was no longer the blues. Whether critics liked it or not, it was a confluence of styles, a conversion from a blues-based band to more of a prog, classically influenced one, maintaining a shouty, bluesy singing style; it was the first indication of an original sound for us.

So, yes, my style did come across to some as quite abrasive, especially before we began making records, but you have to put yourself back in 1974. It's all context, right? As I write in 2022, our collective ears have become much more open. We've heard every style of music, every kind of singer, bands way heavier than Rush, vocalists even shriekier than I used to be. So imagine you're a critic back then in a reverberant arena, there's this three-piece band you don't know and this hairy guy is shouting at you: I get that if you consider yourself more sophisticated than the average music fan, our twenty-six minutes onstage must have seemed a loud mess, but we were truly into it, playing our parts with honest conviction, and raw or not, we were connecting with growing numbers of people. I guess sometimes the official tastemakers are the last to know.

ALTHOUGH IT WAS exciting as hell to be on tour in that way, playing such short sets every night was frustrating. Just when your fingers were starting to warm up, you were off the stage. You rarely had the time to jam out—not even during soundchecks, which were occasional, brief and mostly last-minute, the routine being: plug in, check monitors, dash off part of a song and leave. Meanwhile, we had to be content with writing new songs backstage, in hotel rooms or the back seats of cars with just a couple of acoustic guitars. We got pretty good at imagining how a heavy riff might sound (in fact, some of our heavier numbers, including parts of *2112*, were written that way), even if it wasn't much fun for the drummer. Onstage, however, Neil and I were developing a feel for each other, and how *very* different he was from the fellow who'd previously occupied the seat. John had a good, solid meter, but was a basic, hold-down-the-beat type, whereas Neil had both power and complexity. What made our playing relationship so very special was our rhythmic chemistry, a musical intuition in sync from the start. We shared a love of adventurous fills, odd time

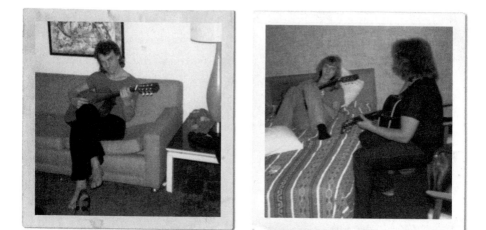

*What a blast! Broke but living in hotels, jamming day and night. Even though Neil wasn't adept, he loved to have a guitar in his hands and plunk away.*

signatures and a bit of well-placed bombast. In the years to come, when he was writing new parts or improvising a drum fill (he'd almost never play one the same way twice) we'd develop a kind of ESP—so much so that we'd freak each other out sometimes, delighting in the moment with a wink or a grin. For a bass player to find a drummer with the exact same mindset is a rare and special thing.

Over the next two months we opened a bunch of shows for KISS, and could not have been treated better. We got to know Gene and Paul and Peter and Ace a bit, hanging out in their dressing room as they put on their makeup and costumes. There was little in their music that we wanted to emulate, but we learned a hell of a lot about the importance of professionalism from them. We were impressed by how they gave it their all every night, and learned a ton about the use of pyrotechnics and other effects, which we'd deploy once we started headlining our own shows. We'd often convoy with their road crew and learned lasting lessons from them about going the extra mile for a show. And importantly, they allowed us soundchecks whenever they could, for which I'll always be grateful. That may not strike you as a big deal, so let me explain . . .

In the early days of touring arenas, bands typically had to deal with extremely loud, triple-barrage onstage volume: wedge-shaped floor monitors blasted your voice up at you, amplifiers blasted you from behind and side-fill monitors blasted *all* the instruments across the stage at a level even louder than the amps. As Ian Gillan first put it in the annals of rock and roll, "Everything louder than everything else." And Nancy wonders why now I can't hear the effin' egg timer?

But what I've just described was the *ideal*; back then as an opening act playing one-nighters with a different band every night, you couldn't afford to bring a monitor guy with you, and with a different person doing your mix almost every night you were walking into a kind of Wild West show. You're in some big barn of a building you've never seen before, with a sound system you don't know and ten minutes, if that, to get comfortable—and that's in the empty building; once it fills up, everything changes because now you have these sound-absorbent carbon-based units called *people* sitting in chairs, soaking up the reverberations and (if you're lucky) making a noise of their own.

The feeling is always a bit out of control at the best of times, a bit disconnected from your instrument (Keith Richards has said that playing a guitar in concert is like holding on to an electric eel, which I think is pretty apt); when I'm playing bass with a huge amount of volume coming at me, it can feel like the strings are fatter than they really are, and my fingers feel sluggish. But as an opening act without even the benefit of a decent soundcheck, with feedback from my vocals squealing up at me and only twenty to forty-five minutes onstage, we'd just have to accept that we weren't going to hear properly. We'd do the best we could and get the heck off. Some musicians adjust to it well, but some never do.

They say what makes baseball hard to play is that it's a game of constant adjustments; the same can be said for live rock and roll. On tour even an established band will have a different set of acoustic problems to overcome every single night, as it strives for a clear and intimate performance in arenas that have been acoustically designed to create a cacophony for the home team. Some cities are renowned for their terrible-sounding buildings. For example, there used to be a place in Chicago called the International Amphitheatre, the most cavernous venue *ever*, in which every strum seemed to morph into an endlessly rolling, thunderous cloud of sound. The crew's joke about places like that one would be "When another band loads in tomorrow, they'll still be hearing the end of our show." Then there was the Rosemont Horizon, in the suburbs of Chicago, with a very squared-off ceiling that slapped back so much noise it was a nightmare for both the mixer and the performer—but not necessarily in the same way or at the same time. Places like that might sound decent out front, but onstage you'd be getting a reflection from somewhere that would drive you batty. At gigs like that, our soundman might come back after the show and say, "Great sounding room, boys," and we'd look at each other thinking, *Huh? Really?*

Bottom line is, in an unfamiliar and acoustically unfriendly building a lot of young bands will come offstage bummed out, thinking they did a shitty job. They're not even sure if they hit the right notes, because some rooms are tuned differently; certain notes become exaggerated, making it hard to tell if your finger was even on the right fret. You're wrestling in an environment with a particular tonality that's not conducive or sympathetic to hearing, and all the while you're trying to sing in key. It's truly trial by fire, night after night after night.

The layman may not fully understand how important soundchecks are to a young band—but you know, come to think of it, not all *bands* do either . . . We once did a bunch of shows where Angel opened for us.* We made sure they got a soundcheck every day, but they never used it. So we'd go out and mess around on their gear and do their soundcheck for them. And *why* didn't they use it? Almost on a daily basis, we would say to the crew, "Where are the guys?" and they would kind of sheepishly say, "Well, they're in the dressing room . . . doing their hair."**

**BECAUSE GENE SIMMONS** and Paul Stanley are both Jewish (their real names are Chaim Witz and Stanley Eisen), I had an opportunity on that tour to reevaluate my own tribal roots. Having cast off the chains of religious dogma, I was starting at the time to look at my family differently; I began to see Jews as a race and not a religion. (Ironically, so did the Nazis!) I wanted to celebrate the talented, the

---

* They were on Casablanca, the same label as KISS, after Gene Simmons brought them on board.
** I should mention that while Angel got a lot of flak for their appearance, they weren't a shitty band by any stretch. They were accomplished musicians with a decent sound. But I guess they had a different set of priorities.

successful and especially the funny Jews (ah, *that's* better), gathering books by folks like Milt Gross, Groucho Marx, Lenny Bruce and, of course, Woody Allen.

In my early teens, wanting so badly to blend in and be accepted at school, I used to deny my Jewish identity. How many times would I be introduced at a gathering as "Geddy. He's a Jew but he's okay"? These small indignities ate away at my self-esteem, but I swallowed them for the longest time, grimacing inwardly, thinking that if the gang thought *I* was cool, then they'd decide that Jews in general were okay. As I grew older, I gained a more mature perspective, realizing that by not standing up to them I was helping to perpetuate a stereotype and even being complicit in fomenting hatred for my own people.

Now I was dredging up the Yiddish of my childhood, working assiduously on my lexicon and my pronunciation.* Billy Crystal is so right when he says Yiddish is "a combination of German and phlegm. This is a language of coughing and spitting; until I was eleven, I wore a raincoat." That's never more true than when Jews hurl curses at one another involving horrible imagery. I translate a couple of my favourites for you: "May your eyes crawl out of your head!" "Leeches should drink him dry!" I mean, who says stuff like that? It's one thing if you're directing it at a figure who deserves it—Hitler, for example—but most of the time this kind of invective is thrown around after some banal argument, like over an unpaid bill. These grotesqueries can get fantastically elaborate, like the ever popular "You should grow like an onion with your head in the ground and your feet in the air." Anyway, by 1974 I had become more confident and began to see with greater appreciation what my parents had endured—that thanks to their suffering, perseverance and sacrifice, I was lucky to be here at all! I silently vowed to never let myself be the token Jew again and began to wear a

---

* I still am. Right until my mom's passing, when she was almost ninety-six and struggling with her memory, I tried to *redn tsu ir* in the hope it would bring her some comfort and help her remember stuff, and I was amazed at how much came back to both of us.

mezuzah* around my neck wherever I went. But when we opened for KISS in Texas, Gene Simmons came up to me, took hold of the pendant and said, "You shouldn't wear that down here. It's dangerous to advertise you are a Jew." That kind of freaked me out, but I thought, *Well, he's an American one, he ought to know.* And, I'm not very proud to say, I took it off.

I should mention that most of the antisemitism I've experienced was in my own backyard. I did come across a lot of rednecks on tour at that time, but their scorn was mostly for the combo of long hair, rock and roll apparel *and* my prominent proboscis. This was the God-fearin' post–*Easy Rider* "Get the gun, Roy" South, where they didn't like men who wore tight pants and looked like women, and Herb "Tiny Tim" Khaury was a handy point of comparison for your average shitkicker; his success did us longhairs no favours at all. Later on that same tour I was stepping out of an elevator with Alex and Neil in Wichita, Kansas, when two dickheads in cowboy hats said to each other:

"Now there's somethin' ya don't see ever' day."

"Yeah? What?"

"Horseshit on legs."

Nice one, dudes.


WE ENDED OUR first stint with KISS in Texas and dashed across America to the suburbs of Chicago to open a show with Steppenwolf and Canned Heat, then flew to Los Angeles for *Don Kirshner's Rock Concert* and ABC's *In Concert*—our first national US television broadcast and also our first time flying first-class—*hell, yeah*. Mercury had ponied up for four seats, which meant one thing to us young sophisticates: free drinks all the way!

---

* Usually given to a Jewish boy on his bar mitzvah, a small, scroll-shaped locket. Inside is a parchment inscribed with Hebrew verses from the Torah. Jewish households will also often have a mezuzah tacked to their doorpost.

We filmed *In Concert* at the Aquarius Theatre—pretty intimidating with the likes of Donovan and Sly and the Family Stone on the bill. When we arrived the next night for *Don Kirshner's*, George Harrison was backstage, but we were way too shy to go up and say hello to *an actual Beatle*. He was there to support his friend Billy Preston (whose manners, I can tell you, had not improved one iota since we last met: once again he pretended that he didn't know us). Also there was the Dutch band Focus, all of whose albums I had at home, and their beautiful solo LPs too. "Never meet your heroes," they say, but those guys were as nice as you'd hope your influencers could be, even if the encounter wasn't much more than a handshake and a few kind words. Not wanting to be that guy who crosses the line from co-worker to fanboy, I always tried to swallow my enthusiasm and play it cool, hoping there'd be an opportunity to talk about their music but never expecting it. For years I never considered myself a peer of my heroes (in truth, I still don't). In time, of course, you realize that heroes are just people—with issues! With their issues revealed, you realize that they, too, have feet of clay.

(LEFT) *The Whisky was a party palace.* (RIGHT) *You can see how out of our "fionce" we were (to use Rush-speak of the period).*

Then it was back on the road to Texas, then the Midwest, driving to and playing Kansas City; Lincoln, Nebraska; Oklahoma City and Wichita in just six days. Headlining four of those gigs were the self-styled psychedelic kings of speed and masters of the universe, Hawk-wind. If ever there was a musical equivalent to tripping, theirs was it: dense and dreamy, hypnotic and not a little demented—in short, a sound that went down well after a joint or two. The last night with them, we had to catch the red-eye to Chicago and on to Toronto right after our set, but had to first figure out what to do with about half an ounce of leftover weed. As you might expect, Alex had an excellent idea. He'd taken lately to rolling mind-bending joints in the shape of airplanes complete with wings and engines and the logo of our own imaginary airline, Zone Airways, inked on the fuselage. To honour this occasion he rolled up one ginormous spaceship as a thank-you gift to the band we'd been supporting. We presented the reefer rocket, they lit it up, passed it aloft around the room, smoked the *entire* thing and hit the stage without missing a beat. I mean, *wow*. That thing would have knocked most bands down, but it was just another day at the office for Hawkwind.

We returned to Toronto to play our first-ever gig at the historic and venerable Massey Hall. That place was packed with memories for me, as I had seen some of my favourite bands grace its stage— Cream, the Strawbs and Genesis to name just three. Now, here we were, standing on that very stage as the opener for Nazareth. What an effin' year it had been! And the gigs kept coming until we were off to the Northwest,[*] also for the first time, then back down the coast to Los Angeles for five nights at the world-famous Whisky a Go Go, sharing the stage with the Butts Band—surely the worst name ever, but which featured two legendary musicians, former Doors members

---

[*] When you're young, you don't get jet lag because half the time you're pulling an all-nighter anyway, but these days a mere one-hour time change fucks me over. I'm gonna need a lie-down after simply typing this paragraph.

John Densmore and Robby Krieger. It was hard to reconcile the club's wild reputation with the dumpy little place we found ourselves in, but playing the career-boosting venue was one of those must-do gigs and an opportunity for us to work on some new songs that we'd soon be recording for what would be *Fly by Night*. O, Stamina of Youth! Since signing with Mercury, we had played more than a hundred gigs. Now it was time to catch our breath, enjoy the holidays and psych ourselves up to record our second album. Terry Brown would be producing, having passed his first test with flying colours, but *Fly by Night* would, of course, be the first with Neil. We approached 1975 with our spirits high, not just as newly bonded friends but a new band united by a dream of making better, more complex music together.

*September 25th, 1974:* (ABOVE) *After about six weeks as an opening act (at times playing for only 26 minutes), we headlined a show at the Agora Ballroom in Cleveland where, thanks to WMMS, we'd developed a wild, raucous, fired up fan base.* (RIGHT) *Pooped and sweaty, but gearing up for a rare event... an actual encore. An encore, really? Hell, yeah!*

# CHAPTER 10

**J**UST ABOUT THE FIRST THING ALEX AND I
noticed about Neil was "Hey, this guy *reads* a lot!" He always
had a stack of books with him on the road, and it made quite
the impression on me to be in the company of someone who,
wherever we were, in the middle of whatever maelstrom, could just disappear into the pages.* Al and I were far more restless. We'd be goofing off half the time, but once Neil opened that book he was *gone*. He
was this fascinating creature we'd found in our midst, and we were two
dogs circling him, sniffing him out, observing his habits.

---

* I was always amazed by Neil's single-minded ability to read, regardless of what was going
on around him or which drug he had just ingested. One night in St. Louis, he got stupid with
the rest of us, then went for a walk in the woods. When he returned, Alex and I were still very
high, but he lay on his bed and opened a book. After half an hour he went to the bathroom,
threw up, then went right back to the page where he'd left off.

---

He was the one who really got us into sci-fi. The fount of all the fantasy we read back then was *The Lord of the Rings*, which the three of us devoured simultaneously, and after which I became a huge John Wyndham fan. I'd never dug *The Chrysalids* when forced to read it in school but taking in *The Midwich Cuckoos* and *The Day of the Triffids* for pleasure was a whole nother world. Among my favourites were Robert A. Heinlein's *Stranger in a Strange Land*, a benchmark book in the realm of sci-fi and fantasy; Mervyn Peake's deliciously dark epic, the *Gormenghast* trilogy; the work of Lord Dunsany, aka Edward John Moreton Drax Plunkett, the 18th Baron of Dunsany, one of the founders of the high fantasy genre (who wrote more than *ninety* books) and Ursula K. Le Guin's *Earthsea* novels. I never quite got into his most esteemed author, Samuel Delany, but thanks to Neil there was suddenly a library full of escapes from the rigors and drudgery of the road. Then, fatefully as it would turn out for Rush, he introduced us to Ayn Rand's *Anthem*, which made sense for us to read since we already happened to be writing a song called "Anthem," though I cannot say I ever grokked its fullness. But I'll save the whole Ayn Rand debacle for later . . .

Neil's verbal aptitude was such that Alex and I suggested he try his hand at writing lyrics. Somewhat noncommittally he said he'd give it a go, and would soon come up with his first, "Beneath, Between and Behind," a modest little epic about the birth, history and present circumstance, no less, of the great country we'd been travelling around—about the decaying American dream and the façade of what it meant to be an American. Its breakneck speed actually makes the song, but when I first tried to sing it, I was like, "Holy fuck, this is impossible. How am I going to sing all these words this fast?" but when I hear it now, it sounds like the crowds of history. It's *supposed* to be busy. Neil aimed high—and never let a multisyllabic word stand in his way—so I had to learn a whole lot about de-emphasizing certain syllables and emphasizing others to wring more emotion out of a lyric and to get its essential, often complex and even profound meaning across.

Back then, we had to write and record songs quickly without the benefit of demos or the time to live with them and consider what was good or bad. It was write it, get it on tape, get it out and then we'd be back on the road. By *Roll the Bones*, when we had more time to digest and be more critical, Neil would have become an even more mature writing partner—without ego or possessiveness about his work, and always open to my needs. Every album there'd be a song or two that I couldn't get behind, but he came to trust me as a sounding board— literally a flesh-and-blood one. For example, "Sir Gawain and the Green Knight," a song for *Permanent Waves* that was replaced by "Natural Science," started out as a very Genesis-style, proggy, fantasy-lit lyric, and Al and I were not feeling it, so Neil let it go. He understood that since I was the person who had to sing the words and emote the feelings behind them, he had to be flexible, even if it meant dropping something he'd written. He'd just say, "I'm just happy to have written it." He was a better man than me.

Typical of young bands, our earliest method of communicating musical ideas was sharing examples of other bands' work, or using abstract terms like "kerrang" or "rizzy"; made-up, onomatopoeic words. As we embarked on the *Fly by Night* album with Terry at the helm, we started to appreciate how *visual* an art form music can be. I know that sounds odd, but since we lacked the benefit of formal musical training, conceiving music as cinema allowed us to express more articulately the size, colour, texture and balance of the sounds we heard in our heads. Terry taught us how to create a soundscape, which was a huge leap forward for us and one that went hand in hand with the lyric stories Neil was beginning to write.

*Fly by Night* is a record of extremes that foretold how we would approach the dynamic flow of all our albums to come, with its hard rockers, gentler moments and, er . . . this event called "By-Tor and the Snow Dog," a song that sort of began as a joke based on the names Howard had given Ray Danniels's dogs—one a German shepherd, the other a much smaller pooch—after watching them scrap. Neil turned

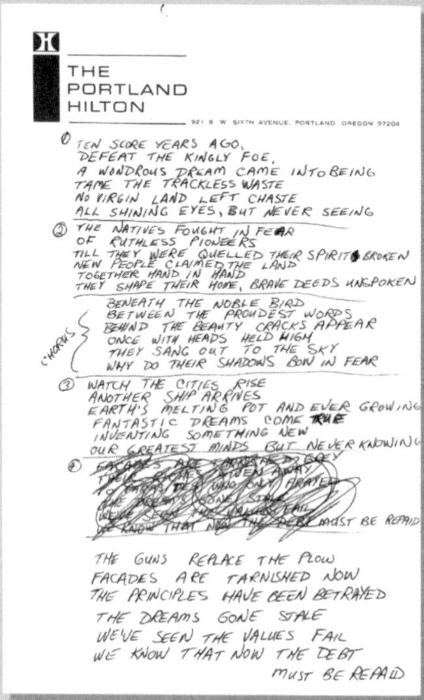
THE PORTLAND HILTON

921 S. W. SIXTH AVENUE, PORTLAND, OREGON 97204

① TEN SCORE YEARS AGO,
DEFEAT THE KINGLY FOE,
A WONDROUS DREAM CAME INTO BEING
TAME THE TRACKLESS WASTE
NO VIRGIN LAND LEFT CHASTE
ALL SHINING EYES, BUT NEVER SEEING

② THE NATIVES FOUGHT IN FEAR
OF RUTHLESS PIONEERS
TILL THEY WERE QUELLED THEIR SPIRIT BROKEN
NEW PEOPLE CLAIMED THE LAND
TOGETHER HAND IN HAND
THEY SHAPE THEIR HOME, BRAVE DEEDS UNSPOKEN

CHORUS
BENEATH THE NOBLE BIRD
BETWEEN THE PROUDEST WORDS
BEHIND THE BEAUTY CRACKS APPEAR
ONCE WITH HEADS HELD HIGH
THEY SANG OUT TO THE SKY
WHY DO THEIR SHADOWS BOW IN FEAR

③ WATCH THE CITIES RISE
ANOTHER SHIP ARRIVES
EARTH'S MELTING POT AND EVER GROWING
FANTASTIC DREAMS COME TRUE
INVENTING SOMETHING NEW
OUR GREATEST MINDS BUT NEVER KNOWING

④ ... MUST BE REPAID

THE GUNS REPLACE THE PLOW
FACADES ARE TARNISHED NOW
THE PRINCIPLES HAVE BEEN BETRAYED
THE DREAMS GONE STALE
WE'VE SEEN THE VALUES FAIL
WE KNOW THAT NOW THE DEBT
MUST BE REPAID

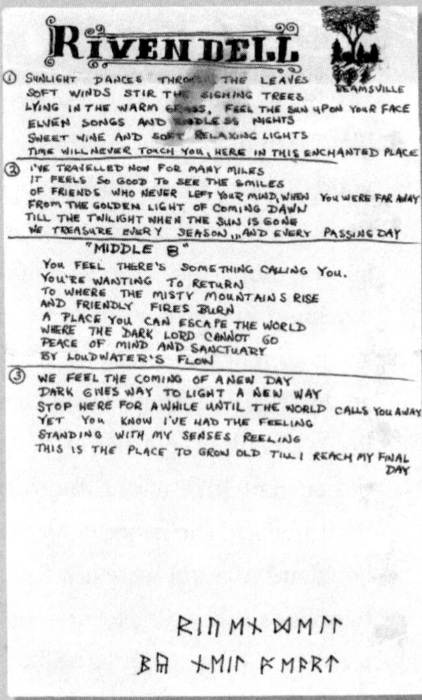
RIVENDELL

BEAMSVILLE

① SUNLIGHT DANCES THROUGH THE LEAVES
SOFT WINDS STIR THE SIGHING TREES
LYING IN THE WARM GRASS, FEEL THE SUN UPON YOUR FACE
ELVEN SONGS AND ENDLESS NIGHTS
SWEET WINE AND SOFT RELAXING LIGHTS
TIME WILL NEVER TOUCH YOU, HERE IN THIS ENCHANTED PLACE

② I'VE TRAVELLED NOW FOR MANY MILES
IT FEELS SO GOOD TO SEE THE SMILES
OF FRIENDS WHO NEVER LEFT YOUR MIND, WHEN YOU WERE FAR AWAY
FROM THE GOLDEN LIGHT OF COMING DAWN
TILL THE TWILIGHT WHEN THE SUN IS GONE
WE TREASURE EVERY SEASON,,, AND EVERY PASSING DAY

"MIDDLE 8"
YOU FEEL THERE'S SOMETHING CALLING YOU.
YOU'RE WANTING TO RETURN
TO WHERE THE MISTY MOUNTAINS RISE
AND FRIENDLY FIRES BURN
A PLACE YOU CAN ESCAPE THE WORLD
WHERE THE DARK LORD CANNOT GO
PEACE OF MIND AND SANCTUARY
BY LOUDWATER'S FLOW

③ WE FEEL THE COMING OF A NEW DAY
DARK GIVES WAY TO LIGHT A NEW WAY
STOP HERE FOR A WHILE UNTIL THE WORLD CALLS YOU AWAY
YET YOU KNOW I'VE HAD THE FEELING
STANDING WITH MY SENSES REELING
THIS IS THE PLACE TO GROW OLD TILL I REACH MY FINAL DAY

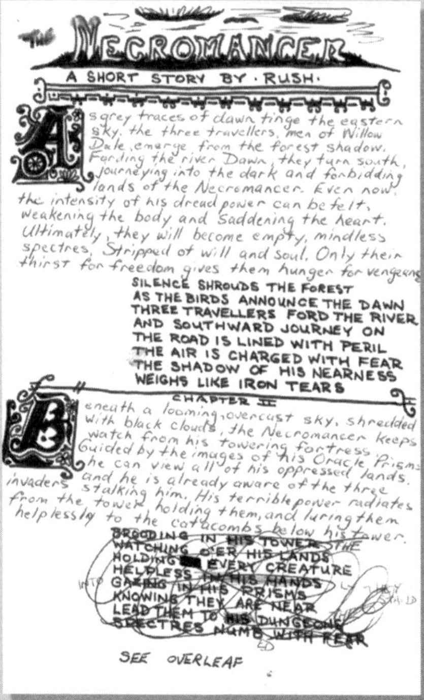
THE NECROMANCER
A SHORT STORY BY · RUSH ·

As grey traces of dawn tinge the eastern sky, the three travellers, men of Willow Dale, emerge from the forest shadow. Fording the river Dawn, they turn south, journeying into the dark and forbidding lands of the Necromancer. Even now, the intensity of his dread power can be felt, weakening the body and saddening the heart. Ultimately, they will become empty, mindless spectres, stripped of will and soul. Only their thirst for freedom gives them hunger for vengeance.

SILENCE SHROUDS THE FOREST
AS THE BIRDS ANNOUNCE THE DAWN
THREE TRAVELLERS FORD THE RIVER
AND SOUTHWARD JOURNEY ON
THE ROAD IS LINED WITH PERIL
THE AIR IS CHARGED WITH FEAR
THE SHADOW OF HIS NEARNESS
WEIGHS LIKE IRON TEARS

CHAPTER II

Beneath a looming, overcast sky, shredded with black clouds, the Necromancer keeps watch from his towering fortress. Guided by the images of his Oracle Prisms he can view all of his oppressed lands, and he is already aware of the three invaders stalking him. His terrible power radiates from the tower holding them, and luring them helplessly to the catacombs below his tower.

BROODING IN HIS TOWER
WATCHING O'ER HIS LANDS
HOLDING EVERY CREATURE
HELPLESS IN HIS HANDS
GAZING IN HIS PRISMS
KNOWING THEY ARE NEAR
LEAD THEM TO HIS DUNGEONS
SPECTRES NUMB WITH FEAR

SEE OVERLEAF

SIR DUHWAIN + THE STUPID KNIGHT

I THE CHALLENGE

AT CHRISTMAS-TIDE
KING ARTHUR'S COURT IN CAMELOT
GATHERED THERE TO SHARE
THE FEAST OF YULE
LIEGES, LORDS, THE LADIES
AND THE GALLANT KNIGHTS
SHINING UNDER ARTHUR'S KINDLY RULE
A PERILOUS HORSEMAN PASSED THE PORTALS
GLOWING ALL IN GREEN
HIS GARMENTS AND HIS HUE OF SKIN
A GHOSTLY VERDANT SHEEN

A BATTLE-AXE
THE GREEN KNIGHT HELD IN GIANT HANDS
CHALLENGING THE KING AND TABLE ROUND
"I OFFER YOU ONE STROKE UPON MY NAKED NECK
BUT SHOULD YOU FAIL-
UPON YOUR HONOUR BOUND"
"ONE TWELVEMONTH HENCE TO SEEK MY HOME
AND SATISFY THY OATH
THY HEAD SHALL THEN BE MINE, BY RIGHT
ONE STRIKE,
ALIKE, FOR BOTH"

A SILENCE FELL
AND THE COURTIERS STIRRED UNEASILY
HERE WAS MIGHTY MAGIC!
TO MAKE SO BOLD
ARTHUR ROSE, EVER FEARLESS
TO GREET THE CHALLENGE
"I WILL TEST THINE AXE OF GREEN AND GOLD"
THEN STOOD YOUNG SIR GAWAIN
WHO WAS NEPHEW TO THE KING
"MY LORD I BEG YOUR LEAVE
THAT I MIGHT DO FOR THEE THIS THING"
AND THE GREEN KNIGHT KNELT BEFORE HIM
DRAWING BACK HIS HAIR AND CLOAK
HIS GREEN NECK WAS SEVERED CLEANLY
BY SIR GAWAIN'S SINGLE STROKE

ALIVE, IT STOOD!
AND HELD IT'S HIDEOUS HEAD ON HIGH
IN STUNNED SURPRISE
THEY SAW THE SPECTRE SPEAK
"ONE YEAR HENCE
I CLAIM THE HEAD OF SIR GAWAIN
THE KNIGHT OF THE GREEN CHAPEL
MUST YE SEEK"...

*Neil's lyric sheets for "Beneath, Between and Behind," "Rivendell" and "The Necromancer," plus an early, spoofily titled version of the ill-fated "Sir Gawain and the Green Knight."*

them into characters in an underworld battle between good and evil, and Terry encouraged Alex and me to experiment with our instruments to create the personalities of the two beasts. It may sound silly, but when we weren't chuckling at what was the first of many inside jokes in our music, we were serious about our first prog rock effort.

Listen to what the rhythm section is doing, especially in the middle section, and consider that Neil had been in the band for only six months, and you will hear what a dramatically different band we'd become. Neil had a catalytic effect on Alex and me, confirming and unleashing all the notions swirling around our heads. Unlike "Working Man," where the meat in the sandwich was in essence a bluesy jam, "By-Tor" was our first song with a *structured* instrumental section. Lyrically speaking, we were figuring out that science fiction could be a very useful literary device for us, one where we could bend or break the rules any way we chose, and with Terry encouraging us to imagine the stereo spectrum as a blank canvas on which we could project a story, "By-Tor" became a prototype for all our future epics.

For By-Tor's growling in the middle-section battle scene, I detuned my E string right down to a loose, flapping string and played it over the rhythm track through a Fuzz-Tone, then gave it repeats with an Echoplex for the *bwow-wow-wow* thing. Then Alex recorded a screaming guitar to represent the Snow Dog's attack. It was like a video game! We didn't consciously think of this at the time, but I realize now that the song is part of a grand tradition of rock and roll battle songs. From that era, ELP's "Tarkus," King Crimson's "Lizard," and "Achilles Last Stand" on Zeppelin's *Presence* are just three that spring to mind. Finally, on the vinyl record there's the run-off groove with snow crystals chiming on forever. Not sure who came up with that idea, but we all agreed it should sound like the story wasn't over—is By-Tor vanquished or just returned to the underworld to regain his strength, like Voldemort?

Most of the songs we've ever written have lasted longer than five minutes, so any vaguely catchy shorter tune has invariably been chosen as the single. "Best I Can" was one of a number seized on for radio play from our first LP "In the Mood" another, but none of them had all the right ingredients for a hit, whatever *those* might be. Sometimes people would suggest to us that if we released such-and-such a song it could be a hit, and we'd respond, "Hah, yes, well. Maybe if someone else covered it." Alex and I enjoyed *trying* to write the occasional short and catchy ditty, but we never really worked out how to pull off such a trick. What we did best was write riffs that were fun and hard to play, not breezy hooks or earworms. We'd always ruin it by thinking up some other part we thought would make the song more "interesting," which coming from us was the opposite of a short and catchy number.

From our second album Mercury chose "Fly by Night," though we never composed it with that in mind. Indeed, just because a song is released as a single doesn't mean it's going be a hit, or even get played— and Top 40 radio has always had a strong aversion to playing Rush. Even without its help, our album would eventually make platinum, but the best the single did on release in America was number 186. I know it's well-loved now, but it's always been one of my least favourite Rush songs. It sounds kinda dinky to me! The first time I heard it on the radio I went, "Ugh." To my taste there was something too sugary, too corny about the chorus. I must have liked it somewhat when we finished it, or it wouldn't have made the record, but it's never wrapped its arms around me.

Recently, Alex and I were talking about the pressure put on us to commercialize our music in the days following the release of *Fly by Night*. Sometime in 1975 we attended a party, and in the middle of the niceties and schmoozing, Neil had a terrible argument with SRO's lawyer. It started out civilly enough but became a heated, abstract discussion about the value of compromise, which as I eavesdropped struck me as thinly veiled disapproval of what he assumed to be Neil's influence on the direction of our music, particularly on songs like "By-Tor and the Snow Dog"—away from the straight-ahead rock of our first record, that is, and deeper into Prog Land. He said something close to,

"Compromise is what the world functions on. *Compromise.* How dare you hurt your partners' promising careers by refusing to compromise?" Nasty shit! Neil retorted simply but firmly that in art or music there can be no room for compromise; it was not a word in his vocabulary. Soon after, the three of us left in disgust.

Neil didn't even know the man, so where did this all come from? Were these the lawyer's own thoughts or was he parroting concerns he'd heard from our management? Were they *all* freaking out because they'd thought Rush was going to be the next Zeppelin or Bad Company? True, singing about dogs in space (Dogs in Space: good name for a prog band, eh?) was a far cry from "Need Some Love," but what they didn't get was that Alex and I had already been going down that road when Rutsey was in the band. In any event, our second album was a reasonably successful follow-up to the first, and we were like, "Better get used to it, fellas, cos that proggie train has left the effin' station."

NOW, YOU MAY be asking why they were so surprised; hadn't they heard it in the studio while recording was in progress? Well, even back then we never wanted management personnel or any other species of business folk anywhere near the studio. We saw recording as a creative process that should never be interfered with—*sullied*—by some boge's "practical considerations," and we stuck to the rule for life. In the long run, our refusal to compromise made them a fair bit of money, wouldn't you say? Even the jam we'd enjoyed during Neil's audition—the one that turned into "Anthem"—was the very song that Ray and Vic named their record company after!

SOME OF OUR early fans were also confused by our new direction, as this next episode illustrates: our career, it seemed, was on the up and up, but we were still mostly opening for other bands, so whenever an opportunity to do a headline gig presented itself, Ray would seize it, and in February 1975 he booked us a week of dates beginning some 800 klicks north of Toronto. When my fellow countryman Neil Young sang, "There is a town in north Ontario," he was singing about Thunder Bay, but I'm referring to an even smaller, more obscure one called Cochrane, where you can still catch the Polar Bear Express,* and where it was cold—like, well-below-zero cold. I mean, like, *thirty-eight-degrees-below-zero* cold. Still, because it was Canada, we were expecting a warmer reception than the one we got.

The local secondary school auditorium wasn't exactly Madison Square Garden, but at least we were top of the bill, playing to a full house seated cross-legged on the floor. Then after the first song . . . silence. Subsequent songs were also met with a disturbing quiet. So we finished our set and said good night—again, to silence and zero applause.

We went back to the classroom repurposed as our changing room, and were halfway into our street clothes when the promoter, a nice-enough fellow, entered the room and said, "You guys are doing an encore, right?"

"Are you kidding?" we said. "Did you see what just happened? They hated us, man. We *bombed*."

"No, no, they loved you!" he insisted.

"*Loved* us? But nobody applauded! You can't do an encore when no one asks for one!"

He was getting upset. "Your agent said you'd play an encore!" he said, clearly not grasping how encores actually work. "Oh, wait. I get it. You guys from the big city need fans to tell you they *love* you before you'll play, right?"

Interesting point, but no, this was getting too weird. We stuck to our guns and refused to go back out.

Meanwhile, out in the venue nobody had left, even though the crew was tearing down the gear and Ian was saying, "It's over, folks, you can go

---

* A 186-mile train ride to Moosonee with special train cars made to carry canoes, snowmobiles and all-terrain vehicles. Canadian enough for ya?

home now." It was like everyone in town had been on that call with our agent and thought we were ripping them off. Now it was getting nasty.

Then Howard informed us that he hadn't booked us rooms ahead of time, having figured there would be plenty available in a local motel up there in the middle of February. In actual fact, the only accommodation he could find was at the lone downtown so-called hotel, which in such a place meant the local bar or beer hall with rooms upstairs — you know, like the saloon in *The Good, the Bad and the Ugly*. Leaving the crew to pack up, we ran a gauntlet through murmuring, disgruntled townsfolk, and another through an exceedingly drunk crowd in the lobby of the dingy hotel where it felt like fisticuffs might break out any second. We took the stairs to our rooms, with one small bathroom for the entire floor. In my barely heated room were what looked like the first lightbulbs ever manufactured, and ropes by the window in case of fire. It's not like we were at the stage where we expected or demanded fancy hotels, but oy vey.

The road crew was worryingly late. When they finally arrived (and, indeed, after a fight *had* broken out in the lobby) they were frozen to the bone, telling us that someone had drained the truck of gas. They'd had to leave it at the gig and run all the way in their flimsy jean jackets (roadies usually wear shorts or light clothing because they work up such a sweat loading gear) and hadn't been prepared for a two-mile jog in sub-zero weather. Ya gotta laugh. I mean, was this the Karmic Wheel fucking with us? We all slept fully clothed, got through the night somehow, gassed up in the morning and bade farewell—or should I say *fled*—that town in north Ontario, with (as the song continues) memories to spare.

BACK IN THE States in 1975, we'd moved up a notch from opener to special guest status (with a slightly longer set), supporting ZZ Top, Blue Öyster Cult, Styx, the Faces, Status Quo, Aerosmith and various others. Working with certain of those bands, we realized we'd probably been spoiled by KISS, and now found ourselves having to bite on the proverbial reality sandwich. At the Winterland Ballroom in San Francisco we were opening for them again, with the Tubes as "special guest," though by the way both we and KISS were treated, you'd think it was a Tubes show with a couple of other bands thrown in for good measure. Things hadn't boded well for us from the start, when on our first night in town our vehicle was broken into and my acoustic guitar and other things were stolen. That was one thing, grumble grumble, but when we got to the gig we found the tension backstage palpable. The infamous concert promoter Bill Graham—who also happened to *manage* the Tubes—had given his band first priority on everything: stage space, soundcheck, the lot. It was a big fuck-you to the KISS crew, and they were not happy. After our set, one of the in-house stagehands ineptly dropped one of Alex's amps off the side of the stage, damaging a speaker. No one appeared interested in taking responsibility for it, the stage crew just sluffed it off, and after Herns failed to get any joy from Graham himself, Alex's Serbian blood began to boil. He proceeded to follow the man around the venue, yelling at him to man up and pay for the fucking damage. Eventually, Graham turned around and, just to get Alex off his back, said, "Okay, okay, I'll pay for it!" but of course he never did. What would have cost him a hundred dollars that day set the tone for our relationship forevermore.

Next time we'd be at the same venue was November '76, for two shows with Ted Nugent and Be-Bop Deluxe. On the first night, just as our intro tape got under way, Ian got a call on the headset to stop the tape for an emergency announcement. Then someone grabbed the mic and said, "Please welcome our good friends . . . Mahogany Rush!" WTF? Ted's stage manager grabbed the mic back from him and did a proper introduction, but the message had already been delivered. As they say, "a fish stinks from the head"; Graham's disdain for us had evidently trickled down to his crew.

The next insult was in 1977. We were now headliners, with UFO and Max Webster supporting, but Graham insisted on adding a last-minute *fourth* band to the lineup. It wasn't until we arrived at the Winterland that we learned he'd dug up some local act called, I kid you not, Hush.* Seriously? Seriously! Yet another fuck-you, and we were not in a position to do much about it. Soon enough, however, we would get a measure of revenge . . .

Bill Graham Productions was by then a national concert promotion company. Some bands, the Grateful Dead, for example, used it for their entire cross-country tours, but we vowed to never do so again in any jurisdiction where there was an option. He had San Francisco locked up, but for some of the state's smaller cities like Fresno or Sacramento, Ray liaised with promoters from the northwest instead. That threatened Graham's sovereignty, his income and his belligerent ego, and suddenly the attitude changed. When we came to San Francisco on the *Moving Pictures* tour in 1980 for a couple of sold-out shows at the acoustically challenged Cow Palace, Bill came backstage to make amends, acting like we were all pals now. We smiled through gritted

---

\* Checking them out online, I note that they had the distinction of being "Northern California's best unsigned band."

teeth as he presented us with a gift of cases of Napa Valley wine with a label that read 30,000 BAY AREA FANS CAN'T BE WRONG. Cheers, Bill. Even his apology was a backhanded compliment. What an effin' vindictive, mealymouthed hypocrite.

I was raised never to speak ill of the dead. So: Cheers, Bill. And fuck you very much.

IN THOSE DAYS a number of headliners, we felt, either gave us a whiff of indifference or a definite insecurity vibe; whether or not that was a mindset encouraged by paranoid management peeps, I cannot say, but it was an attitude that infected everyone on tour. Here is another illustration of the way such backstage politics sometimes played out.

I've told you how important I insist soundchecks are, but I also understand that there can be extenuating circumstances under which a support band cannot expect to be given one: if the headliner is having equipment issues or filming their show, say, they have every right to sort their problems out at the expense of the other bands on the bill. It's their show, after all, and one involving serious logistics. It doesn't matter if the show's at Madison Square Garden or in Medicine Hat; there is always some "assembly required" involving dozens of roadies lugging megatons of amplification, riggers climbing the rafters and hanging the points for heavy and complex lighting rigs, audio technicians tuning the sound system to the acoustics of the room, stage managers dealing with local union or non-union crews and on and on—and all this begins (barring breakdowns en route) around five in the morning. Long before a single note can be played, myriad things can go wrong, which squeezes those precious few minutes you want for a soundcheck. Frankly, every show is an effin' miracle courtesy of that army of people wrestling technology so you can sit in Row 15, smoke your joint and air drum to "In the Air Tonight" (or better still, "Tom Sawyer"). I can also understand why a headliner might be a little stingy as far as the use of lights goes. If they've brought along a complex rig at their own expense, the opening act must reasonably expect an inferior array.

*Nonetheless*, the opener has the right to be seen and given a sound-check if at all feasible; even if support bands are dicks or you just don't dig their music, it's the professional thing to do. But Herns used to speculate that to him it seemed like Aerosmith's system was heavily loaded on over-head trusses to purposely put any opener at a disadvantage, leaving us a minimal selection of side lights and a couple of spots, and the dozen or so times we supported them we weren't once given a soundcheck either. Every day we waited patiently in the stands, but it never happened. Some days we were told we'd *definitely* be getting one, only to watch our allotted time tick away and hear the announcement "DOORS ARE OPENING IN FIVE MINUTES." Was it an intentional snubbing? I prefer to think it was simply that they didn't have their shit together.

Of course it's all water under a very old bridge now, but back then it was frustrating and dispiriting. We were young musicians trying to build a reputation in a strange new world, in debt to our eyeballs, liter-ally fighting for our time, struggling to keep our sanity and egos in check—and most important, trying to keep our dreams intact. No pressure, man! But we knew our job was to get out there every night and, as we say in Canada, just "give 'er." And we did just that. (We also vowed that if ever we became serious and proper headliners, we and our crew would treat our openers generously. I hope we followed through on that promise.)

**TRAVERSING THE MIDWEST** and moving down the west coast, we played some forty shows, twenty-eight of them with KISS, with whom we'd established a terrific rapport. Ace had an outrageous, maniacal laugh like one of those scary clowns in amusement parks that he loved to use and we loved to trigger, so we'd gather in his room, where Herns would regale him with his own road stories while Alex and I smoked joints and listened in like a radio audience. Alex invented a character called the Bag: he'd draw a mad face on a laundry bag with holes cut out for eyes and put it over his head, then push his arms into his sweatpants along with his legs to create a stubby living cartoon with a goofy voice to match.

Gene usually stayed out of it, except one time—right after a couple of girls had tumbled drunkenly into the room (coincidence? I think not)—which is when I first saw a different side of him. One of the girls had grabbed the bag off Alex's head, totally crushing our vibe. Ace and the rest of us were well pissed off, and I asked them to leave. After

*Cream pies and sundry shenanigans onstage in San Diego, the last gig on our tour with KISS.* (LEFT) *The Bag makes a cameo appearance.*

escorting them out into the hallway, Gene followed, grabbed me and pushed me against the wall, demanding to know why I'd given them the boot. "Hey, man," I said, "they were bumming everyone out!" He said, "Yeah, *but* . . ." and he angrily shared with me a few words that could only be described as a lesson in female anatomy. I'll leave it at that. So effin' uncool.

**DURING THAT RUN** in 1975, Rush hit a major milestone: a return to Massey Hall, but this time as proper headliners. Standing on the stage as *our* gear was being set up gave me pause—if I'm honest, a moment of existential angst—to think that for one night the stage would be ours. Was this *really happening?* I looked out at the empty hall, which suddenly seemed so much smaller than all the times I'd seen it the other way around as a concertgoer. I peered up at the second level, where once I had sat alone watching my hero Jack Bruce play the hell out of his Gibson EB-3, and now here I was, about to have my own moment in the spotlight. I know it sounds corny, but I truly got chills and was jangled with nerves right until we hit the stage, when Alex *kerranged* those first notes of "Finding My Way" and I sang, "Yeah! *Ooh* yeah!" to the sold-out house.

I still remember that as the highlight of my life up until then, but I'd be remiss if I didn't mention the *critical* response. The show was mainly reported as a "triumphant return of our local boys," but one pundit described my voice in terms that would follow me around for most of my career—and one, admittedly, that even I use from time to time.

"Lee sounds like the damned howling in Hades," wrote Robert Martin in the *Globe & Mail*. "The music is pretty standard heavy metal stuff, guaranteed to rattle the loose change in your pocket. Still, they must be doing something right, judging by the number of young women who leapt onto the stage to give Lee roses and plant wet ones on his cheek."

# CHAPTER 11

TWO NIGHTS AFTER THE MASSEY HALL show, we moved our gear into Toronto Sound to record our third album, *Caress of Steel*. We would have three whole luxurious weeks to do so, it was summer and we were feeling pretty upbeat despite the ambitious task we'd set for ourselves: our first concept album. (Well, half of one, anyway.)

The prospect of all that studio time was intoxicating, and quite literally went to our heads. We were in possession of a goodly supply of hash and hash oil to spur on our creative juices, but as the author and radio personality Earl Nightingale once said, "Wherever there is danger, there lurks opportunity; wherever there is opportunity, there lurks danger . . ." For us, the second half of that *bon mot* was the most apt.

ONE AFTERNOON AS we sat on the long couch at the back of the control room, the heavy scent of hemp wafting about, one of the most eccentric people I've ever known, the late Canadian musician/painter/writer Mendelson Joe, dropped in. He watched Lerxst, Pratt and me* discussing ideas while mic setups were changed, discussing some more song ideas while amps were EQ'd, discussing yet *more* ideas in readiness for the next overdub . . . What he saw was next to *nothing* going down on tape, and as he left he turned to me and said with his inimitable, only half-joking bluntness, "Well. You guys really know how to waste time." I remember thinking what a funny guy he was, but in retrospect I got that wrong. He wasn't kidding at all. With three weeks of paid studio time and a guaranteed record release, we were squandering an opportunity that he and so many of our musician pals would have killed for. This is why that "spur" to our creative juices came to be known amongst us as our *impedimenta*. Some music critics have noted that consecutive decades of rock music might be characterized to some extent by the most popular drugs du jour—LSD in the sixties, heroin in the seventies, cocaine in the eighties, ecstasy in the nineties . . . In our case, it was an inordinate amount of hash oil. *Caress of Steel* is a really *dry* record; when I listen back to it, there's a lot less echo on it than we thought there was when we were listening back in the studio. The fact is, we were so high that it sounded more reverberant than it actually was.

As the years progressed, we would become so integrally involved in our studio albums' recording process, no matter who was at the helm, that they'd all be credited as co-productions, but more than anyone during the *Caress of Steel* sessions I was the *nudnik*, sitting at the console beside Terry and constantly piping up with ideas. My new favourite question was "Terry? What if we tried . . ." as well as "Terry?

---

* Amongst ourselves, silly banter being the order of the day, our given names quickly became things of the past. Alex was now Lerxst, short for Lerxstpspspsts; Neil was either Pratt, Nels or (as we'd introduce him onstage) the Professor; Terry Brown was Broon and I was simply Dirk or Dirkie Lee, for my pointed, sarcastic, f-bomb-riddled tongue, i.e., "sharp as a dirk."

Shouldn't there be more repeats on Alex's guitar? Terry? What if . . ." I *know* I was annoying, but hey, I was feeling my oats and wanted to try out all the ideas that were popping into my head. I wouldn't go so far as to say that over the years I drove producers and engineers a little crazy, but . . . well . . . Yeah, let's say I did.* I'd watch every little thing with an eagle eye, trying to understand and remember every flick of a switch, leaping on people if they forgot to do the smallest thing, demanding explanations for everything. I couldn't help myself, and I've always been the same. It's partly a matter of control, partly (depending on who we'd be working with) a lack of trust, but most important, it's a compulsion to exhaust every possibility to make the perfect record. I don't want to have to live with errors. Impossible, I know, but what's the effin' point of not shooting for the moon?

*Caress of Steel* was conceived as two distinct sides: one a collection of disconnected songs to rock out and satisfy our need for diversity, the other . . . well, we had some lofty ideas. Before I get to those, I'll deliver on my promise of explaining "I Think I'm Going Bald": another song born of a joke, it was partly a piss take on the title of a KISS song we liked, "Goin' Blind," and partly about the fear of ageing, but mainly about *Alex*.

On tour at the time he was skinny as a rail with long, luscious hair, but was deathly afraid of going bald (the root, so to speak, of his anxiety was that his dad had lost most of his hair at a fairly young age) and for some reason hung up on getting fat. He was always on some fad diet. Neil and I once tasted the Diet Fresca he obsessively drank and went, "*Hool!*"—you know, making a hurling sound—and from then on Howard made sure Lerxst always had "*Diet Hool*" in the dressing room. This led to a tongue-in-cheek lyric about youthful vanity but also how to our generation long hair was a symbol of defiance. In the last couplet, "Even when I'm grey / I'll be grey my way," we were having fun but also referring to how we'd had to push back against criticism of our

---

* After the final playback of *Signals* Terry came up to me, hugged me and said, "Ged, I hate you. And I love you." Uh . . . thanks, Broon, I guess.

evolving style on *Fly by Night*. Little did we know that after the release of *Caress*, that pressure would only get more intense . . .

We'd also been working on a lengthy song of Neil's called "The Fountain of Lamneth," an unabashed deep dive into the world of concept albums such as *Foxtrot* and *Nursery Cryme* by Genesis and Rick Wakeman's *Journey to the Centre of the Earth*, with aspirations to the intricacy of such pieces as Jethro Tull's *Thick as a Brick* and *Close to the Edge* by Yes. Of course, we were nowhere near as accomplished as any of those epic bands, but we desperately wanted to be.

Some critics called *Caress of Steel* derivative. Fair enough. Our influences were nakedly obvious. Like most aspiring musicians we were impressionable and desperate to emulate the players we admired, many of whom were still recording and performing live, and inevitably there were times when we paled in comparison with the real thing. We're all subconsciously influenced by our heroes, but sometimes you don't realize quite how blatant your mimicry is until your music is out there for the world to hear and review—like the time Alex started playing us a new riff he was clearly proud of but stopped when he saw Pratt and me grinning at each other.

He went, "*What?*"

"Dude. You just wrote 'Little Wing.'"*

No one likes being compared with other bands (and comparison is definitely the lazy critic's tool), but we are all inescapably a product of what we ingest. I think of it as going through periods of input, then output: I'll be listening to all kinds of stuff for a while, but when I start to write I have to put it away. When I'm writing or recording, other people's music—even in a restaurant or an elevator—feels like an

---

* I've heard songs by certain artists that sound a tad suspicious, but mostly I defer to a presumption of innocence. Remember George Harrison and "She's So Fine"? Well, the list goes on. There are only five basic guitar chords, you know? Similar combinations are bound to show up. Almost everyone does it sometime or other. Ben Mink told me about a song the Rolling Stones wrote that was identical to "Constant Craving." Their new album was ready for release, and Keith was playing it around his house when one of his daughters said, "Hey, Dad. That's a k.d. lang song!" The Stones gave Ben and k.d. the credit.

intrusion, and presents a danger too. In my desire to create work that's as pure as possible, I get so single-minded that I can't even focus on reading novels; fact-based stuff is fine, but I don't have the patience for anything that demands imagination. I remember times during a playback when I'd hear a word I'd just sung or pronounced a certain way, and realize it sounded way too much like some singer I admired—it could have been anyone from Steve Marriott to Joni Mitchell to Björk whom I'd subconsciously channelled, perhaps just in that one word, but in the end I'd leave it as is, as a nod to my heroes and a kind of Easter egg that only I knew was there.

But it begs the question, doesn't it: When can you say you've achieved a sound or a style all your own? It's basically when your influences have become so diverse that they're no longer easy to trace; they've blended together so thoroughly as to create a stew of your own making. But that's not enough. In my view, it requires a diversity of influences *and* the strength of your individual character. I was a big fan of Amazing Blondel, the Strawbs and other bands in the English folk rock tradition. My pal Oscar and I both loved that Baroque approach to acoustic guitar, and the first great acoustic I bought was a nylon-string Martin because I was trying to emulate that plucking style. Elizabethan tones and melodies had a romantic allure for me too, so it was natural for me to slip that into the stuff we wrote, plus I dug the way Jethro Tull took a variety of classical influences and rocked them up. Complementing all that was the Tolkien and fantasy literature we were reading at the time: we folded it into our music to take it beyond your standard blues-rock. We were like sponges; anything we could soak up from another band had a place in Rush. If it knocked us out, it had a place in our music. I really believe this is what happens with every artist. The more influences one has that are then filtered through one's own personality, the more one ends up with a style and a sound that one can legitimately call one's own. If you have three bands influencing you, you're derivative; if you have a *hundred*, you're original!

It does take time, though. To be honest, we didn't really consider ourselves to have a sound of our own until *2112*, though there were moments like with "By-Tor" when we said to one another, "Ooh, nobody's stupid enough to have done *this* before." We were tasting the stew and spicing it up bit by bit. We were our own target audience, writing music for ourselves on the assumption that there were enough people out there with the same sensibility as us who would dig it too.

Our chops were getting better, that was clear, but of course I wasn't entirely happy—and never would be with any record we'd make. I'd always, always be thinking, *Okay, it sounds good, but god, why didn't I do* this? *Why didn't I do* that? That's why I came up with the expression (with thanks to Woody Allen) "Mixing is the death of hope." I was always in hell during a mix because I wanted it *perfect*. It was like I heard too much; I sensed too many options. For years I imagined that everyone else was to blame for not finding that perfect balance. But now I know that it's the nature of the beast. Mixing *is* compromise.

I've also always found final playbacks painful. I don't hear what I've succeeded at, only my failures. I walk away from it with a kind of post-partum depression. "Post-production blues," we call it. I suffer from a combination of addiction to the perfect moment plus option anxiety. I go so far as to *hate* a record for a while because all I can hear are experiments that didn't amount to a hill of beans. At album launch parties or sitting captive during a radio station interview when the DJ plays a track, I'd always sit there just crushing my fingers, churning inside over all the fucking things I thought could be improved. Gradually, though, the pain subsides as you start to hear the work more objectively for what it actually is. You still hear it warts and all, but those warts aren't quite as big and hairy as you feared.

With our later albums (*Vapor Trails* in particular) I'd stop working on a mix only when it was wrested from my hands. Then the only way out of the depression would be to think, *Well, on the* next *album* . . . If I felt I had fucked up verses on the previous album, I'd focus on the dynamics of verses for the next. Sometimes you're chasing your tail, but you always need that one thing to bring you back to the studio. I cannot stress enough how important it was for us to get better at expressing the ideas we had in our heads, and how much it drove me. I couldn't wait for another chance to improve on myself, pushing to make my influences broader, searching for knowledge, raising my game. For me, that's still what it's all about.

**WHEN *CARESS OF* Steel** was finished, we let the office hear it and . . . well, let's just say that no champagne corks were popped. They were clearly perplexed. Their disappointment was palpable. They didn't get "The Fountain of Lamneth" at *all*. And when they took it to Chicago for Mercury to hear, things got worse. Ray and Vic went into damage-control mode. Knowing there was a tour imminent and that everybody needed to earn some money, they put on a game face and went to battle for us. I have to give it to them; they were total professionals in that regard. It was decided that "Lakeside Park" would be our first single, with "Bastille Day" on the flip side.[*] It got some airplay in the States, more in Canada, but as we prepared to take it on the road, *Caress of Steel* looked unlikely to surpass the sales of *Fly by Night*, and we knew we had a steep hill to climb.

I'm not inclined to reprint any of the bad reviews we received, but I will say that concept albums and prog rock inevitably bring the word "pretentious" to critics' minds, and in the coming months our critics would bandy it about with relish. Neil and I discussed between ourselves what it really means to be "pretentious." The dictionary defines it as "attempting to impress by affecting greater importance, talent, culture, etc., than is actually possessed." We struggled with that. Was that really us? We opted for a kinder interpretation: if the word implied that we were pretending something, well, no. We were *not* pretending, just trying. Maybe our reach exceeded our grasp, but we were earnestly

---

[*] Now we had *two* singles that were my least favourite, although I did later enjoy playing "Lakeside Park" on our very last tour; perhaps I just needed a thirty-five-year break!

trying to write music with a literary inflection; we were attempting to be deeper and more complex than your average rock group. Sure, we were bombastic, but we weren't *pretending* to be anything else! And if we aimed for the stars but hadn't quite enough rocket fuel to get there, so what? No one was gonna stop us from trying.

We were prepared to learn from well-written criticism, but many of those early reviews were ill-informed, badly written or just slagging off a band they didn't think was going to make it anyway. I mean, we were even called devil-worshippers! For the most part, we took note of certain markers: this guy just hates us, so we're not going to bother with him (although Neil wrote a rare rebuttal to Robert Christgau at *The Village Voice*, who called us "the most obnoxious band currently making a killing on the zonked teen circuit"). Well, to riff on George Bernard Shaw ("Those that can, do; those that can't, teach") and Woody Allen ("Those that can't teach, teach gym"): those that can't do *either*, write rock and roll reviews.[*] In any case, I've always tended to believe neither the bad reviews nor the ones that overflowed with compliments. I could always find flaws in my own work, thank you, so if a writer loved a song so much so that he felt there was nothing wrong with it, to me that was no more believable than dismissing it as garbage.[**]


WE HAD WON some goodwill from past years' gigs and kicked off the fall by opening for Nazareth in western Canada, but as we schlepped across the country playing to crowds that were modest at best, we couldn't shake the feeling that we were working our way *down* the

---

[*]   It's just struck me that music critics in those days were akin to internet trolls. They weren't anonymous, but hiding behind their typewriters they did have the power to whack the hive with impunity. The main difference was you couldn't block them.

[**]   In the spirit of open-mindedness, I *will* quote from one of my favourite negative reviews, published after our show in Springfield, Massachusetts, December 1976: "If anyone wonders why they haven't heard of Rush before now, one listen to them provides the answer. With no subtlety, tasteless guitar playing, and a lead singer who had a voice like an overgrown munchkin . . ." *Overgrown munchkin?*

ladder of success. In the early days, whenever we'd had a bad gig or things looked bleak we'd half-joke, "That's it, now we're really going down the tubes." Now, with less than enthusiastic press and radio reaction to *Caress of Steel* making it tough for our agents to score good spots for us, we dubbed the excursion the "Down the Tubes Tour."

Mercury's belief in us was clearly on shaky ground, while our management kept us on the road to work off our increasing debt load with decreasing fees. In the days before MTV or Canada's equivalent, MuchMusic, there was no cross-country music circuit to speak of, and no real coast-to-coast progressive radio network. So not having a sound well-suited to the Top 40 meant that the farther we travelled from Toronto, the harder a time we had getting gigs. It was disheartening to pull up again and again to find a small, shitty club where we could barely fit our gear on the stage. That smelled like failure.*

It wasn't wholly a descent into the abyss, because after a bad gig the next day we might play a better one that buoyed our spirits, but it was definitely a bumpy ride. In our darkest moments, I'd ask myself, *Was the last good gig the future or is it this?* Rock and roll is not a profession for wusses, I can tell you. If you're looking for a sane and steady lifestyle, try elsewhere.

Booked to play the Estevan Civic Auditorium in Saskatchewan, we found the local hockey team had booked a skate-around that same afternoon and refused to allow the ice to be boarded over. In Canada nothing ranks higher than the hometown hockey team, so we had to set up the mixing console on a platform at the edge of the ice at the back, and the lighting console in the wings, and did our soundcheck while the locals skated circles in front of us. When the doors opened, a small crowd took

---

* Speaking of smells . . . At the end of the Maritimes stretch of our tour, I came down with a bad case of tonsillitis and had to fly home right after the Halifax gig to have them removed, while the rest of the guys returned home with the rental car. Lobster was cheap out east, so before embarking on the long drive back, they stopped off at a lobster stand and loaded up the trunk. By the time they arrived in Toronto, however, the ice keeping those briny crustaceans fresh had long melted and the car had acquired a special aroma. They exchanged the vehicle, conveniently "forgetting" to remove them. Our management fought with the rental agency for quite a while over that one.

their seats in the stands at the far end of the arena like we were radio-active. From the stage it looked as if we were playing to empty ice, and it was so effin' cold that when I glanced over at Herns, he had a blanket over his shoulders and was working the lights with vigor to keep warm. Definitely in the running for Most Canadian Gig Ever.

We drove over the Prairies past towns with such awesome names as Swift Current, Moose Jaw, Salmon Arm and Flin Flon (okay, not Flin Flon—it's way up north—but I love the name) and into the stunning Canadian Rockies. I remember waking up in the car as we were ascending and, sticking my head out the window, my jaw dropped at the scale and the gorgeousness of them. I couldn't even see the peaks. That was the very first journey I'd taken across my own country, and it took my breath away—although perhaps what best sums up the sheer Canadian-ness of that trip was looking out at the audience in Edmonton and thinking that I'd never seen so many ski jackets in one place in my life!

In beautiful Vancouver, Nazareth invited us out for some deep-sea fishing. I'd never once been on a fishing boat, let alone on the Pacific Ocean, but salt water was not what I needed to worry about. Though Nazareth's hard-drinking reputation had preceded them, we manly Canadians reckoned we could hold our own. It was only mid-afternoon when we sailed back into harbour on the verge of passing out, but those beefy dudes from Fife were just getting started. "Good fun, lads!" they called out in the hotel lobby. "Bar?" We gave them a big thumbs-up, and headed straight to our rooms and into a deep and blootered slumber.

Over the coming few months across the States we'd open for Blue Öyster Cult, Iron Butterfly, David Essex, Frank Zappa and the Mothers, REO Speedwagon, ELO, Kansas, Styx, Lynyrd Skynyrd, Mott the Hoople, Ted Nugent—and KISS for the last time. Sometimes it felt as if the world had turned topsy-turvy, like we had entered an episode of our favourite TV show, *The Twilight Zone*. Prior to arriving in San Antonio, Texas, the local radio station KISS-FM had put us on heavy rotation for twenty-four hours, and we were thrown a lavish Texas barbecue, treated like superstars—not a band struggling to stay afloat, which in reality we were. At one venue, a former bowling alley and now a country and western bar, the show was a complete madhouse, with tickets oversold leading to people fighting to get in—a first for us! As Howard tells it, one of the good ole boy promoters pulled out a gun when challenged over the door count. Thankfully, a third party present calmed everyone down. (That wasn't the only time Herns had rightfully been freaked out by the appearance of a firearm during a gig settlement. According to him, earlier that year, at a club owned by a certain accomplished ex–Detroit Tigers pitcher, a gun was unnervingly placed on his desk as our money was being counted. Yikes, I'd rather be brushed back by a fastball than an effin' bullet!)

Ten years before us in the industry, the most your average young musician might expect was a hit or two and, with luck, a couple of years of giddy success. (Even the Beatles had plans for when they'd flop; with "Twist and Shout" at the top of the charts, Ringo Starr was modestly sending money to his aunt in anticipation of opening a hairdressing salon.) But by the mid-seventies, a career in rock and roll was an actual prospect. We weren't wealthy, but we were making ends meet and signed on for the long haul. It saddened me when one musician I knew packed it in to go work at his father-in-law's chicken business, but I understood why: he was a sideman, he didn't contribute to writing his band's material, while the three of us were wholly vested in our own music, each with as much to lose as there was to gain. That was worth fighting for. If you're a salaryman in music, what's the difference between being that and a salaryman somewhere else? If you have mounting bills and pressure from your wife to quit, and home is a sad and stressful place, you may come to throw in the towel more easily, but I had optimism and a supportive partner. I had ideals and dreams to sustain me through times of crisis. Quitting music and taking a straight job was inconceivable to me. I had no other skills. During the *Caress of Steel* tour, I considered for the first time that the band might fail, but I persisted in the belief that it would not. It was more like, if failure is a possibility, what am I going to do to prevent it?

# CHAPTER 12

DESPITE THE HUGE AMOUNT OF ROAD travel we were doing, we still had a lot of dead time on our hands. Doing our best to accentuate the positive, we worked on new material in the car or our hotel rooms, and went on a serious sci-fi and fantasy reading binge. As a child I'd never been much of a reader, but with the hundreds of miles we had to cover and Neil's knowledge and voracity for inspiration, I, too, began to devour books, trying to catch up on all I had missed by quitting school.

Neil was *always* reading. He turned Alex and me on to the Russian-born Jewish American author Ayn Rand, and it was in *The Fountainhead* that I found some moral reinforcement against the dire situation the band was then facing. In the novel her protagonist Howard

Roark stands up defiantly for the rights of the individual, and passionately against the concept of artistic compromise. How about that for timing, just as our management and record company were turning up the heat and pressuring us to come up with something more commercial! Rand's book *Anthem* was the clincher. It's a dystopian novella set in a bleak and totalitarian world in which a lone outcast, Equality 7-2521, dares to think for himself, and to the wrath of the tyrannical World Council of Scholars accidentally rediscovers electricity. Neil suggested we use this book as a jumping-off point for a story of our own, and soon it was clear we were developing another concept album.

In February we had four weeks booked at Toronto Sound to record what in many ways felt like our last chance to make a statement about who we were and what we wanted to become. We decided, *Fuck it*, let's do this now or go down trying. I'd like to call it courage, but I'm not sure that in 1976 we were fully aware of the risk we were taking. There are times in life when economic circumstances have an emancipating effect on the decisions you make: one is when you've saved up enough money that you can follow your bliss; the other is when you're at the end of your rope and no longer care about the consequences of your actions. At that moment, we decidedly fell into the second category.

In the dead of the Canadian winter we hunkered down, and straightaway things started to click. We were working much more efficiently than we had on *Caress of Steel*, partly due to the heightened confidence in our playing after so many gigs (almost two hundred in 1975 alone), partly from a measure of defiance and perhaps partly this time from the *absence* of hash oil. We finished some writing left over from the road, laid down the bed tracks and, once all the individual sequences of the "2112" album side had taken shape, came around to the idea of assembling some of the prominent musical themes or riffs for a tongue-in-cheek take on that more famous overture that ends in "12."

I can't recall if it was always our intention to pull that off, but it's likely. I do remember the three of us sitting at the back of the control room with our instruments saying, "Okay, we'll use this riff from this piece, and this movement from that one . . ." and lo, they flowed together pretty well. Neil may well have had the *1812 Overture* in the back of his mind when he came up with the title, and I know he wanted to use a palindrome; "2112" was visually striking, and we just couldn't resist taking the piss. (Maybe still smarting from accusations of pretentiousness, I feel like I have to point out that it was a *joke*—as was the *diddle-iddle-iddle-id-da-da* that Alex put on at the end. Roll over, Tchaikovsky!)

I wouldn't go so far as to call "2112" a symphonic piece, but it certainly had elements in common with symphonic music such as themes and motifs, and its length and multiple time changes made its structure sound more complex and dynamic than *Caress of Steel*. More than an orchestral symphony, it was a raw three-piece rock opera. We didn't even use a lot of keyboards back then, just the swishy, swirly journey through the stars to the Solar Federation off the top and our first taste of orchestration on side two.* I wasn't even using bass pedals much yet; it was on the next album, *A Farewell to Kings*, that I'd tackle Minimoog and Taurus devices.

Alex's ricocheting guitar near the start was inspired by the way side one of Jethro Tull's *Thick as a Brick* ends and side two begins. Having resolved that it was a rock "opera," we set the scene for its totalitarian world with a deliberate pomposity and approached the lyrics the way you would a libretto, with me singing different characters: the innocent protagonist vs. the priests in the temples of Syrinx. I was learning how to use my voice as an interpreter, like an actor does. I had to make myself believe in what I was singing to the point of getting lost in the roles, for the audience would only believe it if *I* believed it.

We wanted the finale to be ambiguous: I took the optimistic view that the priests were vanquished and the temples destroyed, but I

---

* Getting to know our cover designer Hugh Syme better, we discovered he was an accomplished keyboardist. He was a member of the Ian Thomas Band, also managed by SRO, and made two cameo appearances on *2112*, playing ARP synth for the spacey intro and the lush Mellotron on "Tears."

remember Neil talking about the two factions still at war when a *third* party swoops in to take overall control. He and I talked about the Ayn Rand concept of "Sense of Life"—how each of us views the world and makes decisions based on individual values—and in that spirit it felt best not to spell everything out. Was it a rebellion of the oppressed masses or an invasion of liberating forces? That's up to you to decide— and, I believe, one of the essential things that listeners were engaged by and responded to so well.

TO CONTRAST THE singular theme of *2112*, we wanted side two to have as much musical variety as we could muster. "A Passage to Bang- kok," for example, was a travelogue in the mind of an aficionado of fine herbal substances but written by three guys who'd never been east of England (or west of Vancouver). Then a rarity: one song that featured lyrics by Lerxst, called "Lessons," and another by me, called "Tears."

That was pretty much the last time we credited individual works. It's hard to always know who contributes what to the writing of a song, especially when it comes down to the cold business of who gets a publishing credit and who doesn't—meaning *who gets paid*. For example, in some bands a part like a guitar solo is usually considered nothing more than part of the general arrangement and doesn't rate on the pay scale. That's often the reality, but can you imagine "Stairway to Heaven" *without* the effin' guitar solo? Even if that was all that Jimmy Page had contributed, it would certainly have been deserving of a song- writing credit, no? This is why I always hated divvying up the credits; for me, every musical part was integral.

In later years, whenever we'd record at Le Studio in Quebec, we'd hear all kinds of gossip from the staff about arguments other bands had had. The Police, for instance, fought tooth and nail over who would get the B side—because, of course, if you sold a million singles, even the guy who wrote the B side reaped a royalty reward. Well, we had zero hit singles to worry about, so it was easy for us to take the high road, but regardless, hearing that reinforced a decision we were about to take: from *A Farewell to Kings* onward, every song would be divided equally amongst the three of us, all for one and one for all, a working democracy. For the rest of our career we would *never* have to talk about that crap again. And to a great degree it was one of the secrets of our longevity.

Another Rush tradition in the making of *2112* was the Spontaneous Studio Track. The album was just about complete but needed one final musical moment. With less than a day of studio time remaining, we wrote and recorded "The Twilight Zone" on the spot, an homage to its creator, Rod Serling, whom we considered a genius and an inspiration.* Written and recorded in the afternoon and mixed that night, what a breath of fresh air it was both for the album side and our recording methodology. After meticulously and painstakingly grinding through every single moment of the record that far, it was a joy to be so spontaneous—so much so that we'd summon that spontaneity again with "Vital Signs" on *Moving Pictures*, "New World Man" on *Signals* and "Malignant Narcissism" on *Snakes & Arrows*; all were last-minute inspirations.

*2112* took four weeks to record, and all in all it's the album we wanted to make, defiantly oblivious to other people's expectations. We felt triumphant; if we were going down, at least we were going down swinging. Naturally we wanted people to like it, but we had to love it first. We were the Three Effin' Musketeers now. No management in the room, no record company, just Terry and us.

---

* We'd already dedicated *Caress of Steel* to him. We watched the show separately as kids and then together on tour, by which time it was a late-night TV staple, high and huddled round our hotel room set. Serling was a prolific master of tales of fate and irony. He could tell a cautionary tale with a sudden twist not merely to screw you up, but to skewer the human race on the horns of its own foibles. Whenever something happened to us in real life that felt weird or unexpected, we'd look to the heavens and say, "Rod?" and intone one of his famous monologues in that strange clipped, dead-flat delivery of his: "There is a fifth dimension beyond that which is known to man . . ."

You might have imagined that at the end of a good day in the studio I'd give a sneak preview to Nancy or a close friend or two, but no. (She wasn't very keen, to be honest, and kept a respectful distance from our work in progress. She felt that her opinions about my music were superfluous. Early in a tour she'd want to check out the new visuals but was usually more interested in what they were serving for crew meal and would sometimes fly out to see me without attending the concert at all.) I really wasn't *interested* in anyone else's opinions, however sensitive or considered—least of all while we were creating.[*] I wanted us to make our own decisions without being influenced either consciously or unconsciously, even if that meant making our *own* mistakes.

So we were in the dark, and when *2112* appeared to be a kind of hit you could have knocked us over with a feather. I don't mean it was a hit on radio—it was too long and weird for the mainstream—but with the word of mouth and the all-important radio request lines, plus the reaction we'd enjoy in concert, we felt we were really hitting a nerve. It made #5 on the Canadian Albums Chart and was our first to crack the US Top 100, peaking that year at #61 in *Billboard*.

Well, whaddaya know? I have said this before, and so has Neil, but it bears repeating: if we learned one thing from all of this, it was that a young artist's greatest asset is the word "no." It's an immensely valuable word. There will always be pressure on you to compromise, pressure to sell your dreams short, and there will always be people who want you to be something that you're not, *but none of those things can happen without your permission.* My most urgent advice to aspiring artists is always "Be true to yourself and just say no." Oh, and always take your wallet onstage with you. *Bada-bing!*

---

[*]   I do remember Alex and me playing *Caress of Steel* to Paul Stanley when we were on the road together. He looked uncomfortable and clearly did not get it or just thought it weird as hell. Of course, it is an effin' weird record, but remember, we're talking about a guy who sang "Strutter" every night, so it wouldn't have been his bag no matter what.

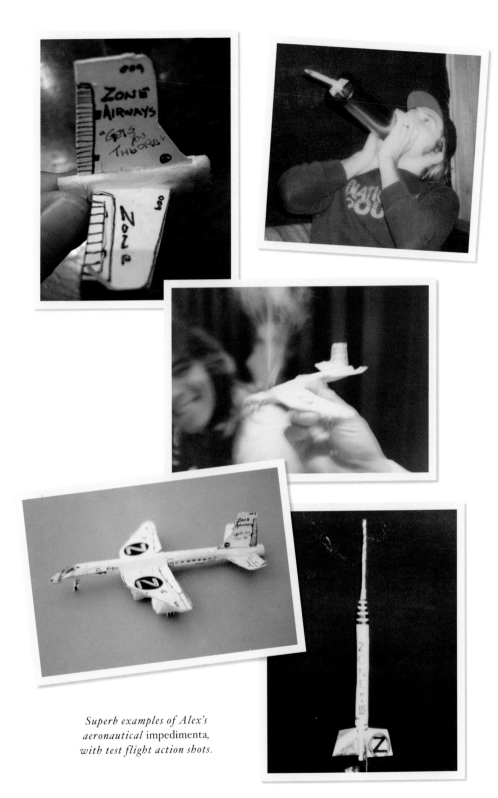

*Superb examples of Alex's aeronautical impedimenta, with test flight action shots.*

*Toronto Sound Studios, 1975 and 1976. The band hard(?) at work. For* Fly by Night, *we were thankful for the luxury of ten consecutive recording days. These would still be tight round-the-clock sessions, but with Terry's guiding spirit we stretched out rather than getting it on tape in a mechanical fashion and under the gun. For* Caress of Steel, *that time expanded to three whole weeks! Good thing we frittered it away smoking too much hash oil. (Oh, and I'm not brown bagging; I swear it's chocolate milk!)*

(LEFT) *According to Wikipedia, Cochrane is located east of Kapuskasing, northeast of Timmins, south of Moosonee and north of Iroquois Falls. Meet ya there for a coffee?*

(ABOVE AND RIGHT) *Alex, Jimmy Johnson and Ian getting ready for the Cochrane after-party.*

HUNK
Proudly Presents
**RUSH**
With Very Special Guests
**MAX WEBSTER**
Monday, September 15th, 1975
8:00 p.m.
Tim Horton Arena
COCHRANE, ONTARIO
Nº 131
Advance Sale $5.00

(LEFT) *Funniest thing about the Cochrane story is, when we returned in September, guess what? We got an encore!*

(RIGHT) *In 1978 we went through a serious "hockey period." Stuffed into the bay of the bus each of us had a sports bag packed with skates and pads, jockstraps and garter belts. Jack Secret and I entertained the others with our complete mastery of ankle skating, the only ways we knew how to stop colliding with the boards or each other.*

(ABOVE) *Touring with KISS and "the Bag" (plus Paul's version in flight).* (LEFT) *We rookies couldn't have asked for a softer landing. "Happy Birthday, Ace!"*

(RIGHT) *October 1975, San Antonio, Texas. A gift from Charlie Applegate, a local high school shop teacher who, with his students, helped prepare the staging for our gig. "I know why they call you Rush — cause all the hell I've done since you guys hit town is Rush — Charlie"*

*(RIGHT) Rockin' the Space Bass, c.'76/'77. (For details, see Geddy Lee's Big Beautiful Book of Bass).*

*(ABOVE) Hanging around my neck is a musical not . . . or is it? Actually, it's a sign of the times: a coke spoon. Strictly for medicinal purposes, you understand. (Yeah, right.)*
*(RIGHT) The Caress of Steel tour was all about keeping your head down, playing hard and hoping for the best . . . but it was hard to shake that sinking feeling.*

*In the midst of our 1977 UK tour, we took a ferry to Sweden for a one-off show in Stockholm, our first-ever Continental European gig. The record company peeps plied us with copious amounts of effin' potent aquavit. Back at the hotel, Alex shared the secrets of the Serbian universe with me, while Neil put on his Geddy Lee disguise. Also: Haute couture Rüsh? Our management's never-ending search for an image resulted in this ill-conceived shot that haunted us for years. Who would have thunk that our lack of image would eventually become our image?*

(ABOVE AND RIGHT) *The* A Farewell to Kings *sessions, Rockfield, 1977. Men in teeny-tiny shorts exploiting the great outdoors for recording purposes.*

(ABOVE AND RIGHT) *Duffo and the Duff-O-Scope.*

(LEFT AND ABOVE) *Lerxst imitating (my) art.*

(TOP RIGHT) *Alex drawing Frank Lee Shyte (in front of the multi-track Studer that tried to eat "Xanadu"); (MIDDLE RIGHT) trying to make an appointment at Advision dressed as Mr. Shyte's manager, w*hile (BOTTOM) *Neil is literally bowled over.*

IN ANTICIPATION OF the album's release at the end of March, we hit the road to promote the thing. And on this tour we sported a new look. When we'd shot the album cover, I was taking fashion advice from Nancy—as Alex was from his wife, Charlene, hence the hat he's wearing on the inner gatefold. To this day, all you have to do is ask him about "The Hat," and Lerxst will shrink down to a two-inch size. Whenever Neil and I wanted to bust his chops (which was as often as possible) we loved to remind him about that effin' hat. It's haunted him for years, poor fellow, but in fairness, none of us looked exactly dressed to kill on that cover. More like for bed. Throughout the "Xanadu" period, I'd wear an even longer white satin robe, with cowboy boots—you know, sort of how Legolas or Elrond would look if they lived in Texas. How does that Glen Campbell song go? "Like an Elfin Cowboy"?

Our stage apparel had always morphed without much rhyme or reason. After Rutsey left the band we left our glitter period behind as well, but still selected items of clothing that made us look more like we belonged on a stage and less like people on the street—albeit never with any consistent image in mind. Then, the summer before on the *Caress of Steel* tour, we had a couple of days off in San Francisco while staying at the Miyako Hotel in J-Town. Wandering through a nearby mall, we found these inexpensive kimonos and for some ungodly reason said, "Here's an idea! Let's wear kimonos onstage!" That's all there is to it. That's how the Absurdly Prophetic Robes (as one critic would memorably put it) were born—right in time for *2112* and the priests of Syrinx.

Our first properly directed music videos, mainly live performances of "A Farewell to Kings," "Closer to the Heart" and "Xanadu" at Toronto's Seneca College Winkler Auditorium, would be largely responsible for establishing that unfortunately enduring image: there I am in all my youthful splendour, sporting a wizardly white satin mantle and cowboy boots I bought in El Paso, singing about the Milk of Paradise, kingdoms full of hatred and philosophers, ploughmen, blacksmiths and artists. It

*My favourite bathrobes.*

was only years later that we found the self-confidence to ditch such misguided and desperate attempts at epic haberdashery and simply walk out onstage in our T-shirts and jeans. It took us a while to grok that our *music* was our image. Slow learners, I guess; good thing we had forty-five years to figure it out.

Following a couple of Canadian shows, we headed straight to the west coast for some club dates in L.A. and then several shows with Styx and Thin Lizzy. The Lizzies were absolutely smashing blokes, a couple of whom, particularly their wide-eyed and exuberant Scottish guitarist, Brian "Robbo" Robertson, *loved* to imbibe the amber liquid—to our occasional peril. One time on a day off in Chicago where we were booked on the same floor of the Holiday Inn on the Lakeshore, we drank such copious amounts of booze, smoked so much devil weed (popped some 714s, aka quaaludes, too) and became so raucous that complaints were made and the front desk called the cops. Suddenly this rotund Chicago policeman barged into the room with a fellow officer. We floundered about trying to clear the air and hide the dope, and Robbo, slurring his words, wobbled over on a misguided peace mission. The rotund cop bellowed, "Back off, sonny. Party's over *now*. Unless you want me to take a closer look around?" Then it was all, "Yes, officer" and "Thank you, officer." *Whew*, close call. One arrest would have made it much harder for us foreigners to obtain another work permit for a long, long time.

Some of the rental cars we drove around the country suffered mightily in the care of us young, bored musicians. We mostly killed time by getting high, reading books or jamming on acoustic guitars, but then there was the time I was awoken by the guys laughing idiotically: sticking out of the strip of tar that seals the front windshield to the car shell was a bristling array of sharp objects: pens, pocketknives and even a "demic" (the patented Rush word for corkscrew, whose etymology eludes me), like a vehicle out of *Mad Max*. Beat that for stir crazy. Another time, somewhere in the South, Alex and I stealthily tied folded strips of Kleenex into Herns's hair as he drove. When we pulled into a Holiday Inn, Herns put on his business face and, as we cackled like hyenas, marched up to the front desk, briefcase in hand, to check us in for the night, oblivious to how his curly locks were daintily adorned with fluttering white ribbons.

By 1976 we could afford an upgrade to the aptly named Dodge FunCraft RV, a family camper van with a raised plastic ceiling that allowed for a bunk above the driver, twee little curtains and a tiny wee table that folded down into bunks so one person could drive while the others slept. There was even a little microwave oven that Lerxst took regular advantage of, mixing whatever foods happened to be on hand—tuna fish, baked beans, hot dogs, Cheez Whiz, you name it—to create, for lack of a better word, an "interesting" casserole. After tooling around in rental cars for so long, squished like sardines and sleeping on luggage, it was the lap of luxury. Challenged once to a drinking contest by the Lizzies, we sat at the tiny table and methodically drank all the Chivas Regal we could. Not to brag, but after being so soundly trounced by Nazareth it was a much-needed win. Even if afterwards there was some, er . . . cleaning up to do.

*If you're going to Alabama / Be sure to wear / Some Kleenex in your hair.*

On that tour, Neil created a rotation schedule for sharing hotel rooms lest we become sick of one another. Not that I buy into all that zodiac freak crap, but Neil, Alex *and* Liam were Virgos with all the anal-retentive tendencies attributed to those born under that sign. They had a need for everything to be tickety-boo that used to drive me nuts. In the early days, Neil would lay out his smokes (John Player Specials; one day he'd even have his Lotus Europa painted the same black and gold as on the pack) like clockwork, and later in life take his

*As the crew grew, Neil's rooming schedules evolved. You'll notice Herns is not on either. He used to get his own room for two reasons: one, he'd be on the phone doing advance work while we were trying to sleep and, two, he liked to keep his room at a temperature only fit for polar bears. Also notice that by 1976 there were seven of us on the road, giving each of us our own room once a week. What. A. Luxury!*

nightly glass of scotch (two fingers) at exactly five (so long as he wasn't working), while Alex kept his workspace fanatically tidy; meanwhile I, your classic Leo, flourished in disarray. It was immediately obvious which side of the studio was the neatniks', and which was mine with its ever-present used coffee cup, cigs and lyric sheets strewn about should I be struck with an idea and want to quickly write it down. If I was working on, say, the melody of a vocal part and liked the way it was coming together, I'd sort of scan the spread with my peripheral vision, hoping that a lyric or theme that Neil had written would leap out at me. Mine was a contrived but *useful* mess.

As I've amply illustrated, touring affords one an enormous surplus amount of time to get high, or read, or both, but for me there was no better distraction than movies. Since I was a child, I could spend hours in front of the tube, lost in *The Bowery Boys*, *The Three Stooges* and westerns with Roy Rogers, Randolph Scott or John Wayne. I grew up watching the humanist dramedies of Charlie Chaplin, Preston Sturges and Frank Capra—*Sullivan's Travels*, *Mr. Smith Goes to Washington*, *Mr. Deeds Goes to Town* and so on.* In my twenties I amassed classic movies on VHS and kept a stack of film compendiums close to hand, *Halliwell's Film Guide* and *The Psychotronic Encyclopedia of Film* among others, and read obsessively about the great directors of Hollywood's Golden Age. It was a labour of love, because in those days there was no internet; you couldn't just google Elia Kazan or Edward Dmytryk. I devoured *Hitchcock/Truffaut*, Strasberg's *A Dream of Passion*, *Kings of the Bs*, biographies of John Ford, Luis Buñuel, George Cukor, Akira Kurosawa and Chaplin, and a couple about the great Orson Welles. After seeing *Citizen Kane*, I read the most respected book on Welles, by the influential French film critic and founder of *Cahiers du Cinéma*, André Bazin. That was my introduction to more than forty books

---

\* I found myself moved by the plight of the naïve and honest man battling a rigged and cynical society, so much so that during one viewing of *Mr. Deeds*, I wrote down some ideas for what would one day become "Cinderella Man."

he wrote on film, including his classic two-volume *What Is Cinema?* and his biography of Jean Renoir.

On board the bus when we got one, comedies by Mel Brooks, Steve Martin and Woody Allen suited us best, especially after a show, when what we needed was to chill, down some inebriates and laugh our heads off. We'd watch *Young Frankenstein* and *High Anxiety*, *The Jerk* and *The Man with Two Brains*, *Take the Money and Run* and *Annie Hall* and every episode we could tape of Canada's own *SCTV* on a loop until we had all the best lines memorized and could incorporate them into the Rush lexicon to regurgitate at will. We could be anywhere at any time, preferably in a boring meeting (that's a tautology, right?) or in a crowded dressing room after a show. We'd toss lines at one another like "Into the mud, scum queen" or "I've gotta go now, I'm due back on the planet Earth" and know exactly what was meant.

We set up what we called "Vector Theatre." We often took Valiums (or Vectors, as Herns called them) to help us sleep while being tossed about in the bunk on rough roads. We'd sit on the sofa, put on a film, pop a "V" and try to stay awake . . . Before long, someone would tilt their head back and nod out, bashing the aluminum venetian blinds, which would clatter and wake them back up while the rest of us guffawed. We usually saved B movies or even lesser films for Vector Theatre because you knew you wouldn't get far past the opening credits anyway, but once in a while I'd throw on a classic drama such as *Citizen Kane*; that particular one led to the inevitable debate over the significance of Kane's last word, "Rosebud,"[*] and along with Samuel Taylor Coleridge's poem *Kubla Khan*, inspired Neil to write the lyrics to "Xanadu." While mixing the intro, I couldn't help but visualize the "News on the March" sequence with the narrator announcing, "Legendary was Xanadu where Kublai Khan decreed his stately pleasure dome . . ." There was no competing with Bernard Herrmann's foreboding musical score

---

[*]  This was long before I'd ever heard the rumour that it was Hearst's pet name for Marion Davies's "tender button."

for the movie, but it was still fun to reimagine it in our own proggy context.

Well into my thirties, movies and books about movies fed my brain. It was a largely solitary preoccupation, as only a couple of my friends had the same degree of interest or patience for old black-and-white films, especially ones with subtitles, but no matter; it's not necessarily a group sport. Film became a gateway drug for me, leading to a range of other visual arts disciplines, especially photography, which would seep into our live shows as I became more involved in the designs for our rear-screen projections; increasingly, I'd come to think of our shows as a mixed media experience rather than simply a musical event. I'd take a harder look at animation and graphic design, which led to an interest in architecture.

These were things I could study my own way, in my own time. In lieu of the formal schooling I'd missed, the museums, galleries and streets of the world became for me a kind of classroom. Much of that became possible only later in my touring life, when I actually *had* days off, but by the eighties and nineties it was not unusual for me to bump into Neil wandering around too, and he introduced me to a game: surrounded by paintings, whether we knew the artists or not, he'd say, "Choose one from each room. Imagine you can take it home to hang on your wall. Which would you want to live with?" It was a sensual and not necessarily intellectual response to art, which led me to wonder which art is best hanging in museums as a gift to the populace and which is just as well gloated over in someone's basement or yacht. I particularly loved the German Expressionists and would always defer to an Emil Nolde or a Max Beckmann if one was there. At a Freudian level I must have been drawn to what the Nazis called "degenerate" art. I liked what the Nazis hated!

# CHAPTER 13

**I**N JUNE 1976, A CERTAIN WEDDING WAS IN THE offing: mine. Nancy and I had decided to tie the knot despite the knowledge that as long as the band lasted, I'd routinely be away from her for weeks and months on end. She was not only willing to take me on, but prepared (she thought) to take on the life of a "plus-one," as she so self-effacingly put it. As I've already mentioned, however, we'd kept our relationship pretty much hidden from my mom, and our engagement wouldn't be official until the two ladies met face-to-face.

Even before that, Nancy had decided to convert to Judaism, taking Hebrew classes, adopting the Hebrew name Leah and going so far as to take a dip in the *mikvah*.* Now, I emphasize it was *she* who made the

---

\* A *mikvah*, or *mikveh*, looks like a mini swimming pool just for one, used to achieve ritual purity.

decision, because I would never have asked her to do it. It really didn't matter to me, but in her wisdom, she knew what an olive branch it would extend to my mother. Nancy was raised a United Church Protestant but harboured no religious feelings of her own; like me, if she was anything, she was an atheist. But having learned from me what Mom's family had endured in the Holocaust, she wanted her to know that she respected her faith and would do what she could to help her swallow the pill of *another* Weinrib marriage outside the Orthodox tradition.

Because ultra-religious Jews do not consider conversion legitimate, Mom's new husband, Max, helped us find a Reform rabbi to preside.[*] I accompanied Nancy to a couple of her lessons, and I have to tell you, I hated them—they brought back awful memories of my own Hebrew school education—but she won *huge* points with me for going through all that crap. The first family dinner, meanwhile, was awkward, but Nancy was a total doll and my mother put aside her reflexive cynicism for the evening. Let me tell ya, my mom could *really* dish if she felt like it, so that was a testament not just to her intestinal fortitude but her natural intelligence too. To accept me dropping out and becoming, of all things, a musician, and now to accept that I was about to be married outside of the faith—Nancy's conversion notwithstanding—was unheard of in the world she'd grown up in, but she understood that the world was changing and, difficult though it must have been for her, throughout her life she'd continue to let old dogmas lie and adapt to new ways.

Now, you may be wondering how Nancy's family accepted *me* . . .

I remember the culture shock of the first time I was invited to dinner. I came from an Ashkenazi Jewish household where the table groaned with great quantities of overcooked foods that tended towards beige or brown—all the hand-me-down delicacies that had made the

---

[*]  Originating in mid-nineteenth-century Germany, Reform (or Liberal or Progressive) Judaism offered Jews a less strict, more modern and assimilated outlook on life: over time in synagogue, for example, family seating was allowed, and women could deliver sermons.

journey from the *shtetls* of Europe, with exotic names like *cholent, kasha, potatonik, farfel, gribenes, tzibele mit schmaltz, schmaltz herring* (clearly, we're big on *schmaltz*), chopped liver and, of course, the ubiquitous gefilte fish. As in many immigrant homes, you had to eat everything you were given, under threat of punishment because, apparently, somewhere in the world Jews were always starving (as if me cleaning off my plate was helping them out). For condiments, there was the ever-present *chrzan* (beet horseradish or, if you like, Jewish wasabi), which shot a rocket up your nostrils and could liven up even the toughest-leather brisket. Very few actual fresh vegetables were ever served; "greens" were either beans from a can or iceberg lettuce (which, I'd like to point out, is barely green). Finally, on holidays Mom would make us a deep-dish matzoh meal pancake called *bubaleh* that you covered in sugar or apple sauce—and devoured before your cousins got their mitts on it. (My dad's specialty had been breakfast, when he'd make his *matzoh brei* and his famous beef salami *versht* and eggs, a tradition I've carried on for my kids and now my grandson, who prefers hot dogs to *versht*, but one must adapt—*right?*) There was also everyone else's favourite, boiled carp, but that, *blecch*, I wouldn't even try. Mom also loved boiled chicken, especially the feet. *Blecch* again! I remember coming home from school to find her cooking up a storm, and her turning around at the stove with a nice plump claw sticking out of her mouth. I was like, "Mom, what are you *eating?*"

"Oh," she said, plucking it from her lips. "Feece! They're delicious!"

So anyway, the first time I sat down for dinner at Nancy's parents' house, I felt like a visitor from another planet. Everything was nice, mind; friendly, polite and . . . *nice*. Nancy's mother, Louise, plated and apportioned each of us a thin slice of rare roast beef, a few carrots and green beans, with a tidy pat of mashed potatoes on the side. I wolfed it down, wanting more but not daring to ask, and since none was offered, waited patiently until we could leave the table . . . and grab a burger elsewhere!

(ABOVE) *Me and my
beautiful bride and the
only photo of me managing
half a smile.* (RIGHT) *Aww,
my buds thrusting me into
the jaws of marriage.*
(BELOW) *Rabbi Lerner,
Nancy's bestie Carolyn,
Nancy, me and Oscar.*

I got along well with Louise, but her father, John, was a little different. When he was young he'd suffered hearing issues that left him with a speech impediment, so he was a man of few words to begin with, but even fewer with me at the table—never rude, but aloof. Raised on a farm at the outskirts of Toronto, he harboured traditional, white, old-school Christian values and perhaps a few old-school prejudices too, and frankly didn't much care for his daughter dating a long-haired, unemployed high school dropout with rock star ambitions. One time I overheard Louise asking him, "What is it about him that you don't like? The fact that he's a musician or that he's *Jewish?*" and just as he mumbled something in return, he noticed me at the bottom of the stairs with my smiling *punim* looking up.

"Oh hi, Mr. and Mrs. Young!" I said with a certain satisfaction, and that was the end of the exchange. Over time he realized that I didn't really have horns (so far as he could see) and we grew to have a fairly good relationship, especially once we realized that we shared a love of baseball, which he'd played passionately as a young man.

So, at the Hyatt Regency on June 20, 1976, Nancy and I tied the knot. It was a small wedding, attended almost entirely by our friends, plus our parents and one couple from each of their families. Alex, Neil and John Rutsey all at the same table (*that* was weird to see), along with my crew guys and the best man, my longtime pal Oscar. Nancy and I wrote our own vows and walked down the aisle to Satie's *Gymnopédie No. 3*. I didn't get high, but everyone around me did (I remember them sneaking outside to smoke up). I *think* it was a joyous event, though you wouldn't believe it from the tense look on my face in the wedding photos. Lighten up, dude!

We honeymooned in the time-honoured fashion at (drum roll . . .) Disneyland. Honest! Then we flew to Maui, where after too many mai tais and piña coladas at Trader Vic's my redheaded bride got sunburned beyond belief, spending the rest of the time in bed—alone, until her skin absorbed the aloe vera and the pain subsided. Then we headed home to say goodbye for what would be some of the busiest years of my life.

*The wheels on the bus go round and round . . .*

Poor girl, I don't think she *quite* realized what she'd signed up for. Frankly, nor did I—although, of course, the person who leaves usually has the easier time of it. I had adventures ahead of me, which she was fine with for the most part—aside from the occasional weak moment when I disappeared up my own ass and didn't call for a couple of days— but then she'd never know what version of me would be arriving home, dead tired after too many gigs in a row or full of myself after the band's recent successes. I'd be used to someone cleaning my room and bringing me breakfast and all the amenities of hotel living. I was like the conquering hero coming home and then it was, "It's *your* turn to take out the fucking garbage!" And while I found it exceedingly difficult to transition to home life, it was just as hard for her to accommodate me as she built her own career . . .

**A SMALL INDICATION** of Rush's rising fortunes was that we could now afford another transport upgrade. Our crew inherited the fabled FunCraft as we rode in a cumbersome new Barth RV and hired a good ol' boy from Virginia to drive it for us. George, or "Jwerg" as we nicknamed him, was at the wheel one day when we felt the ride getting increasingly bumpy. He looked in the rearview and coolly announced in his thick southern drawl, "Fellas, ah think ah see the problem . . ." We looked out the window in time to witness one of our tires overtaking us on the highway before careening off the road. Though we did not appreciate it at the time, I would now say that was a metaphor for our very lives getting ahead of us.

Around this time we were averaging around a hundred and eighty shows every ten months, our bottomless well of youthful energy was beginning to drain and we found ourselves in need of a little something extra. Children of the Age of Aquarius, we weren't too shy about experimenting with drugs, be they the usual suspects like weed or acid, magic mushrooms, STP or pretty much anything other than speed or heroin (we *definitely* considered those last two uncool), so when the notorious white nose candy inveigled its way backstage, we checked it out too without hesitation. In 1977 cocaine was fast becoming the rock and roll touring network's new allure. We were so numbed out by the endless driving and near-nightly gigging that a quick energy burst seemed nothing if not practical. At first, I considered it to be almost *medicinal*, though I now know that was just your typical imbiber's rationalization. We all started out as occasional users, but from '77 into the early eighties it increasingly became a common part of our *impedimenta*.

This may sound suspicious after all I've confessed to you, but I was in fact less experienced and more conservative than my partners when it came to recreational drugs. They knew when they could handle it and when they couldn't, and they would never do anything that would interfere with the quality of their performance, but I'd even given up smoking pot by then because it made me paranoid. You need both a body that can handle it *and* a will to control that body. And I was unprepared for just how much coke would get its hooks in me.

It was all too tailor-made for my situation. I started doing lines after shows with whomever else was hanging out backstage, that plus a couple of drinks equaling immediate rejuvenation and loads of *blah blah blah*, everyone yammering away at eighty miles an hour and each of us imagining we were at the centre of a deep and interesting conversation. I assure you we were not. What may have begun as a lively, inspired exchange soon became twitchy, repetitive and dull, because the reality of being high on blow is that your brain starts to freeze while your mouth keeps motoring on. The moment you run out of words you lay out another line to recapture the night's first rush,[*] but that moment is actually long gone and all you're left with is

---

[*] No, the irony of our band's name in this context is not lost on me now. But it certainly was back then.

too much "schnah"[*] running through your bloodstream, making you jittery and in need of another drink to settle down. It's an inane and vicious circle.

"Bolivian marching powder" being ubiquitous in those days, there were very few people in my life who did not either carry on them that little tell-tale vial with the black screw-top or wear a tiny coke spoon around their neck. I was given one on a necklace, disguised as a musical note pendant. One of my touring pals and I were constantly on the look-out for a "bit" of schnah, and pretty quickly it wasn't enough to do merely one line after the show; he would meet me at the side of the stage during Neil's drum solo or before the encore to do a snort. Or two. Away we'd go, and I could finish the night with a little extra pizzazz.

Now, you may be asking, "Why did you need to jazz yourself up? Didn't you have thousands of people in the audience doing that for you?" That's true, but it was fun anyway, fun and illicit to sneak back, do a line and come charging out for the grand finale. But what began as—we insisted—just some harmless fun proved to be reckless, not least because it did my voice no favours at all; the more coke I did, the more cigarettes I'd smoke, which led to a serious cough and, as an added bonus, trouble sleeping. The very thing I'd picked up as a cure for fatigue ended up aggravating the problem. And at one point we had a driver who, after laying out lines behind an amp or on the monitor board, would announce, "Doctor's office is *open!*" He was a really bad influence because, basically, the doctor's office was almost *always* open.

At the back of my mind I knew I was doing myself harm, plus I had nosebleeds and a crusty nose, but despite my better instincts I kept at it. We started seeing dodgier people at gigs simply because they had some schnah for us. Looking back, that period was not just surreal and not just nuts, but dangerous—if only because, while that

---

[*]   I'm not sure where the epithet originated, but it's likely from the word "schnoz" because, well, that's where you put the stuff.

highly illegal substance seemed cool to us, the range of buyers and sellers who came bearing it were decidedly not. It was after a gig in one Midwestern city that I climbed aboard our bus to find a dealer sitting at the table up front with his briefcase snapped open and his scales set up, measuring out grams for the crew as they popped by to pick up their purchases.

I was freaked out. That briefcase not only carried an enormous rock of coke but had a big-ass satellite phone built right into it too. Not normal—almost no one had cell phones back then. I was thinking, *Who is this effin' guy? He must be a* serious *player.* We found out afterwards that "serious" didn't even cover it; he was a big-time dealer, definitely not the kind of dude we should be associating with, let alone doling out grams on our bus. What the fuck were we thinking? The guy was so dangerous that the FBI was sniffing around our next gig looking for him. Talk about a wake-up call.

As the road trips got longer and the pace of life quickened, I was losing my hold on reality. Even home was no longer a drug-free zone, so I found it impossible to return to the sense of normalcy I had previously relied upon after coming off the road. I remember coming back for a break, only to discover that Nancy and some of her fashion world friends were part of the party drug scene too. There was just no escaping it. We maintained that we had it under control, but into the early eighties cocaine was a road staple for innumerable people with whom we travelled and worked, and it was waiting to greet us when we first recorded in the UK. For some, having a little schnah around during the *Farewell to Kings* sessions certainly helped keep our eyes open, *wide* open, as our schedule went later and later into the night. (I hasten to say that we didn't do any coke while actually recording, but some of those not involved in the session at that moment certainly felt it was safe to do so.)

Finally, a couple of events began to put an end to my romance with toot. One occurred on an off-day in a small town in Texas while on tour: bored and restless, my musician friend and I heard of some punters carousing at the hotel, so we went down and crashed the party—a highly uncharacteristic thing for me to do. Well, it didn't take long before we figured out that there was a girl holding some coke. We persuaded her to bring the party to our bus, but all we wanted was her nose candy, and once we'd done all of it, we made our excuses and asked her to leave. He and I then nursed a quiet and somewhat guilty drink, and when I got to my room for some unlikely sleep, I just felt *awful*. I was disgusted with myself. Taking advantage of a fan just to get a little buzz from some shitty coke? It was truly a terrible moment for me, and one that really *did* awaken me to the trap I had fallen into. Almost.

Sometime after that, I was at a big after-show party in London. I had reduced my regular schnah intake by then and decided that on this particular night I would stay straight, maybe just enjoy a drink or two. As I mingled amongst the guests standing around the room in intimate circles, I noticed that there was little talking going on—or little of interest at any rate—but a whole lot of staring and sniffling and licking of teeth, all nervous and herky-jerky. Everyone was waiting for someone else, anyone else, to invite them to the bathroom stalls for another bump; then they'd return and repeat the whole damn ritual. That was the worst part of it: no one laughing or even trying to tell jokes, the opposite of a pot party where everyone is laughing, even if they don't know what they're laughing at! I mean, how do you make a strung-out person chuckle? The pointlessness of it all was suddenly as obvious to me as the schnoz on my own goofy face.

I pretty much stopped then and there. Over the coming months, I might occasionally have a line and a smoke to see if I really missed it, but the fact was I really didn't, and I've never looked back. Like LSD, I guess it was some kind of rite of passage, something I had to live through. I still had lots of pals who kept on doing it happily, which I figured was fine; I had no right to judge or try to talk them out of it. It was just over for me. I'm fortunate to have been able to simply walk away from stuff like that.

Because I'd been such a quiet kid, I enjoyed the travel and the socializing, the luxuries and the extras that came with being in a band. I felt I had some catching up to do! But even when I dove in, there was always a voice inside me that told me when enough was enough. A part of my brain would kick in and tell me, "Dude, this is a fucking losing road you're on here. This is not you. This is not who you want to be." That voice has served me well throughout my life. In those days, of course, everyone knew somebody who'd OD'd, which served as a cautionary note (if you were smart) but losing my dad at such a young age had really set my clock ticking. For a long time, I never truly believed I'd live longer than he had. It was an irrational thought, but the fear of an early death drove me in two directions at once: on the one hand it made me want to live my life to the fullest, which included hedonistic pursuits such as this, but on the other it probably saved me because no matter how fucked up I was, I always had the good sense to just knock it on the head and get back to my room.

While we're on the topic: I quit cigarettes the same way. By 1983, in the studio producing the Boys Brigade, I was smoking up to a pack a day. I developed a hacking cough and felt lousy all the time, but it only slowly dawned on me that the smokes weren't helping any. Then, with a deadline looming, I looked down at my ashtray, and it suddenly struck me that the worst thing in the world would be to smoke another. I threw the pack away and never took a drag again.

# CHAPTER 14

B Y 1977, WITH SALES OF *2112* RISING AND THE
subsequent success of our live album *All the World's a
Stage*, we were able to headline with some regularity
across North America. Word was starting to spread
across the Atlantic too, particularly in Great Britain, where a small
but fired-up fan base was making some noise. As ever, we were
receiving precious little radio play, so fans had to discover us either
by word of mouth or through the infamous British music press.
*Melody Maker*, *NME* and *Sounds* had a long tradition of discovering,
championing and trashing musical acts, and arguably wielded
greater power in the UK than music publications did in North
America. Maybe they couldn't quite make or break a band, but

without a doubt they could either help musicians or make life hell for them.

It was a wonder, by contrast, that in Canada we were able to discover local or alternative bands at all; with only Toronto's short-lived, low-budget *Beetle* to count on at home, your patriotic hard rock fan barely stood a chance. We scoured the American magazines, *Rolling Stone*, *Creem*, *Trouser Press* and *Circus*, to pick up bits of information about bands we loved, but coverage of our local musicians was almost non-existent.

That helps to explain, by the way, why fans of fringe genres or ground-breaking bands tended to be so fanatically devoted. Ours was a staking-out of tribal territory; claiming a kind of ownership of your cool discovery made you that much more passionate. To be hip to a great band that no one else had ever heard of was like wearing a badge of honour. "What? You've never heard of Van der Graaf Generator? Check out *Pawn Hearts*, man. Their sound is full of dark vibes and cool melodies and they can fucking play!"

To be fair, we *did* have a relatively more adventurous radio scene than in the UK ( John Peel and Alan Freeman being notable exceptions on BBC's Radio 1). Folks of my vintage can remember hearing actual *rock* music sneaking onto the popular airwaves: Traffic's "The Low Spark of High Heeled Boys," the Who's "I Can See for Miles," Zeppelin's "Immigrant Song," the Yardbirds' "Heart Full of Soul," Yes's "Roundabout," the Small Faces' "Itchycoo Park," April Wine's "Could Have Been a Lady" and even Blue Cheer's "Summertime Blues" had their occasional moment in the sun. By the late sixties, music was spreading more rapidly from AM to stereo FM, heralding a golden age for those of us in the bigger cities especially, with freeform and then progressive radio formats, and when that subdivided into target-market categories and radio consultants began to take over DJs' playlists, campus radio filled in where a lot of good and challenging music fell through the cracks. UK radio, meanwhile, remained largely in the thrall of traditional variety shows and all-ages programming. That forced the birth of pirate radio there, unlicenced stations like Radio Luxembourg (based in, uh . . . Luxembourg), and Radio Caroline and Radio Atlanta broadcasting from ships or marine platforms anchored in international waters, but their signals often sounded distant and staticky, and the stations themselves sometimes sank in storms. All of which, to make a long story short, is why the British music press had become so uniquely influential.

*Melody Maker* was the original music paper, the granddaddy of them all, having launched way back in 1926 largely as a circular for dance band musicians. In 1952 a rival came along, another weekly, *The New Musical Express*, which would later introduce the first singles chart to the UK; and in 1956 *Record Mirror* started publishing an album chart. By the mid-seventies, the *NME* was Britain's bestselling music paper, known and sometimes notorious for its less-than-objective coverage—Britain's answer to gonzo, if you like, with its writers as integral to the story as the artists they were writing about—and, thanks to its more iconoclastic critics, had become aligned with Britain's punk movement. Rivalry turned to factionalism, and in 1970 two former employees of *Melody Maker* founded yet another weekly, *Sounds*, establishing themselves as the authority on prog and heavy metal.*

At the ripe old age of nineteen a chap named Geoff Barton joined the British rock mag *Sounds*. He was amongst the earliest journalists to use the term "heavy metal." He liked our music and, in the February 5, 1977 issue wrote a review of *Caress of Steel* with the subheading "Poor man's Zeppelin? Or underrated scions of sword and sorcery rock?" That got us some attention and alerted London concert promoters to us. Soon Ray and Vic at SRO connected with a booking agent named Neil Warnock, who pushed them hard to bring us over.

---

* In particular they flew the flag for the New Wave of British Heavy Metal, with its acronym, I kid you not, NWOBHM—as big an effin' mouthful as the movement itself.

(LEFT) *A rare shot of Neil signing an autograph (and smiling!).*

(ABOVE) *Three examples of the kind of coverage we were getting in the UK during the late 70s. Not all of it was bad! Regardless, it went a long way to boost awareness across Britain and Europe of who the fuck we were.*

Before I get to what I think of as our "Very English Period," though, to illustrate the attitude of the UK music press, I must fast-forward to about a year later, when a writer from *NME* interviewed us in a London hotel. It started off innocently enough but had taken on bizarre proportions by the time it was published. You may have already read about this, but I bring it up again not only to paint a picture of the scene in that era, but also to throw some light on my evolving role as Rush's live front man.

Prior to that interview in March '78, the *NME* had given us decent-to-bad reviews, but so what, we were used to it by then. This guy, Barry Miles, was apparently sent because he was the only one on staff who'd heard of Ayn Rand. When he entered our hotel room, he was polite enough, though it may be relevant to mention that he carried with him a distinctly hoppy aroma from the time he'd just spent in the pub.

His first question was aimed at our stage presence: he wondered why we didn't project more personality from the stage. That was a fair enough question, which deserves an answer here. It was true; I did *not* have the standard entertainer's schtick and didn't talk a lot to the crowd. At twenty-four, I was still learning how to interact with an audience in a natural manner, almost as if we were in a small room enjoying one another's company. Now that the band was headlining and had a longer set, I understood how important some kind of communication was, but it took me years to relax into myself. I truly admire the way artists like Dave Grohl, Eddie Vedder and Tom Waits can chat off the cuff so naturally with their audiences without relying on rock and roll clichés, but I was shy and not a born onstage raconteur; Rutsey had always done the talking when he was with the band, so for me the whole business of projecting was a long, steep learning curve. What's more, by now we'd opened for so many bands who, in my view, yelled insincere greetings and introductions night after night that I was reluctant to jump on the bandwagon. When we toured with KISS I'd stand side-stage listening to Paul Stanley say stuff like, "I got this feeling we can get this place hotter than he-*ell*," which sounded as much like a sales pitch for KISS's album as it did a heartfelt hello. I used to watch the more seasoned acts and think, *Why are they yelling at the people sitting there? You don't have to yell, you've got* amplification. *Just talk to them!* So I'd try that, but felt stupid saying, "How are you, Montreal?" in my naturally soft speaking voice. Then there was Barry Hay, Golden Earring's singer, telling fans every night, "Hey [*insert name of city here*], it's my birthday! I was born here!" (Actually, that one's pretty funny.) I opted for the less-is-more-than-enough approach. I felt the crowd was there to hear the music, so we should just get on with it.

At any rate, the *NME* interview then turned to politics and philosophy, and the vibe became distinctly stilted as Neil and this Barry Miles chap struggled to see eye-to-eye on hypothetical points of governance and social prioritizing: Was socialism in Canada and Europe simply state capitalism? What were the pros and cons of a welfare state? and so on—certainly not the stuff of your average rock and roll interview. We carried on as best we could, but the atmosphere was tense.

Admittedly, we were a little too young and naïve to have arrived at a fully informed worldview. We considered ourselves capitalists but voted Liberal; we thought of ourselves as independent but valued our country's social safety net and national health scheme. We didn't see that conservative and liberal—or even capitalist and *socialist*—were values necessarily at odds. As politely as possible we tried to answer and engage with every argument he advanced, but he wasn't having it. Then, as writers do, he enjoyed the final word *in print*, and published a harangue that bore little relation to the discussion we thought we'd been a part of.

"So now I understood the freedom [Neil] was talking about," he wrote. "Freedom for employers and those with money to do what they like, and freedom for the workers to quit (and starve) or not. Work makes free. Didn't I remember that idea from somewhere? 'Work Makes Free.' Oh yes—it was written over the main gateway to Auschwitz concentration camp . . ."

*WTF?* Okay, now my blood was starting to boil.

The article continued, "These guys are advocating this stuff on stage and on record, and no one even questions it. No one is on their case. All the classic hallmarks of the right-wing are there: the pseudo-religious language . . . The use of a quasi-mystical symbol—the naked man confronting the red star of Socialism (at least I suppose that's what it's supposed to be). It's all there . . . They are actually very nice guys. They don't sit there in jackboots pulling the wings off flies. They are polite, charming even, naïve—roaming the concert circuits preaching what to me seems like proto-fascism like a leper without a bell."

*Deep breath, Ged* . . . To be described as fascists trying to put one over on British rock fans was puzzling enough, but when I got to the part where he invokes the un-invokable words on the gates of *Auschwitz*, I thought, *Fuck you, man.* You have just invoked the wrong fucking thing. With my background? Are you fucking *kidding* me? I get that in the socially polarized days of Maggie Thatcher's rise to power, the UK music media took their mainly left-wing politics very seriously (clearly, *this* dude did), but I still struggle to compose a mature and balanced response. At first, I tried to be kind to him (a very Canadian trait, eh?), to see through *his* lens, but I stumbled, and still stumble, at that abhorrent reference. I don't wish him dead or anything, but he went a bridge too effin' far.

After surviving our "Down the Tubes" tour, we considered ourselves lucky to still be around. We were proud of our victory over those who'd have had us conform and sell out. With our backs to the wall, we had been inspired by Ayn Rand's artistic manifesto on the rights of the individual and the importance of sticking to your *artistic* guns. Writing a rock opera whose protagonist stands up *against* totalitarian rule, we reckoned it shouldn't be too confusing who the good guy was . . . *Should* it? Fans are free to interpret music for themselves as they please, however remote their understanding may be of the artist's intention, but I've learned that both lyricists and critics bear a heavy responsibility—for words (to paraphrase the Buddha) have the power to both hurt and heal. And while we must live with what we've recorded, journalists can stick the knife in and run away. In the end, I can only suggest that we weren't the *only* ones who were naïve that day. And leave it at that.

THE START OF our "Very English Period"—especially for me—cemented an enduring love affair with London and Great Britain, the *NME* episode notwithstanding. In 1977 after the fanfare in *Sounds*, plans were firmed up for a short UK tour (with a one-off gig in Sweden) beginning in June. It was a thrill to play the very towns and venues we had mostly only read about for so many years, and especially triumphant for Neil, for whom London had been a place of thwarted dreams. I know how good he felt about reconnecting with the friends who'd helped him stay afloat his first time there. That being said, we were bemused by our first audience reception. When we hit the stage on June 1 at Sheffield City Hall there was a loud short cheer—then silence as it became clear that Alex's guitar amps had malfunctioned. An awkward start, but when we gave "Bastille Day" another stab, the crowd applauded only as briefly as before: an enthusiastic enough cheer, but one that subsided disconcertingly fast. From then on, whenever I announced a song, there'd be the same burst of recognition . . . and then again . . . silence. It was like a soccer chant, but just a single line from it! Herns (who by now had handed his road manager duties to Liam Birt and become our full-time light-show guy) tried flashing some dramatic effects to prompt a louder response, but still nothing. If we played a signature riff or a solo they knew and loved, there'd be the same momentary cheer . . . then a retreat into expectant silence once more. That's when I realized they were responding to specific musical passages. One of the things we learned from KISS was that if you blow something up real good, crowds will go *yay*—but that was in America. In the UK they went *yay* when you played a riff they loved. They were listening—and I mean *focused* on listening. Ha! How dare they just listen to the music! They most definitely had their priorities in the right place, but it took some getting used to.

Since then it has always fascinated me to witness how a country's character reveals itself in a crowd's response. Audiences in America are boisterous and demonstrative; they've come to party and celebrate, and there's an electric excitement even before the house lights go down. Americans *ooh* and *aah* in response to lighting and pyrotechnics; they'd reliably cheer whenever Herns blanketed them in bright white light or cut lasers across the ceiling, and especially when we fired up the pyro. But we'd have to consciously adjust when we returned home to Canada. I'd never noticed this as a teenaged concertgoer in Toronto, but as a touring performer it was obvious how much more self-conscious and restrained our homegrown audiences used to be (aside from Montrealers, who were so insane that bands sometimes planned their tours to kick off or wrap there). Then there are the Scots, who blew us away when on the *Farewell to Kings* tour we played "Closer to the Heart": they sang along so loudly, almost louder than me, that it gave us goose bumps. Then when we'd travel to South America in 2002, well, *that* was an eye-opener. Rush fans in Brazil, Argentina and Chile are as demonstrative as Americans and know our parts as well as the British, but are almost theatrically emotional, weeping during Neil's *drum solo* and taking it even further when, during "YYZ," they broke out into what sounded like a football song, but one that fit so well into the structure of the song that I thought, *Geez, they've written their own parts.*

AFTER THOSE EARLY UK shows, we were also surprised to find fans lining up behind the venue for our autographs—a first for us! We obliged, of course, signing as many as we could—even Neil, who later in our career would be embarrassed by and avoid that kind of attention. We'd sign tickets and chat with each and every fan, but once word got out, the queues got longer and longer, so while at first it was a novelty that we all enjoyed, it soon felt like work and obligation. In years to come we'd do meet-and-greets after our shows, but even those got out of control, invariably turning into after-show parties, so we relegated them to a strict timeframe before the show. Thing is, each and every contest winner is a fresh bundle of adulation who wants a photo with you and "just a quick word," and when you sign one autograph they want three for their friends as well. So the sad but inevitable fact is that the larger your fan base grows, the more isolated you become. You discover that you need to protect yourself by controlling your fame the same way you have to control your work schedule (and your recreational drugs). I guess that some artists are flattered to stand there all day and all night, but after a while I felt like a kind of personality pollution was coming over me. Believe me, I *like* interacting with fans—that's why I do book tours—but when you're in game mode with a gig of increasing complexity to do, you have less and less of yourself to share.

ONSTAGE, WE'D BEEN showcasing several new songs, an excellent way to work out the bugs and finesse the parts before laying anything down on tape. Terry, meanwhile, found a residential studio called Rockfield Studios, in a rustic spot in Monmouthshire just over the Welsh border, and we headed there straight after the last UK gig with our band crew, a grand total of seven people, for our first recording session abroad, the one that would result in *A Farewell to Kings*. When our buses and trucks pulled into Rockfield's ancient-looking farmhouse surrounded by grazing sheep and cows, and we unloaded what was now an arsenal of guitars, percussion and keyboards, it was like the circus had arrived.

One artist in the Rockfield annals who sparked some nostalgia in us was Dave Edmunds. As teenagers Alex and I had been fans of the band Edmunds was in at the time, Love Sculpture, that did a blistering rendition of Khachaturian's "Sabre Dance"; then in 1970 as a solo artist, he recorded Rockfield's first hit single, "I Hear You Knocking." After Queen used it to record parts of *Sheer Heart Attack* and *A Night at the Opera*, its reputation took off internationally, followed by innumerable notables such as Mott the Hoople, Be-Bop Deluxe, Joan Armatrading and more. Black Sabbath was working in the adjacent studio when we were there, and one afternoon Ozzy popped his head in to ask if he could "borrow" some hash. For years afterwards, whenever Sabbath came up in conversation, Neil loved to furrow his brow and say, "Hey! That guy owes me some hash . . ."

It was the first time we had worked in a residential recording environment, and we found that living on the premises was exactly (as they say in England) what it said on the tin: a rustic, chilled-out yet efficient place, with a snooker table, a television set and a dining room overlooking the fields. (After loading in, a few of the guys went for a stroll, only to be chased across the mud moments later by rampaging cows.) It was a welcome change from eating takeout food while crowding around the console at Toronto Sound; no hassling to get out the door, no stressful driving through traffic to get you there, no one bugging you to do anything but make a record. Furthermore, this was before the internet or cell phones, so we were really off the grid. We'd get up at the crack of noon, drag our butts to breakfast that someone else had prepared and take our sweet time before ambling to the control room and getting down to business. Pretty ideal. In our first few days there we kept typical rock and roll hours, recording noon to midnight in the studio, but soon we found ourselves working later and later into the night until we got it completely back to front, waking late in the day, breakfasting around four or five, working all night long and crashing just as the cows began to moo and the sheep to bleat. (Have you any idea how noisy sheep are?) Nor did it help that Monmouth was only three hours from London and a convenient source of hashish or cocaine whenever required. So much for the idyllic country life.

This would be the first time that Terry did not act as engineer as well as producer. He'd jump in to twiddle a knob from time to time, but most of the heavy lifting was left to the resident house engineer, a funny and affable Irishman named Pat "Duffo" Moran (who sadly passed away in 2011). We nicknamed him Duffo because every time we presented him with a new sound or part that he deemed subpar, he'd scrunch up his face and say, "Ah, that's *duff.*" He cracked us up so much that when we returned to record there in 1978, one of our crew guys created a device called the Duff-O-Scope, which could supposedly detect the "duffocity" of any sound by plugging in and turning the dial.

More seriously, Rockfield presented us with opportunities to think outside the box—or quadrangle, as it actually was. There was a purpose-built echo room that lent unique effects to the percussion, guitar and vocals you can hear on "Cygnus X-1" and "Xanadu," or we could record in the open air, far from the din of the city. Before dawn we set up mics in the courtyard and recorded the classical guitar, synth and chimes for the opening segment of "A Farewell to Kings," capturing some indigenous birdlife on tape in the bargain. (Those avian performers made another cameo appearance on the introduction to "Xanadu," warbling from the rooftops of the quadrangle while Neil played his wood blocks.) For the opening of the title track, Alex walked quietly around a stereo mic as he plucked, moving the guitar across the sound-stage; when you hear it moving from speaker to speaker, Lerxst is actually walking around the courtyard like a troubadour.

Fans often point to Alex's acoustic playing on *AFTK* as evidence of his versatility, so this seems like a good moment to reflect on the man's talent. I know I'm biased, but I do think he's the most under-rated guitarist in the rock pantheon. Rush fans appreciate him, natu-rally, but I don't believe he's gotten his due from the mainstream or critical rock world. Neil and I used to call him our musical scientist, for he is surely one of the great chord inventors, constantly creating his own inversions and unusual intricacies of arpeggiation; he's a fluid and dexterous riffologist, one of rock's most original soloists, a confident and emotive blues-rock guitarist at only eighteen who went on to develop his own blend of heavy rock, blues, classical and more.

His genius is one of spontaneity, his best ideas mostly coming in flashes and sparks that you have to grab in the heat of the moment; get too methodical with him and he'll lose interest. From our earliest days writing together I'd keep a tape machine beside me, even just a cassette player, because so often without even thinking he'd play a figure that was just brilliant, and if I said, "Whoa! Let's build a song around that," he'd often have to listen back, painstakingly learning the very thing he'd only just played off the cuff. Knowing that about him, whenever we worked with a new producer or engineer I'd sit right there in the control room during Alex's warmups and make sure the RECORD button was on lest they miss any happy accidents.

In the early days he composed his solos all himself, developing them incrementally as we played our songs over and over again in rehearsal and onstage, but from *Fly by Night* on, as writing time became limited, some solos had to be written on the spot in the studio, which required a different approach. In the analog age before Pro Tools, we'd create "comps" by bouncing multiple takes back and forth between two tape tracks: first Alex would record five or six solos, while we took note of the most exciting riffs or weirdo moments. We'd encourage him to get outside himself and be more orgasmic with his playing. (He mastered those out-of-the-blue harmonics that Jeff Beck used to do so well; when you hit a harmonic and bend it, that's one of the sexiest guitar sounds you'll ever hear.) Then Broon and I would assemble them into a single performance, trying various combinations until we hit that magical mix. With Alex you were spoilt for choice, which often made it hard to choose, but he came to trust me because, like most musicians left to our own devices, he'd lose objectivity. To no one's surprise, I was very opinionated about his solos. I felt I knew his playing better than anyone, and he usually didn't mind me butting in. Usually.

THE MIXING SESSIONS for *A Farewell to Kings* were booked
at the legendary Advision Studios, where another dream came true for
me. T. Rex, the Who, Caravan and Gentle Giant had all recorded
there, as had Yes: *Time and a Word, The Yes Album, Fragile* and *Close
to the Edge* were either recorded or mixed or both at Advision, and for
us deep-dyed Yes fans, just being in that room momentarily breathed
an air of magic into our project. That was the first impression, anyway.
In the long run, the atmosphere proved workmanlike and unglamor-
ous, devoid of suggestion that between those ordinary walls so many
monumental pieces of recorded music had been created. We just settled in and buckled down to work.

I could go into brain-numbing detail about what mixing a
record entails, but I will spare you (or at least my editor will). Suffice
to say that it's a torturous exercise in second-guessing your ears,
juggling numerous alternate mixes ad nauseam until your hearing
burns out and you don't know which way is up. (This is where producers truly earn their keep.) And out of such tedium and frustration
comes chaos.

AS WE WERE witness to the rise of the punk scene in London that
summer of 1977, with bands like the Sex Pistols and the Clash in the
news all the time, during yet another mixing lull Alex sketched out
a certain Mr. Shyte, a cross between mohawked street urchin and
Frankenstein's monster with a safety pin through his neck. The drawing finished, he wrapped his head in toilet paper with a spoon poking
out from his forehead (*ooh*, so "punk"), then pulled his hoodie over the
top. He then snuck out the back of the studio, reentered via the front
entrance and presented himself to the puzzled receptionist as manager
of Frank Lee Shyte and the Rooten Nazis. He showed her the drawing,
asking to meet Advision's owner to book some studio time for his
rising star. The look on her face was somewhere between polite

confusion and *Are you kidding me?* While we were reduced to giggling like eight-year-olds.

"Is he doing it?"

"He can't be . . ."

"Yeah, he's *really doing it.*"

And in the middle of the fun and games, we came as close as we'd ever come to a true effin' recording disaster. We were working on the mix for "Xanadu" when the master tape machine stuttered on rewind and one spool got momentarily jammed. The tape billowed out and wrapped itself around the transport beneath the other spool as it spun. We all stopped breathing as we heard the only copy of the song crunching in the guts of the machine. In a flash my mind went into triage mode: *Okay, if it's destroyed, we summon the gear, set it all up again, buy more studio time, postpone our flight home, re-record here in London . . .* you get the picture. As we chewed our nails, Terry cautiously freed the tape from the transport mechanism, examined it inch by inch and found that, mercifully, it was badly creased but not torn. We decided from then on to always, always make a safety copy, and right away. That's something you should do anyway, especially if the tapes are going to travel between studios, but since we ourselves had carried the tapes from Rockfield to London, we hadn't anticipated any issues. Lesson for the day: *always* anticipate issues.

I should mention that although our music could not have been more defiantly out of step with current trends, we were all impressed by the public relations savvy those punk bands had, their ability to grab the front page at every turn. And of course, their unbridled energy was admirable. But while their three-chord mantras were fun, for a musician they could be boring—as I'm sure they'd say about us. But without question, one thing that happened was that punk immediately *legitimized* us! When we first got going, we'd been considered a crude prog band; compared to Yes, Genesis or Zeppelin, the perception— the *criticism*—was that we were a pale imitation. But as soon as punk came along, we were up there with Yehudi Menuhin. So they did us a huge favour.

I will admit that I never attended a punk concert, but I did hear lots of tales from our driver Bill Churchman. I know that "from our driver" sounds very rock 'n' roll aristocrat, but our affable East Ender Bill, who explained to me exactly what is required to be a true Cockney (that you must have been born within the sound of the Bow Bells), would tell us terrible stories about having to drive some of those guys around. Yes, the same punk bands that supposedly disdained such luxuries were being driven around *by the same chauffeur.* The main difference being that when he drove us around, there was no danger of us shitting in his car.

*1978, riding to a gig in Birmingham in Bill Churchman's fine Daimler, listening to him tell tales of punk bands... " Blimey, Lerxst! What's that smell?"*

# CHAPTER 15

FTER *A FAREWELL TO KINGS* WAS DONE, WE returned to North America, leaving me precious few days with my new wife. Really, I don't know how she coped, for as we embarked on what we dubbed the "Drive 'til You Die Tour," the more our record sales improved, and the more our homes were disappearing in the rearview mirror.

First we took a cross-Canada trip as fully fledged headliners, then traversed the USA for runs of ten shows in a row, then eighteen, then eleven, at which point UFO joined the lineup. That band, and

*An outtake from the photo session for* A Farewell to Kings, *taken at the Great Castle House, part of Monmouth Castle in Wales.*

(ABOVE) *Pete Way used to stand by the monitors and shout at me during the show about dining on honeydew and drinking the Milk of Paradise.* (LEFT) *Backstage with UFO.* (BELOW) *After gigs, there was always time for a real quaff with the guys: Lerxst and Michael Schenker, Andy Parker and Pratt, Pete and me, Glee.*

particularly the bassist, Pete Way, loved to take the piss out of our songs: one night, the dry ice we'd shrouded the stage with during "Xanadu" dissipated to reveal a pair of fluffy bedroom slippers stuck to the floor beside my bass pedals—complementing, I guess, my kimono. They'd also snuck onstage and placed a miniature Mickey Mouse drum kit in front of Neil's titanic one.

My prog rock inclinations bugged Pete to bits. As I was listening to Bill Bruford's first solo album, *Feels Good to Me,*[*] in the RV to kill time before a show, Pete stormed on board and implored me to turn off the tape. "*Glee*, please! Turn it *off*. Don't listen to that stuff. Don't *do* it. It's no *good* for you, mate."

We all indulged together in the occasional line of schnah, but more than that UFO really loved a drink or four. When we played a dry county in Texas, they couldn't get their heads around the situation and grew visibly upset. Right before they were due to go on, I happened to glance out the dressing room window and saw them in full stage gear with their tour manager in the parking lot, gathered around the open trunk of his car swigging from bottles. At least once on that tour, I'd be backstage listening to them play and hear a *kerplunk* followed by the absence of bass; Pete had fallen off the stage again.

I didn't see him for many years after that tour. Then in the 2000s, he showed up backstage in Columbus, Ohio, with his latest wife, Jo, on his arm. She was an accomplished doctor, apparently, and seemed like a lovely person, yet he looked unhappy and the worse for wear. Not long afterwards I heard that *she'd* overdosed, which must have shocked him back to life, because he eventually made it home to Britain and started touring again. Then in 2020, I heard that he, too, passed away—a couple of months after a car accident and a week after his sixty-ninth birthday. Rest in peace, my old chum, and thanks for making me smile so very often.

---

[*]   I was especially blown away by Jeff Berlin's bass work. Give "Joe Frazier" (the bonus track on the Winterfold re-release) a listen to hear what I mean.

IN FEBRUARY '78 we returned to the UK for the second time in little over a year. We were excited about it but had to learn to adjust. We'd been spoiled by the ease of touring in America, where the venues were mostly new with large and easily accessible loading docks, spacious backstage areas and clean dressing rooms, the whole shebang fully equipped and powered up to run any amount of gear or effects you'd brought with you. It was not the same in the UK back then, with its smaller, older, often crumbling venues: we were still learning about the effect that different voltages and step-down transformers had on the sound of our amplified instruments, and we'd have to load in down back alleys, set up in cramped and drafty dressing room spaces (especially in the winter where there was little to no central heating) and cope with thick fire curtains that were required to be dropped between acts, which affected where you could place your gear, as well as strict safety regulations that constrained incendiary FX.

We weren't using a ton of pyro yet, just one or two flash pots for "2112" and some dry ice for "Xanadu"; lasers would only come into play in the "La Villa Strangiato" period when Howard developed that magnificent fanning-out effect over the audience. Inspired from a young age by Chip Monck's work with the Rolling Stones and Arthur Max's with Pink Floyd, which he felt added a dramatic, even emotional, dimension to shows at a time when few rock and roll acts thought in truly theatrical terms, Herns always went the whole nine yards. We didn't object, except when what he wanted was way too expensive, and even then I'd often fight Ray on his behalf because I really believed in developing the show, but even in our earliest, humblest days when we had no money and were struggling to build our own show, we were spoiled by his imaginative use of limited resources. He made magic with liquid lights à la Grateful Dead, unusual gels and just a few PAR Cans (the kind of light with a direct, narrow beam originally used on roads and the landing strips of airports); Herns was one of the first lighting designers to make full use of them in a concert setting—his first "special effect," if you like. Most bands preferred a broad beam bathing the whole stage in a celestial glow and covering the musicians with changing colours—that's how you make a star look larger than life—but Herns didn't care so much for that. He liked the dramatic dark spaces *between* the beams and the effect created by crisscrossing them kaleidoscopically above us (and he'd make sure there was always lots of smoke in the air because that made the beams even starker and eye-catching). Our egos weren't threatened by that; we were happy to have a light show at all! Bless his heart, there was a bit of a god complex going on there, dancing at his console and sweeping his arms in the air, conducting the lights, like, "Let there be *lights*. For I am Herns, Bringer of Lights, and I will perform for you tonight! (Also sharing the stage with me are three members of a band called Rush. I will make sure that you can always see them as well as my show.)"

To the degree that we could afford, we also started creating little animated moments. On the *Fly by Night* tour we projected an image of the owl from the LP cover that flapped its wings, which wasn't all that sophisticated but went down a treat. We used rear-screen projections from the earliest days and became obsessed with stage size because the depth of a stage limited the enlargement of the projection. With a shallow stage, you'd get a very small image, sometimes just an embarrassing rectangle above Neil's head, so to avoid a Spinal Tap moment, Howard would frame the screen with coloured light. Talk about resourceful.

Our star continued to rise in '78. *AFTK* was generally well received and "Closer to the Heart" even broke into the Top 40 on UK radio. That was the year the Glasgow crowd blew us away singing along on the chorus—the first time anything like that had ever happened to us. We played two nights at the Apollo there, a classic old theatre built in 1927 with Corinthian columns and a severe rake on the stage.* It was

---

* In thespian parlance, a "raked" stage is one that's tilted towards the audience, hence the directive "put that downstage left"—where my mic stand was situated and where I've pretty much spent my entire life.

also really high—fifteen feet, six inches high, to be precise—so that if you stood at the edge you almost got vertigo. At face level opposite there was a balcony that had been built to bounce up and down, and I can tell you, those Glaswegians knew it. Many bands who played that place have testified that when the crowd put the "bouncy balcony" to the test, trampolining with all their might, you stood there in fear it would surely collapse.

The great advantage of playing two nights in the same venue is that the crew doesn't have to pack up and load out after the first show, giving them a night off and us a rare opportunity to unwind with them. So it was on a February night in Manchester in 1978 that we convened in the bar of the Piccadilly Hotel. For a while, Alex had not been very happy. His second son, Adrian, had been born the year before and he was missing home big time. Out of the blue he challenged our stage manager, Lurch, a towering man with a tough constitution, to a cognac-drinking contest. Now, cognac, usually around 40 percent alcohol, is for sipping; no one in their right mind knocks it back in shots, but I think I counted a dozen rounds. Soon words were slurred, voice levels rose, and when a clearly plastered Alex triumphantly slammed yet another glass on the table, he shattered it. I looked at Liam and Howard and said, "You'd better get him to his room," so they put their arms around him and suggested it was time for bed—not least because we had another gig to do the following night.

Those of us remaining in the bar had a laugh about it, then decided enough was enough for us, too, and as we were waiting for the elevator the doors opened and out flew Alex, lying prone on a room service cart. Cue more lunatic laughter and, once again, Liam and Herns rounded him up and escorted him to his room next to mine. Sitting on my bed, I could hear shunting and crashing through the wall like he was moving furniture around. I then heard him yelling out to the street, "Hey, England! You guys are *stupid*. You're all living a thousand years ago! Hey, *you*. Can you *hear* me?"

I opened my window and, leaning out, said, "Lerxst, buddy, go to sleep now. It's late."

"Dirk," he said, "can you believe this? These people are livin' *a thousand years ago*."

"Yeah, Lerxstie, I know. But come on, close your window." I closed my own and began undressing, but he kept calling my name, and then I heard more smashing sounds. He'd torn down the curtains and was soon leaning out his window again, tapping on my window with the metal curtain rod.

"Dirk, Dirk. Don't *go*. Open your window!"

Half-naked now, I pulled back my curtains when the pane cracked apart, showering my room and me with splinters of glass. I looked down to see a three-inch triangular shard stuck in my tightie whities, about an inch from my effin' manhood. Gingerly I removed it, then heard scuffling in the hallway and hubbub all over the hotel floor. I tiptoed over broken glass to the door and looked through the peephole in time to get a fisheye view of a nearly naked Alex running down the hallway with Herns and Liam after him. They were just hustling him back into his room when two security guys charged out of the elevator and banged on his door. He opened up, the curtain draped over him like a gauzy toga, obstinately denying he'd been making a disturbance. He slurred, "Well, I just don't give a shit," and spat on one of them. As we all cringed, mortified, Herns did his best to placate them, earnestly apologizing and promising to sort it all out. He urged them to talk it over in my room, but when I opened the door, there for all to see was the glass strewn across the carpet. Somehow Herns got them down to the manager's office, reassuring them of our normally upstanding character and promising to pay for the damages, and saved us from being booted out in the middle of the night. I curled up under the blankets in that room with no window, splinters everywhere, and fell asleep as the cool February air rushed in.

The next day, poor Alex was embarrassed and humiliated, to put it mildly, even though we knew it was just one of those things that happens when a person's at breaking point. In a fragile state we left to do our second show, and when we returned he went up to each and every employee, shook their hands and apologized. Perhaps because he was so sincere, they were more than cool about it, and even promised to welcome us back the next time we were in town, but the following morning we still left with our tails between our legs.

The test of endurance on the road continued until the end of May 1978. From a professional standpoint, things were bright, as by that time we were firmly established headliners and for the first time even making a little money. Uriah Heep, for whom we'd opened four years earlier, was now opening for us. I say this with no sense of *schaden-freude* whatsoever, because they'd always been perfectly good to us, but theirs was a cautionary tale, the dictionary definition of "coming full circle" and a reminder of how quickly one's fortunes can rise and fall. It's just part of the circle of life on the road.[*]

**BACK HOME, NANCY** and I were headed for our second wedding anniversary. I'd been on the road for about twenty months, spending most of the rest in the studio; in real time we'd actually lived together as man and wife for less than two and at this point there was still no end in sight. Still, we were happy enough on our independent paths, with Nancy ensconced at college and me parachuting in and out of town according to the demands of the schedule makers, and somehow found the time to scout and put a down payment on our first house—a symbol of our commitment to each other and an

---

[*]   Many years later, Ken Hensley, their guitarist and keyboardist, went to work for the Ampeg company and came backstage to see me at a gig in St. Louis, asking me to consider an endorsement deal. Just like when we'd first met in Pittsburgh back in 1974, we were two people at opposite ends of their careers, except that now he was a salesman (he looked pretty much the same) and I was the headliner. That was a weird thing for me.

encouraging sign of the fruits of my labours. It was also where we'd establish some new traditions, starting with boisterous and increasingly extravagant "Christmukkah" parties. As one of only a few families we knew who could afford a house, we threw ours open to an extended family of friends, fellow musicians and several wayward Jewish pals who had never experienced Christmas before. I know it sounds heretical, but like me they were all too used to watching enviously as Christmas was celebrated around the globe without us while we ate Chinese take-away* and watched reruns of *It's a Wonderful Life* and *Miracle on 34th Street*. Basically it was a case of if you can't beat 'em, join 'em.

For the longest time, my sister and brother and I agreed to keep from our mom just how vigorously we all enjoyed Christmas, and we hid those parties or dinners from her for many years. While in many Jewish homes, it was "Don't mention the war," in our case it was "Don't mention the Christmas tree." Sometimes I'd slip by mentioning that we'd had Allan and Susie over for dinner—on like, December 26, so she knew anyway, but we didn't want to rub it in her face. She'd usually be in Florida at Christmastime with Max anyway, which was convenient, but in time we came clean. And you know what? She couldn't have cared less. She embraced it wholly, soon sitting every year at the long table with all the people she loved—people of all religions and ages. Actually, we ended up with more Jews there than those who came by the holiday honestly, but regardless, it showed how far she'd come, from someone upset that I was hanging around in my teens with *goyische* kids to now being part of a mixed-religion family. Far from seeing her grandchildren as mongrels, she loved them to pieces. All her Old World ideas and prejudices, all her pains and fears, fell by the wayside.

---

\* A sweeping exaggeration on my part, based on the stereotype of assimilated urban Jewish folk, as I don't think my mother ever once ordered in Chinese food or any other ethnic cuisine. More likely we'd be munching on an overcooked brisket!

THAT SUMMER WE once again booked time at Rockfield and began work on *Hemispheres*, with side one of another concept album beginning where the journey into that black hole known as "Cygnus X-1" on *A Farewell to Kings* had left off. Side two was equally challenging, with only three songs, one of them a complicated and shifting instrumental inspired by Alex's dreams, which he often related to us at the breakfast table. Now, the telling of dreams is something that will often put listeners right back to sleep, but his were spectacularly, epically, cinematically surreal (in one, he was steering an ocean liner down Yonge Street); whenever he'd embark on another long, wild description at the breakfast table, Pratt would go, "Oh, somebody hit him. I'm getting a headache," but "La Villa Strangiato" is an homage to Alex's dreams—not inspired by any single one but a journey through his subconscious mind (and his overindulgence in marijuana), which meant anything goes—which is why the composition swings from one extreme to another.

Earlier that year, I had engaged an independent and very experienced contractor to build me a custom synthesizer setup that would not only house my modular Oberheim 8 and my Minimoog, but also let me trigger their sounds with my feet via several Moog Taurus bass pedals mounted below: a unique, unified, highly functional keyboard stand. Yeah, right. Not only was he late delivering it, but it was absurdly ginormous. Oh, and one other detail: it didn't work. I could play the synths all right, but the foot pedals did nothing. Nada. Zilch. Zip. I had no way of knowing, of course, but what I was trying to invent was something that only came out a few years later: MIDI, or Musical Instrument Digital Interface, a system that allowed diverse pieces of electronic equipment to talk to and control one another. It was overambitious, I admit, but the doofus I hired had convinced me—at great expense, I might add—that he could pull it off. Well, he couldn't, and I was left with a great white elephant on my hands.

Fortunately, my trusty keyboard techie, Jack Secret, was on the spot. He and Rockfield's electronics maven, Otto, laboured on it for days with, eventually, a modicum of success. It was an important step towards becoming the world's smallest symphonic rock band! Onstage to that point, I'd had to supply the bottom end with bass pedals whenever required to play guitar on my double-neck, and I felt frustrated. I wanted the texture and musicality of so many tantalizing new sounds, but I was primarily a *bassist*. I much preferred to devote my feet to other instruments while concentrating on my one true love.

We were still very much of a mind that we wouldn't put anything on a record that we couldn't reproduce live. A classic example is "Closer to the Heart," in which Alex plays the first verse on his acoustic and then takes a break while Neil gently hammers out a melody on orchestra bells and I accompany him on bass pedals. It's pretty and adds a moment of suspense, but the main reason we composed it that way was to give Alex time to switch to his electric guitar and play the next verse with full-on power chords.

The *Hemispheres* sessions were arduous, intense and slow. We had arrived in Monmouth without any material written beforehand, so we had to hole up in a nearby farmhouse for a couple of weeks and write the entire album before moving into Rockfield to record it. We had underestimated our own ambitions and ended up with a pretty complex concept album that would prove to be much more difficult to get on tape than we anticipated.

We'd always prided ourselves on playing whole songs in one take, live off the floor—not unusual for many bands whose tunes were short and simple, but these more complex pieces were proving more than we could chew. The "Hemispheres" side was divided into bite-sized sections and therefore easier to lay down in one go (even the parts in 13/8 time!), but "Strangiato" was a horse of a very different colour. For days we tried to lay down all ten minutes of that one in a single flawless take, before crying uncle and recording it in three parts that Terry then spliced together. It took us more than ten days to record those bed tracks and overdubs and then to mix them down, meaning by one calculation that we spent more time on that one song than the entire *Fly by Night* album.

We took advantage again of being able to record outdoors for "The Trees" and parts of "Hemispheres," but I don't think the Welsh sun shone more than twice that entire summer. As the work piled up and we all grew beards, despite a brief conjugal visit by Nancy the bloom of being in a boys' club started to come off the rose. Everything took longer than expected. We ran out of time in Wales and had to use the mixing sessions we had set aside at Advision in London to finish recording vocals and guitars. The vocal sessions in particular were the most difficult of my career, and at one point I completely melted down. To give my throat a rest, I'd usually alternate recording time with Alex, but after he'd finished his solos I had to sing virtually every day. That's when I realized I'd made a serious mistake. Never having sung these songs in either rehearsal or concert before, I hadn't gauged if the melodies were in the best key for me or not. At the writing stage, I'd worked out the melodies in a quiet hum or falsetto, assuming they would work. Not. The keys I had chosen were in between, meaning that if I sang in my speaking voice it was too low and without power, but if I sang an octave higher in my patented Geddy Lee range, well, it was too high, even for Geddy effin' Lee!

I did not grasp this mistake until the red light was on, the tape was rolling and I opened my mouth to sing "Prelude." I tried over and over again with force and precision above the heights of my vocal range, frustrated to hear Terry say into the talkback, over and over, "Sorry, Dirk, you're a little flat. Once more, please." Eventually—and the only time in my career that this has happened—I blew my lid and stormed out of the control room to walk it off on the streets of London, blaming everyone but myself—*Why hadn't Terry noticed that?* He's *the damn producer!*—and when I returned to the control room I was still in a huff. I sang again and again and again, stretching my cords for *two weeks* until I got what we needed. Man, it was torture, but I nailed it at last and we tried to reset our brains for the mix.

We took no time off between vocals and mixing to clear our heads, which was a mistake. Terry immediately had trouble with the mixes at Advision. He didn't like what he heard coming out of the speakers. Every move he made, every EQ he added, felt like a struggle, and though we'd been perfectly happy with the mixes he'd done for *A Farewell to Kings* in the very same room, he started to lose faith. He was freaking out. One night back at the hotel after another frustrating session, he suggested we take the tapes around to other mixing rooms in town to be sure the tracks we'd recorded at Rockfield were right and true.

One of them was Trident Studios in Soho, with its legendary, bespoke Trident "A" mixing console. Terrific-sounding LPs such as *Ziggy Stardust*, Elton John's first album (with "Your Song" on it), some of the Beatles' *White Album*, Zep's *The Song Remains the Same*, Genesis's *Nursery Cryme*, the Mahavishnu Orchestra's *Birds of Fire, The Yes Album* and countless others had either been recorded or mixed there. If *ours* sounded wrong in a room with such a pedigree, it had to be on us. Terry put up the tapes and *boom*, not only did it sound like the record we thought we'd made, but we could also clearly hear what tweaks would make it sound even better. I was flabbergasted and very fucking relieved—as was Terry, judging by the colour coming back to his face. I'm sure he'd been starting to doubt his ability to hear, but one listen in Trident and all was right with the world again. No one could explain what hadn't worked for *Hemispheres* at Advision, but one thing's for sure, we were lucky to have grabbed some rare and valuable time at Trident. Musicians, engineers and producers will argue noon and night over which consoles are superior—analog or digital or a hybrid of the two—Neve, API, SSL and so on—but the Trident was truly amongst the best. Most important, it clearly suited the sound we were after for *Hemispheres*. It had a sweeter tone; there seemed to be more air around everything, it was easier to place the various instruments along the spectrum, it coloured the sound in a pleasing way. The top end was sweet, while the mid-range was not overly aggressive and the bottom was smooth. In short, it was *musical*.

After all those months working in the UK, we threw an official playback party for ourselves and some pals, including some from Neil's days in the Carnaby Street souvenir shop. You know by now how much I hate final playbacks, but this time the record sounded awesome to me, different from anything we'd done to date. I felt we'd broken new ground, even if in the effort we had left some blood on the tracks. The intensity and the length of time we were away from home during those sessions took a chunk out of us, and in some ways we'd never be quite the same. We vowed never to set ourselves up for such misery again. We became determined to be better prepared, writing and even doing rough demos *before* setting out to record (even deciding what key the songs should be in!). *Hemispheres* taught us the importance of the word "*pre*-production," a touchstone for keeping ourselves sane, for instilling professionalism while maintaining a balance of work and family.

**WHILE WE'D BEEN** away absorbed by all things Rush, our families were starting to pay the price. Alex was all too familiar with the guilt and longing caused by being an absent father, while Neil had barely been home that year for his daughter Selena, who'd been born in April. They were both ahead of me in the kids department, though that would change soon enough; in the meantime, Nancy and I bought a second house, so that now we had one in town and one in the country. You could say that at twenty-four we were learning how to live the life of the *nouveaux riches*. In reality we were far from *riche*, as a Porsche was my only possession of value, and leased at that. Nonetheless, we were earning and starting to put away a bit of money while paying down *two* mortgages. Life was getting complicated, but we seemed to be handling it. Youthful ignorance sometimes works to one's advantage!

Before going back on the road to promote *Hemispheres*, the band went into rehearsals. That may sound too commonplace a thing to be worth mentioning, but having compared notes with many other musicians over the years, I'm convinced that *no one* ever rehearsed more than we did. Our show had to be tickety-boo or it simply wouldn't jibe. I've talked to other bands who rehearse two weeks and then they're off on tour. The only other exception I can think of was when my pal Josh Homme told me that the band he put together in 2016 for the Post-Pop Depression tour with Iggy Pop rehearsed for well over a month. (It showed. That band was note-perfect and incredibly tight.)

It's not like we enjoyed it. Well, Neil actually did; because he was such a perfectionist and suffered from a bit of stage fright, it settled his nerves knowing the songs inside out. But for Alex and me, rehearsing was dead boring. You play the same song over and over and over and over and over and over and over and over again, and sometimes you're just doing it for the one band member who needs it. Syncing up my sequencers could be a nightmare for everyone else, I'm sure, but Alex drove Neil and me the craziest as we waited for him to get his sounds together: whack the guitar, twiddle a knob, whack the guitar, twiddle a knob, WHACK the guitar, twiddle a knob . . . *Save me, someone!*

So, typically, we'd each rehearse on our own for two or three weeks until we knew our individual parts without having to think about them. Then we'd rehearse as a band on a soundstage for another month before several days of full dress rehearsals in our opening night's venue. To spare my voice, at that stage I'd still only sing the numbers where the guys depended on vocal cues. In later years, I started using a tele-prompter because our shows were so long that I would sometimes forget lyrics, and when we began using props and set changes, it was better for everyone, both band and crew, to know exactly where we were in a song. Meanwhile, all the snippets of film footage we'd been working on for months would invariably only be arriving in bits and bobs, sometimes not even in time for opening night. In the 2000s our show was jam-packed with rear-screen footage, and we were travelling with a full video crew, so we'd have to do dress rehearsals just to get those cues right too. Every song had its accompanying visuals, there was hardly a break from it, and when there was a break, live cameras projected us up behind; all that stuff had to be coordinated perfectly or you'd risk a train wreck.

For me, the toughest thing to prepare for a tour was the simultaneous performance of all the parts we'd recorded separately. It was relatively easy to play our early songs strictly as we'd recorded them, but our later rhythmical and lyrical complexities could be hell to play and sing at the same time. My rehearsal routine was to first learn my bass parts until I wasn't thinking about them anymore; only when I could play them by sheer muscle memory could I attempt to sing the song. That's yet another reason Neil and I bonded so well: he appreciated that I had to learn the kind of multi-dexterous independence a drummer does—and his was mind-blowing, with one hand playing one rhythm while the other hand was playing another and each foot was doing its own thing too. Every limb of your body is thinking as an individual, detached but in sync. When asked once to describe his job, he replied, "It's like running a marathon while doing math equations." Amen, Bubba! Looked at mathematically, the disparate beats might seem to have no business in the same bar, but Neil's genius was making them fit. And while it took brilliance to think those rhythms up, it was rigor, discipline and rehearsal (as well as rehearsal—oh yes, and also rehearsal) that pulled them off.

But muscle memory has its downside. After performing a song hundreds of times, a part of you gets bored and your mind starts to drift. I know it sounds impossible, but I could be in the middle of a song, working every limb on pedals, bass and keyboards, with pyro blasting and lasers swirling all around me and the audience going berserk, while my mind was somewhere else thinking about some other shit. One time in Las Vegas on our R30 tour—unconsciously triggered, no doubt, by the drying machines I'd set up behind me in the place of amp stacks—I found myself worrying in full flight of "Tom Sawyer" how we'd get my son Jules's laundry done before leaving town the next day. Another time in Brazil, during intermission, I'd been bidding at an online auction on a piece of baseball memorabilia and spent half of our second set upset that I hadn't bid enough . . . It's like you're driving a car and make a left-hand turn, then all of a sudden you're like, "Did I just make that turn? Did I even *signal?*" Losing yourself in a song is not *that* dangerous but performing half on autoplay will send the show right off the rails, so you start to invent rhythmical changes to the song, little stimuli, to keep yourself alert.

Speaking of baseball, our *Hemispheres* tour was also the time when my obsession with the game really took hold. I'd left sports behind for years, but reconnected in the late seventies, on tour for *A Farewell to Kings* and *Hemispheres*. Waking up way past noon, my daily ritual was to beg the nice lady from room service to send me up anything resembling breakfast, which I'd eat in front of the TV. It was the dawn of cable, the only things on at that time of day being soaps, infomercials, old movies, quiz shows and—courtesy of the two superstations, WGN Chicago and TBS Atlanta—baseball! I'd watch the Cubs or the Braves and, wouldn't ya know it about me, got so hooked that I made it a point on any day off, in whatever town we were, to go watch a game in the local ball yard; major or minor league, it became my great escape from the touring world, a hedge against boredom and a revelation to me. I was besotted. I became so deeply enthralled by the game—its history, its strategies and stats, its personalities—that the minute I got back to Toronto on a break I signed up for season tickets for the Blue Jays (they'd only entered the major league in 1977, so it was still easy to get good seats then), and after that there was no looking back.

Between October '78 and June '79 we trundled around the globe, playing around 135 gigs, many of them with the same opening bands as before, as well as the Pat Travers Band, Judas Priest, Golden Earring and April Wine. We played so many shows (on one stretch, twenty-three in twenty-four days, travelling overnight from one to the next),

*For any sports fan, getting to suit up with a major league team is the peak of excitement, and I'm lucky to have had several opportunities. I'm pictured here c. 1992 with Big John Ball—I mean Lerxst—ridin' the pine at Anaheim Stadium.*

that I'm sorry to say they're now a blur in the haze of whatever drugs or booze we consumed to get ourselves through.

We had little choice but to tour abroad constantly. It was so hard in those days for Canadian artists to enjoy cross-border recognition that many like Joni Mitchell, Neil Young, Leonard Cohen and the Band fully decamped to the USA. A few, like Gordon Lightfoot, April Wine, the Guess Who and Bachman-Turner Overdrive, were somehow able to score international hits while sticking resolutely to home, but without the benefit of Top 40 radio exposure we had to play countless gigs south of the border, opening for whoever we could, trying to build a fan base in the Midwest that we hoped would expand to the coasts by word of mouth.

Most of the other Canadian bands I can think of didn't have the will, the connections or the good fortune—not to mention Ray's dogged determination to keep us working in the States—to succeed that way. It's not that as a nation we lacked talent. Part of what's always limited so many Canadian acts is the harsh geographic reality: ours is a vast country with a proportionally tiny population, mostly in our six or seven cities huddled along the 49th Parallel. You could drive for days between them before you'd find a venue bigger than the local community hockey rink, while by contrast I was always amazed by the number of Americans who lived and worked in sprawling suburbs or smaller towns, filling out the in-betweens; there we'd play rural towns that were barely on the map but had 10,000-seat arenas. Musically speaking, that meant Canada was a nation of regional enterprise without the economic concentration *or* the flag-waving fervor to grow bigger.[*]

Before the seventies, Canadian media suffered from a small-country mentality: lacking cross-country awareness and a sense of national

---

[*]   Quebec has always been an exception—sort of. It has a kind of critical mass thanks to the unity of its culture and language, but while Harmonium, Diane Dufresne, Octobre, Robert Charlebois and Beau Dommage are local superstars, even they've never commanded a following outside the province.

pride, radio stations favoured music that was big *elsewhere*, taking notice of the scant few homegrown bands who'd won approval abroad but depriving others of the oxygen they needed to grow in the first place. To rescue Canadian artists from this vicious circle, our government decided it had to build a cultural wall between us and the States by imposing "Canadian Content" regulations on domestic radio and television operators: as of 1971, a minimum of 25 percent of all music played on our stations had to be Canadian Content, or CanCon for short, as defined under the MAPL system (pronounced "maple," get it?). The acronym stood for four criteria of Canadianness, at least two of which you had to meet in order to qualify.

M—is the music written by a Canadian?
A—is the artist Canadian?
P—is the performance recorded or performed live in Canada?
L—are the lyrics written by a Canadian?

It was a way of breaking the chokehold American media had on us, legally defining what constituted a Canadian artist and then mandating radio stations to play us more often. Yay! By qualifying in all four categories we now knew we really *were* Canadian! But before you go all *NME* on me and say how ironic it is that we three Ayn Rand–style laissez-faire capitalists welcomed nanny-state intervention, may I remind you that it was the *American* station WMMS that gave us our first real leg up. And only as our success rose abroad were Canadian stations suddenly less reluctant to give us a spin, which *then* helped us find a wider audience in our home and native land.

# CHAPTER 16

IN 1979 WE TOURED CONTINENTAL EUROPE for the first time. We were slated to kick off in Paris, but the gig was cancelled due to a fire in the venue, so now our first show was Poperingen in the Flemish part of Belgium, a bizarre contrast with the multiple sold-out shows we'd enjoyed in cities all over the UK. The tiny venue backed onto a farmer's field, so that when you slid open the doors to the dressing room you got cattle, fences and farmhouses, and you could take a leak right out onto the pasture. Human attendance, meanwhile, must have been under a thousand people, a large portion of which were grizzly bikers who looked every bit as intimidating as in North America. After the show, Herns came to the door and told us a couple of them wanted to come in the dressing room. We were in the midst of changing back into our civvies but didn't want a fuss, so I said, "Sure. Let them in . . . I guess."

The room fell quiet as three gnarly looking dudes clomped in. They strode up to us and said, "Rush?"

"Yes?" we answered warily.

"Excuse us, Rush. Ve just vanted to say . . . that ve are big fans of you, and can ve get your signature, please?"

Whew!

On the way to a hotel in Lille, we passed monuments and memorials to the fallen heroes of both world wars, at Ypres and Flanders Fields and elsewhere, all familiar from our history books. On those memorials, by roadsides, town squares and churches, were listed the names of the citizens who'd lost their lives, and I realized that we were driving over the very battlefields where those men had fallen. It was an eerie feeling that stalked me as we moved across Europe. I related that to Neil, who one day turned it into a lyric about regional chauvinism in "Territories":

*We see so many tribes—overrun and undermined*
*While their invaders dream of lands they've left behind*
*Better people—better food—and better beer*
*Why move around the world when Eden was so near?*

With three days' rest before our next gig, in Oslo, Norway, I scooted off with a couple of my pals for our first-ever visit to Paris, hoovering up as many of the classic destinations as possible, devouring frites and guzzling high-octane beers in cafés. Late into our final night there we realized that, aside from a single credit card, we had no money, barely a sous, but scraped together just enough francs and centimes to buy a farewell *demi bière à la pression* before heading to the airport. Why were we so broke? Well, we had decided that before leaving we simply had to buy three berets, three red scarves and three blue-and-white striped shirts to wear on the plane, so that we could arrive in Norway as *les trois vieux gars de Paris*!

After Oslo, we played Gothenburg, and then Stockholm. I love, love, love being a stranger in a strange land, in a timeworn foreign city, my brain trying to make sense of the language, my senses alive to everything around me, to the feeling that generations have been pounding the pavement beneath my feet before me. By comparison, everything in North America seems so . . . unfinished. I'm powerfully drawn to old things—buildings, photographs, baseballs, even old bass guitars—that for me become windows onto the past with stories to tell. Exploring Europe was making me hungrier to see the world than I had ever been before. I had the bug, all right—big time—but our next stop, Germany, was instilling no small amount of trepidation in me. After all, while

*Zut alors: our assistant Sam Charters, me and Max Webster's drummer, Gary "Stixy" McCracken. On a sad note (why does there always have to be a fucking sad note), a few years later Sam succumbed to the many injuries he sustained from an accident in Toronto. A bright light extinguished in his prime. Mais au fin du jour, mon ami, we will always have Paris.*

I was having a fine adventure, making fresh discoveries, I could not forget that my family was originally from the same continent under very different circumstances—ultimately abducted, decimated and given little option but to *escape* it. And by the time we arrived in Nuremberg, I was rattled to my core.

Still haunted by the hellish stories of my parents' Holocaust experiences, I reflexively thought of Deutschland as the epicenter of evil. When I walked through the bullet-riddled façade of the Grand Hotel in Nuremberg, infamous for figuring prominently in the birth of Nazism, I got chills. I checked into my room, and though it was now a refurbished modern suite like so many others I had stayed in over the years, I could not bring myself to remove my jacket. With a litany of stories from my mother's lips crowding out my brain, I couldn't shake the feeling that during the rise of the worst fascist regime the world has seen, the German High Command might have stayed in that very room! And not just that. I was also painfully aware that this hotel was just up the street from the infamous Palace of Justice where in 1945 the Nazis who'd murdered so many members of my family and destroyed the lives of countless others had most certainly been put on trial. No wonder I was seeing ghosts. Further feeding my wartime hallucinations, when I switched the radio on, I found it tuned to, of all things, the American Armed Forces Radio Network. Thankfully, they were talking about baseball, and the room began to warm as I returned to my senses.

Still, I had to get out. I went for a walk, observing and eavesdropping on people from every walk of life going about their regular day. I bought a frankfurter and sat listening to German being spoken—and was shocked to find, due to its similarity with Yiddish, how much I could understand. And every time I saw someone old, I could not help but ask myself, "What was *he* doing during the war? Where was *she?*" (Geddy Lee, Nazi Hunter? Nah, better stick to my day job.)

The end of that tour was a limp to the finish line—literally. The morning after the show in Hamburg, the plan was to drive promptly to

Mannheim, but Alex injured his finger in his hotel room (during what I must assume was some sort of Serbian mating ritual with Charlene) and had to go to the hospital, where they drilled a hole in his fingernail to relieve the swelling. He then insisted on taking the wheel out on the Autobahn, which as you probably know has no speed limit. Pedal to the metal, he lost control as he noticed too late that he was about to fly past the *Ausgang*—and badly rammed a road sign. The police arrived but spoke no English, while he spoke no German, requiring them to wait two hours for a translator. And then, when he finally caught up with us in Mannheim, he was in too much pain to play, so we cancelled the gig at the last moment, and the following two as well.

We hung out in Zurich for a couple of days as he recovered, and did manage to make it to Holland's Pinkpop, the world's longest-running annual pop and rock festival, with a star-studded lineup including Dire Straits, Elvis Costello, Peter Tosh and, right before us on one of the festival's three stages, the Police. They were riding high with "Roxanne" that summer, and everywhere you went their catchy, reggae-fied melodies put a bounce in your step. Darlings of the press corps, they mugged and cavorted for the paparazzi at every opportunity, and after their set dove straight into a swimming pool that was backstage (only time I've seen that) with all their clothes on—Sting in his effin' jumpsuit. Also back there was a low wall, the other side of which was a concrete staircase leading to the exit. After soundcheck my keyboard tech, Jack Secret, quite possibly under the influence of the demon weed, hopped over it and fell twenty-five feet through the air as Jan Smeets the promoter shouted, "His feets! He's broken his feets!" Howling in pain, Jack was carried by Lurch across the field to a medical tent, whence he was taken to another hospital, but insisted on being brought back straightaway so he could program the keyboards at the side of the stage, even while prone and in plaster. He spent the rest of the summer recovering on his mom's sofa, but man, *what a trooper.*

AFTER THE TOUR, our batteries sorely needed recharging, so we decided to take a six-week break—the first of that length since Neil had joined the band. Then, in midsummer, we moved into a house on Lakewoods Farm in Flesherton, Ontario, hoping to replicate the kind of isolated rural work environment we'd enjoyed in Wales—the bonus being that it was just a two-hour drive away, so we could slip out for the weekends and see our families.

We set up our gear in the basement and hunkered down to write. Our approach to *Permanent Waves* would be a total reaction to *Hemispheres*. Instead of composing side-long interconnecting pieces, we wanted to create songs no more than five to seven minutes long. We were still after big ideas and complexity but thought we'd lend them more flexibility if we freed them from a strict overarching narrative: a small-c concept album this time, loosely tied together by a broad theme. We were determined to approach this album with "crisp professional dispatch,"[*] and as it turned out, everything about making *Permanent Waves* was shockingly painless. We bust out quickly, the ideas flowed and in no time we'd written "The Spirit of Radio."

This was a time when new wave or "alternative rock" was trending on radio across North America, and one particular station just outside Toronto was making its mark with a looser format that, as Neil told the CBC, he found inspiring:

> *I remember coming home very late and as I was cresting the escarpment with all of the lights below of Hamilton and the Niagara Peninsula, where I lived at the time, CFNY Radio was on the air with a fantastic combination of music . . . CFNY's motto was "the spirit of radio." The song itself, musically, is switching between radio stations, with a reggae section at the end, the second verse is new wave, I'm playing like a punk drummer there, and that was all intentional.*

---

[*]  A phrase that has stuck with me ever since I read it in our first *New York Times* concert review. The piece wasn't all that complimentary, but I liked *that* bit.

With a bunch of songs tuned up and fingers in good form, we were primed to start recording at Le Studio in Morin-Heights, deep in ski country an hour north of Montreal and overlooking the Laurentian foothills. It didn't take us long to fall in love with the place—so much so that we'd record or mix the next five, and parts of eight, albums there. It was just five hours from our homes, meaning we could drive there with ease and Broon could bring along his cocker spaniel—our mascot, Daisy or "Ski Bane," the nickname she'd earn for her knack of being unfailingly underfoot whenever Neil and Alex went cross-country skiing.

You feel the province's French influence even before you get to Quebec, as soon as you've passed Kingston on Highway 401 and start seeing vans advertising the classic Quebecois delicacy, *frites avec poutine.** Then you cross the border, and everywhere there are houses with colourful sloping metal roofs (to help the massive snowfalls melt and slide off) and, instead of convenience stores, *dépanneurs*. You approach the teeny village of Morin-Heights and zoom past the local watering hole, the Commons Hotel, where David Bowie, the Bee Gees, Chicago, Bryan Adams, Sting, the Cult, Keith Richards, Rupert Hine, our own Jack Secret and more have been known to quaff a few, play a game of pool or jam with local bands after their sessions up the road.

Most days, sunlight streamed through the studio's floor-to-ceiling windows facing onto the lake, a welcome change from the bunker atmosphere of most recording studios. Most important, the control room featured a Trident A-Range console, which provided the sound we knew and trusted from our time at Trident in London. Making *Permanent Waves* with the Trident from start to finish would give us a continuity of sound—the first time that had happened since our Toronto Sound days. Like at Rockfield, Le Studio's isolated location allowed us to record outdoors, with the added bonus of being able to

---

* Since you ask: poutine consists of a type of cheese curd favoured by the residents of *la Belle Province*, plopped on top of their fries and half melted in a glop of hot brown gravy. Not my cup of tea but the ultimate hangover food.

bounce an amplified guitar across the lake and off the foothills for some truly natural echo; and we were able to create our own tidal pool sound effect for "Natural Science" by recording Neil and Alex gently paddling on the lake.

On the far side of the water sat a four-bedroom guesthouse and a one-room cottage where we lived for the next few weeks, feasting on meals prepared by a celebrated local chef, André-Paul Moreau. We'd also eat at his restaurant, La Bouffe en Broche in Saint Sauveur-des-Monts, a ski town a twenty-minute drive away whose streets were lined with French restaurants, making the place just as busy or busier in the summer as it was in the winter. I was by no means a foodie back then, but in many ways, this is where my interest in food and wine took flight. Every day in the chalet, André would pick a Beaujolais for us, usually a Brouilly, which I knew nothing about other than it was fruity and enjoyable, but the idea of having wine with dinner on a daily basis appealed to me. It felt so *civilized*. My keyboard tech, Jack Secret, meanwhile, was a teetotal cannabis man who preferred Coca-Cola, so Chef André would fill his wineglass to the brim with Coke and announce with a glint in his eye, "Voilà, Jacques, le Beaujolais *Américain!*"

While writing this book I've made it a point to listen to every single thing I've recorded in the last fifty years and make a note of my feelings, however good, bad, indifferent or painful. For want of space (and your tolerance), I can't talk about every album we released (thirty-eight including our solo records)—but right here I'd like to stop and reflect on one song in particular, "Freewill," that over the years has sparked some controversy. I've played it in concert hundreds of times since its release in 1980, and although I always sang it with everything I had, back in the day I may have taken its impact a little for granted.

I accept that every music lover is going to interpret songs their own way; that's just the unwritten contract between writer and fan, it's all in the game. Sometimes the two align, and sometimes not. But over time, every artist also has the right to change the way they originally felt about their own creation. Call it a mark of personal growth. With that in mind, here are a few words about the law of unexpected consequences.

When I was young I ran away from the obligations of the religious household in which I was raised. I felt like I was exercising my free will, but because I was headstrong I didn't fully understand the implications of my actions. In those days I would grab on to whatever ideas supported my aspirations, both personally and as a professional musician. I was trying to forge my own identity. Then, as the band fought to resist the corporate pressure to commercialize, I needed even more backbone and found strength in the Ayn Rand books Neil introduced me to—in particular the artistic manifesto evidenced in *The Fountainhead* and, to a lesser extent, "The Virtue of Selfishness."

In 1979, when he handed me the lyrics for "Freewill," I instantly loved the song. It was a powerful expression of the way Rush was taking control of its own destiny, and also echoed my own refusal of religious dogma, of subjection to the hand of God or, more abstractly, fate. Even if some of Neil's concepts were a bit of a stretch for me, I sang it every night with confidence and pride, offering it to our audiences as a contribution to the time-honoured discussion about existentialism, determinism and faith. It was, in fact, indeterminism that I believe was at the heart of it—the idea that our lives are *not* predetermined—and I hoped that would come across; but in the four decades since, I've seen people play fast and loose with the interpretation of the last lines of the chorus:

*I will choose a path that's clear*
*I will choose free will*

To my dismay, those words have been cited without regard for the song's overall message and used as a catch-all, a licence for some to do whatever they want. It makes me want to scream. Taken out of context, it becomes an oversimplified idea of free will, narrow and naïve, not taking into consideration that even the strongest individual must,

(TOP, LEFT, BELOW LEFT) *Men at work. What a breath of fresh air to have daylight streaming in as opposed to working in a bunker—the reality of 99 percent of studios. I wish I could remember what song we were writing here . . .* (BELOW) *Lyrics for "Entre Nous" and "Natural Science" waiting to be sung.*

to some extent, bow to the needs of a responsible society. Too often it's seized upon as a reckless substitute for common sense.

During the Covid pandemic, I saw this first-hand. When I posted a picture on Instagram of myself wearing a mask, loudmouths were quick to throw "Free will!" back at me, as if those two words alone constitute permission to act without regard for the well-being of others, to ignore science and to rid ourselves of responsibility for the consequences of our actions. To me, it was stupidity taking shelter in poorly thought-through ideology, holding on to the lyric as if it meant "I can be as selfish as I fucking want to be." Well, folks, from where I sit, it ain't that simple. I've read the book *and* the fine print. Life is not so black and white; we live in its grey areas.

I'm afraid that life is too complicated for us to simply "choose free will." You can't just say or do anything, prizing your rights over everyone else's. Generations of scholars (notably the Talmudic ones) have spent their lives arguing in byzantine detail the interpretation of society's rules, because it all depends on *context*: when, exactly, will I choose free will? Over the health of my kids or the happiness of my wife? Over the responsibility not to pass a disease on to my fellow citizens? A caring, functional society needs constraints and responsibilities. Terms and conditions apply.

A vague grasp of complicated ideas is not the same as virtuous independence. Existentialism has been interpreted by some as a licence to behave without regard for societal consequences, but unless I'm mistaken, that's not what the big thinkers like Jean-Paul Sartre or Paul Rée meant; their understanding of free will incorporated a measure of moral responsibility.

I may sound like I'm a grumpy old man yelling at clouds or that I've drunk the Kool-Aid of a quasi-socialist country, but my point of view has evolved with experience as I've watched and cared about what life has thrown at friends, neighbours and strangers alike. We have a social safety net here in Canada that includes national healthcare, daycare and so on—it isn't perfect, but it works pretty well most of the time, especially for those on the lower rungs of the socioeconomic ladder. Living in that kind of society for almost (ahem) seventy years has made me see the world through more compassionate eyes than I had as a youth or in 1979. Sure, we pay more taxes than many others do, but I prefer to live in a world that gives a shit, even for people I don't know. Okay, now I'll get off my soapbox.

*These track sheets exist but the master multi-track tapes they pertain to have completely disappeared, which means* Permanent Waves *can never be remixed. Nor could the original keyboard sounds ever be accessed for live performance purposes.*

*PERMANENT WAVES* WASN'T the only record I worked on at Le Studio that year. I was asked to take the helm on a new album by Wireless and said yes, since I thought the guys were great players and had wanted for a while to try my hand at producing. In December I booked the sixteen-track Good Noise suite on Le Studio's grounds, with winter in full force, the snow shin-deep and the air so cold you could crack it over your knee. I once again packed my bags, said good-bye to Nancy and drove back to Morin-Heights.

Sitting in the big chair was more of an adjustment than I'd expected. It's one thing to sit beside the producer spewing forth ideas about your own music and asking *him* to make it all happen, and quite another to realize other peoples' ideas as the decider-in-chief. The gig requires a good ear, of course, but also a high degree of resourcefulness and imagination, plus a level of objectivity and tact that I had taken for granted in Broon. I would soon learn that a degree in psychology can also be helpful. Above all, if at the end of the day the chips fall just right and you've helped them make a great album, their lives may be changed for the better—but make a stinker, you might be blamed for it but you get to move on and work on something new, while the band pays the true price.

Steve McMurray and Allan Marshall were Aussies who'd moved to Canada via England in 1975 and formed Wireless with Mike Crawford and the ex-Goddo drummer Marty Morin.* I found their twin-guitar sound driving and inventive, all four were excellent musicians and I especially loved Allan's soulful voice and bass playing. They were pros, eager, good-natured and willing to do what it took. We bonded quickly and I had high hopes for the production.

It was a low-budget project, but we got a lot done working crazy hours. Thing is, I didn't yet have a ton of confidence as a producer, and

---

* Steve was a sweetheart. After he passed away recently, of cancer, a mutual friend wrote to me: "He'd beaten it twice, but the radiation couldn't help him. He asked about you and laughed at memories of calling you 'Dirk Yachtfoot,' because you (and your baby son) had such big feet."

after a while the decisiveness that the job required, the pressure of responsibility, the moods and the deadlines were stressing me out. Studio life can be intense. It demands microscopic attention, and nerves can sometimes fray. Musicians swing back and forth from elation to boredom, from confidence to insecurity: they wait for their turn to bare their souls on tape and then listen back, overly scrutinizing every note and beat; working such long hours it's almost impossible to retain a shred of objectivity.

There's usually one guy whose ego needs feeding more than the others', and who constantly tries to wrest control. (Oh, shit. That sounds like *me*.) I remember one time when I was mixing a track for another band, which shall remain nameless, the leader challenged my decision to push the guitar—which *I* felt was the most compelling part of the track—louder in the mix. I made my case, but then the guitarist himself came over and said, "Ged, can you pull back the guitar volume? It's obscuring . . . you know . . ." He glanced over at the leader. "*Him*."

*Mike doing a take while I hold down the E-string to keep it from rattling (what you call a "hands-on" producer).*

That blew my mind. It was like he was under a kind of spell. I said, "Yeah, but it's the guitar that really makes the song!"

He replied (and I quote), "Well, you know, the leader is like the flower, and we are like the weeds. The weeds have to be trimmed back so that the flower can be seen clearly."

"That's a really interesting analogy," I said, "but I just don't see you as a weed and we're definitely going to have *more guitar on this track*."

Wireless, meanwhile, had their shit together—great guys, no real ego trips—but they did *not* back down from whatever they felt strongly about. That was fine by me; I wasn't there to bully them into any particular direction, just to capture them on tape at their best. But it did become wearying. As a member of Rush, I could sit for hours polishing every turd and pushing, pushing, pushing for perfection, but as a studio rat for others, I simply did not have the patience.

Managing all that stuff is the most difficult part of the producer's gig, and is one of the reasons I eventually gave up on that particular dream. It demands so many hours in the chair and so much diplomacy that I never got enough joy out of it. I only have the stick-to-it-ness for my *own* shit.*

**ONE DAY AT** Le Studio, I got a phone call that pulled my brain even further away from the work at hand. Nancy announced she was coming to Morin-Heights. I explained that I was working around the clock, but she didn't care. She wanted to see me that weekend. I thought, *Hmm* . . . We'd been together a lot that summer, so maybe now that I was back at work, she didn't like the separation? I wasn't sure *what* was up. When she arrived, I took an hour's break, and even as I helped her settle into my room, it all came pouring out: she was *pregnant* and scared stiff. It wasn't just the worry about bringing a

---

* We completed *No Static* in the allotted time, and I was pleased with the result. It wasn't a great commercial success, but IMHO it remains a fine and underrated record with some wonderful guitar work and a nice hard-rockin' edge.

human into the world and nurturing it, but having to do it pretty much alone. I tried to be optimistic and reassuring, promising of course that I'd support her every way I could, but you know: that was easy for *me* to say. I was over the moon, but it wasn't *my* body about to go through hell and back. As a touring musician, I could promise the world, but we both knew it was she who'd have to physically raise the child, and in the meantime, what would happen to her plans for a career in fashion? How could she possibly cope with both? And as I sat there uselessly, she just broke down.

In our life together, Nancy has *always* been the one to sacrifice her freedoms for the sake of our children, our home life and my work—even though, at only twenty-six then, she instinctively understood that the road ahead would be toughest for her. This is just one area where so many rock and roll marriages fail. It's an unpleasant fact that few musicians, myself included, are prepared to give up their gig to raise a family. We'll rationalize that we're earning and supporting and so on, and many of us will do our damnedest to pitch in, but for all our best intentions it's our wives and kids who bear the brunt while we get on with our glamorous lives.[*]

Nancy basically cried for two nights. She knew that regardless of what I said, work would always call me and I would always respond. She would never ask me to do anything other, so this new chapter of our lives was something that she would have to shoulder largely on her own, and indeed, as she left with all that weighing on her mind, I went back to work.

**NO SOONER HAD** I reassured her that I'd be there for her than I had to pack up my good intentions and leave her again, this time for the *Permanent Waves* tour. Of course I was worried about her and

---

[*] I believe that it's even harder for producers and engineers to make their marriages work. They're at the mercy of the record they're making and rarely in a position to dictate their own hours. Even if they live near the studio, they're home yet never home.

ecstatic about being a father, but the new record was greeted with such a terrific response that I was caught up in the throes of a rising rock band hitting its stride. I was obsessed with work and however much I told myself (or more important, Nancy) that I wanted to help, I wasn't willing to slow my schedule down. Record and ticket sales were solid and "The Spirit of Radio" was doing reasonably well as (of all things) a *single*, making a radio splash of sorts in Chicago and elsewhere in the Midwest, as well as in the UK.* Our relentless schedule would see us play around 120 more shows before my kid would come into the world.

Soon I was abroad in June on a terrific UK tour, with a milestone five consecutive nights at the Hammersmith Odeon in London, but my mind was elsewhere expecting a long-distance call at any moment, braced for disaster (we Jews are *really* good at that) and feeling worse that I was still away on June 20, our fourth wedding anniversary. I was racked with guilt (oh *yeah*, we're really good at that, too) and couldn't wait to get home.

I finally made it home to my gorgeous, extremely ripe missus. But as we hunkered down, it was soon clear the baby would be late—two weeks overdue, in fact, so that we only checked into Mount Sinai on July 21, when at last they induced labour. Birthing babies was still a pretty formal matter in Toronto back then. Nancy's bestie Karen and my old pal Oscar were restricted to the waiting room, while I was given a surgical gown and mask and accompanied Nancy into an actual operating theatre, where I stood beside her assuring her it would be fine, rubbing her head so nervously to "relax" her and "helping" her breathe to the point that she told me to lay off or she'd have no hair left. Man, they should have given *me* an epidural. I darted out from time to time

---

* It was shorter than most of our songs but at five minutes still not your typical single; even with a radio edit it wouldn't approach the three-minute mark expected of pop songs and could never be a true Top 40 hit. But it brought new fans out to see us and excited the ones we already had, which was good enough for us.

to give updates to our friends and although Oscar had smuggled in a case of Carling Black Label, I was too nervous to even drink.

I watched as the doctors did their thing, and at two in the morning on July 22, 1980, Julian Michel Weinrib came into our lives.* I was choked up just looking at him, but when I asked Nancy if she wanted to hold the baby, she said, "Hell, no. I've got the rest of my life for that. *You* hold him, I need a smoke!" After they took little Jules to the nursery and Nancy to her room for some well-earned sleep, I went home to the Beaches with Oscar and Karen and sat in the backyard with them drinking champagne in the rain, only passing out as the sun came up. Almost immediately, the phone rang with Nancy on the other end. "Geddy!" she wailed. "They brought me the baby, but I don't know what to *do*! Please come over now and help me!" Still in a boozy stupor, I literally threw myself onto the shower floor and turned on the cold water, then pulled on the same clothes I'd worn all night and drove like

(LEFT) *Yabba dabba doo!* (RIGHT) *"Dad? Are you chewing a canoe?"*

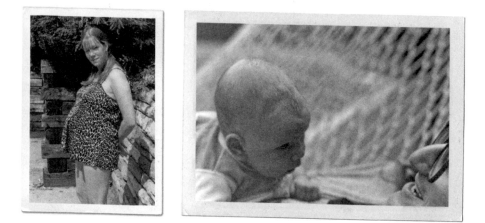

---

\* In keeping with tradition, we gave him the middle name Michel (in Yiddish, "Moishe") to honour my father.

a mad fool to the hospital, parked wherever, ran up the stairs and dashed into her room.

"What?" I said, breathless, sweating bullets. "What's *wrong?*"

With Jules in her arms and a blissful smile on her face she said in her gentlest voice, "Isn't he adorable?"

To quote the immortal Troggs, "Fuck me, Reg!"

AS IT SURELY is for every newbie parent, having Jules at home was a huge adjustment. He wasn't a good sleeper to begin with, plus he was colicky and for some reason hadn't come with an instruction manual. Neither Nancy nor I had ever been exactly early birds, but that had to change PDQ, and it was especially tough for Nancy, who is the Queen of Sleep. Throw in a dose of post-partum depression and you can imagine what she was up against. We hired a nurse to help, but found her untrustworthy and had to let her go. It was a great relief when Nancy's younger sister Barbara moved in with us to help out, but guilt weighed on me once again when I *had* to rejoin the boys for some writing and recording. I say "had to" because the band rules. Right?

Like Big Brother or the monolith in *2001: A Space Odyssey*, "the Band" is ever present. It gives a musician an indisputable reason to run off, regardless of the chaos he may be leaving behind. It is ubiquitous, inexorable and constant. It demands precedence over everything, silently running (and occasionally ruining) your life. Of course, it's of your own making, but it is more convenient to think of the band as an entity separate from yourself. Children, wives, friends and family are left with little choice but to accept being collateral damage of the Band's schedules, obligations and ambitions. It is never your fault. It is the Band's.

Since I was seventeen it had been my life's priority. That had to change somewhat now, but realistically, could it? As the last member of Rush to become a parent, I was also the last to experience the guilt of leaving the family behind and to cope with the tension and messiness that came up every time we had to split. Nancy was for the most part understanding and accommodating, genuinely wanting me to be happy, but she could not entirely hide a measure of resentment, nor not begrudge the lack of sovereignty over her own life. We tried to see each other's point of view, but before we could ever reach a mutually satisfying solution, I'd be waltzing out the door. How many musicians in history have had that same unfinished conversation, the one that ends with "Sorry, baby, I gotta go. The guys are waiting." It wasn't fair but it was what it was. The Band was the excuse and it always won out. But it was a ticking time bomb.

*New Year's Eve 1980. Nancy in her Geddy Lee disguise. (I didn't need one.)*

# CHAPTER 17

**M**OVING PICTURES **WAS THE ALBUM THAT** almost wasn't. We were scheduled to do a live album after *Permanent Waves*, but Cliff Burnstein sat us down in New York and suggested we rethink the plan, arguing that with *Permanent Waves*, from both a writing and playing perspective, we were really getting into gear. It would be a shame, he said, if we didn't go straight back into the studio to record more new songs; we could produce another live album anytime. Psyched by his vote of confidence, it didn't take us too long to realize that he was right. Seizing the chance to write again rather than trundle along playing gig after gig made us feel more in control of our destiny. We spoke to Broon and booked ourselves back into Le Studio for late fall.

So there we were at a farm that belonged to the great expat American rock and roller "Rompin'" Ronnie Hawkins, feeling our oats and writing songs in short order: "Tom Sawyer," "Red Barchetta" and "Limelight" came first, and when for some reason Alex wasn't around one day, Neil and I found ourselves writing the skeletal structure for "YYZ"; I had just come up with the main riff, which he started jamming to, and before we knew it the number had come alive. When Alex joined us, he had a bit of a time learning it because it's really a bass riff and much harder to play on guitar (to play that *digga-digga-digga-dee-dee* with a pick in your hand, you have to double-stroke, whereas a bass player just moves his fingers back and forth) but he got into it, and when he started adding his solo parts, my god, they were brilliant.

In "Limelight," Neil was writing about his own increasing awkwardness with fame; then he drew inspiration from a short story in *Road & Track* magazine by Richard S. Foster, "A Fine Morning Drive," folded in his own love of cars and penned the cautionary tale "Red Barchetta"; the prose style of John Dos Passos heavily influenced his own POV in "The Camera Eye" and a collaboration with Max Webster's wordsmith Pye Dubois helped him create a wide-eyed tale about existential possibilities called "Tom Sawyer." Pye had sent Neil a poem of his called "Louie the Warrior," which he'd refined for our musical purposes while retaining much of its structure and imagery.

By and large the sessions went well, but we had set the bar pretty high for this album and struggled with certain sounds. Almost *everything* to do with "Tom Sawyer" was a struggle. For starters, the great sound we had come to rely on from my Rickenbacker just wasn't right for the song. We tried different compressors, every kind of balance, EQ and amp setting, but to no avail. Out of desperation, I plugged in my seldom-used Fender Jazz and *bingo*! But then, when Alex tried recording his solo, we just couldn't get it to jive with the aggressive fast-paced middle section. He was getting frustrated, until our engineer Paul Northfield came up with a weird idea: "Let's send the amped

(RIGHT AND BELOW) *Talking about "Limelight" reminds me of some sketches Neil drew at Le Studio around this period, humourous projections of how the three of us would surely end up in our dotage. There's a strong connection between what he says in the lyrics and how he imagines himself down the line. Meanwhile, Alex as the gregarious, well-fed proprietor of Chez Lerxst makes sense, but me as a grumpy old baseball fan? Outrageous!*

(LEFT) *Pye Dubois, seen here with his bon vivant smile and my original copy of "Louie the Warrior." This was the second time Neil collaborated with an outside lyricist (the first being with Peter Talbot on "Closer to the Heart").*

guitar sound to a pair of stereo speakers with a set of stereo mics to record it," he said, allowing the instrument to be loud without smearing the bass and drums—as if to put some air around the solo. And it worked brilliantly. Still, there were other issues and the song continued to dog me. I became so negative about it that at one point I asked myself if we should leave it off the record entirely. Can you *imagine?* Rush's all-time favourite song in the can? Doh!

We'd begun the *Moving Pictures* sessions in the fall, and by the time we were rounding third, we were deep into winter. One of the things that sustained us over the months was volleyball, an obsession that had begun during the making of *Permanent Waves*, playing out on the lawn whenever we could, sometimes late into the night after work, fueled by shots of vodka and snorts of schnah (say that five times real fast). We'd even play during the effin' winter, when the kindly studio folks would shovel away the snow and set up lights for us. The only problem was that sometimes we'd get so carried away, we'd stop feeling the cold and our fingers would become stiff and swollen from punching the ball into the starry sky—not exactly conducive to recording. Still, what a release!

Working to a script, we approached each song as if it was, indeed, a cinematic "moving picture." To set the scene for "Witch Hunt," a story

about fear, prejudice and vigilantism, we wanted voices of an angry mob, so we set a couple of mics up outdoors and everyone—crew, band, studio staff—dressed up warmly and gathered around grumbling and shouting, building take upon take until we got what we needed. During the recording, certain inside jokes (and inappropriate comments) found their way into the melee. Among the many *harrumphs*, there was even an "I didn't get a harrumph outta you" from *Blazing Saddles* and, if you listen closely, you can hear Neil yelling something we used to say on the volleyball court if ever someone kicked the ball: "It's not a fuckin' football!" It really does sound like a noisy, sweaty, torch-wielding bunch of rednecks, but in reality, it was a bunch of hosers with scarfs on, freezing their nuts off late on a Canadian night in November.

*MOVING PICTURES* WAS released on February 12, 1981. There was a good buzz and it charted very high, making #1 in Canada and #3 on both the US and UK charts. That resulted in more airplay on classic rock stations and, with "Limelight" and "Tom Sawyer," even some crossover to Top 40 radio. That was nothing to sneeze at, but nor was it a life-changer for us. Outwardly, the tour felt pretty much the same as the previous one; crowds were healthy and boisterous, with additional shows being added in some cities, yet as the tour progressed, things were in fact changing. More demands were being made on our time, more visits to radio stations and more print interview requests. More VIP-type people (or people who thought they were VIPs) who'd never before have admitted they were interested in us but were now showing up at our gigs to check out the fuss. Even management personnel were coming to our gigs! In our early days Vic would come out to see us fairly often—he'd "discovered" Neil, and we could relate to him because he was also a musician*—but Ray usually appeared only at

* Our nickname for him was "Va*Va*Va," like the sound a sax makes.

When our mixing session ground to a halt due to a technical issue, we used the time to shoot videos for three songs from Moving Pictures: "Tom Sawyer," "Vital Signs" and "Limelight." (Like most musicians, Alex plays better when he's being paid—even in Canadian dollars.)

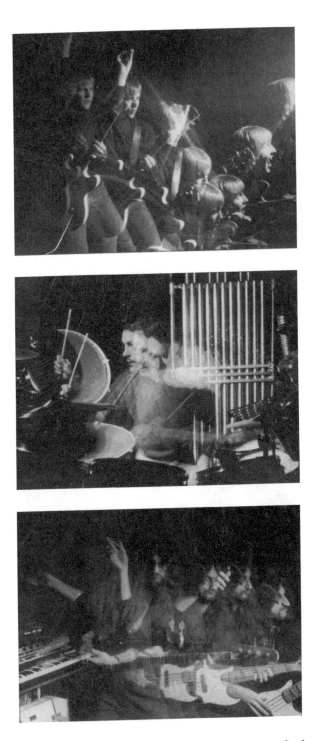

*Early in those sessions, Deborah Samuels and Hugh Syme came to Quebec to shoot photos for the back of the album cover. They were shocked to find I'd grown a beard, and after doing these test Polaroids, they (being Canadians) politely asked me to shave.*

the big gigs or if there was an important meeting. Even after they went their separate ways and Ray became the sole owner of SRO, I don't recall ever having seen him in Davenport, Iowa, or Springfield, Massachusetts. But now he was a fairly regular visitor.

We were flattered to some degree but wary too. Suddenly *everybody* had an effin' opinion about what we should do and how we should be doing it. We kept on keeping on, intent on making our own decisions and our own mistakes, but had to work harder to keep our focus on relentlessly improving the music and the performances. In our liner notes for *Exit . . . Stage Left* Neil would soon write an apology to our fans and friends for not being as available to them as we had in the past, concluding with "After all, we didn't change, everybody else did!"

(RIGHT) *For pretend VIPs.*
(ABOVE) *Parents!* (Actual *VIPS.)*

AFTER THE EUROPEAN leg of the *Moving Pictures* tour, we took a week off, agreeing to meet back in Florida for a November gig at the Hollywood Sportatorium. Pretty odd name for an arena, no? Like an archaeological relic from Roman times: "It's next to the gladiator school, right past the Vomitorium." It was an even odder-*looking* venue, surrounded by a prison-like wall and located at the end of one long and lonely road, making traffic in and out murder at the best of times. Neil had taken his family to soak up some sun in St. Thomas in the Caribbean and was due to fly in the day of the show, but his plane was unexpectedly cancelled. When the venue management learned there was a chance of him not making the gig, they refused to open the doors to the fans lest there be a riot. (The opening act, coincidentally, was Quiet Riot.) Well, that didn't work out too well.

With traffic backed up for miles, rumours were quickly spreading that the show was in doubt, but Alex and I were already at the venue and had decided to do a soundcheck without Neil. When the people outside heard the noise, they feared the show was kicking off without them. They panicked and tried to climb the perimeter wall. Police and venue security overreacted and started tear-gassing fans, and chaos ensued. News helicopters flew overhead as the concertgoers returned fire with rocks and bottles, and eleven officers were injured. It was like a scene out of an effin' action movie! Fortunately, Neil was able to charter a private plane, and once he was in the air with an ETA, the venue felt that although we'd be starting late, it was okay to let the crowd into the house after all. Calm was somewhat restored, but to say the crowd was wild that night is an understatement.

It's important to reiterate that the violence that day had only to do with the panic of fans who felt that they were going to miss the show, and that once they realized they *weren't* going to miss the show, they chilled out. Hence the big pressure at every soundcheck, especially when there are technical problems, to open the doors on time. After that terrible tragedy in Cincinnati with the Who in 1979, when eleven fans were crushed to death, we insisted on not having general admission shows, but we had a real fight on our hands. Promoters and managers love general admission because they can squeeze as many people onto the floor as they like, but while those shows are often more revved-up and raucous, they're more dangerous too. I had to beg people on many occasions to calm down and stop pushing to the front. Security would be pulling people out of the crush or hurling water bottles out, and I hated it. Of course, fans themselves often prefer general admission because they want to get as close as they can to their band, and many bands love to see the sweaty mob pulsating and showing their love, but I was always fearful of somebody being hurt, and the possibility of not noticing someone disappearing beneath the crowd is a very real danger. It's a fine line between letting the audience enjoy itself unrestrainedly and causing a catastrophe. On the occasions we got our way and had reserved seating, it could go to the other extreme, with unnecessarily strict security patrolling the aisles, making it impossible for the audience to express its true fervor.

The fact is, in a big crowd, standing *or* seated, anything can happen. I've done gigs where all of a sudden there's a shoe flying out of the darkness to whack me in the face. Or we get hit by all kinds of weird crap (it's not all bras and panties, you know). People get drunk and pelt coins. Some nights the crew found scary things in the onstage carpet, weird shit like a dart or a bullet; on the *Grace Under Pressure* tour, some idiot threw a disposable lighter at my head, which required several stitches.* Then there are the nights when you have a strong police presence only because the history of the venue has dictated a very strict approach to crowd control. Some nights, after Alex had seen kids getting roughed up, he'd stop the show and start yelling at the *cops*. Sometimes the crew, who always train an eagle eye on the crowd, will tell you in your earphone that there's trouble in the audience and

---

* Other fans, loyal to the core, apprehended the guy and turned him in to security!

ask you to stall before the next song while they take care of it. Sometimes people are stoned or mentally impaired or so overexcited that the line between reality and fantasy gets blurred. In the early days, we poo-poohed the need for security, saying, "We're not a pop band, we don't have crazy fans." But even we do. Really crazy, almost worse because some hear "secret messages" to themselves in our music and feel they have to act on them. Those you have to worry about. One time a fan clambered up onstage and grabbed me by the neck while I was playing and would not let go. I don't know what his intent was, but it was not a loving hug—he had his hands around my throat and the road crew had to tackle him. Scary shit happens! Another time, after I received a death threat, we played anyway but with a ton of extra police, security peeps and metal detectors deployed around the venue. In the end nothing happened, but I felt like a sitting duck up there at the mic, I can tell you.

**WITH *MOVING PICTURES*** and *Signals*, which followed it in 1982, we had entered a new era of success and reward. But a tsunami was brewing, one that threatened to inundate my life. The signs weren't immediately apparent, but they were there had I cared to look. For one, our home in the Beaches had become a magnet for Rush fans: the doorbell rang at all hours, Rush music was played on boomboxes from the street and I was startled at lunch one day by two faces smushed up against the window. The final straw was when I caught a kid in my *kitchen*. He bolted and I ran after him, but he hopped over the fence and disappeared down the street.

Nancy and I felt like we were living in a fishbowl—no way to raise an infant. We took the difficult decision to leave the city and seek refuge in our country place. Far from being country folk, my socially outgoing missus loved all a city had to offer, so it was a drastic move. How the hell was she going to adapt to life in Keswick, Ontario, particularly as her couture label was still in its embryonic stage? Yet it was *her* idea, one of many instances of her putting family before herself. So we sold our beloved home in the Beaches and left our friends behind.

Living in the grand French manor house by the water and playing tennis on my own court was at first idyllic (even if it was hard to convince friends to drive out for a game), and we hired a live-in au pair from Switzerland to help out when I was away working. We were playing at life in a baronial dream state; I mean, we even tongue-in-cheekily named the place Dirk Manor. As sensible as the decision seemed in the moment, our marriage would suffer for it.

**BY THE TIME** we were recording *Signals*, I'd become totally enamored with the sounds my array of synth toys could make: the Oberheim OB1, OB-Xa and DSX sequencers, a PPG Wave and the JP-8 with its trendy arpeggiator fed by an 808 drum box that was the rhythmic core of "The Weapon."[*] It was the beginning of a hyper-competitive time for keyboardists and recording engineers, all seizing on the newest sounds, which were shunned as soon as they'd been used in a popular song. If you knew your way around an oscillator, you could invent your own sounds and build a bespoke library of them, but the competition was nuts. You'd be thrilled to have written a song with just the right sonic texture, only to hear from the engineer, "Sorry, man. That sound is *everywhere*."

Devices were quickly deemed passé as the search went on for the next great synth. At the end of the seventies, all that would be upended by the next generation of machines called samplers. With the Fairlight, E-mu Emulator or Waldorf PPG Wave you could take authentic instruments and voices and blend them with any "found sound" you fancied or sampled yourself. The German-made PPGs were all the

---

[*] That drum pattern was based on a rhythm that my pal Oscar and I came up with during rehearsals on the 808, one that Neil loved and based his own pattern around.

rage at that time, notably used by Trevor Horn, the Fixx, David Bowie, Propaganda, Depeche Mode, Tears for Fears, Ultravox (and, eventually, all over *Grace Under Pressure*). It used both analog and digital technology, and when coupled with its computer add-on, the Waveterm A, allowed you to sample sounds digitally, edit them, then play them on the keyboard. The world, in short, was your sonic oyster. At one point I joked about creating an entire drum kit by sampling the sounds you hear on a baseball diamond: for the bass drum, the *thunk* of the ball hitting the catcher's mitt; for the snare, the crisp crack of the ball hitting the bat . . . The one-upmanship continued as, for example, every studio had to have an AMS Digital Delay, the effect that gave birth to the ubiquitous 1980s gated snare: think "In the Air Tonight," "Born in the USA," "Take My Breath Away," "Hounds of Love," "Paradise City" . . . the list goes on.[*]

You'll often hear people these days crying out, "Omigod, those songs sound so dated!" but I think that many have stood the test of time. It's all about context, of course. When I hear that snare sound on pop rock or faux metal albums, it seems wrong to me, but when I hear it in a dance music context, or in a New Wave or New Romantic number, I think that's where it's most at home because that downbeat was so important for that type of music. When I hear it plastered over something that would have been much better served with a real drummer playing a real natural part, *that's* when I, too, go, "Eek!" It seems so unimaginative and random. In his prime, Phil Collins was one of the greatest rock drummers you could find, so he can do whatever the hell he likes, but with that brilliant and powerful gated drum sound he recorded for "In the Air Tonight," he inadvertently set a bad example for imitators to overuse! It was a sign of the times, for sure, just like the twangy guitar was back in the day for Speedy West. Every period has a sound that becomes its signature cliché.

---

[*]  Strictly speaking, the effect is gated *reverb*, but it was used most effectively on drums and in particular the snare drum.

*SIGNALS* WAS A challenge to record. With so much new material and so many new sounds and rhythms, we were experiencing major growing pains. Thinking more as a four-piece required some serious adjustments. In anticipation of our next tour, we built a compact setup with a shiny new Jack Secret–designed keyboard stand, L-shaped and minimal compared to the brutes of the past. (The ill-conceived Behemoth was relegated to a dark corner of our warehouse, waiting to be scrapped or repurposed as, perhaps, a small vehicle.) I also adorned the sides of my synths with red lacquer to match Neil's latest red drum kit and give our stage a cool, more modernistic look.

Even we had a makeover. Alex looked and dressed more like a member of Duran Duran now, while Neil had shaved off his magnificent Hungarian handlebar 'stache and gone all Depeche Mode. Everyone in the Western world but metalheads and yours truly were cutting their

*What was I thinking?*

hair, and I remained gloriously trapped in the sixties. Sartorially speaking, at least, we'd all evolved from the age of sword and sorcery, donning shiny jackets and colourful shirts with skinny ties, and Alex even took to wearing suits. Finally, around the time of *Grace Under Pressure*, I gave in and chopped my witchy tresses, and what an effin' mistake that was. I hated that lame hairdo something bad and couldn't wait for it to grow back. Unfortunately, it was still on my head at the end of those recording

*Hair, glorious hair!* (TOP LEFT) *1980, still holding out; then in 1983* (TOP RIGHT) *I caved in right before our* GUP *album cover session with the amazing Yousuf Karsh. Catastrophe!* (BOTTOM) *My "Daniel Boone" phase, ugh. There's a simple lesson in all of this, kids: whatever they say, just don't cut it.*

sessions, when we'd sit for Yousuf Karsh. We were so chuffed to pose for Canada's greatest portrait photographer that we graced the entire back of the album sleeve with the result, which was perfect but for one thing: I hated it. He captured us, all right; it's an incredibly honest portrait. When I look at it, what I see all over our faces is the stress of another very tough recording session. Then over the course of the *Grace Under Pressure* tour I grew my hair back, but it morphed into an unfortunate bonnet that got me elected to the Mullet Hall of Fame. It was the best of each world, you might say, but not both. I refer to it as my Daniel Boone phase. Why my wife didn't step in and save me from myself is beyond me. Evidence, perhaps, of how far apart we had drifted?

My expanding keyboard setup all but surrounded me now. Like a newfangled one-man band, I was incorporating longer keyboard parts into songs, then springing back to super-busy parts on my bass, and since our arrangements were still constrained by the desire to reproduce

*Multi-instrumentalist Ben Mink brought his prodigious talents to bear on "Losing It." Busy in the control room bossing Broon around (as usual), I looked up to see that a spontaneous jam band had erupted in the studio, calling themselves the Ziv Orchestra.*

them in concert, much of the bottom end had to come from my netherworld of Moog bass pedals. The synth washes filled the track with richer harmonic content, which in turn inspired me to compose more evocative vocal melodies, notably in the choruses of "The Analog Kid" and "Losing It." I was singing in different keys and lower registers on "New World Man" and "The Weapon." It was the start of a songwriting style that included big washes (or "pads") of keyboard string sounds, sampled choirs and more.

It has to be said, not all our fans were enthralled; indeed, dyed-in-the-wool ones were dismayed by the change of direction, but I was too driven and excited by the sheer newness of the compositions to care. As a band we were terribly aware of the dangers of stagnation. Like that great line from *Annie Hall*, when Alvy is talking to Annie about breaking up and says, "A relationship, I think, is like a shark. You know? It has to constantly move forward or it dies. And I think what we got on our hands is a dead shark." That was truly what the three of us feared the most.

And I'm proud that we didn't look back. Listening to it now after so many years, I'm really diggin' the band's fresh grooves! I'd forgotten how many contemporary rhythmic influences we blended into our own brand of rock. It brings back memories of how much fun I was having playing bass along with those funkified grooves, especially on songs like "Digital Man." Alex worked around them imaginatively too, finding new ways to make his presence known. The urgency of his ska and reggae chops is downright funky at times; there's a blistering intensity all over those songs, especially in his wild soundscapes for the middle section of "The Weapon" and his solo work on "Digital Man." Which is all the more admirable, considering how unsold he was on the whole keyboard thing. I was expanding with such abandon that I'm afraid I was blissfully unaware of his misgivings, which would eventually boil over into feelings of alienation and anger . . . but not for a few albums yet.

In any case, more immediate frustrations were coming to the fore while recording *Signals*. In the past, if Terry Brown had been unhappy with aspects of a song, we'd amiably change things around, but now when he expressed dissatisfaction, there was friction. I felt like I could anticipate his comments even before he made them, wondering deep down if a fresh production perspective—a new producer, in fact—would spur us on to newer things. I kept that to myself for the most part, but dissatisfaction was bubbling under.

There were also a couple of occasions when I felt he was taking us for granted. Once, as I was about to sing the lead vocal for "Subdivisions," he had an idea for an unusual vocal sound, but rather than suggest I take a break and ask one of the crew guys to sub for me at the mic, he had me sing the melody over and over again as he fiddled with

*Is this mic on?*

the electronics until the song went stale and the lyrics became words without feeling. That may sound to you like a small thing, but the goal of a producer, as it is with a film director, is to get as fresh and inspired a performance as possible.

Waiting for the producer or engineer to get his ducks in a row can be tedious for everyone else at the best of times. To stave off the boredom while the tape was rewinding or whatever, I'd bring various instruments into the booth with me. Congas and bongos were among my favourites. Why? Because there's nothing more irritating for the producer to hear when he finally opens up the mic than me making an almighty bongo racket, and let me tell you, I can hold down a beat on the bass but I'm a *terrible* drummer. Another time, the three of us were ready for a take when Broon took a phone call. It might have been his mum, I can't recall, but he was on the blower while, instruments in hand, we waited and waited and waited—when, again, he could have just asked us to take a break. After a while, we realized that he'd even turned off his monitors so he could yammer on the phone! Well, as we got restless and bored, and since he could no longer hear us, we wrote a song featuring a combination of expletives, particularly one beginning with "c" and ending in "unt." We were laughing so hard that eventually we forgot to be pissed off, but you didn't need a crystal ball to see that rebellion was in the air.

**AFTER THE RELEASE** of *Signals*, it was like we'd accidently hit an overdrive button, with life moving out from its normal orbit at warp speed—that is, if a life in rock and roll can ever be described as "normal." There was Nancy out in Keswick, baking the bread, lifting a mountain of household chores, raising Jules on her own, unable to persuade her friends to drive out to the country, shunting her creative ambitions to the back seat while I, as usual, was off on tour. I felt a twinge of guilt every time I left her behind, but I was also entering a period of obsession with my work, blind to how difficult things actually were for my better half.

I'd usually call her after soundcheck from the production office, which was awkward as there were always people about. That was ten years before cell phones became commonplace; when they came out, I'd wander around the arena trying to find a signal, often sitting on a crate at the side of the stage or ending up on a bus in the parking lot—not exactly conducive to giving my all while she's telling me what a tough time she's having. Then I'd be swallowed up by the gig, and only getting into bed back at the hotel would I think, *Fuck, Nance had a hard day, I should call her again . . . in the morning.*

Once again, the burden was on her to figure it out. She'd had enough of the isolation, and soon suggested we buy a small townhouse in the city where she and Jules could live during the week, then spend weekends in bucolic splendour by the lake. Made total sense to me, although of course I'd be away most of the time anyway. She found us a home just minutes from the centre of town (and, as it happens, just a block or so from her old apartment and the scene of our very first kiss) and before you knew it had bought enough furniture to make it habitable. She also located a studio for her and Karen, and voila!, a business was born. They dubbed it Zapata and started making custom-ordered apparel from leather and suede. I'd like to say it was a positive spin of the Karmic Wheel, but really it was wholly down to the awesome, indefatigable, indomitable Nancy Young.

Rosedale was an odd neighbourhood for a rock and roll family to be making a home. At the time, it was a bastion of old and predominantly white money, meaning no rockers (let alone a Jewish one) and *very* few people of colour. Nor were there children of Julian's age on our street or any nearby; old money meant older people, their kids having grown up and moved elsewhere while awaiting their inheritance. On the plus side, any fears we had about fans coming to the door at all hours were quickly allayed—not just because our new neighbours' median age was

(LEFT) *The* Hemispheres *writing sessions near Rockfield Studios.* (BELOW) *The Behemoth's arrival was greeted with awe, exasperation and chuckles in equal measure—the look on Skip's face says it all.*

*The Brotherhood: being stupid men, we decided not to shave until the album was written:* (LEFT TO RIGHT) *Skip, Alex, Ian, Shrav, Neil, Jack and Broon.*

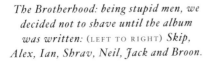

*The never-ending sessions at Rockfield included more recording in the courtyard and, for me, a blessed conjugal visit.*

Evidence that we were cooped up in Wales for too effin' long: after Nancy left, she and I had a long-distance disagreement over what to name our new kitten. She wanted "Katrina," while I preferred the more sensible "Commander Three." Naturally, my compadres agreed with me, so together we faxed a protest, taking the mickey out of her and her friends' hairdos of the day. We weren't high . . . I swear!

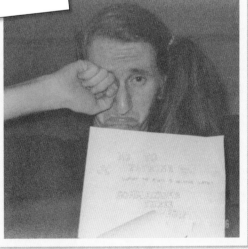

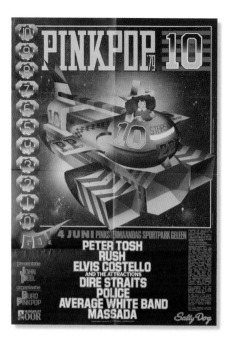

(ABOVE LEFT) *Pinkpop 10, June 4, 1979.*

*On the set of the "Big Money" video, looking dapper (and so expensive).*

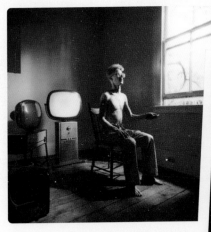

Two test Polaroids (ABOVE) and the final shot (BELOW) by Dimo Safari for the Power Windows album cover. Before settling on the arrangement for his painting, Hugh Syme sent us several of Dimo's shots, which became the catalyst for a "lively" discussion about where the boy (Neill Cunningham) should be looking and whether the antique television sets should be in the picture. I wanted the boy's direct gaze and the TVs to lend an enigmatic dimension to the album's title. The theme of reality distortion would pop up again in both the title track and "Window on the World" on my solo record, My Favourite Headache.

When we returned to the Manor to record parts of Hold Your Fire, we were going through our cowboy phase, entertaining ourselves by pretending to be shitkickers—hats, accents and all. Lerxst killed time during the keyboard sessions to paint me this fine portrait.

*r u s h*

COUNTERPARTS

Of the various accolades we've been fortunate enough to receive (the Order of Canada, the Junos, the RRHOF and others), without question, the most outlandish, most fun, and for that reason our favourite was the Harvard Lampoon Musicians of the Millennium Award in 1993. For me, the highlight of the two-day rage event was when Mark Twain got up to say a few words about "Tom Sawyer," thanking us for the boost in his T-shirt sales.

*Our* Test for Echo *stage set c.1997, as* I *proudly display my first kitchen appliances, including blenders and a fridge encrusted with fridge magnets.*

1 - RAW BASS SOUND GOES IN HERE

2 - SIGNAL PASSES THRU
THE FEATHER REMOVAL DEVICE
(FEATHERS BAD!!)

3 - TO THE SPICER TO GET THE CORRECT BLEND
OF TOP, MIDDLE AND LOW END,
(SECRET SPICE IS ADDED HERE)

4 - NEXT THE SOUND FLOWS TO THE
HEAT CHAMBER WHERE THE SOUND
GETS HOT, HOT, HOT!
(SUGGESTED OVEN TEMPERATURE IS 2112 DEGREES KELVIN)

5 - THE BOTTOM END IS SEPARATED AND
INJECTED WITH "HENHAUS" TASTY SAUCE

6 - IF THE SOUND GETS TOO HOT & SPICEY IT IS
RE-DIRECTED TO THE 'JET-PACK' COOLING
DEFRACTOR" WHERE THE SOUND IS
RECONSTITUTED TO THE CORRECT
THE BLEND OF DISTORTION FOR THAT
"HEAVY HEAVY MONSTER SOUND"

7 - NEXT THE SOUND SIMMERS ON THE
ROTISSERIE FOR APX 2HRS AND 40 MINS *
PERIODIC BASS-TING IS REQUIRED

8 - HOT AND TASTY SOUND COMES OUT HERE

*The cutting edge in hot and tasty bass sound technology.*

(ABOVE AND LEFT) *Behind the scenes during the filming of* The Real History of Rush *for the Time Machine tour.*

(RIGHT) *Director Dale Heslip has clearly never heard a cave dweller speaking Yiddish before.*

basically eighty, but because Rosedale is an illogical labyrinth of leafy streets. Even our friends had a hard time navigating there.

The band, meanwhile, was finally making enough money to invest in our own tour bus, a well-used one that we customized with a stateroom for each of us. That was an exciting idea but impractical, a waste of precious living space, and we soon realized it would be more comfortable to lease a newer model designed specifically for touring musicians. We went from briefly having our own private bedrooms to sleeping on bunks, beginning our life as the "Shelf People."

It was a vast improvement over the cramped car drives we'd endured in the mid-seventies, but it was still exhausting. Our schedule

*In 1980 Rush and Max Webster recorded a song called
"Battle Scar," and when they opened for us on the* Signals *tour,
I used to sneak out and sing my part disguised as . . . a crook.*

was so relentless that we almost always had to drive on immediately after a show. Rare was the night you slept in the same town you'd just played, a recipe for trouble if there ever was one. You'd climb aboard, drink or get high and laugh at a funny movie, then crawl the worse for wear onto your shelf and pull the curtain to try to fall asleep. I often resorted to taking a Valium to knock me out or else I'd wake up sometimes tossed into the air by a pothole in the road. We'd usually arrive at our hotel sometime between four and six, stumble into the lobby and wait half-dead for Herns to give us our keys, then drag ourselves to our rooms to catch as many remaining winks as we could before heading to soundcheck that afternoon.

Some folks love bus life, especially guests for whom it's a novelty; pals of mine would beg me to invite them out to party for a few days, do the truck stops and experience that romantic Route 66 journey across America. And for a few years at least, it was fun for me too, with loads of time to read, especially during a rare day trip or on my shelf the nights I wasn't wasted. I read a ton on the bus and watched a thousand films, while my favourite thing was to have one of the crew guys tape that night's ball game as we were onstage and promise not to tell me the score so I could watch it through the night like it was live—though invariably on my way to the bus after a gig someone would say, "Wow, your Jays really got pasted tonight, eh, Ged?" Doh!

# CHAPTER 18

I N THE EARLY MONTHS OF 1983, ALEX, NEIL
and I reviewed the experience we'd had making *Signals* and
concluded that the direction of the band hung in the balance. We
needed a change. As much as we loved Terry and appreciated
beyond words what he'd helped us accomplish, we felt that we had to
break old habits, learn new techniques and generally challenge ourselves to work in new ways—which could happen only with a
producer from a different background and a fresh viewpoint.

We asked him to fly down to Florida. We climbed aboard our bus
with him, pulled out onto the highway and, after the usual goofing

*Alex and Broon in front of Le Studio during the recording of* Signals.

around, engaged in a painfully difficult exchange. How else could it have been? Broon had nurtured our sound since 1974, watching us grow from the naïve and hungry players we used to be to the accomplished band we were now. How exactly do you tell the only real producer you've ever worked with that you want a change? But as we began to talk, it was apparent that Terry, too, had misgivings; he didn't want to stop working with us, but nor was he sold on the direction we were moving in. He was particularly concerned that the electronic drums and keyboards we were so enamored with diminished the role of the guitar to our detriment. He wasn't wrong, but this was the direction we'd committed to and there really was no turning back. The longer we talked, the clearer it became that, despite his having given everything he had to us, we needed someone new in the producer's chair.

So, sadly but amiably, we parted ways.

We took no joy in saying goodbye. It was a scary feeling to suddenly be without our mentor—you could even have called him a father figure—but it was also exhilarating to consider the possibilities the future held. In reality, with Terry always having our backs, we had kind of lived a sheltered life. We were soon to find out just how sheltered it had been.

WE KICKED INTO producer search mode. Ideally, we wanted someone working in the current London music scene, the hub of some of the most exciting music and musical technology of the moment. A four-night run we'd just sold out at Wembley Arena* would give us different nights to meet different guys, among them Trevor Horn, who'd been a member of Yes and the Buggles before racking up an impressive list of producer credits (ABC, Frankie Goes to Hollywood, Propaganda, Malcolm McLaren, Grace Jones and more). After the first show he asked us, "Have you talked to other musicians about what I'm like

---

* Wembley Arena is a 10,000-seat indoor venue—not to be confused with the massive 80,000-seat outdoor soccer stadium. We were popular but we weren't the effin' *Beatles*.

to work with? You might want to do that before you choose me!" The inference, obviously, was that he wasn't the easiest chap to deal with in a studio and, indeed, to illustrate that, producer Peter Collins would years later tell me a story about working at one of Trevor's studios. On a coffee break, Peter had told him he was having a hard time coaxing a good performance from a certain singer. Horn responded, "Have you tried *shouting* at him?"*

Over the following nights we met Hugh Padgham, who'd made several records with the Police; Michael Kamen, whom we respected as an arranger (he'd arrange the strings on "Nobody's Hero" ten years later); and finally Steve Lillywhite. We loved his work with bands as wide-ranging as the Psychedelic Furs, Johnny Thunders's Heartbreakers, XTC and U2 — and especially Big Country, with their bagpipe-mimicking twin guitars, with a mind to soothing Alex's fears of being overwhelmed by keyboards.

Lillywhite seemed genuinely interested in working with us — so keen that he came to our gig in Birmingham to acquire more insight into our sound, the way we worked and what we were like as people. I thought we got on very well, and soon we were making plans because we thought we had a deal. After the tour we went home for a break but couldn't wait to get started writing. We were totally fired up and thought, Wow, *that was way easier than we expected.* Yeah, right . . .

Less than two weeks before the start of writing sessions, word came in from Ray that Mr. Lillywhite was pulling out. We heard excuses about the project "not being right" for him or some such bullshit, when in reality it seems he'd been offered a chance to record with Simple Minds and was simply blowing us off. Now, there's an expression, I believe, about a man's word being his bond; *this* man's word, apparently, was meaningless. Okay, good to know. No big deal, Steve. It shouldn't be hard to find a producer in just *two weeks.* Thanks for letting us know. All the best, mate, and fuck you, too.

---

* Incidentally, on the night Horn came to see us he sat beside his ex-bandmate Chris Squire, but Squire didn't make it backstage and sadly I never got to meet my hero!!!

Wise in the knowledge that producers can be full of shit, we got back to writing *un*settled, to say the least. It wasn't the best way to embark on a new record, but us being us, we had a few laughs at whatsisname's expense, and even as more prospective producers flew in for meetings we got to work, doing our best to strike a balance between Alex's raging guitar and my latest keyboard sounds, and before long we had "Distant Early Warning," "Red Sector A" and "Between the Wheels."

We suspected, of course, that the best producers would likely be booked months in advance, so I cannot emphasize enough how stressed we still were. *Every* producer we liked and who wanted the gig had scheduling issues. Studio time we had booked was looming, as well as a five-night warm-up stint at Radio City Music Hall in New York. It was no cinch turning the ocean liner RMS *Rush* around! Obsessively preoccupied, I brought the work home with me, talking on the phone most of the weekends to management about producers and engineers, reviewing CVs and listening to records and demos. The search hogged all the space in my brain, making me, shall we say, a less than ideal father and husband. I alienated myself from my own family.

Nancy had opened a salon with Karen in a second-story walk-up at the corner of Yorkville and Yonge. It was a super exciting time for her, but while in my mind I thought I was being supportive, my obsession with finding a producer stopped me from being as happy for her as I should have been. Neither of us acknowledged the crack opening up between us, one that would yawn ever wider and push us into very separate worlds of our own making. Oblivious to her being drawn into a new circle of friends and fashionistas, I assumed she would and could handle everything while taking care of Jules, running the household and supporting me, just as she always had. Actually, she *did* handle it, but my physical and mental absences made it harder than it should have been, and her resentment was festering as her independence was growing. The one constant that held us together was our love for Jules.

AMONG THE LEGIONS of producers and engineers who had come and gone from our rehearsal space in a closed-up ski resort north of the city was an Englishman named Peter Henderson whose engineering and co-production credits impressed us: Supertramp's *Breakfast in America*, Jeff Beck's *Wired*, Zappa's *Sheik Yerbouti* and Paul McCartney's *Wings at the Speed of Sound* were just a few of the albums he'd worked on and sounded terrific to us. Peter came out of George Martin's Air Studios and had been trained by the Beatles' longtime engineer Geoff Emerick. He was a real English public school type, amiable, smart, sporty and good for a laugh, but most important, he knew his stuff and loved music passionately. He was articulate and refreshingly honest with us about aspects of our songs he liked and didn't. He seemed to genuinely dig the direction our new songs were taking, and it was with a great sigh of relief that we hired him.

The search for producers had been stressful, but I believed that talking to all those talented gentlemen about their past work, techniques and attitudes taught me more about making records than any hands-on recording experience I'd had to date. True enough, but as we buckled down to record *Grace Under Pressure*, my optimism would prove short-lived. I liked Peter personally and respected his skills a lot. He really understood what good sound was and how to achieve it. In fact, he may have been the most talented pure *engineer* I've ever worked with. But when it came to producing—producing *us*, at least—something was missing. I know our expectations were high, maybe unreasonably so, but after all we'd gone through to break away from Broon we had something to prove to ourselves. High expectations were warranted. And shouldn't they damn well *always* be?

If memory serves, the first song we had a go at recording was "Distant Early Warning." With a virtual stranger staring at us from behind the glass, we were both psyched up and a little nervous during the first take, but settled in after a couple of run-throughs, then waited with bated breath for his response. But all we got was quiet . . . hesitation.

"Well?" I asked. "How *was* that?"

"Yeah, yeah," he said. "Sounding good, but do you want to try another couple?"

Ah, okay. A normal enough response. So we did a couple more, and afterwards . . . again . . . hesitation.

"Er . . . How was that one, Peter?"

"Yeah. *Good.* Do you wanna . . . come in and listen?"

We were all smiles when we heard the sounds—fat, deep, tough, evocative—very encouraging. Then I noticed that some of the VU meters had been taped over. I asked him why, and he said something about preferring to judge with his ears than be too hung up on mechanical readings. *Wow*, I thought, *that's* confidence. I liked that a lot. Plus, he *was* nailing the sounds and the performances seemed good . . . And yet, and yet . . . it was always "How about another couple of takes?"

It was the template for the entire Peter Henderson experience. We'd do more takes, and more, but never did we hear the words that Broon used to utter: "Guys, I think we've got it!" It was like wringing water from a stone. It was becoming apparent that, as intelligent as his analysis of our music was, he didn't have it in him to be decider-in-chief.

For weeks it was the same at every stage of recording and overdubbing, and when we'd finally gotten to the mixing stage it got even worse. We'd do a basic mix of a song, then innumerable versions of the same mix with 1 or 2dB changes like "Final with guitar louder" or "Final with guitar lower." Now, you always do a few alternate mixes for TV or car radios or keep a "Vocal up" or "Vocal down" mix in the can in case a week later you realize with fresh ears that the balance was wrong, but we'd *never* done so many before. It's nice to have an option or two, but this was nuts—especially for a guy like me who already has option anxiety. We'd spend as many as fourteen hours a day in the studio mixing and listening, mixing and listening, mixing and listening. Deciding which takes would actually make it to the album took forever. We kept our feelings to ourselves and a "mustn't grumble" attitude, but quietly it was wearing us to the bone.

That long, cold winter took a chunk out of us as a band and me as an individual. I had invested so much of myself to find the perfect producer, then pushed so hard for decisions during those frustrating sessions, that I ignored all the signs of my dereliction of duty to my wife and son. And after the sessions, it *still* wasn't over for me, as I had to take the tapes to my old friend and brilliant mastering engineer Bob Ludwig, sift through the multitude of masters and assemble the final version as it exists today. It stood up pretty well in his finely tuned room, though I was dissatisfied with the bottom end I was getting from my Steinberger bass guitar, and Bob had to work some magic to bring more of it out on a couple of the songs. At the end, my nerves were too frayed to be excited, but hey, what won't kill you makes you stronger, right? (What idiot ever said *that?*)

*Band portraits by Alex during the* Grace Under Pressure *sessions.*
*Think we look stressed enough? And there's my effin' stupid hairdo again!*

THE LAUNCH OF MTV in 1981 had already revolutionized the music industry. Doing videos was now de rigueur and every band, even ours, was urged to produce a breakthrough one. Budgets and production values were rising, at times exceeding some bands' recording budgets! Think about that for a moment. Record companies were willing to spend more money on the video than *the record itself.* That insane concept gives you an idea of the power MTV had back then.

Because videos so obviously aligned with my love of movies, I became the point man for most of Rush's visual projects, but I learned very quickly that making videos was *not* the same as making movies. To start with, Rush songs were never going to make the Top 10, so the higher-ups funding these things (with our future royalty money, I might add) had little motivation to advance us a quarter million dollars for whatever extravaganza I had in my head. My Big Ideas were invariably rewarded with a reality sandwich: "Well, we'd love to do this, but we don't have Steven Spielberg's budget."

Still, we were intrigued by the possibilities because so many of the songs we wrote were ripe for visual exposition. Neil's lyrics were filled with arguments and ideas, protagonists and antagonists, fantastic vistas and epic stories—ideal, you can imagine, for a plot line and an inventive director. The challenge was that we'd always hated spelling out the meaning of a lyric, and it felt corny trying to act out a literal-minded five-minute screenplay in a low-budget way. Another challenge was that both management and record company wanted us to appear in the videos, and we were not keen. Directors making a Rush video found themselves with a set of challenging preconditions, not least that we weren't exactly fashion icons or matinee idols. Neil refused to appear unless he was playing his drums for real, *and* we insisted that whatever story a director wanted to tell would have to somehow interpolate shots of the band without appearing intrusive or gratuitous. (If you ever wondered why cyborgs in a futuristic totalitarian dystopia have Rush on their all-seeing monitors—or that Neil doesn't appear at all—well, now ya know.)

In future years, we'd turn away from stories in favour of a more high-concept or abstract approach (like the guy strapped to a pole in "Stick It Out," off *Counterparts*) where the intermittent appearance of the band didn't seem so jarring. So we made them, all right—as artfully, we hoped, as anything else we did—but it was compromise after compromise, and my ardour soon dissipated. In any case, as time went on they became less important as a marketing tool, and we pretty much stopped doing them altogether, switching our attention to films for our live shows, where we could take our inside jokes and comic ideas and throw them up on the screen, sharing our goofy sense of humour with a dedicated audience and without the approval of record companies, TV channels or anyone else.

*Grace Under Pressure* was well received[*] and "Afterimage," "Distant Early Warning," "The Body Electric" and "The Enemy Within"[**] got a surprising amount of video play on MTV and its Canadian equivalent, MuchMusic.[***] Were we darlings of the small screen? Well, Alex's Simon Le Bon coiffure notwithstanding, there would be no Top 10 Buzz Clips for us, but it was good exposure.

FROM MAY THROUGH November 1984 we toured the album across Canada and the US, this time around playing "only" seventy-seven shows in six months. We'd told Ray that the era of twenty-three days in a row without a single one off were over. We were playing longer sets now, which took a greater toll on us, and our new rule was three gigs in a row, max. Neil brought along a bicycle and spent off-days pedaling long, long rides to clear his head of rock and roll routines; one time he rode

---

[*] It reached #4 in Canada, #5 in the UK and #10 on the *Billboard* 200, where it made platinum (that is, it sold more than a million copies). In 2014, *Guitar World* placed the album on its list of "New Sensations: 50 Iconic Albums That Defined 1984."

[**] Directed, respectively, by Tim Pope, David Mallet and the team of Annabel Jankel and Rocky Morton.

[***] MuchMusic began life as a weekly rockumentary show called *The New Music*, on CityTV in Toronto, and in that format actually predated the American behemoth.

the more than ninety miles from Milwaukee to Chicago—some nice, light exercise after playing a two-and-a-half-hour show the night before. Seriously, the man was a monster both on the kit and his two-wheeler. As you probably know from books he'd later write like *The Masked Rider*, his love of bicycles led to a passion for motorbikes. He was a road guy through and through, but what he really dug was the lifestyle outside of the band when he could travel in relative anonymity.

*My* version of heaven, meanwhile, was flying; for most of the tour we still rode the bus, but for transatlantic flights since *A Farewell to Kings* we'd been taking the Concorde. Now, *that* was an effin' amazing machine, flying just shy of Mach 2, so high that when you looked out, the clouds below had disappeared and the sky was black—you know, like in outer space! To get from New York to London in just over three hours was like having a long meal in a cramped but gourmet restaurant, and the best part was that when you arrived it was early in the evening, with time for a nightcap and bed at an almost respectable time—without being jet-lagged.

We'd also started treating ourselves at the very end of North American tours by chartering a small plane to get us home quicker. It was during the last gig of that leg of the *Grace Under Pressure* tour, in Providence, that Alex and I noticed Neil looking agitated behind his drum kit. We thought it was fatigue at first, and indeed he was exhausted, but this was different. He kept it together but was evidently having an anxiety attack and pretty much running on fumes. We barely made it through the show before clambering aboard the Learjet we'd hired. Drinks in hand, we sat in close quarters across from one another (Learjets were fast but confined), until about thirty minutes into the flight, when Neil looked up at us and said with a moan, "I've just *got* to get off." We told the pilot to land asap, and fortunately he was able to put us down at the Rochester airport in a matter of minutes, where Neil was met by a car and driven home across the border—leaving us shaken because we'd never really clocked that he had a serious fear of flying.

FOR YEARS HE'D hidden it pretty well by being funny about it, razzing us about the dangers of aviation and once even making T-shirts with a picture of a bus with wings, emblazoned THE BUS WON'T FALL OUT OF THE SKY. Before a gig in Jacksonville, Florida, in 1980, he'd handed those around in the dressing room, not registering that we were in the hometown of Lynyrd Skynyrd, whose Convair CV-240 ran out of fuel and crashed, killing (among others) the band's singer, Ronnie Van Zant, and guitarist Steve Gaines. Fortunately, one of our crew had the presence of mind to rush in and point out that terrible coincidence, and poor Neil put them away before anyone was offended.

Anyway, after the Learjet incident, we were all shaken and worried—not least because we knew the next time we'd be seeing him would be at Pearson Airport for a flight to Tokyo. That would be his first and last trip to Japan, but not only because of his fear of flying . . .

We had always been reluctant to go to Japan because we wanted to bring along our full North American show, and the time and cost of shipping all that gear was prohibitive. Japanese companies guaranteed they could replicate any band's stage setup so accurately that you'd never know the difference, so most Western bands playing there never brought their own, but we were skeptical. Finally, though, we worked out a compromise, bringing just some of our gear and leasing the rest when we got there, and off we went to do a mere four shows in four Japanese cities: Nagoya, Fukuoka, Osaka and concluding at the famous Budokan in Tokyo.

I was excited but disoriented (so to speak) by both the massive jet lag and the utterly unfamiliar culture. For a start, I was quickly disavowed of the notion that Japanese eat sushi morning, noon and night. (Not so! It's expensive and rich and usually saved for special occasions, although that didn't stop Lerxst one iota from tucking in as often as he could.) I was knocked out by the mash-up of ultra-modern and traditional Japanese architecture—the way, for instance, you might see at the end of some alley between two skyscrapers an old Shinto shrine tended by a priest in *yukata* and elevated *geta*. Likewise with the fashions on the street, where you'd be just as likely to see women in classic kimono and obi as you would hip fashionistas or a multitude of identically uniformed school children. It was also the first place I'd been where I needed a card with the hotel's address on it, in Japanese, to find my way back; you could have dropped me a block away and I'd have been totally lost, as not only is Tokyo's layout incredibly confusing but finding a passerby in 1984 who spoke English was next to impossible.

The concerts were a culture adjustment too, as you might imagine. First, you went on super early, around six p.m.; then once you'd started to play, you'd be looking out on a sea of black hair bobbing up and down like puppets on a string in time with the music (well, *sort* of in time). They seemed so oddly robotic that we found ourselves stifling laughter up onstage, but still, the crowd did seem to be enjoying the hell out of the show.[*]

We had a day off before the Osaka show, and our concert promoter, the legendary Mr. Udo, treated us to a day at a *sentō*, or bath house. It felt odd disrobing and bathing while female attendants walked around us with complete disinterest. They led us to a row of massage tables separated by tall privacy screens, where a second set of women in white-skirted uniforms and short white rubber rainboots greeted us impersonally, motioning us to lie down and proceeding to wash our hair and scrub us from head to toe as we joked with one another through the screens. I felt like I was in a car wash, where I was the car. After they'd dried our hair and poured us drinks in the lounge, we dressed and headed back to the hotel almost literally glowing.

After such a unique experience, we were all in a terrific mood and gathered in the bar to happily pound back a few more drinks, until Neil left to use the men's room but failed to return. One of the crew looked

---

[*]  What we did not know at the time was that following a riot at a Deep Purple concert at the Budokan in 1973, the enthusiasms of Japanese rock and roll audiences had become strictly curbed.

The three of us wandered around Japan, Hong Kong and China in a state of awe, accompanied by the Boozecan International before things took a turn (as you shall see . . .).

for him in the lobby and called back to us, "Hey, guys! Neil's having an argument!" We ran out and there he was, berating a squat, tough-looking man who was fighting with a woman. Neil had apparently been outraged to see him beating on her while the front desk people and security nonchalantly went about their day. Now the man was shouting back at Neil in Japanese, fairly obviously telling him to mind his own business. They shoved each other, at which point Alex got into the guy's face too, and then the hotel staff started yelling at *us*, urging us to leave the lobby and, as far as we could gather, assuring us that this was solely a matter between husband and wife. We were so incensed that we continued yelling at him to stop, but our protestations only made it worse. As security pushed us into the elevator and the doors closed on us, we watched in horror as the thug punched the woman in the stomach and she fell to the ground.

We went up to our rooms stunned, confused and fuming. What in the fuck just happened? It was like we had entered a completely different Japan, one of brutality and indifference. The next day, our translator explained that the man was heavily tattooed, which—especially in Osaka—meant he was a member of the yakuza and that no Japanese would dare confront him. Suddenly I understood why there had been signs in the bathhouse declaring NO TATTOOS—code, in fact, for NO YAKUZA. We still weren't ready to let it go, however. We tried to argue that it was barbaric, demanding to know why the hotel would do *nothing* about it, but it was all too confrontational for him and we were met with silence. In that moment, I felt the full collision of West meets East. It's naïve and typically North American to think that a foreigner could begin to understand, let alone challenge, such a complex and age-old society, especially in the midst of a first, short visit, but still, as far as we were concerned, there was no justification for what we witnessed. It was an abhorrent and violent act, surely, by any standard. For us, at least, the bloom was off the rose. We were depressed, no one more than Neil, who was so disturbed that he vowed never to return to Japan, and never did.

# CHAPTER 19

FTER THE HOLIDAY SEASON OF 1984, WE
moved into Elora Sound, a rural studio about two hours'
drive from Toronto, housed in a barn opposite a farmhouse. It was large enough to accommodate our gear and a
proper multi-track recording facility, so that this time around we could
make more sophisticated demos. We'd never had the time for proper
ones before, perpetually on the road and diving into the deep end of
each new record, so now it felt luxurious to be able to do some serious
prep work before laying down the real thing. In the early days, Neil,
Alex and I would bang out songs on bass, guitar and drums, with maybe
a keyboard I could zing over to if some extra melody or texture was
needed, but as I became more comfortable behind the keyboards, I

began to compose on them more often, which is why our music got quite dense in that period. With all the technology we were juggling and the multi-layered approach to writing that was developing, demos were not just useful but necessary.

We hunkered down in the cold Canadian winter, working flat out from Monday to Friday and going home for the weekends—a good thing, since my son, Jules, would be turning five that summer and it was becoming harder to leave him for extended periods. Nancy and I had been living parallel lives, as for the past two years Zapata had evolved to produce seasonal lines with Canada-wide distribution, using unusual fabrics that she and Karen found on buying sprees in Paris and Italy. We'd drifted apart, and it was beginning to show in public. Many in the fashion crowd that Nancy spent time with when she wasn't being a mom didn't even know she was married, let alone to some guy in a rock band. Being my "plus-one" was not enough for her; she was determined to carve her own path free of that association. Because of my absences and deepening obsession with my own career, I'd become a ghost in her life. I was complicit in letting us drift into separate orbits, because when our schedules did jibe, I just went along with it as she did, ignoring the depth of dysfunction. The more you live as independent individuals, the harder it becomes to think as a couple, and increasingly, we were having trouble finding common ground. Not knowing how else to handle it, I simply returned to my work as usual.

WE STARTED ON some arrangements with our new producer, Peter Collins, whose name had come up in conversation with Gary Moore when we gigged together on the *Grace Under Pressure* tour. Peter had re-recorded an old song of Gary's, "Empty Rooms," that we all thought gave it more power and glory, so we'd asked to meet him. The person who walked into our dressing room was not a person who looked like a hip record producer, but rather a small man with a beard and glasses, someone you'd expect to find behind a desk in an accountancy, but we quickly warmed to him and hired him to helm *Power Windows*.

Not being schooled musicians, Neil, Alex and I had learned few of the fundamentals your average songwriter knows as a matter of course. Approaching things instinctively without hard and fast rules had served us well and, dare I say, made us more original, but we were up for it when Peter suggested that this time around we try on some basic principles. Rather than simply accepting the way we'd written a song, he'd ask us to try it in different keys or tempos. Sometimes he'd suggest a reductive approach, breaking down a verse or middle eight, eliminating certain instruments to make room for more dynamic parts to come. He believed strongly in injecting surges of energy or detail as a song went along—either with a sound effect, guitar line or keyboard flourish— arguing that a one-off event or a sudden change in feel will give a song longevity. His style was never dictatorial; he respected that we'd done well enough in the past without him. But he wouldn't hesitate, cigar in mouth, to snap his fingers and say, "Sorry, chaps, this part just isn't working. Do we really need it? If not, let's just *shmeiss* it."

The first time he said that we laughed and answered, "Um, '*shmeiss*' it?"

Although Peter is Jewish, I don't think he realized he was using a Yiddish word that actually means "to smack or whack." He'd insist, "Yes! Erase it. *Shmeiss* it. Get *rid* of it!" If a part was just okay, rather than keep it on tape and risk second-guessing himself later, he'd say to our engineer, "Jimbo, *shmeiss*." If an assistant wasn't working out or the catering wasn't up to snuff, he'd grin and ask, "Shall I . . . *shmeiss* him?" I loved it. This was one decisive effin' dude, a producer in *action*. With his take-command attitude, his love of cigars and his ever-so-slight resemblance to the stout but diminutive Edward. G. Robinson, voilà, "Mr. Big" was born, and so from us it was, "Yes, Mr. B. *Shmeiss!*"

We settled into the Manor Studio in Oxfordshire. Described by one British newspaper as "the high altar of 1970s rock," it had most famously produced Mike Oldfield's *Tubular Bells*, as well as XTC's *English Settlement* and *Ghosts* by the Strawbs, which I especially liked. After completing basic bed tracks, the stage was set for the grand entrance of Andy Richards, an expert keyboard and synth man who had worked with Frankie Goes to Hollywood, Propaganda and Grace Jones, and specialized in creating innovative sonic textures. Not only was he a confident and knowledgeable programmer, but once the tape was rolling he turned into quite the flamboyant performer at his array of keyboards, flinging his arms aloft like the Phantom of the Opera and holding court throughout. Peter insisted we give him full licence to play all over the tracks, which had me concerned that our songs would be overwhelmed, but I went along with it, giving Andy the "image fixes" he asked for.

Alex, meanwhile, had to have been wondering where his guitar would fit into all of this. He spent a lot of time in his room, valiantly working out his parts on a portable tape machine or distracting himself by trying his hand at oil painting. Outwardly he acted like a total pro and never threw a wobbler. It's only now—almost forty years later—that I fully understand what he was really going through. Why? Because I recently asked him about it face-to-face. And this was his response:

"Up to that point," he told me, "whether writing, rehearsing or recording, we'd always worked together, but Peter came from the school of hiring outside musicians, and on *Power Windows* that's how I felt he looked at *me*. So I sat in my room for three weeks, and while those tons of sounds sounded cool, to me it wasn't who we were. I *resented* that. I was like, What am I doing here? But I adapted. Then for *Hold Your Fire* I spent a lot of time working out guitar parts on my little TEAC, thinking I'd get ahead of the curve, but when I played them for you, you were like, 'Mm. Hmm. Mm-hmm,' and I was like, 'Oh, *really?*' Then on the first day of recording, we were working on 'Prime Mover' with so *many* people in the studio, and I played you a little riff from behind the console and you said, 'I don't like that!' And

I said to myself, 'I'm gonna put my guitar down. I'm out of here. I don't want to do this anymore.' Then five minutes later, you caught on and said, 'Why don't you do that thing again?' but it was too late. I said, 'No. I'll just play whatever you want me to play.' I felt a lot of friction and unhappiness back then. Ged, you know how you get bossy in the studio sometimes, because in your mind you see *everything*. You're so in control. I'm much looser by nature, while you're very planned and methodical. But of course the more work we did, the more open we became. The more you came to trust me . . . "

*Oh, crap!* I've already admitted that at times I certainly can be Mr. Bossypants, but hearing that after all these years makes me feel a fool. How on earth could I have been so blind to what he was going through, not just as my writing partner, but as my dearest friend? In the name of progress and experimentation, I had made him feel diminished. In hindsight I wish we'd talked about our feelings back then. It's more than interesting to wonder what might have changed about that album had we done so . . .

*AIR Studios, Montserrat, where for three weeks we recorded guitars for both* Power Windows *and* Hold Your Fire. *Here is proof of how hard Neil and I worked, while Alex (not seen) is in the bunker, playing his fingers to the bone. Cruel, yes, but fair.*

THEMATICALLY, *POWER WINDOWS* is another of our small-c concept albums, one that deals with power in various forms. The lyrics of "The Big Money," for example, decry the cold, passionless use of the Almighty Dollar—money for money's sake—but also acknowledge its power and sexy, irresistible allure, which was something we were experiencing for ourselves at the time; not being pop stars churning out lucrative hit singles, we'd had to earn our reward slowly, the hard way, playing gazillions of gigs, and at last our record sales were starting to reflect our efforts. But was Big Money changing us? Yes and no. For one thing, with our management working to keep us on the straight and narrow, we always had one eye on practicality, always putting our dollars back into our shows, but now were able to splurge on certain luxuries. Crossing the Atlantic by Concorde was one of them, living more comfortably at home was another and we were driving nice cars, but it never changed our work ethic. There was never a feeling that we had it made in the shade.

True to his name, Mr. Big felt that a couple of the new songs deserved "the full Montevideo," as he liked to put it, proposing not just an orchestra throughout but a full-blown choir too. We hesitated. It sounded extreme, obviously, and we were also wondering how we'd ever replicate this multitude of musicians and singers in concert, but we succumbed with a "Fuck it, sure, why not," figuring, at least, that with all the samplers and synthesizers at my fingertips, we could pull it off live.

For "Marathon" and "The Manhattan Project," Peter called on Anne Dudley, whose work we knew from Art of Noise, Lloyd Cole's *Rattlesnakes* and Trevor Horn productions like Frankie Goes to Hollywood's "Two Tribes," and Malcolm McLaren's "Buffalo Gals." The respected composer and keyboardist Andrew Pryce Jackman wrote the parts for the choir and led them at Angel Studios, a recording and mixing complex built around a lovely old wooden chapel in North London. Then we moved to the legendary Studio 1 at Abbey Road, a room so large that it can accommodate both a 110-piece orchestra and a 100-piece choir. I mean, Anne Dudley conducting members of the London Symphony Orchestra in the most revered studio in pop history—does it get better than that? And playing *our* weird music? It was literally breathtaking; you could not wipe the grins off our faces if you tried. I spent the whole time wandering around taking photos and eavesdropping on the exchanges between the musicians, mostly droll complaints about having to play the number too often, what a wanker the producer was, etc. It's a different vibe with that kind of working musician, grizzled veterans, longtime union members with thick skins—although maybe not so unlike hardened roadies, who also only notice the things at a gig that are being done incorrectly, i.e., how *they* would have done it better. That's just human nature.

Those sessions were spectacular from every perspective. It's really why we gave Peter his nickname; no idea was too big for him. We had made as different a record as we possibly could, yet it was still true to us. For all the choir and orchestra and keyboard magic, it was still a hard rock record. We were just adding more *music* to our music. People often say that less is more, but in our case *more* was simply more *better*—and although the mixing sessions were arduous and complex, I was starting

*Liam and Mr. Big in Abbey Road's historic Studio 1. Irritatingly, my camera and all the film from that orchestral session were stolen on the way back to Canada with the rest of our gear, so this is the only photograph I have of that magical day. If you're the thief, could I at least have the negatives back, please?*

to accept that they would always be that way for me. In the often difficult two and a half years since we'd parted ways with Broon, we had finally found what we were after. After the stressful confusion that was *Grace Under Pressure*, Peter Collins had delivered a record we were proud of—and for the longest time it was my favourite record from that period.

**AFTER ANOTHER GRAND** tour of America in late '85 and '86, it was time for yet another album—our twelfth in only thirteen years. Work much? After such a warm and successful collaboration with Mr. Big, how could we not try to do it all again with the same team? So the schedule for *Hold Your Fire* replicated much of what we did on its predecessor and then some. It was truly an international production, recording in five different studios: the Manor in Oxfordshire, Ridge Farm in Surrey, AIR Studios in Montserrat, McClear Place in Toronto and Guillaume Tell Studios in Paris.

At the writing stage, Lerxst experimented with sounds in his home studio, while I got up to speed with a music writing program for Mac computers that let me visually compose, sequence, control and record my various instruments—well enough to create sonic sketches I could then play for Neil. We returned to the Manor in large part because Neil loved the way his drums sounded in the high-ceilinged stone end of the studio there, then relocated to the UK's oldest residential studios, Ridge Farm in Surrey, a mostly seventeenth-century building in a farmhouse that dated back to the Middle Ages, when men were men and most of them were short: if you didn't watch yourself stepping through the doors, you'd lose a chunk of your forehead on the lintels or ceiling beams. Enhancing the mediaeval atmosphere was a pig farm located upwind of us, which made even the shortest ramble a malodorous excursion, but yes, it was a *lovely* rustic setting.

Once again, Peter insisted we go whole hog, this time on "Mission." In addition to strings, he wanted an authentic old-school English brass band, like the ones he grew up hearing. Honestly, we thought it an odd idea, but he was so psyched up that we let him go get it done on his own. Then it was time to torture poor Lerxstie once again by returning to the tropical splendour of Montserrat, where he'd be confined to the bunker that was AIR Studios—cofounded by the Beatles' producer George Martin—until most of the guitar tracking was complete.[*] The strings that Peter wanted for "Mission," as well as "High Water" and "Second Nature," would be conducted and arranged by Steven Margoshes, the accomplished Broadway composer, pianist and long-term collaborator with Jim Steinman. And as if a string section wasn't enough, Peter wanted a gospel choir for the outro of "Prime Mover."[**] It was an unusual idea for a Rush song (though you might say it underscored the song's theme of "anything can happen") but blended in so subtly that I don't think you could accuse it of being over the top. Finally, for the first time ever a guest lead vocalist featured on a Rush song: we brought in the charming and enormously talented Aimee Mann to sing with me on "Time Stand Still." We wanted something haunting from someone who sounded angelic, a voice that floated down from the heavens, and she delivered exactly that. She's such a great vocalist (not to mention a really talented singer-songwriter) and couldn't have been more accommodating and professional. We were like schoolboys crushing over her.

AT HOME, NANCY and I had drifted about as far apart as a couple can while still cohabiting. She had little interest in my working life and was thriving independently with Zapata. I respected that but was alien to her professional milieu and at a loss as to how to bridge the

---

[*]    We were lucky to be there one more time, as only two years later Hurricane Hugo hit the island, destroying 90 percent of its structures. The studio and most of its equipment were damaged beyond repair, and Martin had to shutter it.
[**]   I was about to type "Mr. Big cannot stop thinking big!" but I think it was actually my idea. I guess he got us all thinking big.

chasm. When I'd first come home, of course we'd have the big hug and the big kiss, but we were wary. Even if at first it's a bit spiky, at heart you're happy to see each other and don't want to crush the buzz. Do you really want to get into the heavy shit? No, you want to start canoodling and being a couple again. But we were sometimes like two cats circling each other in the alley, checking each other out, like, "What the fuck? You smell different!" And yet *not* talking stoked the fires of resentment too. If you don't talk, you stop knowing how the other person is feeling. That's a serious warning sign, but instead I'd make assumptions that Nancy was cool with this or that—to the point of saying, "I'll just come home a day later. She won't mind." Or *she'd* make the assumption that because she had so much on for a fashion show the day I was home, we could just as well see each other a few days later. Then all of a sudden, you're sitting there looking at each other like you're strangers. With a minefield between you. You've booby-trapped your life together.

Typically, things would build and build until *just* when I had to head back on the road. We'd have been civil for the duration, but then, *man*, would we get into it. But we were never able to reach a conclusion because, right when we were getting close to the bone, I'd be off again with a "Sorry, I *can't* do this right now. I gotta go." Almost as if it were . . . intentional? You're not sure, but you do know one thing: you can't solve it right now because you've got to be on that plane in twenty minutes. She'd be pissed off, but it never entered my mind to change my flight or cancel a gig to *save my marriage*. If that sounds stupid, well, it was.

At last, we agreed to seek counselling. Maybe an objective party could help sort out what we could not. At least we both had a willingness to go; *that* was a good sign. It was awkward at first, of course—finding the willingness to open up to a stranger is never easy—but it was worth the trouble. Our therapist made some observations that hit home both literally and figuratively. For one, she pointed out that we had been together, on and off, since we were seventeen and in a sense had both run away from our families and into each other's arms. Rebelling against the life our parents wanted for us, we had unconsciously but intentionally orphaned ourselves, the result being that not only were we lovers but also parents to each other too, helping "grow each other up." The therapist suggested that now that we were adults (sort of), we had outgrown the rules of our original relationship, which was why they no longer felt good. No grown-up wants (consciously) to be romantically involved with a parental figure.

She encouraged us to refresh our view of each other and see if there was still a boyfriend/girlfriend attraction there. She gave us some exercises to do, the most memorable being to try to "talk" to each other for twenty-four hours at a time without using words. That one had us smirking, but we tried it. I'm still not sure how it was meant to work, exactly, other than making us actually *see* each other better and simply be physical again in our communication. Regardless, what she said about reinventing the terms of our relationship stuck with us and, slowly, we began to treat each other with more consideration, more like on a date and less routinely like co-residents.

As we mended our relationship (and resumed actually talking), we became fantastic arguers. Once we got over the hump, we found we could fight fiercely without fear that one of us was going to walk out. But that was only possible because we'd learned to listen to each other. As Robert Fripp has put it so profoundly, "Listening is a craft. Hearing is an art." I find that a major reason for the failure of many couples is they don't really hear what's being said—not just the words, but the subtext. It's all too easy to take something your partner says at face value and not grasp what's behind it; that there may be real pain underlying what they're trying to share.

Speaking from experience, I can tell you that when you're separated so much of the time, you lose the art of hearing and communicating. With me on the road so often, we started seeing ourselves as separate entities; the only things we were really sharing was some property and our beautiful boy, which just wasn't enough. On the road you spend all your time with bandmates and crew and fans and so on—in relationships that are utterly different from the kind you have with a girlfriend or wife—and if she joins you out on the road, it feels like an invasion. You're unavailable to her the way she needs you to be.

Anyway, these are some of the things that I learned in that difficult time, all of which said to me "I don't want to let this woman go." I've always found Nancy incredibly attractive both physically and intellectually. Yes, she's a beautiful, sexy redhead, but first and foremost she's smart as a whip, with intuitive superpowers! She's also fiercely independent and strong willed—and maybe because I had a very strong mum, I've always been attracted to strong women. She's also always had an innate sense of right and wrong. She has a deep, deep well of kindness, and not only for her friends; we both take our friendships very seriously, but her heart will be broken by something she's read in the paper (she's a voracious reader of books and newspapers; she has a great capacity for human interest stories) and the next thing I know, she's reached out to that person and donated money to help them. To top it off, she has a bubbly, vivacious personality, she's quick-witted and very funny; better still, she's never without a story or the juiciest gossip. I was immediately enamored with all that when we first met because I'd grown up such a quiet, nerdy kid, and more than forty years later, whether locked down at home or eating our umpteenth dinner in a row alone together while on holiday, they're still qualities I cherish.

We refreshed our view of each other's professional work during that period too: I balanced my time between home and studio better, and in public she stopped denying her connection to the band. I even started going to her fashion shows, though at first I felt like an intruder in her life. The few friends she introduced me to looked at me strangely. As I mentioned earlier, some of them didn't realize she had a husband, let alone one who looked like . . . well, *me*. But I remember being so impressed by the clothing, the hip choice of catwalk music and the way Nancy and Karen looked in action—so in command, all of it theirs and *nothing to do with me*—that I found myself welling up with pride.

There was still plenty of relationship work to do, and it wouldn't be the last time in life we'd seek help, but the counselling gave us such a jump start that after only several sessions we didn't feel the need to return. I don't think I'm betraying confidences, by the way, to mention that my bandmates were also feeling similar domestic pressures; with growing kids of their own, the need for them to change their work habits was just as evident, which in the ensuing years would significantly affect the way we went about our business. Would it be too much to claim that we were, at last . . . growing up?

**AND SO** . . . back to work. ("Sorry, honey, I gotta go!") We spent about a month mixing *Hold Your Fire* at Studio Guillaume Tell in Suresnes, an old village in the western suburbs of Paris. That time remains a highlight of my recording life. There's so very much I'd like to tell you about it, as it really was the beginning of my love affair with the city, the country and the culture—in fact, there's a lot I *have* written but has been excised from this book for want of space (I do go on a bit, you know), but there are a couple things I'll squeeze in here: a few years prior, when it was clear we'd be working in Quebec more often, we'd all decided to take French lessons and signed up with Berlitz, the international language school. One of their teachers would come to the gig in whatever city we were playing, and between soundcheck and show time, the three of us would sit for a forty-five-minute lesson. Pretty nerdy, eh? It was super useful, though, and a great way to pass the time backstage. Now it was definitely paying off. For Neil and me, this was a great Parisian adventure. With all the time we had on our hands in between mixes, we were free to check out museums and restaurants and what have you; Lerxst, however, tired of it pretty quickly and started to spend an inordinate amount of time at the apartment, smoking pot and watching *Star Trek* in French.

Once in a while, a French friend of our producer Peter Collins would join us for dinner, regaling us with stories of his travels. One night he brought us to a tiny but lively bar. I'm not sure if the place actually had an official name—he referred to it only as the "Gypsy Bar"—but I know it was in the heart of Montmartre, a stone's throw from the dome of the famous Basilica of Sacré-Coeur. There we slammed back vodka shots, ate slices of saucisson and listened to the musicians jammed into the corner of the room—usually a duo consisting of a violinist and guitarist or bassist with a decidedly Django Reinhardt vibe. One evening, Peter's pal whipped out a harmonica and played along from his seat, while others sang from theirs. It was like a scene from a 1940s movie set, another *époque* come alive. (Paris, like Istanbul, is among the few cities I know where you can feel so entirely transported back in time.) In the wee hours we'd drunkenly stumble out (again!), bewitched by the smoky atmosphere. One night in Paris truly can be like a year in any other place.

WE TOURED THE album in North America from October 1987 until May '88, finishing up with seven gigs in the UK, and on the Continent just one in Holland and two in Germany. It was after the last of those European gigs, in Stuttgart, that I was confronted with a different moment of personal truth. Travelling together apart from the band was one of the ways Nancy and I had resolved to rebuild our relationship, so she flew in to join me for a road trip across France in a rental car. Pulling out from the venue, I saw a group of fans clustered at the exit holding signs aloft that read RUSH FAN CLUB OF ITALY. They saw me, too, and tried to wave me down for autographs, but I reflexively braked, reversed and made a getaway. But then, as they grew smaller in my rearview mirror, I was hit with a major pang of guilt, like, *What the fuck is wrong with me?* Here was a handful of fervent fans who, knowing Rush weren't playing their home country, had travelled far to see us wherever they could. All they wanted was a few moments of my time, yet I bounded away like a scared rabbit. What was so threatening to me? I had to ask myself, *Is this who I am now?* I hated how I'd handled it. I hated the negative energy I'd generated. And by the time we got to our hotel, I vowed that from then on I'd chill the fuck out and turn the negative into positive for everyone concerned. I believe I've done pretty much so ever since.

In the excitement of the moment, fans will often lose their sense of propriety, so in such encounters it's up to us to take command of the situation. A smile does wonders to calm folks down, and then all you really need to do is sign a quick autograph, exchange a couple of words and wish them the best. No biggie. It's win/win: they're happy and I'm guilt-free! Done right, the whole drama is over in a minute or two. But there are of course times when one needs to put up boundaries. I mean, I've had fans ask me to sign something while I'm standing at a bathroom urinal with my dick in my hand. How am I supposed to respond? "Uh, sure, pal. Just hold *this* for a moment, will ya?"

Neil felt that adulation was corrosive. When not on tour, being just Joe Blow on his motorbike or having a coffee in a truck stop, he was the friendliest guy you could meet, but by the mid-eighties he wanted nothing more to do with the extraneous things that came with being Neil Peart the famous drummer. He was fundamentally shy, but fiercely guarded his personal space, partly on the principle that the only thing he owed the audience was a great performance. Alex, on the other hand, can almost be *too* accommodating to fans. If someone wants a hug, he'll give them a hug; he comes across as so sincere, so sweet, that fans invariably feel like they've just become his new bestie — and the next thing you know, they're hanging around the end of his effin' driveway waiting to be asked inside. And then they want to marry him. But you know, you do have to draw the line somewhere, so I used to say to him, "I have to teach you how to be a little bit of a prick, Lerxst. I'm good at it." And he'd say, "Dirk, *teach* me!"

Then there's the "I hate to bother you" right when you're dining with the missus and the kids and in the middle of a mouthful of steak. But hey, it comes with the territory, so rather than get uptight about it, I just swallow hard, and before you can say "Matsusaka beef" it's all over. The WASP that she is, poor Nancy has never gotten used to it, so for years whenever I was surprised by a fan in the street, she'd take her embarrassment with her and walk ahead until the deed was done.

There are some situations you have to avoid, such as when confronted by rude or aggressive fans, or in crowded places like a mall or airport—or worse, when professional autograph scalpers pretend to be fans. I've seen scalpers resorting to all kinds of ploys to make a few bucks off my scribble. Some would ambush us outside our hotel in the rain, even dragging children along with them to give their plea legitimacy. I have zero time for that crap.

You have to acquire a sixth sense about who is real and who is not. When you live in the public eye you develop all kinds of radar. I can sense people circling from two blocks away as first they try to make sure it's actually me and then build up their courage to make their approach. That way, I have the time to prepare myself for the encounter, to determine if they mean well or not. I also like to think I've developed the ability to clock if they're talking to me as *me* or to "Geddy Lee"—my *image*, the character in their imagination. It's odd when that happens, when "Geddy Lee" has become a kind of costume I inhabit. It's ironic that for me as a kid, rock and roll musicians were embodiments of superheroes; I was never going to be Superman, I couldn't leap tall buildings . . . but I could make music! Well, what goes around comes around. So I certainly don't mean to sound judgemental. I understand why it happens and I've learned to live with it, but it can be awkward when fans are so involved in their own relationship with your image that when they meet the real you they find it difficult to act normally. I'm guilty of it myself: after the Blue Jays won Game 6 of the World Series in Atlanta in 1992, my brother and I were invited to the celebration in their hotel. The hero of that game was the great Dave Winfield, who laced the double that drove in the winning run. At the party I went up to him and said, "I'm so happy to meet you. Congratulations! I think I was the happiest person in the stadium when you hit that double."

To which he quite rightly replied, "No, *I* was the happiest person in the stadium."

And as I realized what a fool I had made of myself by talking to the Great Dave Winfield, not the real person, all I could do was chuckle with embarrassment and say, "Oh . . . Right."

We once met a fan who was so exuberant and funny that over time he earned our trust—to the point that we gave him full backstage access. In varying degrees he became friends with all three of us and was welcomed into our homes, becoming privy to much of our private lives. I assumed that he had made the leap from fandom to bona fide friendship, but it eventually became apparent that he had either lost perspective or never really had it in the first place. He began to cross some lines, betray some trusts and presume intimacy—to the point that I had to ask him what was going on. To which he answered, quite matter-of-factly, that he thought his actions justified because "all the songs on your recent album were written about me."

*Huh?*

At first, I wasn't sure if he was joking or not. When I explained that this was a mad notion and patently untrue, he looked at me in utter disbelief, like *I* was the one who was confused. Well, yeah, I was confused, all right. I mean, how had I misread the signs? It freaked us all out, leaving us no choice but to sever communication with him. After that, I'd occasionally see him in the audience, and I'd wonder if he had sorted himself out. I truly hope so.

On the flip side of that coin: in 1979, a young fan knocked on the door of my home in the Beaches and asked me for an autograph. I sort of smiled and brusquely obliged. (Those were still early days; today my home is a definite no-go zone.) Soon afterwards, this polite, clean-cut kid started a Rush fan club, in the process befriending some of our office staff, who let him backstage at some gigs. He was always on his best behavior, and over time we got to know each other a little. He also became friendly with Nancy, offering to run errands for Zapata, and once in a while did the same for me. He also had an evident talent for photography and started shooting the band in concert, and by 1989, his studio work had become so accomplished that we hired him to shoot the album cover portraits for *Presto*.

Over the years I watched him become a well-respected photographer and videographer, shooting numerous iconic portraits of Canadian celebrities and becoming our number one lensman, doing all our cover shots and the bulk of our press and concert photography. His name (as

(ABOVE AND OPPOSITE) *Teacher and pupil: Andy MacNaughtan and me at Turnberry Golf Club and Resort, Ayrshire, Scotland, on a blustery day in April 1992, looking out to Ireland in the distance.*

you've likely guessed if you're an avid reader of album liner notes) was
Andrew "Zulu" MacNaughtan.

Andrew introduced me to the world of gay people. He let me in on
the language, the jokes, informing innocent little me, for example, that
gay people were sometimes referred to as Friends of Dorothy; if he saw
someone around who got his gaydar tingling, he'd nudge me and say,
"F.O.D." He was a great, gossipy pal who could really dish when he was
in the right frame of mind. He took me to my first gay club, in San
Francisco—sort of challenging me to go. I went, and the bouncer
checked my ID at the door. While I was thinking, *Wow, I must look
younger than I really am*, he looked up and said, "You know this is a gay
club, right?" and I thought, *Is my straightness* that *obvious?* Usually
when we were on the road, though, before Andrew had a boyfriend,
he'd go out on his own. It's good that he was so independent, because

if you're gay and want to meet people, that requires some action on your part—especially in the very heterosexual world of rock and roll. He wasn't going to find what he wanted to get his rocks off backstage at a Rush show!

Another bonus of having him on tour with us was that he also helped me with my own amateur photography. We talked a lot about art and music, and he was even my fashion advisor. On the road he liked to take me shopping for a new shirt, anything to make me look hipper than I really was. We'd talk about the work of André Kertesz, Paul Strand, Alexander Coburn, the British photographer Julia Margaret Cameron (who, being a female photographer, was ignored in her time, but now early prints of hers are museum pieces) and the great New York crime photographer Weegee. Sometimes we'd just go out walking with our cameras, and because like me he was a collector, we'd go to shops and meet dealers and talk about art with them. He had truly transcended from fanboy to dear and trusted friend.

Those were the days before we found it prudent to protect ourselves from crazy fans by checking into our hotels under pseudonyms. Soon we'd be having a blast thinking up the stupidest cover names,

*Andrew in his natural habitat—working
the pit at The Gorge, Washington, in 2011.*

different ones for each tour. I first paid homage to my hero baseball players: Hank Greenberg, then Moe Berg (both Jewish, you might have noticed), so imagine my surprise and joy when in Pittsburgh in 2002, a concierge handed me a copy of the Colorado Rockies rooming list, revealing that the star right fielder Larry Walker, ex of the Expos, was checking into hotels under the name of . . . Geddy Lee!

Sometime later, after laughing my head off watching *Superbad*, I became Mr. McLovin, which embarrassed Nancy to no end whenever she joined me on the road and had to announce herself as my wife to the front desk. Lerxst, goof that he is, took pleasure in changing his name as often as possible mid-tour, driving Liam nuts as he'd have to notify each and every hotel down the road: Harry Bagg, Dr. Karl Zbourg and, as I recall, Mike Oxonfire (go on, you can work it out), while Pratt called himself after his favourite *Family Guy* character, Brian Griffin, as well as Johnny Gilbert, the announcer on *Jeopardy!* Lerxst pushed the limit on one tour with "Colonel Dick Hertz," but Liam gave him such a hard time that he modified it to Dick Burns and finally Richard Burns—but not before threatening Liam with a nickname of his own, Shitty McCuntcock. Thankfully, not even Alex had the balls to go through with that; instead he dubbed one of our band-crew golf tournaments the "Shitty McCuntcock Invitational." Yes, kids, rock and roll is a serious business. A word of warning, though: when you're checked in under an outlandish name, don't lose your key, as you'll have to show proof of ID to get back in your room.

**PARTLY AS A** strategic move to give us a nice long break before returning to the whole studio-album-tour cycle, we recorded a number of shows from the *Power Windows* and *Hold Your Fire* tours for a live album and video called *A Show of Hands*. Where *All the World's a Stage* had been, I felt, too raw and *Exit . . . Stage Left* too processed, this one got it just right, sounding authentically ambient and ballsy yet tight as well. Being an assemblage of recordings from five cities over two tours, it represents one *ideal* night from that period; in practice it was a blessing because we could forget the tape was rolling and play our best at our most relaxed. Listening to it as I write this chapter is an unexpected pleasure. I mean, I'm barely cringing! I'm reminded of the seemingly impossible, constantly evolving and extraordinarily complex technological system we devised in order to continue as a three-piece. I can't think of another band mental enough to attempt such a setup, let alone stick to it for almost thirty years. The cover, meanwhile, with its Constructivist-inspired version of us rockin' out, derives from me seeking out examples of works by Moholy-Nagy, Popova, Rodchenko in galleries (particularly the Russians; I thought the posters from the early days of the Revolution were cool), which led to conversations with our go-to graphic artist Hugh Syme about the direction the album art should go in. It remains one of my favourites.

With the help of my keyboard guru Jim Burgess and his peeps at Saved by Technology, a computer and audio-video retailer in Toronto, we'd developed a multiple-hard-drive system that in concert allowed Jack Secret to load a different set of sounds for each song, dialling up large digital files one step ahead as the show progressed. He would also load a duplicate set of backup drives, so if one failed (and that *did* happen once in a while) he could flip the failsafe switch and we'd play on without delay. That kept Jack and me on our toes, for sure.

The system also had a variety of different samples and notes programmed to the same keys, which required me to memorize a completely different keyboard and pedal layout for each song. The key two octaves above middle C could be a brass patch for one song, a special effect or choir sample or twenty-second rhythmic piano piece for the next; then, for a song such as "Subdivisions," the keyboard would function normally. It was a constant, hair-raising matter of memorize it and don't effin' hit *that* one by mistake! Talk about a nightly tightrope walk—on my hands *and* feet. (And to think that just because I can't prepare both appetizers and a main course in time for dinner, my wife thinks I can't multitask . . .)

When you're onstage, you're connected to every nuance of the show. I'm playing bass, but that's just the start of it. I'm a human neural net, a musical cyborg. My brain's first priority is to sing in key; the second is to make sure I'm playing the right notes in the right order; third is the choreography of foot pedals and keyboard switches; fourth is listening to everyone else and making sure that every technical aspect of the show is clicking in. So when we go to a new section and a lighting effect didn't happen or the screen has gone down, or when the audience isn't digging the show, believe me, I am painfully aware of it.

One gig in Denver or Phoenix, disaster struck minutes before the show. By that time we had a pretty elaborate system in place, when keyboards were an integral part of our sound and each of us was a one-man band with electronic pads, foot pedals and so on. And when the system failed, it *failed*. So, right before we went on, the whole computer system went down and the drives wouldn't load or respond. We delayed the show for as long as we could, until I finally said, "Fuck it, let's start," and went on with just one old-style keyboard with two basic sounds to choose from. I announced that we were having technical issues and hoped aloud that we'd get through it. And of course people didn't give a shit. The show went down a storm. At the end of the day, you forget that all people are really there to see is you play and sing. When a string breaks and Alex has to stop and change his guitar, the audience will usually applaud (if it's done quickly enough).* It makes the show more memorable for them, though for us it's an "uh-oh" moment. In the old days any sudden breakdown used to shake us up.

Being so dependent on technology is a dangerous way to live. At one of the last shows we ever recorded, in Toronto, we hit the stage and as usual I clicked on a very long, complex sequence that we all had

---

* Bass strings rarely break, but it does happen. John Paul Jones recently told me that he has never broken a bass string in his entire career!

to play along with—but this time there was a momentary lag. Like half a beat. Like if you're watching a movie and the lips are moving but the words are coming out a split second later. We were all completely flummoxed. Neil adjusted his performance, but Alex wasn't following, so we had to adjust back to follow Alex, and I was screaming over to the side of the stage, "It's out of time! It's out of time!" We had a duplicate, "redundant" system but Jack couldn't hear the problem. He was oblivious, looking at me like, "Huh?" and I was like, "Can't you hear that? Reboot!" which is what he eventually did. I'm not sure the audience was aware of the lag, but they were surely aware of me freaking out for some reason. Which is really the last thing you want the crowd to see, especially at the very start of your show.

That kind of thing happens only once a tour, but you never know when it's going to strike. There are always little fuckups or "clams" due to human error, of course, but the ones when technology fails can really fuck you up because you don't know how to react and you can't have a huddle onstage to discuss it. In retrospect that can be the funniest part of the night but in the moment, of course, it's a train wreck—especially when your choreography of instrumentation is down to the microsecond and one missed beat shoots the whole thing up the spout. The big test then is how to recover, but there's no handbook that I know of entitled *How to Get Out of a Train Wreck Onstage*. Instead, there's this psycho-kinetic communication going on between the three of us as to who to follow to get out of the disaster zone. Some bands just stop the song and restart it, but we'd stupidly forge ahead pretending no one would notice if we sorted it out quickly enough.

I used to wonder what it would be like to tour with a band where I could just play bass, where I didn't have to sing and do my dance like a trained monkey on the keyboards and sixteen other instruments. It's a secret dream of mine. That must be so much fun. But can you imagine? I'd probably bum the whole band out because I wouldn't shut the fuck up on bass.

# CHAPTER 20

A SHOW OF HANDS BOUGHT THE BAND A six-month break from one another, and when we got together again we were refreshed and ready to go at it hammer and tongs. Peter Collins had moved on with other acts, so we called upon someone we'd hoped to work with on *Grace Under Pressure*, Rupert Hine, and this time our schedules aligned. Roop had produced several of my favourite records with Brand X, U.K., Bill Bruford and Peter Gabriel, overseen the creation of some bloody good and modern-sounding records with the Fixx and Howard Jones, Stevie Nicks and Tina Turner, and was a fine musician in his own right with his Thinkman project and his band Quantum Jump. I knew his name from as far back as *I Can See Your House from Here* by Camel, an album that Oscar and I adored. On it was a beautiful, slow-moving instrumental called "Ice" with one of the most delicate and lovely endings of any song from that progressive music period, featuring one of the truly great guitar solos of the late seventies, played by Andrew Latimer; IMHO it ranks up there with the likes of Clapton and Gilmour.

Right out of the gate, Roop made some unexpected observations about our work, and one of them was about the way I enunciated certain vowel sounds when I sang. He had picked up on a long "e" sound that I tended to lean on too often—like when I sing "ee-lectrical" in "The Pass," and the one for which Paul Rudd makes fun of me in our 2011 short film *I Still Love You, Man*, going "Tom Saw-yee!" He encouraged me to make different shapes with my mouth to give my voice a slightly different character. Perhaps to the layman it sounds silly (and it *looks* ridiculous), but mouth shapes greatly affect what comes out. If you've ever seen how seriously actors do their warm-up exercises backstage, you'll understand how important it is to have your facial muscles relaxed and pliable.

There are many more techniques. Some singers like to stand way back from the mic and belt it out, while others sing more softly and work the mic up close, moving in and out depending on the level of breathiness they want; to intonate better, some work with only one ear cup of their headphones on, while others plug one ear with their finger so they can hear their "inside" tone. Sometimes I'd record an intimate part early in the day when my voice was still waking up and a little hoarse, as it gave me more of a gravelly character,[*] but when I'm singing in my upper range, like any muscle my vocal cords need to be well warmed up and loose. Some singers drink scads of water or an organic "throat-coat" tea, whereas I'm happiest just sipping on coffee.

---

[*]  John Lennon famously sang the electric version of "Revolution 1" that way, not opening his mouth after waking until he lay on his back on the studio floor and gave the song his everything.

Each new Rush album gave me another opportunity to improve as a player and a songwriter, but especially as a singer. Likely it became so important to me because of all the heat I took for my voice over the years. Sometimes my attitude was, like, *Hey*. Don't like the way I sing? Well then, I invite you to fuck the fuck off and move along to something more suitable to your sensitive tastes. But most often, to meet my own standards if no one else's, I worked hard at improving my range, and trying endlessly as a songwriter to develop better melodies.

In the early days, as I've already admitted, I abused my voice by smoking and doing cocaine during shows. How I survived that period, I'll never know, but in the last fifteen or so years of touring I took care of my voice much more carefully. I was rigorous about my diet because by then I had a local throat specialist who gave me a list of strict dos and don'ts: no dairy, no spicy foods, no overly acidic foods, and I wasn't supposed to drink—particularly not white wine because it has more acidity. He also recommended I not talk on days off, which dramatically affected my lifestyle on the road. Once we'd stopped doing back-to-back shows, I'd spend my days off alone in my room or walking in

search of great wine stores *shtum*, completely quiet, only breaking my vow of silence at dinner with Lerxst. I'd avoid whispering because that's actually harder on your voice than talking. I pretty much stopped doing interviews on the day of a show for that same reason. (Good excuse, eh?) Life could get a bit boring, but it was imperative to be in the best possible shape for our epic-length shows.

By far the worst was singing with a cold or the flu, which I did far too many times. That was a special kind of torture. With our "the show must go on" attitude, we resisted cancelling unless it was absolutely unavoidable, and I went onstage with tonsillitis, croup coughs and even a bloody nose, swallowing blood (with this nose, that's a *large* amount of blood) and feeding a spittoon throughout the show. When I was sick, my bass tech Skully would also keep a shit ton of Kleenex and a wastebasket at the side of the stage, running out between songs with hot tea, lemon and honey.

One time my ears became so congested that my trusty ENT doctor in Toronto had to puncture one of my eardrums to drain the fluid out, simply so I could fly to the next gig. (During decompression at altitude, fluid in your sinus cavities can become excruciatingly painful and leave you partially deaf for days. That's a *whole* lotta fun.) I screamed blue murder when he did it. Leaving his office I noticed a young boy in the waiting room, pale as a ghost, staring at me in horror. And I said with a wink, "You're up, kid."

Even though I'm not performing these days, whenever I get a ticklish feeling in my throat, I'm still seized by the fear I lived with for so many years that I might have to cancel or, worse, I might lose my voice halfway through the show. That was something the other guys never had to worry about. They had stuff to play through but none as overtly noticeable as when the singer's voice was in trouble. Alex playing through his arthritis was tough, and Neil hurting from tendinitis was bad, but he's not as wussy as me and would stoically soldier through without anyone noticing. One April in Austin, I woke up with that *Oh, woe is me!* thing, but it wasn't a cold. Spring comes early in Texas, the trees were shooting their spores into the air, and I was having an extreme reaction to them. My voice held out that time, but on numerous occasions it went completely—in Ottawa once, it was gone after the third song, and I was squeaking the rest of the night. I was in hell. It sounded like shit, it was a nightmare, but I got through the show. Then I came off the stage and bundled myself up, and everyone came into the dressing room to tell me how great a show it was! What the fuck? Are you deaf? Do people have such low expectations of my voice that when I sing with what is so *obviously* a sore throat and a plugged-up nose, they think it sounds just the same? (That's a rhetorical question, please.)

In the last ten years of my touring life, I've never been seen without a precautionary scarf, even at soundcheck, which made me the butt of crew jokes. It sounds neurotic, but it's not hypochondria, I swear! Athletes are the same. Dave Stieb of the Blue Jays told me that some pitchers won't allow air-conditioning to blow on their pitching arm.[*] The sense of responsibility is crushing. You can talk to your bandmates and you can talk to your manager, but no one will pull the plug on a gig except the guy who's not feeling well. They just look at you, like, "What you gonna do, Dirk? You gonna cancel the show or not?" So, it's up to *me* to disappoint 20,000 people at the last minute. Of course, you *never* want to make that call, so you cross your fingers and go for it anyways. At the end of a tour, I'd feel so elated. I'd be like, "Yay, I can get sick now! Come at me, baby, gimme all you got!"

UNEXPECTEDLY, DURING THE *Presto* sessions—and especially coming from a keyboardist—Roop argued that on our last record, synths had led Rush astray. He wanted a return to our basic trio sound, and to mostly use keyboards as enhancements swirling around that

---

[*]   Athletes are famously superstitious, of course. So much so that walking onto the field, they'll hop over the foul line. "Step on a crack, break your mother's back."

solid core. Naturally, I didn't feel we'd drifted that far off (while Alex clearly did), but I had to admit that the preponderance of synthesizers was having a detrimental effect, at least, on my sense of humour. Let's call it "digital stress." It takes a tremendous amount of focus to wrestle wild noises and fashion them into melodious sounds. You don't want to use a preset right out of the box because everyone has access to that same sound; you have to adjust it and mold it into something original, and all that trial and error soon has you feeling like you've been sucked into a vacuum, like your brain has become fused to the machine, soldered to the diodes and oscillators. Which will make your head hurt. So even I was ready to get physical again.

We wanted to build the production on a strong foundation—a great-sounding drum room—but weren't happy with the options on the current Toronto studio scene. We'd been spoiled by that high-ceilinged stone end of the room at the Manor, so for the first time since *Grace Under Pressure*, back it was to the warm familiarity of Le Studio in Morin-Heights, with that gorgeous picture window overlooking the lake. The songs were in good shape, we breezed through pre-production and

*A case study of digital stress: the three of us, plus Rupert and Stephen, have been disturbingly synthesized. (I can't imagine which Serbian in the control room created this.)*

before we knew it we were done, ahead of schedule and ready to record solos and vocals at Maclear Place back in Toronto. Mixing was then done in the UK at a new London studio complex called Metropolis, a marvel of modern science with brand-spanking-new control rooms and state-of-the-art gear. The entire production process went swimmingly.

On evenings off Rupert took us to some of his top London restaurants and arranged a dinner with his pal Bob Geldof, who, for all the flack he gets for being too earnest about world affairs, was a cool and funny cat who had us in stitches with stories and jokes—including, as I recall, this one:

So, these explorers are travelling up the Amazon through the Brazilian rain forest. The first night, they're sitting around the campfire and hear drums. They're alarmed, but the guide says, "Don't worry. Drums fine. When drums stop, *then* trouble."

So, the next night, same thing. "Drums? Don't worry. When drums *stop*, trouble."

Then the third night (of course), the drums stop. They look to the guide in fear, and he says, "Uh-oh. *Bass solo.*"

*McClear Place studios in Toronto during the*
*Presto sessions. Rupert Hine and Stephen W. Tayler*
*at the console and some goofball behind.*

**THE BACKDROP WE** used for the *Presto* tour was an oversized reproduction of an antique carnival poster originally painted in oils that I found hanging on a wall in my friend Jason Sniderman's[*] home and immediately thought would look terrific on our stage . . . flanked, of course, by two gigantic inflatable rabbits. This tour was the first to feature props in addition to our usual animated sequences and film clips, which meant expanding our crew to include carpenters and stagehands—or, as they became known, Wrabbit Wranglers. I'd always admired the way Pink Floyd used inflatables in their shows, and this was the first time we'd tried them ourselves, the difference being that we took them to surreally comic extremes.

We ended up milking those bunnies for quite a few tours, and when it was decided they were getting tired we asked ourselves how we might kill the gag. So we literally killed it. We had one bunny shoot the

*Nothing to see here—just a Jew and a giant rabbit.*

---

[*]  Jason played the superb piano work on *Presto*'s "Anagram" and years later on "The Garden" from *Clockwork Angels*.

other one. We gave one of them an arm that rose up with a double-barreled shotgun in its paw, and at a certain point in the show, with a flash pot for the BOOM, he'd fire it, and onto the back of the stage we projected an early Disney-style cartoon tracing the circuitous trajectory of the angry, fanged, cigar-chomping bullet, eventually finding its way into the other bunny, which deflated in a puff of smoke. Rather than the bitter social critique of Floyd's *Animals*, we went for a goofy joke, but to our horror we'd hear the audience go, "*Oh-h-h-h.*" Worse, the bunny that was shot would not deflate fast enough sometimes and just stagger there, sagging tragically, so even though the cartoon then showed him being taken to Heaven by two sexy rabbit angels, we kind of bummed the crowd out every night! Rush's fans are very sensitive types, I guess. Be warned: getting into gags is a tricky business. Show business is hard, but comedy is harder!

IT SOUNDS LIKE a cliché, but as we all travelled, worked and lived together over that hugely busy period, our crew was very much a family to us. We'd catch up and joke around with them at mealtime, trying to make ourselves available and remain close with as many as we could. As we convoyed from state to state and gig to gig, we'd sometimes take turns riding with the drivers to chew the fat and stay sensitive to what their lives were actually like as they drove all night, slept all day, stocked up at truck stops and communicated with one another on CB radio. (Neil initiated that, as a matter of fact; he was always curious about the working lives of others and greatly respected what the guys did for us.) As the band grew in popularity and the show became more elaborate—with lasers, live cameras, props and more sophisticated animation and film presentations—the army grew ever larger, incorporating cameramen, video technicians, a director and more, and the idea of being buddies with every single one of them became less realistic. I like to think that over the years we had a tight and sincere vibe with all

our crew, but it wasn't easy and we may not have always been successful. It was a twenty-four-hour thing. To give you some idea of what I'm
talking about, here's a brief rundown of the roadie's routine:

The riggers are in first, at five, six, seven a.m. They and the lighting
crew used to have shirts that read:

FIRST TO COME

LAST TO PULL OUT

Having driven all night from the previous venue, the riggers hang
the points, then stick around to make sure there are no problems for
the sound crew once the PA system is raised. After that, they and the
drivers sleep all day in the bus or a hotel, and the next time you see
them, they're rubbing their eyes and grousing as they arrive for dinner.
At the end of the evening, they pull the show down, clamber into the
buses and do it all over again — ten, twenty, thirty times in a row.

Once the points and lights and sound are hung, the band crew
arrives to set up our gear onstage. They're the last to arrive and because
they've gotten more sleep they're jokingly considered a little more
"Hollywood" than the others. All three crews then work all through
the show, so there's really no rest for anyone — and as our team
expanded to include carpenters assembling the risers and a plethora of
props, they, too, would have to be there the whole time, waiting to tear
it all back down. Even during the performance, no one got to hang
around. Everyone had cues as to when and where they had to be, multiple jobs to carry out with their earplugs in, and on R40, with its retrospective theme, some were given roles that involved walking out on
the stage as part of the theatre of it all. The fact that a show as elaborate as ours was set up and torn down in one night was a minor miracle.
By then we'd be hauling ten semi-trailers full of equipment around
with us — we'd come a long way from carrying our cables in a few Coca-
Cola crates.

Travelling with such a large contingent was like a circus (with animals, even, albeit inflatable), and being away from home and any sense of normal family life for so long inevitably stirred up myriad issues for everyone, be they substance abuse, marital stress, money matters or what have you. As in any family, there were some naughty boys, which sometimes meant a troubled visit in the middle of the night. And as I was the most engaged of the three band members when it came to day-to-day decision making and the business side of the band, the four a.m. knock would usually be on *my* hotel room door.

We had a driver who came to me in the middle of the night really coked out and upset that his habit had gotten the better of him. He told me he was worried about being well enough to be at the wheel the next day. That was pretty damn responsible of him, I thought, though I wasn't convinced his problem was as bad as he feared. I thought he mostly needed to talk to "the boss" for a minute, to unburden himself,

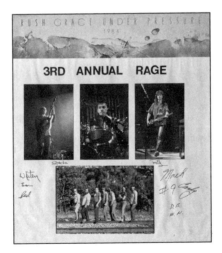

*Not only did our drivers (and riggers) take us out for dinner, they also presented us with personalised mementos such as this signed and framed photo. It meant a lot. Sadly, we lost a few good folks along the way; of those pictured here, only Arthur "Mack" MacLear (right, second from the end) was with us to the end—a stretch that began in 1978, lasting thirty-seven years.*

which was the nature of our relationship. I listened to him as best I could and asked him if he wanted us to seek help for him, made a few suggestions and then he went away. And happily that was that.

But not everyone comes to you with their issues before it's too late. There were other instances when I'd be the last to know. More than once, someone was found lying comatose in the parking lot who had to be rushed to the hospital, or someone else was discovered passed out in one of the stalls. One fellow we sent to a rehab place in Minnesota left the centre after a couple of days without telling us. Unbeknownst to us, he'd gone AWOL from the facility, then showed up for the next tour, thanking us for sending him there and pretending that everything was fine. Then in the middle of the tour, when we played a university arena where the sports medicine staff kept their supplies in the dressing room, he broke in, stole some drugs and was subsequently found slumped over in the bathroom. He survived and was hugely contrite, but we had to let him go.

I felt like a fool for having worked so closely with someone and not seen the signs. I felt responsible. How could I have been so oblivious? Not to realize that I had someone working for me who was so strung out made me wonder where my fucking head was at. And he was in dire shape. Yes, we'd sent him to rehab, but after a supposed recovery, I hadn't made sure he ever finished his course. I didn't understand the depth of his addiction, nor did I realize how the mind of an addicted person works. After we'd parted ways, he would contact me for money and, of course, I couldn't trust what it was really for. I felt so conflicted, trust had been broken and I turned away, never speaking to him again. Years later, after he really did get clean, he was still working in the business and communicated with Neil and some of the crew, but I still felt so betrayed that I couldn't bring myself to reforge the relationship. And eventually he passed away. My failure to forgive bothers me to this day. Yes, he was the one hiding his habit from *me*, but he was in my employ, and I should have been hip to it. Then again, when you clock all the lies you've been told, it's hard to simply forgive and forget.

It sometimes felt like in addition to being the bassist, singer, keyboardist, day-to-day business guy and all the rest, I was amateur therapist and counsellor to the crew, but it's not like it happened every day. Still, when it did, it usually ended in tragedy. Yet another chap who worked for me turned out to have a drinking problem that got so serious I could smell it on his breath at soundcheck. On the road, every employee becomes you or your bandmates' rep, meeting with technical salesmen, music store people and the like, who of course would smell it too, so I thought, we can't have someone representing us in that condition. After I asked one of our production managers where all the booze was coming from, he started secretly marking the bottles we provided with the crew's supplies of foods and snacks aboard their bus, noting who went in and out in the course of the day. Sure enough, huge amounts were disappearing and were linked to the comings and goings of a certain individual. Liam and I had an intervention with this fellow and reassured him that if he had a drinking problem we'd help, but the guy denied it, denied it, denied it, only for us to find him passed out in the parking lot a week or so later. The drinking had given him heart issues and he ended up in a hospital in Seattle. After that, he was too embarrassed to see me and never worked for us again. At one point he reached out, and I put him in touch with a counsellor in Toronto, but he wouldn't finish the program. And he, too, passed away.

Every band has stories like these, a lot of which are born of loneliness. It's difficult to work for a band, to keep the hours that roadies do and have normal relationships, let alone a normal life. Even if the type of person drawn to this type of work is often not in search of a "normal" life, you can't help but feel somewhat responsible for them when things go really bad, but it is the nature of the music business. (Fortunately, we've never had a problem with someone in the actual band, but many bands do, and that must be just *terrible*.) It's a tough way to live, way tougher than people realize. Certainly not as glamorous as it's cracked up to be.

In the end, I do believe we and our crew enjoyed a mostly mutual respect, because many stayed with us for years, even decades. Liam worked for us from age seventeen to sixty—that's *forty-three years*; Howard worked with us for forty; our head driver, Arthur "Mac" McClear, drove for us pretty much every tour from 1978 to the very last, in 2015. We shared hundreds of thousands of miles and countless experiences, watching one another and our respective families grow, often physically distant yet always close at heart. In the early eighties, the drivers would even arrange an Annual Drivers Dinner at which we were the special guests. That was really touching; I mean, whose drivers take them out to dinner? Sometimes things went south and people went their own way, but for the most part it was on good terms. Neil used to refer to Alex and me as "the guys at work" as much as he did the crew, and we were happy to be considered that way.

*Towards the end of every tour we took a shot much like this one—us with our entire road family. I wish I had the space to print them all.*

# CHAPTER 21

ACK IN CANADA AFTER SOME FAMILY
time, the band was champing at the bit to return to
writing. In late August we holed up at Chalet Studios in
Claremont, an hour's drive north of Toronto, where we'd
spend ten weeks deep in demos for *Roll the Bones*—by far the longest we'd
ever spent in pre-production. It was idyllic there. Between the studio
and the bedrooms was a games zone and living room where the crew
could yuk it up around the pool table playing Scoozball* while I topped

---

\* You may have noticed Scoozball mentioned in the liner notes for *Power Windows* and
wondered what it was. Invented by the crew, Jimmy Johnson, Larry Allen and Skip, it was a
variation on pool in which you got points for doing all the *wrong* things: calling the wrong
shot, sinking the cue ball or bouncing it off the table, that sort of thing.

---

up the bird feeders and kept an eye out for evening grosbeaks and gold-finches. But a more sinister vibe was encroaching on our space. In and out of the studio, it was impossible to ignore the large-screen TV tuned constantly to CNN as it broadcast updates on the Iraqi invasion of Kuwait and the impending conflict in the Persian Gulf. As war became inevitable, we would often stop and watch in stunned silence at what was unfolding far away from our little creative paradise.

Still, songs surfaced fast. To nail the spirit of "Bravado," Neil had in mind the line "going for it regardless of the outcome" from John Barth's *Tidewater Tales*,[*] but seldom have I sung a line from any song that rings so true to me in my own personal experience as "We will pay the price / But we will not count the cost." Being so determined to be a musician and breaking my mother's heart in the process; the damage I'd done to my family life and my most important relationships . . . In all these instances I naïvely thought I was prepared to pay the price, but I didn't really know what that was until it was tallied up and presented to me. Anytime you follow a dream, there is a hidden cost. If you're lucky, it just won't be too dear.

Most dramatic was the way the title track came to life; seldom had Alex and I been more in sync while writing a song. We wanted to funk up "Roll the Bones," so after he created a pattern on his drum machine (he's the best drummer you've ever heard who can't actually play the drums), we jammed to his downtempo rhythm, starting with a set of choppy guitar chords to give me lots of room for a funky bass line. Harking back to our Toronto roots, we then threw in an old-fashioned, Mandala-style blue-eyed soul organ slash to boost the riff-o-matic funk machine (yeah, white Canucks *can* get funky!) as we approached the still unwritten middle section for which Pratt had written a set of quirky rhyming couplets—a kind of ode to hip-hop. Glancing down at the lyrics, a half talking/half singing melody slipped out of my brain that fit the song like a

---

[*]   Many years later John Barth would also be a major influence on *Clockwork Angels*.

glove. We had such a blast goofing around that we mooted adding a special guest to deliver it. First we imagined a female, then maybe Robbie Robertson with his rich, deep voice, then John Cleese either doing his Upper Class Twit of the Year or dispassionate BBC broadcaster, but during the actual recording sessions, after we detuned my guide track voice with a harmonizer, we decided to keep it just like that.

Who knew that it would be considered controversial? When it came out, some fans *hated* us doing it, while some classic rock radio stations refused to so much as play it unless we cut out the so-called rap. Seriously? For heaven's sake, it was more a rock number with a spoken-word section. True rap comes from bona fide rappers with legitimate street cred; it's about *context*, people! To us it was no different than injecting some reggae and ska rhythms into the middle of "The Spirit of Radio"—just another of our many influences, little jokes and quotations, tossed into our musical stew. We were proggy hard rockers having fun with words while paying respect to a serious art form.

It's worth noting that *all* rock and roll was born of Black music. Where would Zeppelin, the Yardbirds, the Stones or even Rush be without the blues or Motown? Nowhere, that's where. Was it legit rap? Of course not. We didn't come from that experience, and never pretended we did. We were tipping our hat to the best of that genre, using electronics to keep a certain distance from the real deal, and we were sponges absorbing everything we could, but we were not trying to culturally appropriate! That Rush was copping rap was a stunningly shallow interpretation perpetuated by the very conservative world of commercial radio. For a while then, some radio stations wouldn't play Rush—*any* song by Rush—or even utter our name on the air, even if privately some DJs loved the song. Why? Because just our *name* was too associated with hard rock or prog rock, which didn't fit their format even if the song did. (As I've said before, for years we weren't really suitable for any format, not until "Classic Rock" came into being. We had to hang around a long time to qualify for that!) *Roll the Bones* was released when a multitude of musical genres were breaking out, and Neil, if nothing else a listener who rarely dismissed anything unfamiliar out of hand, was impressed by the rhyming and cadences and language of rap. He was analysing it in his own way and trying to bring a bit of himself into it. Oh, and having some *fun*. It was supposed to be fun, but Rush in the minds of many had to be *serious*, so we got an adverse reaction.

It's also worth noting that, as is often the case with hip-hop itself, the controversy obscured the actual content of the song. Isolated though we were in the countryside, the large screen TV we had to pass on our way into the studio made sure that we couldn't miss what was going on in the world. Stunned and heartbroken though we'd been by the news of John Lennon's murder while we were making *Moving Pictures*, our music hadn't been affected because it was already written, but we were in the early stages of writing "Roll the Bones" when Saddam Hussein's invasion unfolded before our eyes. It still wasn't, like, "Hey, let's write a song about the burning oil fields in Kuwait," but it did affect our mood, and chances are it was smouldering in Neil's mind while he was working on the lyrics. "Roll the Bones" is more generally about fate, how life is a roll of the dice, and chances are he was thinking about people being blown up in a war that had really nothing to do with the people themselves. I don't remember him specifically talking about it, but it's not a stretch now to read those lyrics and imagine that they contain a subliminal reaction to the way war waged by generals and politicians will snatch control from ordinary people's lives. Neil was *always* observing and absorbing. As he's written in his books, he loved to keep track of the graffiti and signs (especially church signs) he noticed through the window of our car or tour bus and write down the funniest or most remarkable or most ironic ones. Again, I don't remember him looking at a road sign and bursting into song (although when *Rush: The Musical* opens on Broadway . . .), but he really did silently consume and digest it all; it would work through his system and suddenly there it would be: new, often topical material.

*Put a bunch of grown-ups (did I say "grown-ups"?) on a well-stocked bus with miles and miles to kill, and shit happens . . . And when Andrew MacNaughtan is your assistant and a photographer, oopsie: evidence.*

The sessions for *Roll the Bones* were even more efficient than those for *Presto*. For starters, Neil nailed almost all his tracks in *one take*. Seriously, he completed ten tracks in something ridiculous like four and a half days. I did my best to pick up the gauntlet, and we ended up finishing all the bed tracks in record time. Take it from me: ten weeks writing and rehearsing *will* pay off. More important, the two albums we did with Rupert and Steven are very fond memories for me, all the more bittersweet for Rupert's succumbing to cancer on June 4, 2020, at only seventy-two years of age.* Rupert was fun and lovable and, above all, unflappable. I *never* saw him upset. He would never start an argument or engage in friction in the studio, always keeping an even keel no matter how much he disagreed with you—a major reason he was such a successful producer. Whether jamming with the guys or dishing gossip, he was a charming and engaging fellow and always good value at the dinner table. We remained pals even after we stopped working together. He was truly a "lovely jubbly" gent who radiated much more light than heat.

AFTER *ROLL THE* Bones' release and tour, we pondered next steps for the band. We'd worked with three different production teams since Broon, and I'd learned a helluva lot about making records. In spite of the confidence that the three of us were now more than capable of producing ourselves, I also understood the benefits of having someone objective around—someone to keep an eye on the shop and take care of the innumerable decisions that come with the territory.

With the advent of grunge from the American Pacific Northwest, attitudes towards rock and recording were reverting to a heavier, less corporate sound, and we loved what we heard in the music of bands like Nirvana, Pearl Jam and Soundgarden. To be honest, I wasn't as

---

* "Only" seventy-two? I suppose that's a pretty good life, but speaking as someone pushing seventy, it seems way too effin' soon!

well-versed a grunge freak as Neil was, but I dug the energy and the live-off-the-floor vibe. Soundgarden's power and song structure were particularly impressive. While to my ear Nirvana played with a free-wheeling, reckless abandon, they weren't so much "heavy" as a grungy yet melodic pop sensation. But most important, a ton of what came out of the Seattle scene was fresh, exciting and inspiring—a new take on the American sound. We were keen to get a new game on too, harnessing the refreshed rock vibes to a skill set we had honed over the twenty-plus years since the "new guy" joined us.

Reviewing our last few albums, we realized that sonically something serious was lacking. Even when I'd sat in the mastering suite with our longtime mastering engineer, Bob Ludwig, and listened to the final mixes of *Roll the Bones*, I'd recognized with some disappointment that the tracks lacked scale and power, especially at the bottom end, and now we all agreed that it was time to make a more aggressive and heavier-sounding album.

Alex was adamant about sticking strictly to a three-piece lineup with no keyboards at all. I agreed with him, but when we loaded into Chalet Studios and he saw my usual keyboard setup, his nose got a bit out of joint. I mean, he must have already told me ten thousand times that he didn't want keyboards on the album. I tried to stress to him that, as with *Roll the Bones*, I would not use them as a writing tool, only to add judicious touches to the arrangements, but he was leery and there was immediate tension at the start of those sessions. That sort of thing has been the death of many a band, but fortunately we *never* had arguments or even lengthy words. I know it sounds incredible, but in forty-five years, though feelings about this and that sometimes simmered below the surface, we never once came to blows. We were too busy talking about stupid things! We'd sooner make jokes about going into the Hall of Farts—this little area of the studio that was the only safe place to go if you were on the brink of a gaseous episode. That's the kind of mentality we had at work—as I said, plain *stupid*.

We weren't going to waste our time fighting. As far as the keyboards were concerned, I was true to my word, and we moved on . . .

I've consistently described Alex as the funniest man alive, but he's also a Serb. He gets very emotional, very heated, and is perfectly capable of flying off the handle. Many times in meetings, he'd explode, but never at *you*. It's not personal, it's at the universe. When you use logic to try to deal with him, he kind of . . . slowly . . . calms . . . down . . . but it takes a while for the steam to dissipate. Apparently, his mother had a similar attitude. His father used to say, "Sometimes when I look at her, you can tell there's something on her sleeve!" (Alex has always told hilarious stories about his parents, fully taking on their language and accent. Early on I picked up some choice Serbian curses from him, as well as several useful phrases I could use to suck up to his mum, saying, for example, "Ja сам јако добар дечко"[*] and then wagging my finger in Alex's direction and saying, "Он није добар дечко."[**])

We called once again on Peter Collins. For all the excesses of the two albums we'd done with him, both *Power Windows* and *Hold Your Fire* sounded bigger, bolder and frankly better than both *Presto* and *Roll the Bones*, and his expertise and decisiveness were valuable assets. We also listened to a wide array of engineer-type dudes' demo tapes, seizing on one with a set of big, fat, ballsy sounds. This dude's name was Kevin "Caveman" Shirley, a South African resident of Australia but living at the time in New York City. Kevin was an awkward-looking man, burly with big hands and a round head. You could put a scruffy beard on him and he'd look like a caveman—hence the nickname. I think he called *himself* that, but we liked it because in that moment we were so digital and he was so analog; soundwise, he was back with the so-called rock and roll dinosaurs. He flew up to Toronto to meet us, and the interview was shockingly direct and unfiltered. He held nothing back, saying that many of the sounds on our recent records were either bad, wimpy

---

[*]  "I am a very good boy."
[**]  "He is *not* a good boy."

or too effect-driven, and made a strong case for going back to basics. He was an analog man to the bone, asserting that he could help us make the best-sounding record we'd made in years. Oh, *really?* That took some nerve, but we didn't hold it against him. We liked how confidently opinionated he was and gave him the job. But could he deliver the goods?

The moment we entered the studio, Kevin took over our sound. He assessed the ways we'd become accustomed to record and straight-away challenged us to do things *his* way. And let me tell you, there was no point in arguing with him. If ever I tried, he'd say something like, "Why do you want to use *that* sound again? It was shitty!" And he'd beg Alex to "stop using that fucking pedal board!" Well, we'd chosen him for a reason, and decided to give him enough rope to hang himself. But he didn't. He knew exactly what he was doing, and we got better sounds than we'd expected, bolder and more energetic yet still raw.

Then I was in his line of fire. He pulled out an Ampeg head someone had resurrected from the garbage, plugged it into some Trace Elliot cabinets of mine and insisted on EQing it himself; cranking the shit out of it, miking the cabinets in a way only he knows how, and on every track had me use my early-seventies Fender Jazz Bass, which I hadn't played in years. Then he got Alex playing in the studio instead of the control room to get that natural resonance between guitar and amp. He was fearless in the face of Neil too. When Neil expressed concern about the sound of his hi-hat, instead of delicately twiddling a row of knobs on the console, Caveman simply *moved the mic*. That was so effin' old school! Far from being dependent on the range of high-tech EQ gear available, he went straight to the source. Neil had been a lesser fan of his attitude at the start, but now he charged into the bed tracks and, like a man possessed, recorded all eleven songs in just three days.

At that time, incidentally, I wanted to bring a more percussive, rhythmic approach to the way I hit the strings, and developed a kind of flamenco approach to playing. It was partly inspired by watching Les

*After recording bed tracks at Le Studio, we relocated to McClear Place in Toronto, where (can you tell?) we were sent a ton of hats from the only grammatically challenged team in the NHL. Go Leafs go!*

Claypool of Primus onstage and listening to players like Flea who switched seamlessly from a slap style to traditional yet still adventuresome rock. What accidentally made my style unique was that I was pretty much a *failed* slap player. When I attempted it, my strings sounded too clicky and lost *oomph*, so I developed my own finger technique to produce an aggressive rhythmic approach that retained my signature twang, and what at first sounded weak and weird in the context of Rush provided a different but still powerful backbone.

*Counterparts* was greeted warmly by our fan base, and all that appreciation was reflected in the chart positions. "Stick It Out" became the #1 rock track on radio and the album debuted at #2 on *Billboard*; only the excellent Pearl Jam prevented us from claiming our first #1 album debut, and we certainly didn't begrudge them that. The subsequent tour was also successful, but we disappointed our management and agents by limiting it to North America, stopping in mid-May after only fifty-four shows. Because I had promises to keep and responsibilities to fulfill.

**I HAD BEEN** wanting to expand our little family for a couple of years, but Nancy was unwilling to even consider having another baby, especially if I intended to maintain my rigid work schedule. She saw the value in Jules having a sibling, but she was a career person herself now, with little appetite for housewife drudgery. Our conflicting desires led us to seek marriage counselling for the second time, which helped. Persuaded, at least, that I was sincere in my willingness to be as close to an equal partner in raising a second child as I could, Nancy reluctantly gave in. But as Mother Nature would have it, we were unable to get pregnant and had to accept that a second child wasn't in the cards.

Of course, we had a perfectly happy little family with Jules, who in the summer of 1993 was celebrating his thirteenth birthday, which meant . . . bar mitzvah time! We hadn't raised him religiously, but I still identified as a "cultural" Jew, proud to play a part in my family history and the race of people who had overcome so much simply to survive. As such, we felt it would be right as well as fun for Jules to have a bar mitzvah of some kind, even if it was improvised or, shall we say, unorthodox. My plan was to take him to the Holy Land so he could get a sense of his people and some of their history. Neither Nancy nor I had been to Israel either, so we considered it an education for all of us.

I'd heard innumerable stories about Israel, of course, and was impatient to experience it for myself. I wasn't interested in seeing the rabbis or the bankers—I knew what *those* guys looked like. It was the Jewish proletariat I was interested in. I wanted to see Jews in all their capacities, waiting tables, cleaning streets . . . the jobs, in other words, that in North American society would have been left to

*Nancy taking shelter from the Egyptian sun. Unlike us Semitic types, redheads just ain't cut out for the desert life.*

other immigrants. I wanted to see if there was some guy like me, a third-generation Pole on *top* of a pole, fixing an electrical cable! I wanted to see the breakout, the *anti*-stereotype. I used to joke about that all the time with Jewish friends: when your doorbell rang and someone came to fix your toilet, would they look just like me? Was it a kind of bizarro world in which everyone looked alike, like they all came from the same Polish *shtetl*? When I read Michael Chabon's fabulous novel *The Yiddish Policeman's Union*, I loved that the characters in his imaginary version of Israel situated in Alaska were all that: the head detective was a Jew, and so on . . . It was Chabon's version of Israel that I was looking for!

We toured the length and breadth of Israel from the Temple Mount to Bethlehem, Caesarea, the Golan Heights to the Dead Sea, climbing to the top of Masada and back north to Haifa, and unavoidably visited the harrowing Yad Vashem—the Holocaust Remembrance Center—which had me in tears. It's hard to express how profoundly distressing it was, but put it this way: I felt I had no good reason to be standing there. Like I shouldn't even exist. It felt like a miracle that I was even there to see it with my own son. Knowing that the line had carried on should be a cause for celebration, but you don't feel like celebrating when faced with all that horror. Your heart bleeds for every family, of course, but most of all it bleeds for your own.

Then we went to Egypt for more sightseeing, accompanied by our friends Peter Mensch and his wife, Melissa.* We were fortunate to have been able to arrange the services of a hugely experienced Egyptologist, a personable and informative woman who'd once worked for Anwar Sadat. On our first day in Thebes, she walked us around the temples of Luxor and Karnak, leading us to a wide-open circular area, in the centre of which was an ornate pink granite pedestal with a scarab perched on top.

---

* Peter was one half of the highly successful management team Q Prime, with Cliff Burnstein—the same Uncle Cliff who signed us to our very first record deal on Mercury Records.

The guide told us that we were on a holy site where a statue of Pharoah Amenhotep III had once stood, attracting people from all over the world since ancient times. She explained that walking around this scarab seven times, clockwise, would bring good luck and fertility for those in love. Well, as soon as Peter heard the word "fertility," he grabbed Melissa's hand and walked around it *fourteen* times just to be sure, and then I took Nancy by the hand and dragged her around it too—just a modest seven times—as she giggled, "Oh, this is ridiculous!"

Well, within three months, not only was Nancy pregnant, but Melissa was pregnant with *twins*. Hand on heart, this is a true story. As the lyrics of "Presto" go, *I'm not one to believe in magic*, but what in Amun's name?! When our baby girl arrived, we wanted to name her Cairo after the experience, but Jules, being the conservative young soul that he was at fourteen, insisted it was "dumb" to name someone after a city,* so to keep the peace we amended Cairo to Kyla, which he endorsed wholeheartedly.

I wrapped the *Counterparts* tour in anticipation of Nancy's due date, fully pledged to set time aside away from work and be properly engaged in the first year and a half of my daughter's life. Nancy's experience this time around was a lot more relaxed than fourteen years before; in 1980 everything had happened in an operating room, with me dressed in full hospital gown and mask and looking over the nurses' shoulders. But now we were in our own delivery room and I was an active part of the birthing crew. Nancy, a big believer in better living through chemistry, happily accepted the epidural and actually fell asleep during her contractions. I will never forget having to *wake her up* because it was time to give birth. I was literally hands-on, bringing Kyla Avril Weinrib-Young into the world and cutting the cord myself. One of the happiest moments of my life.

---

* Adelaide? Cheyenne? Florence? Phoenix? Leon? Not so dumb!

IN FEBRUARY 1996 we brought Peter Collins back to produce our new album, *Test for Echo*, at the legendary Bearsville Studios, our first-ever recording session in the US of A. In its thirty years of operation, more than two thousand albums were made there by artists including Metallica, Patti Smith, Todd Rundgren and the late, great Jeff Buckley. It was a friendly and accommodating place, but we felt quite isolated. Our snowbound recording sessions were accurately represented by the *Test for Echo* cover art, which shows a lonely inukshuk standing vigil over a barren, snow-covered landscape with nothing but a row of satellite dishes in the background, but the title of the album was really about *technological* isolation. Social media was burgeoning, we were well into the Age of Information, but were the most important signals of human communication getting through the noise? "Is this mic on? Is anybody *out* there?" "Test for Echo," the song itself, was asking what is relevant in a five-hundred-channel universe. Everyone was up to their necks in technology, but was anybody listening? Happily, when the album came out in September it was pretty well

*"Taking a break from my face."* (LEFT) *Men with Goatees, circa 1985.*
(RIGHT) *As Kyla pops into a* Test for Echo *mixing session in 1996, all that remains is my soul patch, which hasn't left my* punim *since.*

received, hitting #5 on the US charts and #3 in Canada, and making a strong showing in the UK and across Europe.

The tour consisted of sixty-eight shows, from October through to July of the following year, and with the gigs billed as "An Evening with Rush," it was our first without an opening act. We did that mainly so we could play longer. With sixteen studio albums in our pocket, we had a lot of music to cover in only two hours; this way we could play three or more, with a twenty-minute intermission to catch our breath. We sprinkled songs from *Test for Echo* over two sets, dramatically ending the first with side one of *2112*, almost in its entirety, kicking off the second half with "Test for Echo" and still having the time for six new songs and a wide range of older material.

Free from having to accommodate other bands' gear, we could build up our show to any scale we desired. No set changeovers made for a much more relaxed atmosphere backstage and allowed us to fine-tune the acoustics for the entire evening before the crowd filled the house. It was better in every way. Charlie Watts once said of the Stones' routine, "Work for five years. Twenty-five years of hangin' around." Well, with less hangin' around now, we could arrive promptly, do a healthy soundcheck and all our backstage business and get onstage earlier. Technically and psychologically it was an improvement, which made for a superior performance. It was all very civilized.

I once visited Josh Homme backstage before a show on his tour with Iggy Pop. There was a total party vibe going with really loud, super-hip music while Josh poured tequila shots all around. Iggy stayed sober in his dressing room, but the rest of us were totally in the groove and I was thinking, *Wow. Is this what a normal dressing room is like? With people having . . . fun?* Sorry to disappoint you, but our backstage was very quiet. We *never* had music playing, just the sounds we ourselves made while warming up. We needed structure, a peaceful routine to keep us healthy and sane and composed for the stage. We'd sometimes welcome family in, but even that could get hairy with children running amok, raiding the buffet and chasing one another around the couch while Neil growled as he tried to read. That may well have been why he eventually demanded his own dressing room, but in any case all three of us preferred a quiet refuge to a party zone. I know a lot of ballplayers who are the same: when I used to visit Mark Langston when he was pitching for the Cleveland Indians, he'd be really friendly in the afternoon, during batting practice or whatever, but then he'd disappear, and if I ever asked what was up with Mark, I'd simply be told, "Game day."

During intermission in later years, here's what thrilling things would happen: first we'd fight for the bathroom. Then Neil would have a cigarette, I'd check the baseball scores to see how my fantasy team was doing and Alex would dive into his iPad. *That's* how exciting it was backstage with us. The last thing we needed was to see people.

But at the *end* of the show? Different story (when we weren't doing a runner to the bus or the airplane, that is). There was always a need to decompress, to come down from your adrenaline high, so after showering off, even if stuck backstage in some shitty dressing room after the show, it was nice to tuck into an elegant bottle of Burgundy and a beautiful piece of meat that our road chef, Frenchy, had prepared (plus, for Alex, a fine fatty). After a couple of bottles we could be a shindig unto ourselves, but there was often a line of people waiting outside to say hi, so we'd open up the room and what followed would be some form of party, if never a full-on bacchanal. On nights we had to fly out, I'd usually have indicated to the road manager which people I wanted to see and which I didn't, and we'd have a code of simple gestures to indicate when we needed the room cleared. And if we were getting sloshed, there'd be no missing Liam's disapproving face as he tapped his foot and looked pointedly at his watch. At least he was still working. He had to ensure we could make the flight, fly to the next city, get to the hotel, check in, all the rigamarole. He couldn't relax until we were all tucked away; last to turn out the lights, first to get up in the morning. Then do it all over again.

# CHAPTER 22

EAST GLACIER PARK, MONTANA
The lobby of Glacier Park Lodge, East Glacier Park, Montana, was built more than 3/4 of a century ago. The huge 40-foot long timbers supporting the lobby are Douglas Fir, while those used to support the verandas are Cedar.

*Photo by Eric E. Christianson*

Hey Dirk—
Greetings from "The Healing
Road." I pulled into this joint
today, and decided to stay
another day. I've been doing some
great hiking out here, but I'm
2-scared of the bears, so I walk
along singing "Big Frank" songs—
my voice is a guaranteed bear
repellent! (But just in case, I also
carry a pointy rock, for Grizzly-
smacking... yeah right!) Thanks for the
fax in Van, man. John Ellwood

POST CARD

MOAB, UTAH

Oaxaca

HE END OF THE SECOND LEG OF THE *TEST FOR Echo* tour was planned so we could finish close to home, with our final three shows in Toronto, Quebec and Ottawa. Nancy and I drove to our cottage in northern Ontario; for Alex it was golf season and the links were calling his name, while Neil headed off to his lake house in Quebec. It was an idyllic summer. On July 29, my forty-fourth birthday, he sent me his yearly "Prattfax." Neil never missed sending me or Lerxst a note on our birthdays, even if the bulk of it was an update on *his* life. This one in particular is difficult for me to reread . . .

He described in great detail how the Quebec summer was treating the family, how he was getting over the elbow tendinitis that had hampered him on the road and a book he was writing that he referred to as "Landscape with Drums," about his adventures on our most recent tour, onstage, backstage and riding his motorcycle along the backroads of North America. He joked lovingly of how he had been mandated "a mornings-only work schedule" by "Their Royal Female Majesties," his wife, Jackie, and nineteen-year-old daughter, Selena, and proudly related how Selena, whom he'd dubbed "The Princess Warrior," had spent the whole month of July with them, and how, now that she was a licenced driver, was ready to head out on a road trip of her own before the September semester at York University in Toronto.

Just short of three weeks later, the morning of August 11, 1997, I received a phone call from Ray. He was barely able to get the words out of his mouth: "Yesterday . . . Selena was in a car accident."

I sat down before I could respond. "What? What *happened?* Is she okay?"

He shared the few scraps of information he had, and it was as bad as it could possibly be. She'd loaded up her Jeep Wagoneer and hit the road. Neil had escorted her on his motorcycle partway, stopping in Hawkesbury, Ontario, where they got out and gave each other a big father-daughter goodbye hug. She drove away along Highway 401, just west of Brighton, when she somehow lost control of the car. It flipped. And just like that, she was gone.

As Ray described to me the terrible moment when the police had appeared at the door of Neil and Jackie's lake house and broke the news that their daughter was dead, I sat in the bay window of my home, stunned and staring blankly out over the lake, the sun shining brilliantly but the world around me falling dark. I felt paralyzed. Nancy and I were in a daze. Terrible images looped around in my head . . .

Ray soon called again to say that Neil and Jackie were returning to their Toronto home, so we packed up and drove to the city. I managed to call Alex, who was staggered too, struck dumb. We arranged to meet but I was in such a fog that I couldn't decide when the best time would be: That night? The next morning? Nancy and I were second-guessing ourselves over and over. What should we do? Phone them? Send a note? Go over now or later? Would Neil even *want* to see us? Would he and Jackie prefer to be alone in their grief?

Alex, always the more demonstrably emotional, was the first to act. My memory of that exact moment remains foggy, so I recently asked him to remind me what exactly he did back then. "I was playing golf when I got the call from Ray," he told me. "I went straight home and spoke to my friend Syd, because he and his wife had gone through the same experience two years earlier when *their* daughter was killed in a car accident, and he and Cindy have both since become grief counsellors. I asked him what was the right thing to do, and Syd said, 'As difficult as it is, you need to go to their place as soon as you can, sit with them and let them talk. Talk about Selena. Say her name a lot. Make them feel like her name's not being forgotten, because that's going to be one of their greatest fears—that she'll be forgotten. Just keep saying her name. Keep saying her name.' It was difficult to do, but I did it. After Neil poured a bunch of scotches, I toasted Selena. I said, 'To her memory.' And I remember Jackie looking at me, like, *'What the—? A toast? Now?'* But Syd reassured me that it was the right thing to do."

I'll never forget the scene Nancy and I walked into the next day: family and friends in total despair, heartbroken, hysterical. Neil was in a profound but manic state of shock. He fell into my arms and as I held him said, "*You* know . . . *You* know!" He wasn't just saying that because I was a parent and could guess at the unfathomable and devastating pain of losing a child, in his case an *only* child; in his mind we were connected because I, too, had a daughter. Around us was a mad scene, a grief-house. No one knew what to do or how to behave properly, so some drank and smoked, some snorted, and it went on like that for days and nights with everyone who knew and loved them arriving to give them whatever solace they could. It was, of course, to no avail.

Jackie was grief-stricken beyond anyone I had ever witnessed, as the family, even Neil, tried in desperation to console the inconsolable.

It sounds morbid, I know, but having grown up exposed to stories of the Holocaust and my many forebears murdered during the war, and then my father's death and the year of mourning that followed, I've always considered myself to be more familiar with death, more well-versed in it, than most of my friends. Death was no stranger to me, but not since my mother on the night of my father's passing had I seen anyone suffer even close to this way, in such pure and scorching pain. No amount of experience could have prepared me for the cruel and heart-wrenching loss of the child of people so close to me. In the natural order of life, children are meant to survive their parents, not the other way around.

Then came the funeral, which was unbearable.

After a number of days of a hellish wake, Neil and Jackie decided that remaining in Toronto or even Canada was untenable. Everything they looked at, everywhere they might go, would be nothing but another awful reminder of their lost girl. So they flew to London, England, where they could hide and grieve for the months that loomed. But when they arrived, they found the city in mourning for the loss of another princess: Diana. She had been killed in *her* car accident just eleven days after Selena. The papers, the TV and the radio blasted on and on about it, and for Neil and Jackie there was no escape.

Close friends and family members took turns going to London to make sure they had some company from home. Neil and I stayed in touch by fax, as I struggled to relay news from home — anything I could think of to lift his spirits in the slightest. We began riffing on "English Gossip," sending each other absurd headlines from the many trashy English tabloids, anything for a smile. When all else failed, we relied on making jokes at the expense of our favourite and irresistible target, the lovable Lerxst. Razzing him and his idiosyncrasies always amused Neil. Our latest dig concerned Alex's recent obsession with Super

Blue-Green Algae, a product he was taking daily, whose numerous health benefits he was constantly espousing. Pratt dug up articles from periodicals such as the Berkeley *Wellness Letter* about how the "miracle vitamin" he was ingesting was nothing more than "pond scum." It became a running gag. I was thankful that there was *something*, however insignificant, that I could joke about with him.

That December, I flew into London to spend a few foggy days alone with them. Staying at a nearby hotel, I would walk across Hyde Park to the flat they were renting with my heart in my mouth, gathering my thoughts and bracing myself for the emotional visit to come. By then, Neil was motivating himself enough to care at least for Jackie, who was still beyond solace. He kept his mind and body occupied by teaching himself to cook, going out for groceries and preparing their meals, and when I'd arrive he'd usually be in the kitchen making dinner. I'd do what I could to somehow lighten the load they were carrying. I'd try regaling Jackie with stories and juicy gossip from home, occasionally succeeding in getting a chuckle out of her. (Alex was much better at making her laugh. According to Neil, he was one of the few people who really could. When she refused to eat, he apparently said, "Well, you can start a new career as a supermodel." My god, I'd never have the nerve!)

One night, they booked a table at a nearby restaurant. They did it to please me more than themselves, but in my view it was good for them to get out; any contact with the real world had to be considered progress, and despite the underlying sadness, we ended up having a nice evening. Man, that trip was tough. It went by quickly, but our goodbye was painful in the knowledge that until the next visitor they'd be alone with their sorrow.

It was Ray who created a kind of firewall around them, fielding whatever larger issues arose during their self-imposed exile. In the twenty-four years since Neil joined the band, Ray had become more involved with all of us on a personal level and was by now a dedicated family man with four kids of his own, so this tragedy rocked him as hard as any of us. If anything positive could be said to have come out of that hellish time, it was that he formed a closer friendship with Neil, who slowly came to regard him not just as his manager, but a trusted confidant. Ray valued that deeply and would be faithful and attentive to Neil through thick and thin, right to the end . . .

During that painful London period they sought help from a grief counsellor. "Dr. Deborah," as they called her, explained that they were suffering from a kind of post-traumatic stress disorder and did all she could to start them on a healing path, but their life in exile and agony dragged on for months. And then Jackie started suffering from chest pains. On their return to Toronto for medical examinations she was diagnosed—unbelievably—with *lung cancer*. It was deemed inoperable and her fate, too, was tragically sealed.

Neil kept telling me, as he told everyone close to him, that she was willing herself to death, unable to live in a world without her beloved daughter.

They left Canada again, this time bound for Barbados, where they had rented a peaceful villa and arranged palliative care for Jackie. During that time we stayed in regular contact, me sending him news and reading material and he, between updates on Jackie's condition, doing his best to keep his head up by informing me of the island's birdlife.

Jackie's condition worsened, and a mere ten months after Selena's death, she succumbed to "the loss she could not bear," as Neil wrote to me, slipping away on June 20, 1998.

Those of us looking in from the outside were utterly incredulous— "appalled" is the word—that one man's world could be so completely and mercilessly blown to pieces. We were all now at a *total* loss as to how to comfort him, and while this may sound like a trivial concern in comparison, we had no more of an idea how to move forward with our own lives and careers.

As the year dragged on, I kept in touch by phone and fax with Neil. He spent the dregs of summer back in Quebec, trying to get a grip on life, rambling around the lake house amidst the ghosts of his family. As usual, I received a note from him on my birthday:

> *As you can imagine, not too many birthdays have been commemorated by me in the past year — in fact, I've only paid attention to two: Selena's and Jackie's. However, I've been diverting myself by dabbling in habits of former years, like rowing, motorcycling, and hammock-dozing, and it seems somehow right to have a go at writing you my usual midsummer greeting and update.*

He said he had some "beeswax" to deal with in Toronto,

> *And then it will be time to* PREPARE FOR THE FUTURE. *And that my friend is some scary shit!*

What he meant was that he was planning to set out alone on his motorbike. It would be the beginning of the *Ghost Rider* journey that would take him up to Alaska, then down the coast to see his brother in British Columbia, but that's as far as his plans went. We had joked on the phone about meeting up somewhere along the way like Fargo, Missoula or Pocatello, but his call never came. As he rode on out, he became increasingly elusive, words from him arriving fewer and farther between. He would say that riding helped him "ease his little baby soul," but Alex and I worried about him constantly as he roamed, trying to outrun his pain. He travelled incognito, losing himself in the landscape and the company of strangers. You never knew when the man himself might reach out, so at home a disparate network of concerned friends coalesced; anyone anywhere in North America who'd heard from him or even vaguely knew his whereabouts would keep the others informed.

Throughout that time I'd occasionally receive seemingly anonymous postcards from Alaska or Mexico or who knows where, addressed to "Gary Canada," Neil's pet name for me, and signed off by one of his various pseudonyms such as Hank Kimball (the guffawing sales guy on *Petticoat Junction*) or Brian Griffin (from *Family Guy*): smoke signals that he was okay. Ish. To keep myself from going completely nuts, I also set out on a series of trips. As Neil himself was discovering, just moving around can be a helpful distraction.


**TO CELEBRATE NANCY'S** birthday, she and I decided to cycle around Morocco. We flew to a town in the High Atlas Mountains called Ouarzazate and began our journey down to the Sahara. And yes, we did the typical tourist thing, riding camels into the desert and spending the night in a Berber camp, dining and sleeping in a tent loosely constructed of sticks with ornate carpets laid over them. And just like in the movies, I woke up in the middle of the night to find that the wind had blown away one of the carpets and I'd been sleeping on a pillow of sand. I lay awake for the longest time, gazing up at the starry universe, lost in the awe of it all.

The next day, we hopped on a bus to a lovely hotel called Domaine de la Roseraie, lush and ornate and set against the mountainous backdrop. Arriving tired and sweaty, dishevelled in oh-so-chic, sand-caked Lycra biking clothes, we grabbed our room key and quickly headed off for a shower and a glass or twelve of champagne. We were given one of two suites in a private bungalow at the far end of the grounds, past the rose beds that gave the hotel its picturesque name. Our door opened out onto a small square patio, with an identical door opposite. As I put the key in the lock, the other door opened and a lovely young woman and an older man with long, shaggy blond hair emerged. His eyes and mine met for a moment, bemusedly taking each other in, and then we went our separate ways.

I said to Nancy, "Was that *Robert Plant?*"

She said, "Sure looked like him," but we were more focused on a refreshing drink, so we let it go. After we were cleaned up and sufficiently sophonsified with champagne, we went to the restaurant for our dinner, and as I was sitting there, sure enough, the man himself came over and introduced himself. We gabbed and he was as charming as can be.

Back home not long after, the management office relayed a message to me. Some crackpot claiming to be Robert Plant, the receptionist said, had been trying to get in touch with me. He was quite insistent and left a mobile number.

"Oh," I said. "Actually, it *could* be him."

Turned out he was in town with Jimmy Page for a Page/Plant show. I explained that it was only recently that Neil's wife had passed away and I wasn't yet up for going out in public. He was very understanding, and candidly spoke of recovering from the terrible loss of his own.[*] He said to me, "Sooner or later, you have to get back to living your life. And in my experience, sooner is better than later. I insist you come to the show." Well, I could hardly refuse such a big-hearted invitation, so I said okay and called up Lerxst, who was also feeling quite low at the time. He perked up, and we headed together to the Amphitheatre, where we were treated royally. Robert told us about a recent trip he'd made to Havana and then sensitively asked how Neil was bearing up, before we were led to the monitor mixer at the side of the stage from which we could watch two of our all-time musical heroes play. We were in seventh heaven. After the show we thanked them for their generosity of spirit and returned home full of music and lessons about life and loss and the importance of trying to get on with it—a difficult lesson, but one I took to heart, and in times of loss since then, which have been all too frequent, I do think of Robert's words.

---

[*] In 1977 his five-year-old son, Karac, had succumbed to a viral stomach infection.

# CHAPTER 23

IN THE TWO YEARS THAT FOLLOWED, I CAN
honestly say that Lerxst and I never entertained the notion of
carrying on together without Neil. There was nothing to talk
about. We simply kept ourselves busy as best we could, leaving
the band in a state of suspended animation. I knew that one day I'd
return to music of some kind, but I had no idea if Rush would ever
record or perform again.

Before the tragic events of 1997 and 1998, I had planned to do
some songwriting with my pal Ben Mink. He and I had first met in
1979 at a party at Phase One Recording Studios in Toronto's East End,
when he was playing electric violin and mandolin with the band FM.[*]
In only a few minutes we found ourselves laughing uproariously over a

---

[*] He'd later find tremendous success writing, producing and performing with the
immensely talented Canadian pop and country chanteuse k.d. lang.

mutual love of *Yiddishkeit*, in particular our recollections of the language and disgusting foods of our parents' generation, almost as if we'd grown up in the same household. We had a lot in common—almost too much, since our parents were all Holocaust survivors.

Like Ben, I had a passion for pastrami and in the course of my life regressed to all the stereotypical staples of Jewish cuisine: gefilte fish, pickled herring, *kishke*, lox and of course bagels. Dishes my mother used to make, *cholent* and *potatonyik*, had taken fond residence in both our memory banks, as did another we adored as kids—*mish mash*, a combo of overcooked penne (no such thing as al dente in our households) and *p'tcha*.* After a forty-year friendship now, Ben and I are still reduced to being eight-year-olds together. Just this morning as I was sitting down to write this, he called me to say he's going to an ear doctor. "My hearing is stuffed," he said. "It's some extreme blockage, maybe a piece of *klopsz*," which instantly brought back memories of both sight and smell that totally cracked me up: my mother used to make *klopsz*, a kind of meat loaf, from some kind of mystery meat, I couldn't tell you what. I was convulsed at the mere mention of it.

Where was I? Oh yes—our music. Every time we occasioned to jam we'd been amazed by the synchronicity of our playing—not just in terms of timing but *feel*. It was like, "Wow, you play like me!"

"No, *you* play like *me*."

So, comedically, my relationship with him was no less preposterous than the one I had with Alex, but musically it was a different matter. The chemistry I enjoyed with Alex was the way we filled in each other's gaps. He has a wild and spontaneous creative heart, while I generally take a more considered approach, and the admixture clearly made for a happy and prolific partnership; Ben and I, by contrast, are two peas in a

---

* Calves foot jelly. In Polish, *galareta*, or *gala* for short. An Ashkenazi delicacy usually served on a little tray like pâté. One time, at a party attended by a fussily groovy crowd, Ben and I snuck a slab of it onto the buffet table and stood back to watch. As the fashionistas stumbled on our hidden delicacy the looks on their faces were a joy to behold, and our laughter so alienated us from the well-clad crowd that we had to leave the party in hysterics.

pod. We were both constantly improvising and composing at the same time: "Ah! That could be a verse! That could be a chorus!" I'd start a sentence and he'd finish it. So this album was constructed very methodically. Ben used to say, "All we need is a good six minutes." It might take an hour of useless playing to get those six minutes, but there'd be a song in there. Not everything about us was similar, though—he was well-schooled in the basics of musical theory, for example, while I was a play-it-by-ear musician—but still, we wondered if our similar backgrounds and sensibilities could bear creative fruit. If nothing else, it would be an interesting psycho-sociological experiment: nature, nurture or *nudnik*?

Then in 1997, towards the end of the *Test for Echo* tour, we had loosely made plans to get together in Toronto and see if we could get past the Yiddish jokes to write some music. But disaster struck Neil's life, and our would-be collaboration fell to the wayside. As time dragged on after Jackie's death, I found myself badly in need of somewhere to

*When Rush was touring with Ben's band FM, he and I would crack up over old-country words that our parents used to use. One was* rötz, *meaning "snot." When I was a kid out shopping with my mom and she'd finally had enough of my sniffling, she pulled a gross, makeup-scented Kleenex from her handbag, put it to my nose and commanded in broken Yiddish, "Öfshnahtzen de rötz!"*

put my emotions, something to do to take my mind off all the woe. Creating music was what I did, so I spoke to Ben about reviving our plans. Hanging out together as easily as we did was a welcome balm for the soul, but could we take it to a more professional level? And would the friendship survive getting serious? We decided to give it a whirl.

He came to Toronto for a couple of days in my home studio, and, with Neil's cataclysm still at the forefront of my mind, the first song we wrote was "Gone," a ballad about loss. We spent hours arranging and recording parts for it, but in the end I decided it was too emotionally raw. I wasn't comfortable releasing it for the public, and it remains in the vault as an extremely well recorded "demo."[*] Still, it was a spark, definitely the beginning of something. I stayed with Ben in Vancouver, settling into daily writing sessions that ended up lasting weeks at a time, putting sketches in fits and starts onto tape and paper, and after a few months we'd amassed enough songs to consider actually making an album. Working through to early 2000 before approaching a producer, he soon learned what a mental case I was to work with, but he put up with my relentless and uncompromising nature and my nagging, obsessive eye for detail as best as he could.

We thrived in our work, writing, jamming and experimenting all the time. I always keep notes of ideas, words, a turn of a phrase, questions I want to ask life and see if life answers me back. I was inspired by Neil's lyric writing; I'd become experienced in the art of it by proxy, singing his verses and wrestling with him over their phrasing (while learning not to be afraid of tackling lofty ideas). With Ben, it was a collaboration from the word go. He was for me the perfect sounding board. "Window on the World," for example, stemmed from a ridiculous conversation we were having about online pornography (I think magazines liked *Wired* were speculating at the time about things like

---

[*] I recently discovered a second song that we left off that album, called "IMUR," also a highly polished demo. I can't for the life of me think why we didn't use it. Must have run out of time when we were in Seattle.

teledildonics) and people surfing cyberspace and finding a window onto some sexual paradise.

This was at a time of expanding digital capability in every walk of life, with even home computers being able now to record an almost endless number of tracks—which was both a blessing and a curse. Like Lerxst, Ben was exceptionally good at conjuring up sounds and effects from his computer, and as we became more seriously involved we found ourselves going to greater extremes to produce our "garage" demos. I milked every drop of his expertise, encouraging him to build multitudes of violin and viola tracks (I even learned the difference between violins and violas!) to simulate large string sections that would be unaffordable in the real world. He was so good at it that I couldn't help but write parts for my own imaginary in-house orchestra, and after the impressive results he'd produced with k.d. lang, I also trusted him implicitly when it came to recording vocals. He heard nuances in my voice that he encouraged me to exploit, and I believe the end result counts among the best performances I've committed to tape. At times our mutual tolerance was pushed to the brink by the long hours and the family pressure that all the intercity travel brought to bear, but we got through the pre-production with our friendship intact and were now poised to make an actual album.

In July 1999, I received my annual birthday Prattfax. "If the first is the year of sorrow," Neil wrote, "the second is the year of emptiness." There were, however, tiny signs of light piercing through his darkness. He'd begun to show up in Los Angeles, as our good friend and photographer Andrew MacNaughtan was living and working there. Bit by bit, Andrew introduced Neil to his small circle of expat Canadians as well as some Los Angelenos he'd befriended, among them the ex-Torontonian and Kids in the Hall member Dave Foley and the hilarious Matt Stone of *South Park*. God knows, if anyone deserved to have a few laughs at that time, it was Neil. Whenever he was in town they brought him a modicum of joy, but it was also through Andrew that he'd started actually *dating* someone in San Francisco, an event that left him "confused and bewildered by the Great Mystery of Woman." That first attempt at securing some female companionship did not work out, but thankfully he did not give up, nor did Andrew, and his next encounter would be entirely enchanting—with a woman named Carrie, who when they met was working with Andrew. And in a year would be Neil's wife.

Even more stunning was Neil's report that back in Quebec he'd also experienced some positivity on the musical front.

> *I responded to that bewilderment by going and beating up my drums! It was the first time I had played in almost exactly two years (since our last show in Ottawa in 1997) . . . I was surprised that the "tools" were still there. I could play everything I could back then, as well and as fast, only the transitions between figures were a little rusty. And it felt pretty good.*

He went on to describe how he had booked the back room at Le Studio and set up his yellow Gretsch drum kit there and was playing on it for a couple of hours at a time. It gave him "somewhere to go and something to do," he said, and characteristically, when he attempted to analyse what he was getting from his playing, he couldn't help but dive deep.

> *From the first day, a strange thing happened, as I played along through various patterns and tempos I suddenly realized that what I was* really *doing, on a subconscious level, was playing my story. Not in a concrete way, of musical and lyrical themes, but more of an abstract approach—"this is that part". . . and I meandered through passages that were slow and sad, heavy with anger, fast and rhythmic "travelling music" and (yes) the Anthem of Redemption . . . Not only did I possess the technique of playing music, but I possessed the spirit of it, the voice, the ability to "tell my story."*

My jaw dropped as I read this. It was incredible to me that after all he had gone through and was surely still fucked up about, he had the wherewithal to grapple with describing the essence of artistic expression in such hopeful, forward-looking language. He went on to say,

> *I realized that while I might be ready to play again, I was not ready to work again. Not yet, anyway. So I put my drums away for a while, but knowing that the power was still there, and that I could do it if I chose.*

He concluded by saying that he was telling me all of this not only because it was my birthday, but because this date marked our twenty-fifth anniversary as bandmates (after all, he joined the band on my twenty-first birthday back in 1974) and he wanted to let me know "where I'm at in those departments."

Rereading the letter today not only reminds me of the depth of that man's artistic soul, but of how much he valued our relationship at that very difficult moment in his life. I don't think I'm flattering myself to think that for him it was also a lifeline.

**BACK IN CANADA,** a new millennium and back to work. Ben and I were now well into planning our recording sessions. *My Favourite Headache* was a reality and we needed a producer, or at least an engineer or two. Most producers I had reached out to seemed more interested in working on a Rush album than my own solo effort, which I suppose was understandable, but pissed me off nonetheless. Ben and I said *fuck it*, we'll find a likely engineer or two and produce the damn thing ourselves instead of waiting for some big shot to do it for us. After all, between us we'd already made dozens of albums and could manage on our own.

One engineer who stood out was Adam Kasper, one of the grunge scene's quintessential engineer-producers, who'd also worked with Queens of the Stone Age and the Tragically Hip. He knew Matt Cameron well, having worked with him on Soundgarden and Pearl Jam albums, which was a bit of synchronicity for me because Matt had been one of the first drummers who came to mind when I started thinking of rhythm partners for my project. In a flash we were booked to record

*Yours truly with Daniel Seguin, Ben Mink, Adam Kasper and Matt Cameron in Studio X, Seattle—an awesome way to start my journey into the unknown. Terrific players and a welcoming city filled with people who did nothing but talk about music. Right on!*

in April at Seattle's Studio X (formerly Bad Animal Studios, owned by Ann and Nancy Wilson of Heart).

Obviously, Matt was a very different kind of drummer to the guy I normally worked with, but I was looking for a fresh rhythmic vibe that would stretch my imagination. He's a solid as hell but humble, "stay-at-home" drummer with incredibly good taste, who instinctively knows just what a track needs. He takes his brief extremely seriously and doesn't stray beyond it. I remember him commenting during those sessions about one particular fill he had just played, saying something like, "I'd like to do that one again. Right now it's too *Hey, look at me.*" What a lovely, modest man!

It was awesome, meanwhile, to see how a city I had played in so many times when it had no musical reputation worldwide had become such a vibrant mecca. It used to be a dormant, hippie-ish town but had now exploded. Everyone I met there, whatever job they were doing—the guy carrying my bags into my hotel room, the woman driving my taxi—was a musician. Seattle was a town populated entirely, it felt, by young grunge artists, a town of musicians and musicians' musicians! Moreover, since I came from a more competitive and disconnected music scene, I was impressed by how these people seemed always ready to play on one another's projects and be supportive of new things the others were doing. (The terrific *Temple of the Dog* album is just one example of that.) I have to say I felt a lot of respect when Kim Thayil and Krist Novoselic dropped in to say hi. I was forty-seven, almost twice their age—an elder statesman of rock! It was a yardstick of how long I'd been in the game that here was a younger generation that had grown up with our music and wanted to hang. There was a great rapport between everyone in the studio, a free-flowing atmosphere that yielded terrific results. We worked civilized hours, dined out at cool local eateries, sampled Washington state wines and generally had a great time. It went much too quickly but remains one of my fondest recording memories.

One great advantage of doing my own album was that I was free of all Rush rules and regulations. I was free to fill up the soundscape with multiple bass tracks if I wanted . . . and so I did! On the title track, for instance, I laid down four of them: one straight and bottom end, two chordal parts and another distorted in the upper range to mimic a lead guitar. I didn't have to worry about the Lerxst Wall of Sound, I could hog the soundscape. On the other hand, when it came to layering instruments, the album was both a revelation and a nightmare. At times I went completely overboard, making life as difficult as I could for myself. Whenever I thought we were close to finishing a song, more ideas would pop up that I found irresistible. *Plus ça change . . .*

I also had to accept that my writing and playing styles are inextricably bound up in the way Rush sounds, so if I wrote something that sounded Rush-like, then it would be perverse to take a detour around myself. Mine was the only voice Rush had ever had, and I couldn't escape me! In the meantime, there were other avenues to explore, like using the keyboards as a major writing tool without fear of recrimination from Alex; we could use guitar sounds that were less distorted and Lerxst-like if we wanted; and since I wasn't thinking in terms of having to reproduce the album onstage, I could experiment with stacking loads of vocal layers. As a result, the record is more lush than Rush.

To help us finish and eventually mix the record, we reached out to David Leonard, who Peter Collins had raved about to me.[*] Ben and I got on incredibly well with him, and we soon became three amigos working long hours in both Vancouver and finally Toronto. I was proud as hell of the work we did and especially blown away by the mix David did on "The Angels' Share," which I think is one of the best pieces of music I've ever written. The final mix pretty much brought us all to tears. I couldn't have made the record without him and the rest

---

[*] Before me, David had worked with Fishbone, John Mellencamp and, most notably, at Prince's Paisley Park studio, which he pretty much built himself . . . and lived to tell the tale.

of the team, and I was elated to have found another band of brothers. Music is a collaborative art. I know there are people who can play every instrument or dictate exactly how they want it to be and push everyone else around, but I see it as interconnection, reciprocity, affinity and, ultimately, an expression of friendship. There have been so many bad solo records that reveal how important collaboration is and how the greatness of so many bands is down to the happenstance of those players meeting and working together.*

The album peaked at #52 on the *Billboard* 200 chart. I had wanted it to do better, but I was proud of it nonetheless. Ben's commercial experience notwithstanding, we were never deluded enough to aim for a smash hit or even hit singles. It was more than enough for Ben and me that it felt so good and that we hadn't killed our friendship in the bargain—although we did have to take a few months away from each other after it. Because (I don't know if I've mentioned this) in the studio I am quite the . . . what is the word . . . *bossypants*.

There is one more song I'd like to mention before returning to Rush: "Slipping," which I wrote mostly on piano. While I love to rock, and rock hard, there's a quieter part of me that aspires to simply write basic, beautiful melodies. I've never figured out how to satisfy both sides of me in equal measure, and more often than not the gentler side has taken a back seat, but this one is as vulnerable as I've ever allowed myself to be. It's so personal that I could never have done it with my band. It's a good example of why you have to occasionally venture out—to see what you might reveal about yourself. In a way, it's about my life with Nancy. (I couldn't have said so at the time, but now that I've written about my married life in this book, I can out myself.) It's an apology for my failings as a human being in love, for every failure to

---

* My favourite exceptions include Thijs van Leer's and Jan Akkerman's albums outside of Focus; David Sylvian's after Japan; you could make the argument that Peter Gabriel's solo work has superseded his work with Genesis; and I remember liking a couple of tracks from Mick Ronson's *Slaughter on 10th Avenue* after Bowie summarily dismissed the Spiders from Mars.

understand, every failure to be considerate enough, every failure to act when I should have and for the pain my self-absorption caused.

Not that she noticed! In fact, nobody in my family made so much as a peep about the record. But you know what? That's okay. I don't demand it of them. I imagine it's weird for them. I didn't seek my bandmates' approval either, but I got a nice nod and a note from Neil. Alex was not very expressive, other than saying the guitar sounds were not to his taste. Nor did anyone ever suggest Rush play a song from the record (should we ever reunite), any more than one from Alex's solo record, *Victor*. We considered those things personal business.

Actually, I had little time to consider *any* of that, let alone suffer my usual bout of post-album depression, partly because I enjoyed a boatload of confidence in myself as a songwriter independent of Lerxst, but mostly because, finally, a Rush reunion was indeed on the horizon.

# CHAPTER 24

I N FEBRUARY OF THAT YEAR I RECEIVED another Prattfax, this time from Santa Monica, where Neil had been living for a month or so. He wrote:

> *I'm happy to report (like so happy). The reason I'm here at all is the woman in my life, Carrie . . . and it has to be said that Andrew got it right this time . . . I was telling Leaf [Liam] the other day that it's as though my life has gone from a nightmare to a dream. And that's pretty cool.*

Pretty *effin'* cool. Their romance had progressed so quickly, in fact, that he'd rented an apartment in Los Angeles. This came as a surprise to me because I'd never envisaged Neil as an LA kind of guy, but god knows that after he'd been beaten to a pulp, he deserved some love in his life. He went on to talk about how he had given up smoking, joined the YMCA and worked himself up from the physical wreck he'd become over those terrible two and a half years—ingesting whatever alcohol or drugs he needed to numb the pain—to this person now telling me, "I'm in the best shape of my life." This was all blowing my mind. He sounded like a completely changed man. I mean, quitting *smoking*? I couldn't have been happier for him. (Actually, I knew that one wouldn't stick. He loved his smokes too much and would soon be lighting up again—once an hour from now on, almost to the minute, as if an alarm had gone off in his head.)

Then came the real bombshell. He wanted to get together in Toronto (a place he had avoided for obvious reasons), not only because he wanted us all to meet Carrie, but so that we could discuss his "seeking gainful employment."

First he wanted to discuss the parameters of our work schedule. He did not want to return to the old regime, he made it clear, lest it take him away from the new woman in his life for weeks at a time. He'd been given a second chance at happiness, and he wasn't going to fuck it up by not being there for her. Then came a wedding invitation. Whoa! This was getting real, and fast.

**MAKING THE NEXT** Rush album would surely not be easy, as Alex and I were dealing with a still-fragile individual. Neil had proven to himself that he could still play at a high level, but he needed to build back his strength. He'd not been in an intense lyric-writing environment for more than four years and would need to find the confidence to put pen to paper again, while wrestling with a multitude of raw emotions. You have only to listen to "The Stars Look Down" to get a sense of that. Inspired by A. J. Cronin's novel of the same name, it plops you right in the seat of Neil's BMW as he roams around North America trying to make sense of his devastated life. It's a conversation between his mind and the cosmos as he asks, "What the fuck did I do to deserve this much pain?" and the stars look silently back down at him, leaving him to answer the question for himself.

We spent a couple of weeks drinking coffee and talking, not playing much at all but getting back in sync with one another. At the start, the music wasn't exactly what I'd call *vibrant*, and in truth I was secretly worried that we had run out of joy juice. To take the pressure off, we decided just to jam for fun before knuckling down to any actual songs. That did get us into gear, and before long Neil had come up with a *pile* of lyrics.

We put together a version of "Earthshine," but when it was clear the song didn't pass muster, we threw it in the trash and started from scratch. To have written something that so clearly sucked really shook our confidence. Those early doubts and difficulties established a frame of mind where even the slightest good idea seemed precious to us and worth keeping for the master recordings. Over the long sessions, that would prove a curse, but just the fact that we recognized our errors of judgement was a good sign. The same happened with our earliest take on "Out of the Cradle." Then, little by little, we became more discerning and less afraid to rewrite anything that sounded weak. We found ourselves on a roll, and more songs like "The Stars Look Down" started to come together fast.

I wish I could tell you how or why these were the first rabbits we pulled out of the hat, but I've written so many songs in my life that I cannot remember the genesis of every single one, and in any case the process of creation is so ineffable. Whenever a new song comes together, pardon the cliché, there's magic in the air. If you're lucky, that is. In a perfect world, a riff leads to a lyric that leads to a melody that starts to snowball. But very little of *Vapor Trails* just happened out of the ether. Often it was a process of grabbing and holding on to an idea that seemed to have potential, working hard on it, relentlessly polishing until we'd gotten to what we felt was a good place. But then I'd take a break and not listen to it for days, and time and again when I returned to the material with fresh ears, it was patently not good enough. That's why *Vapor Trails* took so long. There was so much insecurity and second-guessing that it was the most neurotic of any of our sessions.

Some songs, like "One Little Victory," were born out of ideas Alex had come up with in his home studio in his off time. He'd assembled a crazy instrumental soundscape with all these wonderfully strange textures, and I remember thinking, *How do I get into this? How do we make sense of it together?* Methodically, I took it apart and rearranged it, then applied some lyrics Neil had already written that had no home. That's a song that also benefitted from the chops I'd developed while recording *My Favourite Headache*, particularly with the vocal melodies. Combining our strengths that way, we had a triumphant, galloping song to get Rush back into gear.

There was endless to-ing and fro-ing and grinding away, and very delicate exchanges with Neil in regard to any lyrics he'd written with reference to what he'd been through. One of my fears at the time was that, after all he'd suffered, his lyrics might be too personal for me to sing. I sometimes had to push him to strive for a greater universality to allow both the listener and me into the story, to allow for our own interpretation and emotional connection. If it didn't have a certain universality, I'd just be ventriloquizing *his* pain. A perfect example is "Ghost Rider," which was so clearly autobiographical. We made subtle changes to the point of view simply by using "you" instead of "I." That may have been tough for him to swallow, but in my view it's almost always good to broaden the scope of a song. There's a time and place for deeply personal, singular expression, but relatability is essential, and I believe that "Sweet Miracle," "The Stars Look Down," "Vapor Trail" and "One Little Victory" all benefitted from a more inclusive approach.

I was no longer up for recording late into the evening, so I'd stop around five or six and head home for dinner with the family, and of course when Carrie was in town Pratt would do the same. But Lerxst is very different. He'd stay behind, smoke a few joints and disappear into the guitar tracks, playing through the night. The next morning, I'd have the immense pleasure of hearing all his new parts and experiments for the first time. That was a big change for us—and especially for me. We had to trust one another not to fuck up a song when left to our own devices—or more precisely in my case, not worry the parts to death—because if you're not around while the thing is being recorded, you lose some of the right to criticize it later. Sure, we'd still all put our two cents in, but we were giving one another much more latitude than we ever had before. This was especially important for me. I was letting go of my compulsion to control every moment of the sessions. It was good for my sanity, and good for my family life too. I guess I had finally become an effin' adult.

Lerxst was dead set against two things this time around: guitar solos and keyboards. So as not to make waves (or, indeed, wave*forms*), I put my experience working on *MFH* to use, layering my vocals to create the kinds of textures I'd have otherwise obtained from synthesizers. That was a blast, especially on songs like "Peaceable Kingdom," where I mashed together harmonious and dissonant backing tracks. As we got more serious, however, the curse I alluded to a page or two ago came into play. Keeping so many recordings from the writing and demo stages became a real problem. In the past, we'd have re-recorded them "for real" in-studio, but there had been such a sense of relief at finally finding our groove, and we'd been so fearful of losing one iota of vibe, heart or even rawness, that we kept almost *everything* and now came down with a bad case of "demo-itis." That's a condition I'd heard other bands complain of, but had never experienced myself: it's when you become so in love with the nuances of each and every part that you think them impossible to beat. Sure, you can replace a track with a better sound, but you become stricken with fear that you'll never catch that same lightning in the bottle again. Demo-itis strikes deep, into your life it will creep!

Still, we persisted in building numerous songs like that, painstakingly piecing parts and pieces together. It became our overriding method and, in the end, why the album sounds the way it does. It's not a blueprint I'd recommend any band to follow. But it wasn't until the mixing stage that we understood what a slippery slope we'd made for ourselves. The *Vapor Trails* mixing sessions were as close to torture as I've ever experienced. After a year of labouring over the songs, we needed to be *wowed* . . . and we weren't. We'd spent so long sweating over every note that we'd disappeared up our own asses.

The tracks from the demo stage required an inordinate amount of EQ or compression to bring them up to snuff, sometimes even sending guitar parts back out to an amp and re-recording them from there. To quote the Troggs again: "You gotta put a little fucking fairy dust over the bastard, ya know?" But while you can improve any particular sound, the accumulation of EQ risks adding white noise and/or distortion that you can't always hide in the mix.

It didn't matter what kind of mix our poor producer Paul Northfield presented us with, we were not happy, and soon he was pulling out what was left of his hair. We wanted to hear the "magic" we felt when we wrote the songs back in January, and now it was November. We needed a fresh pair of ears, so I reached out to David Leonard again to pick up the slack. We settled into Metalworks Studio, which he knew well from mixing *My Favourite Headache* there. Located in the bowels of an industrial mall in Mississauga, it's a mundane hour's drive from Toronto—but, as it turned out, just long enough for Lerxst and me to review the previous night's mixes and make notes. Countless mixes were burned and then destroyed over the three effin' months we spent there, hundreds of CDs generically labelled "Car Mix #3" and the like. *Three months.* Listening to those endless variations was the only thing that made the drive to the wastelands of Mississauga tolerable, but still, at that point it was psycho-mixing. Christ, we did the entire *2112* album in four weeks.

By the time the last mix was done, in February 2002, I was frankly shellshocked. All that option anxiety had burned me out. But now I had to fly to New York for the mastering sessions, yet *another* round of minute, painstaking sonic decisions that demanded ears far fresher than mine, so I asked David to join me at Masterdisk to make sure I didn't fuck up those pristine mixes of his.

But then he caught a cold. He was so stuffed up, he felt like he had cotton batten in his ears. Scratch any help from him! I went through the mixes with Howie Weinberg, Masterdisk's head engineer, instead. We tweaked things here, there and everywhere, but he kept comparing the levels of our mixes with other albums he had recently mastered— including one by Limp Bizkit—saying, "We gotta make this album *loud* so when the songs hit the airwaves they don't sound quiet compared to the ones before or after it." Those were the days of the so-called Loudness Wars.[*] With digital tech, mastering engineers felt they could boost output levels further than ever before and with impunity. Uh, not exactly. You *can* master records loudly, but ultimately a sonic price must be paid. There's *always* a ceiling to the amount of level you can boost, even on a digital recording, and if you don't pay close attention, the transient responses and dynamic peaks are cut off or "clipped," which stops the song from breathing properly. The song becomes loud and powerful but also relentless; nuance is lost, and it's fatiguing to the ears.

With David sick and both Lerxst and Pratt fucked off on their long-overdue holidays, I was by myself. Everything sounded great to me at Masterdisk, but it was a false positive. Remember how we hung

---

[*] *Definitely Maybe* by Oasis is widely credited with being the first CD that blew other songs out of the jukebox thanks to producer and engineer Owen Morris's "brick-walling" technique. Some of the albums notorious for pushing the limit included Metallica's *Death Magnetic* and *Californication* by the Red Hot Chili Peppers. Today, streaming services have put an end to competitive loudness practices with Audio Normalization. I think, by the way, that the Loudness Wars helped spark the debate over which was superior, digital or analog, and created a whole nother red herring.

on to those early, spirited performances from the writing sessions, despite the sounds not always being up to snuff? Well, in fairness to Howie, the boost in level and compression had started to reveal the subtle digital distortion and sonic artifacts that had been around since those tracks were recorded. Now they were coming back to haunt me.

Every day I was getting pressure to approve and deliver the album. I left the control room exhausted and, as I flew back to Toronto, felt confident that I had a terrific set of powerful masters, but when I got home and listened back to them on various sound systems, I thought I was going mad. I started hearing tiny flaws everywhere. My good wife implored me to leave for our own holiday already, so I took my CDs with me to St. Croix in the Virgin Islands, resolving to manage the situation from paradise.

What followed was a barrage of panicked calls at all hours to and from Masterdisk.

"Guys, I hear a bit of distortion at the thirty-second mark of 'One Little Victory.' Can you lower the levels a bit?"

"Okay, Ged, but I'm not sure I hear it. I'll send you new ones. Down a dB or half a dB?"

"Well, *I'm* hearing it. Try a half."

"Okay, okay. How 'bout I do the first thirty seconds down one dB and edit it onto the master? The distortion will be gone and you'll still have the power of the rest of the track?"

"Okay, yeah. But also . . ."

This went on for days, with every one of my nerve endings bristling on the surface of my skin. It was system overload and I was an effin' mess. I badly needed to soak my head in the ocean lapping at my door. Finally, I let the sea water wash over me and Zenned out a bit. But when I got home I couldn't listen to the record at *all*. It would be ages before I could do that. I avoided it at every turn. It wasn't music to me anymore, just a raw connection to my nervous system. But I couldn't do a thing because the album had already gone to press.

The worst part was that I couldn't appreciate what we *had* accomplished. We had reunited, brought Neil back into the fold playing as great as ever, spent fourteen months writing and recording a complex, emotive and intriguing album and were now planning our first tour since 1997. These were great songs, there was a lot to celebrate, but I was in no mood to party.

HAD YOU ASKED me two years earlier, while I was writing *My Favourite Headache*, if Rush would ever tour again, I'd have said, "Unlikely." In my heart of hearts I couldn't accept that the band was done, but I had no real reason to imagine Neil would ever rekindle his spark. Yet here we were! The tour rebooting Rush would kick off in Hartford, Connecticut, on June 28, 2002, and run until November for sixty-six shows, so we definitely weren't going into it half-heartedly, but still we couldn't be sure if it would be the first of many or a kind of grand farewell. It was great to see Neil fired up again, but we were taking nothing for granted. There was still a heaviness to his demeanour (anniversaries would always be a dark time for him), but he was spirited by his new marriage and his welcome back into the fold. And do you know, together again that entire time on the road, the only things we ever brought up from the past were the idiotic moments, the funny stuff, the goofy inside jokes that had become part of our own private legend. Never the sad stuff, not once.

First rehearsals will always be bumpy, but this time around—perhaps inevitably since we hadn't played together in five years—we were *crap*, sounding like a bad Rush cover band. After a couple days, though, we were becoming a pretty good one, until we finally hit our stride, and as we shook off the rust we found ourselves flush with optimism, eyes wide open, hyperconsciously aware of the second chance we'd been given.

In hindsight, it was also the beginning of what I refer to as our own "Costanza Method," after the *Seinfeld* episode "The Opposite," in which George complains that everything he does in life is wrong, and

Jerry says, "If every instinct you have is wrong, then the opposite would have to be right." We didn't believe that *everything* we'd done had been wrong, but we had developed a certain tunnel vision. For example, we'd always turned down requests to play live on television because we thought that rock bands looked dumb on TV, but what happens when you say no more often than yes is that your management starts to say no on your behalf without bothering to discuss it with you. You should always retain the right to say no only when you have full knowledge of the situation, because you might just surprise yourself. So with Rush 2.0, instead of rejecting opportunities out of hand, we resolved to take some chances. In fact, our first Costanza Decision was to stop limiting our North American tours to the USA and Canada, and finally go to Mexico and Brazil. We were embracing change, unafraid to make some new mistakes!

Another thing I approached differently was my gear. By now, the ergonomic in-ear monitors and solid state devices and pre-amps I was using in pursuit of a better tone rendered amp stacks onstage quite unnecessary (even if they *looked* cool). During rehearsals for *Test for Echo* in 1996, it was obvious that the shrinking of my rig had created an imbalance with Alex's on stage right, and I thought, *Why don't I take the piss out of all of that?* I asked the crew to find me a stack of kitchen appliances, and soon the following items appeared stage left: one Commodore Deluxe Shake Maker set, one Osterizer Deluxe 2-Speed Blender, one Proctor-Silex Deluxe Juiceit Oscillating Strainer, one Beatrice Deluxe #2 Manual Meat Grinder and one Morphy Richards Deluxe Automatic Toaster. A shelf unit was built for it all, but an awkward space remained between my actual bass amp and Neil's drum kit . . . which, naturally, I filled with a Frigidaire Deluxe Refrigerator. That fridge attracted a growing encrustation of fridge magnets Pratt collected on his motorcycle rides between shows, and Herns installed a powerful bulb inside so that during the show I could open the door to take out a drink and an unearthly light would blast

(TOP) *At SARSfest in Toronto with my Maytags.* (BOTTOM) *On tour in Brazil, with Neil's drum tech Gump hiding behind the dryers.*

out, like out of the briefcase in *Pulp Fiction*, all the way to the back of the venue.

By the time rehearsals for the *Vapor Trails* tour were upon us in 2002, I had decided to lose my onstage bass amps *altogether*; all I needed was a rack to sit beside my tech, Russ, at the side of the stage, and one small mic'd amp under it. Neil's drum tech needed something to hide behind, though, so the crew and I tossed some more ideas around, moving conceptually from kitchen to laundry room, and bingo!, in a used-appliance store on the outskirts of Toronto Liam happened upon three Maytag coin-operated dryers. We removed the heating elements and installed glow lights inside to enhance the tumbling. Night after night I took great delight in the smiles on some fans' faces and the looks of total confusion on others, like, "I don't understand. Are you joking or *what?*" Seriously, I've never fielded more questions about any one thing than those effin' dryers.

The goofiness of my stage gear was just one aspect of our loosening up onstage. It had started for Lerxst on the *Test for Echo* tour with just a few plastic monsters, Godzilla and a herd of dinosaurs atop his amp racks; then his crew assembled a harem of worshipful Barbie dolls holding up tiny signs of love and admiration in front of his foot pedals. Then for some reason we got heavily into a pirate motif: Neil would wear an eye patch, while my bass tech taped a stuffed parrot to my bass strap so it sat upright on my shoulder, and at the end of "The Temples of Syrinx" I would sing the last line in my best Bluebeard voice, "Arr, matey, we are the *pirates* of the Temples of Syrinx." I imagine that some of our more earnest prog fans thought we'd loosened up too damn much, but there was no putting *that* genie back in the bottle. Next, the absurdist comedy crept into the rear-screen material. Ben Mink created an intro tape for us, replicating the theme to *The Three Stooges* TV show, which we all watched religiously as kids, with Curly, Larry and Moe photoshopped as me, Pratt and Lerxst. We were aware that many of our fans—the younger ones, at least—wouldn't get the joke, but we never cared. We thought of those characters as representative of our inner selves: riotous, rude and inane, three scrappy boys, three morons just like us. They were our totem, our touchstone. It had been a heavy five years, but here we were, Three Effin' Goofs, back on the road again.

**AND JUST LIKE** that, opening night was upon us. As I prepared for that first show in Hartford, it wasn't lost on me how miraculous the moment was. Neil had travelled to the edges of despair, yet somehow found his way back to do what he was born to do. As we stepped forward again into the light, beneath my calm demeanour my emotions were bubbling madly—and when I glanced at my partners' faces, I saw that I wasn't alone. Stepping out of the dressing room towards the stage, we could feel how electric the atmosphere in the venue was. We were all fighting our nerves, no one more so than the big guy with the drumsticks in his hands, who was visibly agitated while waiting to get on with it. Each of us was lost in the moment in our own way, but of course his hill had been far and away the toughest to climb. Then suddenly the strains of "Three Blind Mice" faded and it was time to hit the stage. The crowd's roar truly took me aback. I had almost forgotten what any kind of applause felt like, but this welcome was utterly tumultuous. We ploughed into "Tom Sawyer" and as our nerves settled Alex and I converged centre stage to check on our friend—our first mid-song meeting around the drum kit in five whole years—and found ourselves both grinning ear to ear and choked up not only to be brothers in arms again but knowing that our fans had not forgotten us. I was forty-nine with no serious physical problems to speak of; Neil and I had maintained a gym regime and were in good physical shape; Alex was Alex; we were middle-aged men returning to a gig that many teens could only dream of, and still it never felt like a job. There are some days when we bitched and swore at the prospect of three hours of warbling and chewing up our fingers, but at the end of every show we knew that we'd actually done something for a heap of people and sent them home happy. That was the life we'd chosen and I was goddamn thankful for it.

THE TOUR MARCHED on triumphantly, crisscrossing the country, revisiting old places and pals we'd lost touch with and encouraging them to do a cameo turn onstage and take laundry out of the dryers. One especially notable cameo would come in 2004, when we played Irvine, California, and Jack Black stepped out onstage in the middle of "2112," stripped to his boxers, threw his clothes in the dryer and posed on top of one of them as the man in the star, then hopped down, slid over to me on his knees air-jamming, jumped up again and disappeared. What he may not have been aware of was that his boxers had slid down at the back, immortalizing the moment as that of "Jack Black's Crack."

Those dryers created quite a buzz backstage at the largest gig of our career. The SARS benefit show on July 30, 2003, otherwise known as Toronto Rocks, was a one-off fundraiser for Canadian frontline healthcare and hospitality workers, as well as the tourism industry, which was suffering so from global restrictions during *that* pandemic. We were on holiday following the *Vapor Trails* tour by then, but we immediately agreed to participate, even before we were apprised of the lineup: the Rolling Stones, AC/DC, the Isley Brothers, Blue Rodeo, the Guess Who, Sass Jordan, Justin Timberlake and many more.

The day of the event, we met up at Union Station in downtown Toronto and were taken right backstage by train. I remember walking off and seeing only a small part of the crowd, having little idea how many people would show up; the organizers were prepared for maybe 50,000 or 100,000, but that would swell to just shy of half a million.

Waiting for our cue to go on, we were standing stage right when an elderly gent climbed up and asked to meet Neil. As I've said before, Pratt suffers from bouts of stage fright, and as this was the largest

*Cameos courtesy of the Blue Man Group and Jack Black.*

(TOP) *Every time I look at this pic of the stage markings from SARSfest 2003 in Toronto, I have to chuckle: "Stones—Keith's Rack; AC/DC—Guitar Risers; Rush—Dryers."* (BOTTOM) *This photo was snapped by Neil's security man and motorcycle riding buddy, Michael Mosbach. I'm so glad he did!*

crowd we'd ever played for, he was deep in his tense, pre-gig zone, so when this white-haired chap approached I could see him turn with a stern look, like, "Can't you see I'm *busy?*" Only as the man passed me did I recognize him. I gestured at Neil, caught his eye, pointed and mouthed, "Char-lie *Watts!*" Neil's eyes opened wide and his mouth broke out in a grin. He immediately pulled out his ear monitor and shook the legendary drummer's hand. Pratt, of course, was a big fan of Charlie's, especially his jazz work, and clearly the respect was mutual, so it was great that they could share a few moments before we had to hit the stage, and even when Charlie said, "I'm going to *watch* you," Neil was unfazed (almost). What a terrific buzz!

Then we went on and, my god, the view: people as far as the eye could see—the very horizon was moving. It's an amazing feeling to play to such a crowd. I have tried many times to describe it, but maybe never successfully, so here goes again: before you hit the stage, you have the knowledge and the confidence of months of preparation and playing. You know the material by every possible metric. Still, however much you've warmed up in the dressing room, that first song is always about shaking off the cobwebs—especially if you're singing—even if up there I do look like an organ grinder with everything but the tin cup, more than anything I'm focused on singing in key. On a good night, once I'm locked in, I enter a sort of dream state. I'm in awe but can't just stand there gawping, I've got a job to do, and my brain sort of lifts off. That kind of awareness has always fascinated me: when you feel jacked into every little thing that's going on around you but in another sense you're not really there at all. The motor functions of your brain are firing on all cylinders, your fingers are flying up and down the neck of your instrument, but your thoughts are somewhere else entirely. You might be thinking about what's coming up *after* the song you're actually playing, or worrying about those people security is pushing around down in front, or thinking, *Wow, there's a hot chick in the third row! She must think the Stones are about to come on* . . . and yet somehow you make it through the gig. At that point I'm living the music, it's become an extension of me. My fingers are connected directly to my brain and my heart is spurred on by the crowd. I'm sweating, hyperaware, lost in the moment. I'm aware not only of my partners, but of every soul in the building. I have a psychic peripheral vision that makes me feel connected to everything. And when the three of us are in that same mode, there's no feeling like it. I miss the synchronicity of that partnership the most—both the skill set and the emotional turbo drive. There's no more rewarding experience I've ever had on earth, with the possible exception of . . . Okay, hey, wait a second. Just calm down there, please. If you thought I was gonna say something stupid like "an orgasm," well, I wasn't. I was going to say "a glass of 1978 Musigny."

IN OCTOBER 2002, we crossed the border into Mexico City for our first-ever gig there. I couldn't wait to be a tourist, incognito, but it wasn't so straightforward. I was unprepared for the security the promoter customarily provided visiting entertainers; he told me that kidnapping of high-profile foreigners was almost a legitimate business there. Yikes! I didn't see anything out of the ordinary at the airport or when arriving at the Four Seasons, so as we pulled up I told my management peeps Pegi and Shelley that as soon as I could dump my bags, I'd want a car to take me to the main square, Plaza de la Constitución, for my first walkabout. We piled into an SUV and headed downtown, when I noticed that we'd been part of a convoy of *three* vehicles. Then in the historic Zócalo (as the locals call it) I became aware of an array of big men in bulky black suits flanking me about twenty feet away on either side. "Peg," I said, "are those guys for *me*?"

"Yes, Ged." She nodded. "And they're armed."

Every major rock band who'd ever toured had played Mexico— except us. Another instance of Rush's tunnel vision. We'd been approached to play Central and South America before—for instance at Rock in Rio, the world's biggest annual pop festival—but either the timing was wrong or our management hadn't prioritized it. Now, when we saw the enormity of the stadiums we were scheduled to play, we wondered why we hadn't known how big a fan base we had. Why did it take us so long to get there?[*] Much as I hate to point the finger, particularly so many years after the fact, I can only blame SRO. They'd either failed to do due diligence or failed to inform us. In fairness, we'd long been limiting international touring for the sake of our families; even prior to his tragedies, Neil wanted more family time, to the point where he didn't want to play in the summer at all, or ski season either, so Ray was focusing on closer, less costly destinations.

We'd been forewarned that "Closer to the Heart" was a fan favourite in Latin America, so, having given it a rest after playing it on every single tour for twenty-five years, we added it back to the set. But we were wholly unprepared for the reaction. The fans who'd waited to see us all that time rocked out with authority. They knew our music really well and whooped it up at least as passionately as our Texas crowds had on the other side of the border. Old and young, all were dancing, fired up in a way I'd never seen before.

In São Paolo, Brazil, I was similarly unprepared for the size of the throng of teary fans on the ground. We posed for pictures, signed some autographs and then gathered at the hotel bar to consume unwise amounts of Brazil's sweet and highly alcoholic national cocktail, the caipirinha. Lerxst led the charge, of course, consuming twelve of them and staying up long after the rest of us had retired, completely plastered. Go, Big Al! Or should I say, "Go to *bed*, Big Al!"

At the press conference the next day, we were overwhelmed.

---

[*] One explanation for our "secret" success in Brazil (and Chile for that matter) is the huge South American bootleg and counterfeit record industry; our actual sales far exceeded what our label accounted for. But that must also be the case for almost every big international act. The goofiest thing, it turns out, is that *Profissão Perigo*, the Brazilian version of *MacGyver*, had been using parts of "Tom Sawyer" for its theme song; the show was popular enough there to spur sales of *Moving Pictures* and the rest of our album catalog. Thanks, MacGyver!

Paparazzi? For *us*? Like proper pop stars, Alex and I stood there in a bombardment of flashbulbs and then, like nice, polite Canadian boys, responded to as many questions as we could from a pack of reporters who, judging by the number of autographs we were asked to sign, were also rabid Rush fans. Inevitably, the first question was "Where is Neil?"—which had always been a difficult one to answer but was particularly sensitive in light of his recent tragedies. Lerxst and I explained as succinctly and delicately as we could that he simply couldn't handle it. Then we toured the city, flanked as in Mexico by bodyguards who never left our side (although these ones were a bit more discreet). The executive kidnapping business, we learned, is booming there, too.

The next day we flew to the coastal town of Porto Alegre for our first show. The plane was tossed about by some fiendishly wet and windy weather, making several in our entourage pretty damn nervous. Ever since Buddy Holly and company went down in that Beechcraft Bonanza in 1959, every rock band flying in a small plane has had reason to be fearful, but for some reason I never, ever am. We can be thrown upside down and inside out and I never get nervous, nor does Alex, but that one was as much a white-knuckler for us as it would have been for Neil. (*He'd* wisely elected to ride instead, having brought his motorcycle to South America, which in turn freaked out Ray, in fear that Neil would be waylaid by banditos.[*]) Then when we arrived, we were greeted with the news that our gear was drenched, the monitor desk had blown up and our front-of-house guy, Brad, was going to have to feed us a compromised mix from the side of the stage.

Meanwhile, more than 30,000 exuberant fans from all over the country waited undaunted outside the arena for half the day in the rain, and then another couple of hours inside, entertaining themselves by chanting, waving flags and singing Rush songs a cappella. From

---

[*]  Just my opinion, but I think one reason we'd never played South America before was that Ray had been projecting his fear of foreign places onto us.

backstage I thought I could hear them chanting, "Hush! Hush! Hush! Hush!" until I was told that the Portuguese pronounce the letter "r" like an "h." Ah-*hah*, got it now!

We were blown away by the range of generations who came to celebrate our music with us, and even more surprised by the large contingent of rockin' females—a first for us! It has to be said that by that time, even in North America, generations of fans were coming to see us—fathers, daughters, sons and little ones (we'd been around that long), but I did *not* expect it in Brazil. Seeing all those families brought home how popular we'd been there for quite some time, and I was floored. The entire crowd seemed to know every lick and lyric, dancing from start to finish (how do you even dance in 7/4?), bouncing up and down like on an arena-sized trampoline and punching their fists into the air. They not only knew the songs inside out, singing along to the changes in tempo and key of "YYZ" but added what sounded like new parts too. This happened at every gig we played there, so tight it was as if they'd all rehearsed it together before we got there. In time we understood that it was born of soccer culture: a rockin' version of a soccer chant adapted to our music.

The rain abated for a day, but returned with perfect timing for the show in São Paolo. After many delays, we kicked off at ten, but the show hung by a thread throughout the night with little to protect us from sideways-blowing gusts that soaked the stage and spritzed the electronic gear, giving me the occasional shock from my mic and making Neil's electronic drum kit go haywire. He improvised around the screwed-up sounds his drum pads were spewing out until the system simply gave up the ghost. Meanwhile, I'd never seen an audience like that in my life, close to 60,000 Brazilians pleading with us to play their favourite songs, dancing and (no exaggeration) weeping with joy. We played on as best we could, spurred on by their resolutely undampened spirit, but as we pranced about the stage, throwing shapes like rock and rollers do, we were seriously mindful of the danger of electrocution. It was treacherous. I mean really, we could have easily slipped on our asses or been fatally zapped.

But the real test was yet to come. It's rare for bands with shows the size of ours to play São Paolo and Rio back-to-back because the 425-kilometer drive is just too long for a convoy of trucks to pull off in a day with time enough left to set up, but thanks to another management/promoter cock-up, that's what we were booked to do. By the time our exhausted crew dragged their sorry heinies off the rickety Brazilian buses, they were already six hours behind schedule, but being the pros they were, they helped one another every way they could to get the show up in time—even after discovering that much of the gear was still wet from the night before, in particular the onstage carpet, and that the power grid had grounding and insulation problems. Halfway through the afternoon, the main cable arced and blew out the connection, cutting off power to the sound system. Concerned for our safety, our production manager wouldn't let us play a note until that was resolved. With throngs of people gathering impatiently outside, we ran out of time for soundcheck, and the film crew that had accompanied us to South America couldn't do a line check either. We'd have to go on cold and hope for the best.

Happily, it was one of those nights when the band was totally locked in. Neil's electronics were back in form, the crowd of more than 40,000 was in fine voice, giving us a recording we could all be proud of. The arena was like a steaming cauldron full of gyrating noodles over a fire stoked by the band! It was a miracle, really, for the moment the show was over it began to pour again, right onto our poor, tired crew as they loaded out, and soaking the carpet so completely that they had to leave it behind,* and in the process my excellent monitor man, Brent Carpenter, slipped off the ramp of one of the trucks and dislocated his shoulder. They worked through the night, then drove to

---

\* It was subsequently cut up and sold on eBay, probably by a local promoter.

the airport and unloaded everything yet again onto pallets for shipping to Canada. Back at the hotel later that day, I joined them by the swimming pool bar and thanked them for working more than *forty hours straight*. After the brutal schedule they'd endured, they were an exhausted ragtag collection of people awaiting their flight. There was no end-of-tour party like we'd usually enjoy, barely time for a pat on the back, because management and our penny-pinching comptroller were so concerned about losing money on the South American tour after shipping our equipment by air, but I wanted to buy the crew at least one damn libation. As the rain dissipated in the tropical heat, we drank and hugged goodbye, and I was moved by the thought that there'd have been no show (and, as such, no recording) without these guys—pure and simple. Heroes, all.

Some hours earlier, after Alex, Neil and I had dashed offstage into the waiting van with our wives inside and sat back sweating with towels around our necks and glasses in our hands, and as we made our way through the jam-packed streets of Rio, Neil looked out at the traffic lights and neon above the clubs flaring through the rain-streaked windows, and said, "Well, I guess you could say we are now truly an international band. Cheers!" and it struck me at that moment that at last he was fully, truly, happily back in the fold, ready to take on whatever the next phase of Rush would throw at him. More than anything else, *that* was something to celebrate.

# CHAPTER 25

AFTER THE FOURTEEN-MONTH GRIND making *Vapor Trails* plus the hectic tour that followed, I was in no hurry to even think about another album. But then Ray, never one to miss an opportunity, pointed out that our thirtieth anniversary was fast approaching (thirty years, who'd a thunk it?!), that a tour to mark it was imperative and that we couldn't go back out on the road without something new.

Actually, the prospect of presenting the first retrospective of our long career was appealing, packed with possibilities, and he was right, it felt too easy and even exploitative to simply tour—that just wasn't how we rolled. But even if we could put the memories of those *Vapor Trails* sessions behind us, could we write and record new material in time? It was then my pal Jason Sniderman suggested that instead of writing new songs, we consider covering some favourites from our formative years—a nod to the bands who made us want to be musicians in the first place: the Who, Buffalo Springfield, Procol Harum, Blue Cheer, Love, Cream . . . *Hmm* . . . Rush as a cover band? A thoroughly cool idea. A new recording, but instead of a heavy *mental* project, a quick and joyful release. There'd be none of the usual agonized fretting over whether the songs were good enough, since they'd have already passed the test of time. We'd record them in short order, and they'd neatly dovetail into the retrospective theme. All we had to do was play 'em like we meant it!

Everyone lit up. In direct contrast to the fourteen painstaking months that we'd spent labouring over every minute of *Vapor Trails* "in the box" on our computers, we recorded the tracks for *Feedback*[*] live off the floor at breakneck speed, tweaking the guitar and bass in the control room and *boom*: the EP was finished in little over a month. Just like the old days! Now we were armed with something to build a show around that would be unlike anything we'd done before.

Aside from their virtuosity and complex songwriting, one major thing that our favourite bands from the UK had in common was a flair for theatre: Jethro Tull, Pink Floyd, Genesis and Yes in particular all knew how to mesmerize with oversized visuals, surreal cinematics, high concepts, funny and dramatic presentations. They were our inspiration. I saw Tull play Toronto's Maple Leaf Gardens on June 4, 1972. Oscar and I had listened to *Thick as a Brick* together countless times, devouring every tasty morsel of music until we had it memorized, but the stage show opened up a whole new dimension. It began with the house lights still on and a work crew sweeping the stage. One by one

---

[*] Neil came up with the title partly because feedback was such a hallmark of the period; the bane of live rock and roll, a constant annoyance that robbed me of my hearing in the 2.8K cycle range. But *Feedback* also represented what we were trying to do: feed some respect back to the music that helped make us what we were.

they shed their overalls and picked up an instrument; they were, in fact, the members of the band, who then launched into an hour-long enhanced version of the album, interpolating (to use a word one often saw on prog rock LP covers of the era) snatches of other songs and suddenly stopping for, say, Ian Anderson to answer a telephone or the bassist, Jeffrey Hammond-Hammond, to deliver a faux weather report or news broadcast. At one point a man in a scuba suit walked across the stage; at another the lights went out momentarily, coming back on to reveal a Bedouin tent, out of which the guitarist, Martin Barre, emerged to deliver a crunchy guitar solo. It was as close to rock and roll meets *Monty Python* as you could get, the first time I'd seen such a mix of deft musicianship, complex songwriting replete with odd time signatures *and* a healthy dose of humour. A bar set that high was inspiration for any ambitious young musician, while reminding the nineteen-year-old me to take my music seriously but not *myself*.

Long before *Feedback* and the R30 tour, our shows had featured short film clips, animated sequences and computer-generated art, but now we were moving to the next level. Pratt came up with the idea for an overture, a medley of photos and film clips underscored by musical excerpts that would trace the course of our career. We brainstormed a short introductory film that featured characters and logos from our album covers coming to life, handing the baton to one another in a time travel sequence and ending with live action of one of our older fans (played by Jerry Stiller, George Costanza's dad on *Seinfeld*) waking abruptly from a Rush dream and fearing he'd missed the show.

As anyone who knows me can attest, I'm not a very price-sensitive guy, and my Big Ideas ran over budget on a regular basis: once we'd seen how fans on the *Signals* tour loved Joe Flaherty's appearance onstage as the hopelessly unscary Count Floyd from *SCTV*'s *Monster Chiller Horror Theater*, we understood that a bit of a laugh was a welcome breath of fresh air at a heavy prog show and worth spending money on; hence the gun-totin' rabbits on the *Presto* tour (Disney-style animation does not come cheap) and the *Rush in Rio* fire-breathing, cocktail-swilling carnival dragons (those were effin' *expensive*). Poor Herns had to make his presentation after mine, and because his initial drawings would also include the moon and enough rocket ships to get us there, he had the toughest time choosing which to scrap. Every tour we fought to fund our technicolor dreams—like the robotic rotating screens he'd later come up with for the *Clockwork Angels* tour. I used to love all that wrangling—real Broadway stuff! Each and every tour we had to choose amongst screens and scrims and explosions and lasers and whatever, always wanting more, which meant a bigger lighting rig, a bigger crew, a longer convoy of trucks. There was often resistance from management, but one of the costly things Ray did love was the live cameras used to project us onto the seventy-foot screens above the stage. Why? Because that meant he could sell seats way to the back of the arena. *That's* how managers and promoters think—suddenly a crappy seat is not a bad seat!

I was often secretly amazed by how much rein my trusting partners gave me, but of course they cared about creating a stunning show too. By that time it was already pushing three hours long, a line we were loath to cross because it was so hard on our bodies and vocal cords, and because we didn't want to incur the onerous overtime charges of union-controlled venues; in a place like Madison Square Garden, where you could be dealing with as many as ten different unions, you could run up a pretty stiff bill. That's one of the reasons Pratt suggested we create the "R30 Overture," a crafty way of having a "new" song for fans *and* keeping us to our time limit.

We had, at long last, tripped upon a unique image for ourselves: a combination of complex and melodic progressive hard rock presented in an abstract, absurdist, self-deprecating package. To my knowledge, no other band (except maybe Primus) has taken their own personal goofiness to such an extreme. The success of R30 also told us that it was okay to revel in the past every now and again, so long as we kept adding fresh ideas and one eye keenly focused on the future. We were determined to never become the proverbial dead shark—a fate we'd seen end the careers of all too many other bands.

By the *Snakes & Arrows* tour in 2007 we'd be fully committed to "An Evening with . . ." as a three-hour show split into two halves with no other bands on the bill, and the production budget would grow exponentially. We were even more intent on filling the time with crazy props and absurdist filmmaking, going further out on a limb than ever by appearing in the films ourselves. In *The Real History of Rush* on the Time Machine tour, we played characters rooted in our own ethnicities: I became Gershon, a Yiddish delicatessen owner (with Kyla as Kugel, Gershon's daughter); Lerxst played Slobović, an obese Serbian inventor; and Pratt became O'Malley, an Irish beat cop sipping on scotch and making pithy, cynical remarks; plus young versions of ourselves in an oom-pah-pah band called Rash playing in the deli. I invented Slobović to channel the inner Lerxst. From the time he was a skinny teenager, he'd always looked in the mirror and saw only Fat Lerxst, so "Slobović," a mash-up of "slob" and the terrible Yugoslavian alcoholic beverage slivovitz, was the perfect Serbian fat man.* A lot of serious, thoughtful work goes into preparing a tour, you see. It's not *all* fun and games.

The goofiness extended to our onstage personae too. I guess that when you've endured something as serious as Neil had but come back from the edge, you just don't sweat the small stuff the same way anymore. We became looser, more celebratory, more like our real-life selves up there. On opening night in Hartford in 2002, Alex broke into a verbal improv like the ones he'd only ever delivered in rehearsals to break the monotony and entertain the crew. In front of a live audience now, and giving Neil and me no warning, he stepped up to the mic during "La

---

* Lerxst's enormous fat suit took the costume/makeup department ages to wrap around him. The day we filmed was one of the hottest that June, and we were working in an abandoned café that had zero A/C. Between takes, the poor sweltering guy had to have sections of the massive costume removed to blow some cool air onto him.

Villa Strangiato" and sang "Hey Baba Reba!" (from Frankie Yankovic's "Café Polka," a drinking song his parents used to enjoy with their friends). That improv turned into a regular nightly stream-of-consciousness featuring such topics as "While My Guitar Gently Vomits" and "Chris Isaak on Acid." For the times he wandered into oblivion or painted himself into a corner, Pratt worked out a drum cue that signaled it was time to wrap it up—like in the vaudeville days, when they'd give a performer who'd outstayed their welcome the shepherd's crook.

A majorly pressing issue, meanwhile, was how to top my laundry dryers. Their spin action had added a subtle bit of energy to the show, so I asked myself what other machines moved, tumbled or turned, and presto!, chicken rotisseries popped into my head—the kind you see in restaurants and butcher shops with that orangey-reddish glow, turning the chickens around and around—and the "Henhouse" was born, complete with rotating rubber chickens. I wanted to waft a roast chicken aroma into the crowd, but that was too difficult to achieve in large venues (we even considered sneaking a real chicken in amongst the rubber ones for someone to munch on, but that wasn't practical either), so instead we had guests or crew members walk out mid-show in a chef's hat, completely ignoring the crowd and the band in full swing, to matter-of-factly baste the chickens— and sometimes even Pratt's drum kit for good measure. (You would not believe the number of fans I meet to this day who actually believed those were real chickens roasting in the Henhouse. Nice prop job, team!)

THE NORTH AMERICAN leg of our *Feedback*/R30 tour of 2004 came with a stab in the heart for me: the death of my old friend Oscar Peterson Jr.

We'd kept in touch over the years, even forming a band on the side in the early days called the Midnight Marauders, jamming in Rush's rehearsal space in East Toronto after hours—not playing serious music at all, just letting off steam with whacked-out pseudo-country and mock-disco songs. He was well-liked by everyone in Rush, band and crew, and was a regular visitor whenever we recorded, popping into the sessions at Le Studio, where he made a cameo appearance as President Ronald Reagan on "The Jack Secret Show," a spoof late-night variety show that the band and crew used to tape for laughs. As I became more successful and travelled farther abroad, however, our friendship had suffered. I told myself it was down to me being away so much, but there were other things at play. He worked on and off as his dad's road manager and helped him out in his home studio. He loved it, he told me, but they had a falling-out and he found himself unemployed as my fortunes continued to rise. I tried to help out, but he was a proud dude and resolutely refused to burden me with whatever he was going through.

Then he showed up out of the blue at a gig in 2003, striding into our dressing room and delivering his usual "Yes, sir!" and though I felt guilty that he had had to make the first move, it was like I'd seen him just the day before, and we picked up right where we'd left off. But not long after our reunion, he became ill. Diagnosed with a brain tumour, he underwent surgery that rendered him paralyzed all down one side of his body. He then spent a few months in a care home, where I visited him as often as I could. He loved dogs, especially big Newfoundlanders, so I'd bring along my little cairn terrier, Duke. Duke would hop up on his bed, walk all over him and lick his face until he was in convulsions, helplessly looking to me to rescue him, but I'd just sit back and let it happen because I so loved to hear him laugh. Soon after that, I'd just done a show in Philadelphia, when I got the terrible news that he'd passed away at his home with his partner, Louise, and their kids at his side. His passing was crushing for me and everyone who knew him. I think of him often. I loved that man.

IN THE FALL of 2004 Rush made a long-overdue return to the UK and Europe. These were the first gigs there in more than twelve years. We packed up the full R30 circus and crossed the ocean to kick

off the fourteen-show tour at Wembley Arena in London. To mark
the occasion, it was suggested by management (at the eleventh fucking
hour, as usual) that we film the elaborate show with a view to releasing
it on DVD. Because the decision was made so late in the game, we had
no choice but to record one of the shows later in the tour, at the cavernous and quite creepy Festhalle in Frankfurt, Germany.

This venerable old neo-Baroque building holds particular significance to any child of the Holocaust, thanks to the part it played in
Hitler's Germany before and during the Second World War. On
March 16, 1936, Hitler stood at his lectern to deliver a hate-filled
speech and declared that the swastika would be the new official flag of
Germany. And on November 8 and 9, 1938, almost sixty-six years to
the day of our performance, the Festhalle had been a scene of terror
for the Jews of Frankfurt as they were forcibly gathered under its
ornate glass-dome ceiling to await transport en masse to various Nazi
concentration camps. I was chilled by the thought, glancing throughout the show at the spot from which the Führer once ranted. (Since
then, I've learned more details about that building's dark history. In
1945 it was bombed and badly damaged, then rebuilt, the only acknowl-
edgment of that terrible moment for the Jews being a plaque in the
rotunda. A footnote. Creepy enough for ya? It was for me.)

But that trip will always be most memorable for the time I got to
spend with Shelley Nott. I've lost all too many friends, companions
and workmates along the road, and one I still miss enormously is her.
(I know that I've probably told too many stories of people I've known
dying but, well, such is life—or such, it seems, is mine . . .) As our daily
wrangler handling press and production requests and any other matter
that needed on-the-spot attention, Shelley spent the bulk of her life
between 1996 and 2008 travelling with us and became my steady day-
off dinner companion, many an evening patiently pretending to be
interested in my stories about fine wines. She made my life on the road
in the 2000s so much more tolerable. Any night I asked if she was free

for dinner, she always said, "Yes!" but never let me pick her up from her room, insisting on meeting in the lobby because she wouldn't be seen without her makeup and full-on goth regalia. Nor would she ever go out in the sun to join us for a drink by the pool with her pale complexion and black fingernails. "Oh, Mr. G," she'd say. "I can't! We People of the Night never go out in the sun." Despite that, when one time we had three days off in Calgary, she agreed to go hiking out in the Rockies near Banff under summer skies, with little bells tied to us to scare the bears away.

She was an absolute gem of a human being. (Yes, Virginia, goths are humans too.) After she had a terrible breast cancer scare and felt she was living beneath the Sword of Damocles, I resolved to take her to see as many places as possible while she was well. On the *Feedback* tour in 2004, we rambled around the UK, making a stop at the Fat Duck in Berkshire, just as its chef, Heston Blumenthal, was making an international name for himself with his take on molecular gastronomy and amazing theatrical dining experiences; later we drove through northern Italy into Switzerland, through charming mountain villages where we stopped for espresso, Bündnerfleisch sandwiches and deep breaths of the bracing Alpine air; in Zurich at the exclusive Baur au Lac hotel, we drank too much wine and Calvados; in Paris she and Nancy did some serious shopping, we had an over-the-top meal at L'Ami Louis (drinking far too much excellent Burgundy and feasting on their famous Poulet de Bresse) and I escorted her to every interesting place I could think of—although the only one she really wanted to see was the Catacombs. When I asked her why she wanted to go there so badly, she looked at me as if it was self-evident and said, "Skulls, Mr. G. Skulls."

Sometime during the early part of the *Snakes & Arrows* tour, she'd fallen in love with one of our new lighting crew guys, married suddenly and moved to Nashville with him. Cancer survivors can't afford to waste time, I reckon, and she'd fully embraced a chance to start a new life, but wow, that girl could keep a secret! For a while, apparently, it was all parties and happy times, but as the fall of 2007 approached she told me she wasn't coming to Europe with us as she'd had a relapse and needed to return to Canada for surgery and treatment.

Dammit, it was all to no avail. Before the end of January 2008 she passed away, and I was crushed. (I still prefer to think of her as simply being "out of town.") To keep her spirit alive and rockin', on the following tour I had some T-shirts made to wear onstage every night, one with the initials "SN" surmounted by a seashell—her nickname was Shell Belle—and another with one of her favourite expressions, "Keep the Rawk."

The last time I ever saw her was in the hospital. She got terribly upset when I walked in. Because, you see . . . she had no makeup on.

*"Skulls, Mr. G. Skulls."*

# CHAPTER 26

ELL INTO SPRING OF 2006, ALEX AND
I wrote songs for *Snakes & Arrows* in my home studio
while Neil sent us lyrics from California. He wrote
"The Larger Bowl" in one creative burst as a pantoum
word game he'd tried for a long time to get into our songs. The origin
of the pantoum is Malaysian and Indonesian, with echoes of the inter-
woven rhythms of gamelan music: in it, the second and fourth lines of
each verse become the first and third of the following one.* Very smart
man, Neil! (He extended the pantoum theme to the album cover
featuring a Leela game—a precursor to Snakes and Ladders originally
created by Buddhist saints and sages in ancient India, called The Game

---

\* I actually broke the pattern by turning the second stanza into the song's chorus, but it's
otherwise sound.

of Self-Knowledge,* in a sense a user manual for conducting oneself through life's trials with grace and hope.

It was a pretty idyllic time. Lerxst and I gabbed and joked, drank coffee and jammed for hours on end, recording every riff, every idea. Being the more technically minded, he'd wrestle with the gear, plugging stuff in and messing with compressors and such, while I stood back, and at the end of the day he'd doze off on the sofa as I sorted through the recordings. Such was the level of trust we'd achieved after working for so many decades together that we no longer cared who came up with what idea. Every once in a while I'd ask, "Lerxst, how is this sounding?" and I'd hear him answer drowsily behind me, "Huh? Oh yeah. Sounds great, Dirk!" All that mattered was the end result. (The playfulness and ease with which we wrote is summed up in the title of the album's all-instrumental track, "The Main Monkey Business," which comes from a remark my mother once made about a relative of ours: "I have a feeling," she said, "he's up to some monkey business." "What kind of monkey business, Mom?" I asked. "You know," she said. "The *main* monkey business.")

By March, Pratt was back at his lake house in Quebec enjoying the cross-country ski season, so Lerxst and I decided to brave the snow and hang out with him a bit. Instead of sending tapes and communicating by email, we wanted him to hear the rough demos in our presence so we could talk about them on the spot and face-to-face. He heard a new direction in the music that Lerxst and I had sort of sensed but, being so deep in demos, couldn't perceive objectively: a lot more blues-based riffology, a folksy thing (especially on "The Way the Wind Blows") and a tinge of Eastern mysticism, elements we'd used in the past but that were now layered in a more sophisticated way. That was typical of Rush. We'd experiment on a couple of records, then come

* "Leela" is the Hindi word for "game."

up with *2112*; we'd experiment on a couple more, then come up with *Moving Pictures*; a couple more, and then you had *Power Windows*. Finally, you can hear that *Vapor Trails* and *Snakes & Arrows* were stepping stones towards *Clockwork Angels*.

To produce the record, we'd hired an American producer/engineer named Nick Raskulinecz, who had produced a couple of Foo Fighters albums, including *All My Life*, which won a Grammy for Best Hard Rock Performance. (Dave Grohl hadn't been happy with the original version of the record and re-recorded the entire thing in just two weeks with Nick at the helm.) This energetic young man was in his mid-thirties but seemed *much* younger; his manner was *very* "'Murican"—I've never met anyone before him who used the term "badass" so often;* and he was over-the-top unabashedly *excited* like we'd never seen in a producer. Unruly enthusiasm was his stock-in-trade, which I was starting to understand would be good for us grizzled old veterans to be around, but he also expressed his ideas in detail and with nuance.

In November we moved into Allaire Studios, a sprawling compound and residential studio on a secluded hilltop near Woodstock, New York, where a year before Neil had recorded an instructional video called *Anatomy of a Drum Solo*. Our time there was creative and exuberant. The state-of-the-art studio and estate overlooking the Catskills suited us well—like being back at Le Studio in its heyday. With *Vapor Trails* behind us in every sense, we were looser and more confident. The way we'd been welcomed back by our fans, the success of *Feedback* and explosive fun of the R30 tour, Neil's happy marriage—all had settled our nerves.

Nick's approach to recording the rhythm tracks was to be as live and loose as possible. On previous records, Neil would have typically played his parts to pre-recorded guide tracks, and we still used them

---

* When we first met him, he called our music either "badass" or "kickass" (no one had ever done *that* before) and told me that Taylor Hawkins of Foo Fighters never, ever called him by any other name than "Kickass."

for certain things, but this time the three of us were mainly out in the studio playing together as one to give him some true live vibes. And whether I was in the studio or grooving at the console, it was a delight to see our new muse in action. "Hey, man," Nick would say. "How about trying *this*?" and then sing and air-guitar or air-bass the parts for us. With his vocabulary of brash Americanisms—"That's badass," "Wha-at?," "Fuck, yeah," "Killer, dude!"—and every onomatopoeic utterance he could invent to describe a particular sound he was after, it was hard to keep a straight face, but he was nothing if not authentic. He may have been raw and unsophisticated but musically he was no bumpkin. He had an acute ear and could actually play all of those instruments to some degree, so that his gestures even made visual sense (most of the time). Above all, he was good at sniffing out the slightest hint of complacency on our part, and was determined to push us above and beyond—to dig deeper and play, in essence, more like ourselves. And goddamn if he didn't say what was on his mind, constantly reminding us that first and foremost we were a hard rock band and should be playing more like . . . well, *Rush*—the Rush he knew and loved, but making new music.

In some ways the *Snakes & Arrows* sessions were our happiest ever. We were all at a contented stage of our lives, and after walking on eggshells during the finicky and more technically driven *Vapor Trails* sessions, we were enjoying an easy and confident working relationship. With the possible exception of the *Permanent Waves* sessions, they were my favourite of our entire career. For once, I was actually happy with the work we had done!

WE STARTED GETTING offers from unlikely places because people who'd been Rush fans in their teens were now grown up and in the workforce. A generation of them now occupied positions of power and cultural influence in the media, in law, in Hollywood, even in politics.* We'd been turned into animated characters for TV on *South Park* and *Family Guy*, and for the first time were invited to appear on an American talk show *and* in a bona fide Hollywood feature film.

Was it that the mainstream was starting to notice us or, more likely, that Rush secret agents had infiltrated the mainstream? John Hamburg, the director/writer of *I Love You, Man*, was a Rush fan who felt that we—or more to the point, our extremely dedicated followers— should anchor the bromance backstory of the film; the movie's co-star Jason Segel told us how he'd played a Rush fan before, in the TV show *Freaks and Geeks*; and one of the producers said to me, "You know, during development of this project, I asked John, 'What if Rush won't do it? What's your plan B?' and he told me, 'There *is* no plan B.'" (Wow, that blew me away!)

That movie did a lot for our reputation, drawing us out from cult status and into an odd kind of mainstream acceptance. Then we

*Nancy is a very discreet person, so I was shocked when, without hesitation, she plopped herself down in Stephen's chair!*

<hr>

* Sorta. We used to joke that we couldn't wait to get a Rush fan in the White House, and we actually got close when one of them started working for Obama's merchandizing team.

jumped from the silver screen to the boob tube. We'd pretty much avoided TV since *Don Kirshner's Rock Concert* and *In Concert* back in 1974, as we felt that bands like us never came off sounding powerful enough on the box, but with our new resolve to challenge ourselves according to the Costanza Method, when we were asked onto *The Colbert Report* we responded with a most emphatic *yes*.

We were already huge fans of Colbert and *The Daily Show*, and totally psyched. We walked around the studio with smiles on our faces but shivering. (They keep those places cold to prevent those on camera from sweating, to cool the equipment and to keep both crew and audience alert and responsive.) In the mercifully warmer greenroom, Stephen told us that his director was a Rush fan who'd been badgering him for ages to have us on the show, adding, "*My* character is willfully ignorant. The best thing you can do is to let me be the idiot, and everything will work out fine."

Okay, message received: "Do not try to one-up the host!" (He's so hilarious, that would be hard no matter what.) We sat obediently on our stools as Colbert delivered his barrage of "questions" that were really jokes, like, "You're known for some long songs. Have you ever written a song so epic that, by the end of the song, you were actually being influenced by *yourselves*?" and "You are yet to be inducted in the Rock and Roll Hall of Fame. Is there any chance your next album will be called *That's Bullshit*?" Neil, surprisingly, was the most voluble of the three of us. After we'd all signed Stephen's hand, Neil quipped, "I don't wanna see that on eBay," which brought a slow grin to Stephen's face as he realized he wasn't the only funny one in the room.

So yes, suddenly some pretty cool people were standing up and showing they weren't afraid to admit to liking us. There were people, we realized, for whom being a Rush fan had been a rite of passage at a certain time in their lives, and later as accomplished adults were discovering a commonality with others like them. Finally, they could share the almost secret passion they'd harboured from all those years ago, when for so long it was uncool to dig us. *Colbert* and *I Love You, Man* suggested that the winds of change were finally blowing in our favour. Not that it kept us up at night or anything. We still had many influential detractors— some of whom, for example, sat on the board of the Rock and Roll Hall of Fame. (What was it we were going to call our next album?)

**SHORTLY AFTER FILMING** *I Love You, Man* and while on tour in California, I was informed that John Rutsey, at only fifty-five, had died of an apparent heart attack related to complications from diabetes. Although we'd lost touch and I hadn't seen him in years, the news came as a terrible jolt. His passing at such a young age felt sad and unfair. At the funeral, Alex spoke well and generously of his old friend, while I wrestled with my feelings, and a flood of memories from a more innocent time, both good and painful, filled my mind. I didn't speak, but had I, I'd surely have told these two stories about him . . .

John was mischievous and at times captivating, telling us once about his neighbour's haunted house and the headless man who lived in it. We didn't believe a word, of course, but as the evening progressed and we got higher and higher on an assortment of acid, dirt weed or both, he called to us in a whisper, "Come here, quick! There he is. There he is." We looked out across the yard and, sure enough, there was a shadowy figure sitting with his back to us . . . without a head! A trick of the light? A shifting shadow? Was he simply bent over? At first we laughed. Sort of. Then we didn't at all. Freaked out, we took another peek, and just like that the man was gone. And to this day I have no idea what we really saw.

Then there was the gloriously sunny day at the end of the summer of '69 when John invited me to drop acid with him (Purple Owsley microdots, if you must know) and attend the Rock and Roll Revival concert at Toronto's Varsity Stadium. The air was thick with incense as we literally tripped around the grounds, enjoying each other's company and grooving to a fantastic variety of bands from the Doors to Bo

Diddley to John Lennon on his first post-Beatles outing. It was almost a love-in! John was *up* that day, and that's the way I choose to think of him now—deeply into music, with a wicked sense of humour that could crack up the room. He was my bandmate for six years, at an indelible, incredibly formative time in both of our lives, and for all that could make him difficult company at times, I'm forever grateful that we shared the beginnings of a fantastic journey.

**WHILE LERXST AND** I were enjoying our leisure time in so many ways throughout 2009, Neil and his wife had a baby. Olivia Louise Peart was welcomed into the world on August 12 with joy as Neil embraced his second chance at parenthood. It did not go unnoticed that she had arrived just two days after the anniversary of the date on which Selena had departed. I can only imagine how bittersweet that moment must have been for my friend. Shortly after the birth, he invited us to California to meet the little gal face-to-face, and at the same time discuss plans for the band. He'd vowed to be as involved and attentive a dad as he could be, which would require more careful and considerate scheduling than ever on everyone's part.

It had been almost three years since we'd started work on *Snakes & Arrows*, and more than a year since our last show, and Ray was pushing to get us back on the road in time for a summer shed tour. Seeing as 2010 would be the thirtieth anniversary of *Moving Pictures*, he also suggested we perform that record in its entirety in concert. Around that time a number of bands were reviving classic albums onstage— just about everyone, in fact, from the Beach Boys to Public Enemy— but we'd never done it and were intrigued.

I also thought we might assemble all our instrumental tracks together on a new album, updated with a brand-new, epic, wordless piece, which would also give us something new to play on tour. As much as Pratt and Lerxst liked that idea, it merely became a catalyst: it sparked

Pratt's ambition to write an epic-length suite of songs that would comprise our first concept album in almost twenty-five years, built around Pratt's interest in steampunk, a sub-genre of sci-fi he described as "the future as seen from the past"—a futuristic world made of Victorian mechanics. All through December we shared articles and visual ephemera as the cogs in his brain cranked into gear. What we first referred to as "Steampunk Serenade: A Work in Progress," we conceived as occupying two sides, with the story unfolding in three parts: "Caravan," "Carnival" and, early on, "Caravel." In its development from concept to a recorded piece of work, it morphed from "Serenade" to "Steampunk Rhapsody," and finally *Clockwork Angels*.

As Lerxst and I beavered away, I had a strong sense that we'd reached a new point of understanding, of solidarity as writing partners. Starting with *Snakes & Arrows*, my bossiness was giving way to confidence as I trusted Alex's taste and ideas more than ever before. After forty years, our partnership had finally hit its stride! To ensure I wasn't kidding myself, I recently asked him how he'd felt, and (thank goodness) this was his response: "Making *Clockwork Angels* was a fucking joy. I never felt happier working together. By then you'd started saying to me, 'I'm not coming in tomorrow, so just go ahead and do your thing,' and I was like, 'I love this guy!' I was happily smoking pot and doing my thing! And if the next day you came in and didn't like what you heard, instead of us getting our backs up, we'd just work on it some more. That's maturity, I guess."

Although I do think that album represents a step up on our songwriting learning curve, it wasn't effortless. The lyrics Pratt first sent us were very much works-in-progress that required a lot of trial and error from Lerxst and me. The earliest version of his story played out like a swashbuckling adventure, which did not easily translate into a heavy rock context without sounding melodramatic or overblown. The story line led too easily to me singing less like me and more like some kind of posing progster—too full of pomp, too full of himself. Lerxst and I wanted it much more current and harder-edged—not like Gilbert and

Sullivan with electric guitars—and at times we even wondered if the concept mightn't be better suited to a single side after all. What's more, Neil had been inspired by Voltaire's classic satire *Candide* (early on, the main character's name was Candido), and while there was a lot to like in what he wrote, I felt that if the influence were not so obvious we could make the story more our own and broaden its universality.

One line from the first draft of "Caravan" did speak loudly to me: *Can't stop thinking big.* Those words captured the way I've always felt about making music and pretty much everything else I've ever put my mind to. As the song evolved, Neil embellished it to *In a world where I feel so small, I can't stop thinking big*, which put me right back in my bedroom as a kid, dreaming of escape from my lonely dead-end life after Dad had passed away. It was so personal to me that I knew it had to be the chorus of the song, and that I had to find a melody strong enough to make it resonate with listeners as meaningfully as it did for me.

We first showcased this fascination with steampunk and the very beginnings of the concept album on our Time Machine tour, which was divided in two legs—from July to October 2010 and from April to July 2011. The set list comprised a variety of tunes from the past, the whole of *Moving Pictures* and the two new songs, "Caravan" and "BU2B" (standing for "Brought Up to Believe"). Both got some serious radio play, and the new absurdist films we'd made to accompany the show all went down a storm, which boded well for the future of what would become *Clockwork Angels*.

And as if that wasn't enough, John Hamburg, the director of *I Love You, Man*, offered to shoot a sequel of sorts for this tour, appropriately called *I Still Love You, Man*, with Paul Rudd and Jason Segel reprising their bromantic roles as fans who sneak backstage during a Rush show and finally meet their heroes face-to-face. We screened that one at the very end of the show as a treat for our audiences after sitting through that three-hour marathon. As George M. Cohan wrote in 1904, "Always leave 'em laughing when you say good-bye."

It was a tour of tremendous highs, but also of worrisome lows. On the one hand, on a glorious summer night during the Festival d'été outside Quebec City, more than 80,000 people attended our Plains of Abraham gig—our biggest headline show ever. On the other, the Time Machine was plagued by health problems. Neil's ears became infected by the summer's heat and humidity and further aggravated by his ergonomic in-ear monitors and the earplugs he used to muffle the sound of his motorbike as he gunned down the highways from show to show. It got so nasty that, even stuffed with antibiotics, he had to resort to large over-ear headphones (now you know why he's pictured wearing them in photos of that tour). Over the years he'd become increasingly vulnerable to infections but pushed on with characteristic stoicism. Lerxst, meanwhile, was suffering from stress on his heart brought on by a bleeding ulcer, and episodes of sudden overwhelming fatigue and shortness of breath were becoming the norm. He'd had them before, on and off the road, but now, as his doctors struggled to find a cure, it was weighing more heavily on our minds. And then there was an incident involving Alex in St. Louis that freaked me the fuck out.

After enduring the mugginess, we did a couple of shows at high altitude in dry Colorado (where they put a cup over my mouth and nose[*] and gave me a blast of oxygen to help me combat the dizziness and sing more easily—not, in fact, so unusual for performers in Denver), then plummeted into the sweaty Midwest. I knew people in St. Louis, some of whom were employees of the Cardinals baseball club, others in the wine business, and whenever we played there we were treated to terrific meals and rare Burgundies at various eateries in the Central West End. On this particular, quiet Sunday evening in August it was still around 31 degrees Celsius, with 80 percent humidity, when we met up with two friends for dinner. Alex, ignoring the heavy toll that switching atmospheres was taking on our bodies, joined us after *two rounds* of golf; I

---

[*]  A big one, naturally.

think he played *thirty-six holes* in that effin' heat. We emptied bottle after bottle, and then he went outside with one of our pals to share a joint in the sweltering summer night, while I remained indoors, waxing extravagantly about the finer points of Richebourg or some such self-indulgence. After about ten minutes I happened to glance through the bay window and saw him with his head down on the table. I dashed outdoors shouting his name, but he didn't respond, while both of our friends looked on in stunned silence. I totally freaked out, fearing he'd had a heart attack. I lifted his heavy head in my hands and tried to slap him awake. He was breathing but completely unresponsive. I slapped him harder, yelling, "Someone call an ambulance!" One arrived almost instantly, and miraculously, just as the paramedics were lifting him into it, he began to revive, even finding the wherewithal to crack a joke or two through his haze. I phoned Liam to tell him to meet me at the hospital, and there we waited well into the night for news. Finally, a doctor told us Lerxst was awake in the ICU. He suggested it had been heatstroke but wanted to keep him overnight for observation and on an IV to rehydrate. What a relief, but man, that was one of the scariest

(LEFT) *Having scared the shit out of me, there the fucker is, in the ambulance smiling!* (RIGHT) *And fourteen hours later onstage I was like, "Hey Lerxst, remember how I thought you were dead last night?"*

moments of my life—and, quite frankly, part of me wanted to brain him. Depriving himself of sleep to play golf on a day from Hades, then drinking vino for hours, *in his condition?*

He returned to the hotel the following morning, clearly shaken, then slept for several hours. He still insisted on doing that night's gig, which being outdoors was hot as hell, but got through it okay and made it to his fifty-seventh birthday five days later—still around, hallelujah, to be greeted by us all with celebratory T-shirts.[*]

**THE TOUR ROLLED** on through to October, when we returned to Brazil and played our first shows in Argentina and Chile—the latter being another country where we'd badly underestimated our popularity. This had become an embarrassing habit! Our show there took place only days after the rescue of thirty-three miners trapped in a collapsed shaft in Copiapó, which surely contributed to the euphoric atmosphere. The crowd was absolutely incredible, and the next day a newspaper headline read RUSH PAYS CHILE BACK FOR 40 YEARS!

In October we returned to the studio to finish *Clockwork Angels*. We still had more than half the album to write, but the concept was coming together both lyrically and musically. As I look back on correspondence Neil and I shared, I'm reminded of several of the books and visuals beyond *Candide* that inspired him: Robertson Davies's *Deptford Trilogy* for "Carnies," various Cormac McCarthy novels for "Seven Cities of Gold," John Barth's *The Sot-Weed Factor* (which was in fact a retelling of the Candide story) for "The Anarchist," Daphne du Maurier, H. G. Wells, Jules Verne, Joseph Conrad, Herbert Gold and several others, plus ongoing conversations with his friend and steampunk pioneer Kevin Anderson. That rich stew had already influenced the vibe of the Time Machine tour and was a precursor of

---

[*] Actually, he played *great* that night. But seriously: effin' golf, man. It'll kill ya!

more to come as Neil hammered away with a relentless energy. It makes me dizzy to think of how vast a creative database operated in that man's mind.

The remaining pieces of the puzzle were "The Anarchist," "Carnies," "Seven Cities of Gold," "Halo Effect" and my personal favourite, "Headlong Flight." Wait, no . . . "Anarchist" is my fave . . . or is it "The Garden"? Each song had its own trajectory and, at times, issues to overcome, but fuck me, as they came together, I really did start to fall in love with them. There have been moments in Rush when I have had an inkling, a visceral feeling that we were working at the top of our game: *2112*, *Permanent Waves*, *Moving Pictures* and *Power Windows* come to mind, and, speaking now, *Clockwork Angels*. But I didn't have that inkling at the time. I was too busy, head down, deep into the *doing* of it to appreciate the quality of the work. Not so with Pratt, who was confident we were onto something special from the start.

Unprecedented, meanwhile, was the absolute faith and respect Pratt now showed Nick Raskulinecz, allowing him to stand inside the studio when the red light was on and actually *conduct* him with a baton. He gave Nick pretty much unfettered freedom not only to suggest drum part ideas, a huge enough thing, but to dare to air-drum the suggestions, pushing the Professor himself to the limit. I could not believe my eyes, but Pratt, so far from seeing it as interference, took Nick's gestures in the spirit of a click track, a helpful and quicker way to get a better result, and even more than that, trusted Nick to help him come up with patterns more complicated than he might have come up with on his own. Nicky, need I add, was in badass heaven.

Most songs came together synchronously, each with their own flavour but flowing into one another. Compared to old Rush songs like "Headlong Flight," they have a furiousness that doesn't feel too fast. I listen to some of our earlier songs now and wonder, *Where's the fire? Where are these guys running off to?* It was like someone had sped up the tape, whereas now we'd finally figured how to be furious without rushing it. Now we sat right in the pocket. There's a heavy mass to songs like "The Anarchist," "Carnies," "Headlong Flight" and "Wish Them Well" that shows how much more settled we were in our relentlessness. It was like we were drivers seated comfortably on a steaming, careening locomotive, confident of keeping it on the rails. The record feels heavier and tougher, but also delicate and richly melodic whenever a song's sentiment calls for it.

As I alluded to earlier, not everything came together so easily. Neil had developed a character known as the Pedlar whom he described as "a kind of amorphous phantom who drifts through the story, prompting soliloquys from the major characters"; in his mind, this person was a "provocateur, an enigma, in disguise," someone who keeps whispering things in your ear (*What do ye lack?*), and as such an important device for exposition in a song of his own. Were this a novel with the space to develop such a character, Lerxst and I could see Neil's point (and he was in fact already working on a novelization of the story with a writer friend of his), but within the more limited confines of a rock opera we felt it would be easier to convey his presence by way of a leitmotif or just a musical mood complemented by some story notes with the lyric sheets, as we'd done for the Starman on *2112*. With so many songs already segueing nicely, another big representational piece of music with dialogue felt bulky and superfluous. With it, Lerxst and I were afraid of gilding the lily, of bloating the opera. We'd be losing focus. We hoped to accomplish the same thing by making the mood more ominous to represent the Pedlar's malevolent spirit, like you hear in "Carnies."

Throughout the sessions, the Pedlar Conundrum persisted. Neil kept on making his case for more character exposition, and we did try to make it work, eventually reducing the Pedlar's presence to one simple line that appears twice on the album—but even that line had its controversy. He wanted me to sing or say "What do *ye* lack?" but every time I tried to sing "ye," I felt like a pirate with a peg leg and parrot: "Urrgh, matey. What do ye lack?"[*] and Lerxst would double over laughing. So I suggested simply replacing "ye" with "you," but in the end, Neil volunteered to voice it himself. Done deal! That and the addition of story notes worked for everyone. So, if you listen to the very end of the album's title track, you can hear Pratt whispering it himself.

Nick felt that a few of the songs would benefit from orchestral treatment (*every* producer wants their big moment), and recommended we hire David Campbell, with whom he'd worked earlier in the year on the eponymous Evanescence album. Because Rush was such an insular group, I was eager to hear how David's arrangements would be delivered by his own hand-picked LA session players. Back when we'd first put strings on "Marathon," I feared that the orchestral treatment would soften our music—reduce its rock-and-roll-ness, make it too flowery. It can also go wrong when you give the powerful parts that are supposed to be the rock band's job to the orchestra. You end up with something pseudo-Beethoven. But recorded with the right amount of ambience in the mix, it need not diminish the power of the band. It was Terry Brown who in our earliest days had introduced us to this notion of "perspective": what do you want the listeners to hear and, when they're closing their eyes, to see? Too much of the string section can indeed make a song too syrupy; too little, and why did you bother? Somehow, David Campbell's instincts were so finely tuned that he added very little that was either inappropriate or superfluous.

We'd worked with orchestras before, but watching it all go down juiced up my adrenaline and gave me goose bumps. Just as it had in earlier years, it seemed miraculous how compositions that had begun as a humble bit of noodling on my bass could take such a giant step beyond. With all his experience, David seemed to see inside the way

---

[*]   A side effect, perhaps, of too many gigs making fun of "2112" in my pirate voice with a stuffed parrot on my shoulder?

*Ocean Way Recording, LA, January 18, 2012.*

we'd structured our songs, where the spaces sat, where he could add strings without getting in the way. And the ensemble, man, were they pros. Rush rehearsals were a matter of learning the notes by rote and repetition, but these people—being trained to play, you know, the latest James Bond score, or sit in the orchestra pit for *The Book of Mormon* on Broadway and read those little black marks without thinking—read David's scores and nailed them on the first pass. I used to make fun of them, like, "Huh? You read while you play?"

WE ASKED ANDREW MacNaughtan to fly in to video the session. He arrived dead-tired from his flight and, as he weaved around the studio that day, didn't seem himself at all. He worked unusually slowly and tentatively—and on the following Monday, when we gathered in a studio he'd rented to shoot the cover photo and some publicity stills, he still wasn't at his sharpest. Then a couple of days later, returning to our hotel from a morning tennis match with our management rep, Andy Curran, I walked into a kerfuffle in the lobby. Police were standing around, but hey—this *was* Hollywood, so . . .

The moment I closed the door of my room the phone rang. A distraught Andy was on the other end, saying that Andrew had been found in his room, dead from heart failure. These words sounded nonsensical to me. I struggled to understand. I hung up the phone and sat on the bed trying to gather the wherewithal to call Nancy. Ever since Andrew had worked as her assistant at Zapata, the two had been very close, and he and his partner, Alex Kane, had become part of our extended family. The call, as you can imagine, was simply awful.

The rest of the day moved as if in slow motion, and when Neil and Alex and I spoke we were too numb from shock to say anything of consequence. Pratt was at home trying to console Carrie, who, having worked with Andrew when she and Neil first met, was as stricken with grief as he was. Nick, Lerxst, Andy and I ended up in the bar drinking until after it closed. I resisted going to my room, knowing it would get all too real once I was alone with my thoughts. I struggled to understand how someone so young—just forty-seven—could be struck down so suddenly. Yet again, I was flummoxed and angry that the hold we have on life is so tenuous. My dad was only forty-five when he died as a result of the hard labour forced on him for five years in the camps . . . but *this*? This was not supposed to happen. In an instant, one of my closest friends—who'd exhibited no signs of serious illness—was gone. But the fact was, he was a nervous sort who had struggled over the years, on and off, with bouts of serious anxiety. He'd been prescribed various medications that at times had a debilitating effect on him—primarily fatigue. Sometimes the cure can be worse than the illness, and in this case, officially determined to be organ failure, may well have contributed to his death. To be overwhelmed by one's demons that way is a lonely, rotten way to end such a brilliant life.

Not to draw attention to myself, but I have to say that sometimes it feels to me that those bouts of existential angst I suffered as a child were justified, even prescient. After my dad passed, my obsession was further fed by the multitude of stories I was told about all "my" people who had died in the Holocaust. As an adult, what with all the casualties of the road, the inordinate number of deaths of friends and colleagues, I felt increasingly vulnerable. Trying to make light of it, I guess, I'd often recall the *Three Stooges* episode in which a cake gets stuck to the ceiling and Symona Boniface says to Moe, "You act as though the Sword of Damocles is hanging over your head," but seriously, I sometimes feel that's how I've lived my life.

Andrew had recently founded a charitable organization called Art-GivesHope, launching it with the release of a book of photographs he'd taken in West Africa, called *Grace: Africa in Photographs*, the proceeds of which went to families in Africa affected by HIV/AIDS. Stepping out that way from the entertainment business had meant an awful lot to him, and he was justifiably proud of the stunning shots he'd produced to help people in need. In the days that followed, I thought a lot about the clean-cut teenager who'd first shown up on my doorstep in the mid-seventies asking for an autograph. His final gig had been to take photos of us and make us laugh.

*CLOCKWORK ANGELS* WAS released in June and did very well out of the box, as they say, hitting #1 on the Canadian album and *Billboard* rock charts, and landing just shy in that magazine's Mainstream Chart at #2. Most gratifying was that fans seemed to really dig the record and were getting into the concept. I could now divide my summer amongst idling on the dock by my cottage on the lake, joining production design meetings with our team in the city to design the *Clockwork Angels* tour set and actually learning how to perform the songs that we'd spent so much time writing and perfecting in the studio. You'd think that such intimate familiarity with the material would make that process somewhat easier, but no. Arranging songs piece by piece is quite another thing from performing them live on bass, vocals and keyboards simultaneously. And take it from me, a few of those songs were motherfuckers to sing and play at the same time. To illustrate the struggle, I include an email status report I sent to my partners while in rehearsals that July.

*July 12, 2012*
*WHO WROTE THOSE IGNORANT SONGS?*
*deep into it . . . geez, Louise, can we hire a singer? seriously, I'm getting there with the new stuff . . . but wtf!! There are 3 effin c-nts on this one for me . . . Anarchist chorus, Carnies verses and the almost impossible pre-chorus of Headlong . . . got the first half of it but the 2nd? forget it . . . Leke, YOU sing that, o.k.??*
*that's it from Deke's bunker of hell*

Neil responded in kind, saying that he was taking a day off from "The House of Pain" and sending us a clip of him practicing that, with the help of the Action Movie FX app, ends with a missile blowing up his kit and himself with it. *Yep, they blowed up real good!*

Once the big wheels of the tour ground into gear, having that string ensemble onstage was a life-changing experience. It was fascinating for me to work with David on the arrangements. I loved watching him in action, seeing how quickly he could turn material around for several older songs we thought might also benefit from strings. Professionally,

(TOP) *Cover your valuable violins! And dudes, your man buns!* (BOTTOM) *"Xana-dooooo!"*

I learned a ton about melodic writing, while personally I felt fortunate to have taken on such a likeable ensemble and socialized with them as often as possible. I grew up in the raw, unschooled rock and roll circus—just like the kid in *Clockwork Angels* who runs away to join the carnival—while these people had taken a very different route, getting properly schooled, earning degrees, cutting their teeth as hired hands and so on. It really lifted my spirits at soundcheck every day to hear them share their stories.

From the very first day of rehearsal, we were jazzed up to be surrounded not just by so many experienced musicians but also by so much *sound*, layer upon layer of fresh, subtle melodies that made the songs we'd been playing for countless years feel new again. I was amazed by the extra juice they were bringing to the performance by rocking out so wildly. (Speaking of extra juice, they weren't prepared for the heat coming off the flamethrowers we'd rigged to jet up behind them during the show. I know where to stand onstage when those fiery fuckers go up and how much you feel it—the whole back of your body is suddenly very hot. So standing where they were standing? Oh my lord.)

We had a team I'd worked with and trusted implicitly: my bro and producer, Allan Weinrib, and director Dale Heslip. They'd been in charge of set design and film production of our shows for years. They embraced the steampunk concept, and, to complement the sumptuous set we'd introduced on the Time Machine tour, tasked several animators with bringing that weird world to life in a variety of styles. One of our old favourites was Crankbunny, aka Norma V. Toraya, who'd created the segues for all the *Moving Pictures* songs on the Time Machine tour, and would later make more segments for us, notably an awesome intro film for R40. Her work is deceptive: at first blush it's all lush flowers and whimsical critters out of a Victorian children's book, but in fact it's so overripe that seeing it on the enormous concert screen makes you reel, like someone's spiked your drink. Teletubbies on ecstasy! The depth and range of her imagination always blew us away.

The cherry on the cake was a new intro film, the story of two gnomes and a troll—the Watchmaker's snarky, mischievous guardians played by Lerxst, Pratt and me, whose main purpose in life is to torture the poor taxman (played by Jay Baruchel). It was our cheeky, *Wizard of Oz*–style challenge to the idea of the existence of God, designed to leave you wondering if lunatics have taken over the universe.

IN APRIL 2013 we convened in Los Angeles to rehearse for the second half of the tour, which was due to kick off immediately after our induction ceremony at, wait for it . . . the Rock and Roll Hall of Fame. After fifteen years of eligibility and being endlessly asked by the media, "How does it feel to be overlooked once again?" we'd developed a healthy fuck-you attitude towards this particular award, so now that it was actually happening, we hardly knew how to respond. Did we care, all of a sudden? I mean, *really* care? At first not much, to be honest, but as the news sank in we did warm to it. Personally, I was happiest for the legion of fans who had been fiercely outspoken about our exclusion for so many years; it was a reward for them as much as it was a pat on the back for us.

A good number of friends and family came down for the presentation—our parents too, my mom beaming nonstop. It was her first time in Los Angeles, and she was ready to party. I've never written about this side of her, but she *loved* attention, and being recognized from *Beyond the Lighted Stage* by so many fans in and outside of the venue really lit her up. "I feel like a regular celebrity!" she said.

We had each prepared a speech, divvying up responsibilities and making sure not to forget to thank our closest people in the heat of the moment. In the car on the way to the venue, Lerxst was in his own world beside me as he practiced his, and I recall being surprised how much he was gesturing with his hands. It seemed incongruous in the context of what I *thought* he was going to say, but I had my own speech to think about, so I dismissed it. It didn't occur to me that he had something else "on his sleeve," as his father used to say.

Waiting in the greenroom before the show, we were characteristically calm. I mean, how can you get nervous about a thing you've convinced yourself is not important enough to care about, right? We, as well as inductees former and current, were leaned on rather heavily to attend a pre-show party and mingle with donors to the RRHoF who'd paid extra for the privilege of rubbing elbows with the stars. Neil would have no part of it, but Alex and I grudgingly agreed to go, joking in the elevator, riffing on all the posers as a couple also headed for the proceedings stood uncomfortably by. We had little tolerance for those types of schmooze fests and usually stayed for as short a time as was optically acceptable. Seated in the theatre after that, I was delighted to chat with Spike Lee, whom I hugely admire, at Public Enemy's table next to ours, but when Joan Baez took *her* place nearby, to my lasting embarrassment I realized that she was half of the couple who'd had to endure Alex's and my misbehavior in the elevator. Ouch.

Speech after speech, performance after performance, the inductees were honoured and the cameras panned around the venue, lingering over the more famous people in attendance—actual luminaries such as Jack Nicholson, Oprah and Harry Belafonte. Tension built as I began to feel a sense of—okay, I'm *admitting* it—importance creeping into the air and under my skin. Over the course of the evening, various musicians such as Tom Petty and Tom Morello, Jackson Browne and Chuck D also made a point of saying something nice to me. How could I maintain a façade of indifference in the face of all that? Well, I will be honest: I couldn't. I was seduced by it all. It felt like sweet surrender.

When in his opening remarks Jann Wenner, founder and editor-in-chief of *Rolling Stone*, uttered the words "from Toronto," before he even said our name, the audience absolutely exploded. He looked shocked, for from that moment it became clear that a sizeable portion of the audience had come strictly to celebrate our moment in the sun, and their

(LEFT) *A speech for the ages.*

(BELOW) *No fool, Super Dave knows who to party with. (She stayed later than me!)*
(RIGHT) *And you know these guys.*

(RIGHT, LEFT TO RIGHT) *Dave, Taylor, Nick Rasculinecz, Neil, me and Al.*

raucous applause sent shivers up my spine. After his introduction (during which he was booed), he approached our table and bent down, whispering in my ear, "Wow . . . Just incredible!" The man who'd been the dartboard for Rush fan vitriol over the years, the very one they presumed had single-handedly kept us *out* of this hallowed hall (and had all but ignored us in his magazine), was visibly shaken by the love we were now being showered with. Gotta admit, that too was a sweet moment.

Some of the speeches that followed were effin' long and self-indulgent—yeah, that's right, Flavor Flav, I'm talking about *you*, man. But finally it was our turn. From the podium Taylor Hawkins and Dave Grohl gave a rousing, and I mean *rousing*, presentation. They were so effin' funny, especially when making fun of our *2112* album cover shots, that they had us in hysterics, but their vigorous endorsement of us as musicians, of what we meant to musicians like them, was what really made the evening worthwhile.

Then they called us up. Neil delivered a speech as full of wit and wisdom as anyone who knew him would expect, but for me the finest moment was when he said, "All the previous inductees into this pantheon of rock are like a constellation of stars in the night sky. Among them, we are one tiny point of light . . . in the shape of a maple leaf." When I delivered my bit, thanking our fans for the dedication that made the award a reality, the way Taylor was hopping up and down with glee, I thought he was gonna jump out of his shoes. Finally, I turned the mic to Lerxst and glanced back at the teleprompter where the speech he had written was ready to roll. But no-o-o. Ignoring it completely, he surprised us all with an enthralling, two-and-a-half-minute piece of mime, acting out his feelings along our journey, the years of work, the fatigue, the exhilaration of playing, the persistence and the disappointment, the fuck-you of rejection, the disbelief at finally being accepted, the sense of pride and gratitude towards the gallery—all with gesture and pathos and the words, *only* the words, "blah blah blah, blah blah blah," over and over and over again. Neil and I were nonplussed to say the least, but kept smiling up there for what felt like an eternity. Standing behind him as we were, we couldn't appreciate the nuances of his performance, and at one point I leaned over to Neil and said, "*I'll* hit him with my award, and *you* drag him off the stage, okay?" It felt to us like he was bombing, although he was anything but. That speech left a lasting impression on everyone there and on everyone watching from home when the show was aired on TV, and it would become a regular thing for the rest of the tour to see people in the audience with signs and T-shirts with those three simple but eloquent and revelatory words.[*]

ROCK & ROLL
HALL OF FAME

Date: Thursday 18th April 2013
Location: The Nokia Theatre, Los Angeles, United States
Transcribed by: Polly Graf

Geddy Lee (continued): And on behalf of my two partners, I have to thank the most passionate, most dedicated, incredible fan base around the globe. That's you guys... For not only supporting and encouraging our musical progress over the years but for the insistence of their voices which has most certainly led us to this evening. We share this honour with you. Thank you.

Alex Lifeson: Blah, Blah, Blah. Blah, Blah, Blah, Blah, Blah. BLAH, BLAH, BLAH, BLAH. BLAH, BLAH, BLAH, Blah, Blah, Blah, Blah, Blah, Blaaaaaah. Blah, Blah, Blah. Blah, Blah, BlahBlahBlah? BLAH, BLAH, BLAH, BLAH, BLAH, Blah, Blah, Blah, Blah, Blaaaaaah. Blah, Blaaaaaaaah. Blah, Blah, Blah, Blah, Blah! Blaah, Blah, Blah, Blah, Blah. Blah! BLAHBLAHBLAHBLAH! BLAHBLAHBLAHBLAH!

Blah, Blah, Blah, Blah, Blah, Blaaaaaah. Blah, Blah, Blah. Blah, Blah, Blah, Blah, Blah, Blah, Blah, Blah, Blah, Blah, Blah, Blah, Blah, Blah, BLAHHH, Blah, Blah, Blah, Blah. Blah, Blah, Blah. BLAH. BLAH, BLAH, Blah, Blah, Blah, Blah, Blah, Blaaaaaah. BLUH BLUH! Blah, Blah. Blah, Blah, Blah, Blah, Blah, Blah! BLAH, BLAH. BLAH, BLAH, BLAH, Blah, Blah, Blah, Blaaaaaah. Blah! Blallallallallallalah... Blallallallallallalah... BLAHBLAH? BLAH! BlahBlah, Blah. Blah, Blah, Blah, Blah, Blah. BLAH, BLAH, BLAH, BLAH. BLAH, BLAH, BLAH, Blah, Blah? Blah, Blah, Blah, Blaaaaaaaah. Blah, Blah, Blah. Blah. Blah, Blah, Blah, Blah, Blah, Blah. BLAH. BLAH, BLAH, BBBBLAH, Blah, Blah, Blah, Blah, Blah. Blah, Blah, Blah, Blah! Blah, Blue, Blahblah. BLUEBLAH! Blah. Blub, Blub, Blub. Blub, Blub, Blub. BLAH, BLAAH. BlahBlah... BlahBlah... BlahBlah

48

---

[*]    I don't know how Flavor Flav felt to be upstaged so, but after we got our award and finished our performance, Chuck D looked at Alex and said to him, "Man, that was performance art!"

# CHAPTER 27

FTER THE *CLOCKWORK ANGELS* TOUR, the three of us largely went our separate ways. Neil devoted himself to being a dad and husband while working on the novelization of *Clockwork Angels* and indulging his love of vintage sports cars and motorcycles, occasionally going out on jaunts but mostly fine-tuning his "Silver Surfer" collection with pride and joy. (They were all silver but one, in fact: his 1964 black Shelby Cobra. I don't know much about cars but that beast was always my personal fave.)

Lerxst, meanwhile, escaped from the noisy wear and tear of our rock and roll life by fine-tuning his golf game and partnering with some fellow enthusiasts to build a course north of Toronto. Mentally, he was wholly fired up by the challenge of designing it but was hampered by the same arthritis and the heart and digestive issues that had been building while on tour. In truth, though he was consulting various doctors and trying a range of new medicines, his condition was worsening. The break from touring and recording couldn't have come at a more opportune time for him.

On May 28, 2014, our family was gloriously expanded with the arrival of our first grandchild, Finnian Moses Weinrib—from which day forward I would assume yet another identity: that of "Zaidy" Lee!* I won't hide that I was overcome with emotion. For years I'd watched Lerxst's eyes fill with love whenever he told us stories about his grandsons, and I rolled my eyes and thought, *yeah, yeah,* but now here I was looking at my own and tearing up. Who knew? It's just pure love. Wait and see, you'll know it when it happens to you!

At the close of summer, Lerxst's health reports weren't good. He was in terrible discomfort and had finally been diagnosed and recommended for surgery. Basically, he suffered from bleeding ulcers exacerbated by his stomach having somehow moved too high up into his abdomen, putting pressure on those ulcers and his lungs, which in turn gave him shortness of breath and arrhythmia. But if that wasn't enough to worry about, something was also stewing in Pratt, who was suddenly insistent on meeting with us and Ray less than a week after Alex's operation. He was on a tight Canadian promotion schedule for his latest book, *Far and Near: On Days Like These,* and told us there was no other option. This did not bode well. Being so intransigent, especially considering Lerxst's condition, was quite unlike him, but obviously something serious was up, so we agreed to his date.

We met at a regular haunt of ours. Out of the hospital for only four days and unable to even bend forward with ease, Lerxst walked in slowly and struggled to take his seat, sitting bolt upright, fighting any show of discomfort for the sake of getting on with the meeting. Tension was in

---

* Based on the Yiddish word *zeda,* Zaidy or Zaidie or Zayde means "Grandfather."

the air, which was supremely out of character for the three of us. After some uneasy repartee, Neil got to the point. He didn't want to tour in 2015. He told us he wanted to delay any gigs for at least a year to spend more time at home . . . and added that he was pondering retirement.

*Boom.* The "R" word.

We were silent as he told us how proud he was of *Clockwork Angels*. It was our best piece of work, he said, but hard to top, and he feared that the wear and tear on his body would soon start to let his playing down. Even if it didn't, he could no longer justify leaving Olivia for the sake of touring. He needed and *wanted* to be a more consistent presence in her life.

However incontrovertible those arguments seemed, we tried to challenge them, but nothing moved him until Lerxst admitted that after all the physical issues he'd endured over the past few years, he *too* was close to being done with touring. As I sat there in shock—he'd never shared those feelings with me before—he went on to say that he would much prefer to tour sooner than later; before, that is, his health got worse. Hearing that, Neil's face scrunched up. He was clearly exasperated. He pointed his finger at Lerxst and said something to the effect of "Before this meeting I said to myself that the *only* thing that might weaken my resolve was if Lerxst really wanted to tour now . . ."

We sat in silence for a while. Then agreed to sleep on it.

**IN EARLY NOVEMBER** I left town for London, where I was thrilled to perform with the Who for their fiftieth-anniversary fundraiser for the Teenage Cancer Trust, and it was just as I arrived that I received an email from Neil with the subject header "My God. You Bawstid." Here is an excerpt that illustrates our mindset after that tough meeting in Toronto (oh, and it might help to tell you that at this stage in our lives together, our nicknames had evolved. Neil was now

"Peke," Alex was "Leke" and I was "Deke," while "Ekes" became the plural form of address*):

> *Ekes:*
>> The one *door I had left open—*
>> The one *little lever.*
>> *Fuck.*
>> *In all my plans for NOT working next year, and maybe even embracing the R-word (and I don't mean R40)—in all my intentions to continue my current mode-of-life, for my own sake and for Olivia's—*
>> the one *door I had left open in my made-up mind was . . .*
>> *That if Lerxst really wanted to do it, and felt he might not be able to in 2016, why, then I'd have to go along.*
>> *And the fucker goes and plays that card . . .*

Calling Lerxst a "fucker" was just a good-natured jibe, of course. He'd never have given in were it not for his love and respect for the man. He wrote that our meeting had led him to a night of pacing in his room and saying *fuck* a thousand times, but by the end of it he was resolved to do as Lerxst wished without complaint.

He then went on to say:

> *But now, back home and forcibly redirected, I am feeling more like another R-word: "resigned"—it is what it is. Embracing my fate, graciously accepting the inevitable, I can view it as a necessary challenge—reorient my focus and my energies . . . Start to think about a new drumset design . . . About what weird songs we might play . . . About (yikes!) a new drum solo . . .*

---

* I recently came across another email from Neil, from when he was ill and struggling with words: "Hey, Deke. I have a vivid memory of the birth of that nickname. And so much else. It had been the answer to a crossword puzzle for the hockey maneuver, DEKE. And just after that, you mistyped your sign-off that way too. It was too great to pass away."

I responded as positively as I could:

*Ekes*

> *so many things to discuss . . . now that Peke is R-worded . . .*
> *First let me say Peke that anything we can do to give you more access to home time with Olivia is certainly fine by me and totally understand the situation . . . so if rehearsal time in LA is helpful let's do that . . . so you can be home more readily . . . As for the schedule . . . I am happy to let you and Ray work out most of it as suits your life best . . .*
> *Anyway . . . let's try and make this as painless as we can and something that we can enjoy as much as humanly possible despite the number of F-bombs that will be coming from the middle of the stage . . .*

*I remain your obedient Jew*
*Deke*

It was good to get that much off my chest, but my heart did sink further when I read Alex's response:

*Ekes,*

> *I, too, am resigned to this likely being the last tour we play together. I'm sad and relieved at the same time; I love playing together so much and will miss it terribly but also feel guilty that I've stabbed you in the heart, Peke. As Deke said, whatever makes it more comfortable for you.*
> *. . . I remain, without a clue,*
> *Leke*

It was my turn to say "*Fuck.*" The exchange had cast a shadow over our future, but I was determined to move forward, to gather the team and design what would become the R40 tour. We had dodged a bullet and, true to his mantras, "Mustn't grumble" and "It is what it is," Neil returned to work without complaint, but I knew in my heart that it was not the last we'd hear about the R-word. "Retirement," it seems to me, is an incongruous word for a musician to use, and definitely not a concept I had—or have—ever considered. I couldn't even countenance the word. When he first mentioned the possibility, I instinctively thought, *Ridiculous! Musicians don't retire, artists don't retire. They either work or they don't, but they always leave themselves open to when the muse may strike again. The door must always be left ajar, open to the possibility that feelings can and often do change, so why impose finality on it?* But I pushed those thoughts away as best I could and hitched myself once more to the wagon, pouncing on a tour concept I'd had in mind for a while: a theatrical Rush retrospective but in *reverse*. A *de*-volution of sorts, not only musically but visually and three-dimensionally too.

**THE SHOW WOULD** begin in the present day, with the songs and look of the stage set right where the *Clockwork Angels* tour had left off, in our own steampunk universe; from there we would move back in time through the phases of our career until, at the end, we'd be reduced to our humblest beginnings, the elaborate stage sets dismantled and replaced by a simple drum kit and a pair of amps on chairs in a generic high school gymnasium—a replication of my first-ever gig with the Dusty Coconuts, back in the Fisherville Junior High auditorium in 1967, competing in the Battle of the Bands.

For years I'd attended plays and musicals with Nancy in London and New York, and now those hundreds of hours were paying off.[*] I'd always

---

[*] The rear-screen projections for "The Wreckers" on the *Clockwork Angels* tour were inspired by a Miyako Odori performance I once saw in Kyoto, where the musicians and geisha played in front of a Hokusai-style ocean backdrop made of numerous cut-out waves pitching in time to the music.

been in amazement watching set changes—when, say, the stage would start to turn in the middle of the act, or the scrims would lift and reveal something entirely new. In the theatre, it's perfectly normal to have stuff change before your eyes; you'll even see the *actors* move the furniture about as they set up the next scene, and yet when the lights come up again on full, you still believe it! In rock and roll, on the other hand, there's kind of an unwritten rule that you never break the so-called third wall; you never see the mechanics, you never see the Wizard of Oz behind the curtain, only the magic that's being performed. And I thought, wouldn't it be great to bring that sensibility into a rock and roll show, where you actually see the roadies move things about? In my mind I pictured set changes throughout the show, requiring our carpenter team, dressed in red *Moving Pictures*-style overalls, to replace the sets right in front of the audience, and over-the-top exaggerations to clearly announce the many eras in the history of Rush. Rewinding to the seventies, for instance, when stacks of amplifiers on the backline were de rigueur, we piled them sky high—although of course they were empty boxes, with "Dirk" and "Lerxst" custom logos, mine fashioned after the Ampegs I used in that period and Alex's after Marshall.

Excitement rose after full dress rehearsals in Tulsa, Oklahoma, when it was clear that the reverse-retrospective idea was going to work well. That held true for opening night, May 8, 2015, and for the first week of shows; but pleased as I was, it hurt that the number of shows on the books was so small. Pratt had agreed to do thirty, which Ray pushed to thirty-five, but that meant no UK, European or South American dates. That we'd hit only the biggest population centres of North America was frustrating as hell for me. It seemed so inadequate, so unfair to our fan base, but I had to calm myself by considering things philosophically: after all that Neil had lost, survived and to a degree regained, that he was able to muster up the enthusiasm to come back at *all* was a miracle. Everything we'd accomplished after 2002 had to be viewed as a bonus to what was already a terrific and fruitful career.

Listening to *Clockwork Angels* just the other day I was almost shocked to hear how well it hangs together, but back then Neil was the first to hear it. In essence, that was why he retired: as early as when he'd heard our earliest demos, and again when we all listened to the finished album, he clearly thought, *We can't beat this.* He was deathly afraid of going onstage and not playing as well for our audience and for *himself.* Yet ironically, on the R40 tour, he played better than he'd ever played. He was a bit miffed, actually, because he knew he was playing at his peak but felt that neither Alex nor I were patting him on the back often enough. He told other people that he was disappointed, but I swear I sat at the side of the stage every night and watched his drum solo in awe of him. Look at any backstage footage of that tour, and there I am: listening. I never even took my in-ears out. In the end, though, it wasn't that he didn't want to play in Rush anymore; he didn't want to play anymore *at all.* He'd already lost one family and wasn't going to risk not being there for Olivia.

These were the things I told myself in my brain, but my heart didn't want to listen. So I clung to the "maybes," and there were a lot of those going around . . . *Maybe Neil will have such a great time on this tour that he'll relent and we'll add another few more weeks of shows? Maybe after a break at home he'll want to come back and do another leg or two? Maybe after a year away from the touring grind he'll feel recharged and hungry for the challenge once again?* Then there was Alex's health to consider. His arthritis presented a threat to his playing, which I know weighed heavily on him, but he seemed to be handling all his issues pretty well; the surgery had worked, and at least some of his problems had disappeared or faded into the background. It was why I refused to call it a farewell tour. If there is one thing I've learned in life, it's—to quote my old partner—"anything can happen." There have been more than a few artists (you know who you are) who've said goodbye and then come back looking foolish, past it or simply like they needed the money. I refused to milk our audience that way. If it was really going to

(TOP) *I wish to hell I could remember what* The Amazing Lerxst *did to astound us at this moment on the* Snakes & Arrows *tour, but it's clear he's taking some pride in it.* (ABOVE) *Perhaps his pedalboard cheerleaders could tell us?*

(LEFT AND BELOW)
*Was success going to our heads?*

*Allaire Studios near
Woodstock, New York, where
we made* Snakes & Arrows.
*What an effin' stunning room
to record live in.*

(LEFT) *This was the only spot
I could stand where my bass
pickups would not buzz.*

**Amp Concept for Geddy**
By Dale Heslip
February 20, 2010

(LEFT) *One of Dale Heslip's models for the* Clockwork Angels *show.* (BELOW) *Crankbunny's animations.*

*Are we having fun yet?*
(ABOVE) *Gluttons for makeup
punishment. We loved it;
well, maybe not so much
Neil, but he was a trooper—
as was actor/writer/director
Jay Baruchel.* (LEFT) *What
a bunch of clowns: Liam,
beloved road manager
Donovan "Poolie" Lundstrom
and longtime friend
and stage carpenter
George Steinert.*

*Roasting in the fires of hell? Nah, just Anaheim.*

*Maestro Paul Rudd conducts the Clockwork Angels String Ensemble*

be the end, then so be it, but before the tour kicked off I certainly wasn't prepared to make that kind of public pronouncement. I held on to shreds of hope, and whenever I was asked, I simply said, "It's most likely our last tour," but nothing more definite than that.

The tour marched onwards and gathered steam, with fans who'd maybe heard rumours that this might be our last, or at least that there had been no announcements of gigs abroad, coming out in droves from all over the world. Night after night we saw them holding up signs with the name of whatever country they'd travelled from, and every time I saw one I secretly hoped that somehow we could convince Pratt to extend the tour. There were, however, only so many times I could bring it up without stirring up an uncomfortable atmosphere. And I really did not want to be responsible for a bad vibe on what could very well be our last go-round.

Then Neil started having new health problems. After a couple of long days riding his motorcycles through the rain, his feet had become soaked through his boots and he developed an extremely painful infection. It was diagnosed as a fungus that grew into eczema, psoriasis and bacterial infections. He tried using ointments, but they only made things worse. Whatever joy he felt from playing well—and as I've said, he was playing as well as I'd ever heard him play—was draining on account of this agonizing ailment. Uber-stoic person that he was, cancelling or rescheduling a couple of weeks of shows was not an option; he stubbornly insisted on playing through the pain, and that was hard to watch. He could barely walk to the stage without wincing, yet he beat the hell out of his bass drums night after night. As he described it to us: "By the end of the second leg I was walking on two raw stumps."

As we moved from northeast to southwest, the final gigs loomed larger, and I had to keep the sadness bubbling under my surface in check. I think I put on a pretty good front, and I suspect Lerxst felt the same, but Neil was on the upswing. After a week's break at home, his feet were starting to feel better. I think he knew that he was on the home stretch and that he felt good for fulfilling his obligation to

(BELOW) *Me and my brutha from another mutha, tour manager Craig "C.B." Blazier (who I first met at our first gig with KISS, in 1974 when he was their monitor mixer).*

(ABOVE) *Donovan takes a rock and roll selfie while refuelling in Gander, Newfoundland.*

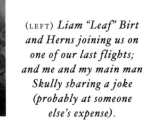

(LEFT) *Liam "Leaf" Birt and Herns joining us on one of our last flights; and me and my main man Skully sharing a joke (probably at someone else's expense).*

us—particularly to Lerxst—and couldn't hide his growing happiness. I believe he was the only person in the entire organization getting happier with every step closer to the end; he even produced a batch of T-shirts celebrating his imminent freedom that showed him on his motorcycle with his arms wide open, the words BRING THAT HORIZON HOME TO ME! emblazoned above the scene.* He seemed oblivious to the looks in the eyes of our longtime crew members that to me betrayed a sadness that *their* ride was coming to an end too.

Then in Los Angeles, ineluctably, came the last show. As I sat alone in the back seat of the ride to the venue I felt edgy, at odds with myself, fighting it, trying to be calm, trying to treat it like just another gig, but filled with foreboding. Before I entered the Forum, I stopped to look and take it all in, and knew it would be a day of conflicting emotions. We went about our regular soundcheck routine but spent more time chatting with crew than actually playing, and all the while I had to make great efforts just to appear normal. Then it was dinner as usual as we got ready for the show. Jokes were made, but not as many as usual. Neil spent most of the time in his own dressing room with his family and friends, where I suspected a much happier mood prevailed. He was about to be set free. As I write, the phrase "Two Solitudes" comes to mind. That's the title of Hugh MacLennan's novel about the lack of communication between English- and French-speaking Canadians, but surely apt here too. There were two dressing rooms that night, which might as well have been two different worlds; if not a nation, certainly a *band* divided. I happened to overhear Liam saying that Neil requested something he'd never done after any previous tour: he wanted his dressing room case not to go back to our warehouse in Toronto, but instead to the Bubba Cave in LA, his inner sanctum and private office/garage where he kept his Silver Surfers, motorcycles and writing desk. That was the moment that sealed it for me—this was truly his final gig.

---

\* He used the same photo and title on the cover of *Far and Wide*, the book in which he recounted his version of the very events I'm talking about.

Just before going on, Pratt came into our dressing room as usual, we joked around as usual, headed for the stage as usual. But the bundle of feelings we all brought out onto the stage with us were far from usual. We played our hearts out that night, and in between the playing I made a point of taking as much of it in as I possibly could. It was a corker of a show, and I could see people in the audience with tears in their eyes. As always, I felt incredibly alive and aware of everything in the room, but this time on a purely emotional level, and as we got closer and closer to the last song, I had to fight off the lump forming in my throat.

Before going on, Alex and I had suggested to Neil that he might want to cross the invisible line between his drum kit and the front of the stage and come down to take a bow, but he refused. One of his unwritten laws was never to leave the comfort of his riser to venture into our territory, so after we'd played the very last notes of "Working Man" and he'd stood up to take the three photos on the opposite page of the two of us and the audience, I assumed that that was that. But as I was doing my damnedest to say good night to the crowd without losing my cool, I felt a tap on my shoulder. I looked back to see that the big guy had hopped down to give us a hug after all. Then we all three took our final bow on centre stage. And it was over.

Neil ran to his dressing room, where his family and friends were waiting, and Alex and I went to ours. We hugged, then changed our clothes in silence to get ready for the party. I don't think I've ever felt such mixed emotions. We were happy to be in each other's company but hardly felt celebratory. We knew we'd need several stiff drinks to put on a happy face.

As LA was now a hometown gig for Pratt, his hands were full with his guests, and I cannot recall seeing him the remainder of the evening. Our final contact that night was the onstage hug. He had even cordoned off a section of the party upstairs for himself and his friends and family. Some of his guests made their way out of there to have a drink with us, but he did not, and neither I nor Alex ventured in. It was a disconcerting

*Photos taken by Neil from his riser at the Forum, August 1, 2015.*

way to end it all, but I told myself to remember that over our forty years together, Pratt had become increasingly uncomfortable in party situations, especially with a lot of people he did not know.

Whether it was a fabulous party or a wake, I couldn't tell, but we hung around drinking long enough for our band crew guys to load out and join us for a toast before we left the venue. I departed high from the buzz of a momentous show, but emotionally drained and weary of the conflict within me. Part of me was convinced it was over, yet still I clung to a tiny shred of hope for the fate of my band of forty-plus years.

On the plane home, Lerxst and I and our families were quiet, worse the wear for both the late-night revelry and the past week's emotional roller-coaster ride. The following morning, just as had so often happened after a tour or a recording session, and once the intensity had subsided and the adrenaline in me had stopped pumping, I awoke in my own bed sick with a bad cough that would linger for weeks. After spending a week at home with regular visits from my grandson, which is always a tonic that brightens me up, we piled the dogs into the car

*Nancy took this shot minutes after our final show.*

and took off north to our lake house to spend some quiet time by the rippling water. I'm not so sure that being so alone with my thoughts without distraction was the best thing for my brain at that particular moment, but my body certainly needed some rest.

It's said that depression is really repressed anger, and I admit that ending the tour after only thirty-five shows had left me frustrated and resentful. I tried to take the high road but couldn't hide my disappointment. I was so effin' proud of the tour we had designed and the quality of our performances right up to and including that last show that it felt to me like we were gaining steam, not grinding to a halt. Which is why I still held out hope for a change of heart from Neil. I was left feeling that the party was over just as it was peaking.

I understood that Pratt deserved the new life he had chosen for himself, but choosing to end his career had also ended mine—with Rush, at least. Alex was readier for a change than I was, due to his health issues, but even he felt this tour should have been longer. He no longer viewed touring as a long-term thing for him, but thanks to surgery he was feeling better by the day, and after all the work we'd put into *Clockwork Angels*, he too wanted to bring it to more people. Yes, we were free to hire another drummer and reinvent the band, but we felt that our essential identity was inextricably tied up in all three personalities and expressed in the music only we could create together. It was out of the question to find a replacement—and at the time it never entered our minds. Lerxst and I could continue composing together, but not as Rush. The circle was broken. However we proceeded, it would have to be as something else, something new, but I was in no shape to imagine how.

There had never been a debriefing after the tour, nor any talk about the future. We had gone our separate ways, leaving behind an elephant in the room. At the end, Neil had never actually said, "That's it, guys, I'm done. It was great, I love you, but now I'm out." He led us to believe that retirement was imminent but he never actually said goodbye. We knew that *this* tour was over, and that he wouldn't be touring for a while, if ever, but he never said whether he'd work with us again or not, one way or another. In any case, there was much unfinished business to attend to in the immediate aftermath of the tour. There were the R40 film edits and soundtrack mixes to approve, and myriad decisions relating to one we'd recently made, to sell our publishing rights. Although we were in fairly regular communication, the subject matter of those emails presented few opportunities to goof around, and little personal vibe was in evidence. At the end of August, as Lerxst and I tweaked the final version of the film and we watched our reverse retrospective playing out on the screen exactly as I had hoped it would, an odd feeling came over me. I felt proud but also pensive and aloof, and I left the screening early.

**I DECIDED IT** was time to reach out to Pratt, one-to-one, about anything outside of the mundane business-related decisions that for months had been the sole focus of our so-called conversations. I loved what I was hearing in the R40 mixes, blown away by his solo and how he'd nailed it on the first night we recorded in Toronto. Hearing it again made me want to tell him just how proud I felt, so I shot off a short note:

*August 29th, 2015*
*Hey Peke*
 *I hope this finds you doing well and enjoying Quebec I assume . . .*
 *I'm just catching up on all the mixes and wanted to say the drum solo sounds fucking awesome! . . . is it from the first night? because as I told you at the time I thought that you killed it that night man!! The structure is super cool and really shines through with all the effects and melodies too . . .*
 *Hope all is well otherwise . . .*
 *xoxo*
 *Deke*

Well, that certainly broke the ice.

*Sep 4, 2015, 8:59 AM*

*Sa-Mo-Ca*

*Deke!*

*Thank you so much for that note. It was weird that in the rehearsals and early days of the tour, as I drafted out that solo's theme—a guy sits down at the drums and plays a story—and eventually developed it into what I thought of as "the soundtrack to an imaginary movie" (for the DVD I'm calling it "The Story So Far"), nobody ever said nothin'! Even back in drum rehearsals with Gump, he never said a word about it, and not you guys, or Brad, or anybody. I guess it was just the reflex of "He already knows he's good—we don't have to tell him," but having pushed myself so far out of my usual comfort zone, and with that ringing silence after every time I attempted it, I had to think, "Hmm—maybe it's not working . . ." But sheer will carried me toward what I thought was a worthy goal, and the "final frontier" for me in terms of approaching true spontaneity—letting the eventual structure grow out of itself, as it were, rather than to fit an arrangement, as I used to do.*

He went on:

*Toward the end of the tour Carrie asked me if I was looking forward to that last show, and I said, "You know what? I'm looking forward to October." Thinking of how things would settle into a comfortable and rewarding routine by then. Weekdays at the Cave, two mornings a week at the Y (boo), and the rest of it more-or-less on Planet Olivia.*

*I have volunteered to help in the library at her school every second Tuesday—the perfect retirement job for me: Assistant Librarian!*

*. . . Let me know your whereabouts and plans, and . . . don't be a stranger!*

*Le Pique*

That last bit hit me hard. I could sense through those simple words—volunteer, school, retirement—just how much it meant for him to be home and present in Olivia's life. If "Assistant Librarian" was about as ambitious as he cared to be for the foreseeable future, who the fuck was I not to applaud the kind of life he wanted for himself. I had been blinded by my own self-interest, putting partnership ahead of friendship.

As Nancy and I departed for another UK walking trip, I found myself in a more positive mindset. As we huffed and puffed our way over the hills and down the dales, I worked on sorting myself out. Between the cliffs, the fog and the surprisingly attractive sheep we saw (seriously, bighorns are incredibly good-looking!), I breathed in the good air and pushed out the bad. When in doubt, get the fuck out— out into the world to take in something fresh. By the time Nancy and I dragged our sore feet to that journey's end, I had widened my horizons and regained a little context to my life. I still had regrets about that last tour being so severely truncated, but I knew that those issues were mine to own and I had to stop assigning blame for them. Now I needed to plot a direction for my own personal future.

Then I heard from Pratt again.

It was April 12, 2016. Our lawyer and close friend David Steinberg[*] had just paid him a visit in Los Angeles. After they talked about his future, Neil felt obliged to reach out to Lerxst and me with an update on his domestic bliss:

---

[*]  In the 1980s he drummed for a variety of bands, including the Dead Boys with Stiv Bator. Yes, Virginia, there *is* life after rock and roll!

*... a while back Olivia, in her genie guise, was hanging in the kitchen while I started dinner, after a pleasant day at the Cave, and she asked me what my three wishes would be.*

*After a moment's thought, I said, "You know, I only have one wish right now—more of the same, please!"*

*I like the 9 to 5 writing life here at the Cave, messing about with cars, and doing whatever else I feel like. Like Mark Twain defined work: "Anything you'd rather not do." So I avoid stuff like that—except for the Υ, because of course it's . . . nessa.*

*As far as songwriting or drumming, they simply do not enter my mind. Maybe someday—never say never—but not now.*

*Basically, "I'm very shallow and empty and have absolutely no ideas."*

*And I like it! . . .*

*Meanwhile, I hope all is well with youze and yours, as it is with me and mine. I miss you and ethereally smoosh your cheeks.*

*XOXO . . . ¡El Pico!*

There you have it. "Maybe someday—never say never—but not now." The elephant in the room was shrinking. In the meantime, it was plainly time for Lerxst and me to get on with gettin' on.[*]

IT WAS IN late August, and Nancy and I were back in London prepping for another walk, this time across England's rainy and mountainous Lake District. We were sitting in a neighbourhood restaurant when I glanced down at my phone and saw an email from Neil—not just to me but also to Alex and Ray. Curious, I opened the message, and as I read it my stomach was tied in a knot:

---

[*] More recently, David told me, "We talked about a lot of things that day and it was overall very enjoyable. He greeted me at the door with a huge hug and actually picked me up off my feet. I won't forget that. He was a big, strong ape. But he was determined not to play again."

*So . . .*

*I've got a brain tumour.*

*Sounds like a joke right there, I know — but alas, no joke.*

*I've felt it coming on this summer, got to my local doctor Monday,*

*then a guy at Cedars-Sinai today, and — it's real.*

*Going in for an operation next Wednesday.*

*Trying to keep it private, but . . . I had to share it with youse.*

Gut-wrenching shock. Disbelief. I wrote back immediately, my response pure emotion: *WTF? Details please.* Only Ray responded, telling me that he'd just been with Pratt, Carrie and Olivia at his cottage, and that Neil had not been himself, distant and quiet. Imagining that it was a case of depression, they saw a doctor as soon as they got back to Los Angeles, and there the truth was revealed. Pratt was still digesting the news himself, and nothing more would be known until after the surgery, but the fact that they got him into surgery so fast did not bode well.

Nancy and I sat gobsmacked, powerless to do anything except numbly proceed with our hike as we awaited the results of the surgery. We had to do *something*, and after all, walking had always helped me sort things out before. We spent the next week climbing up and down the rain-soaked Eastern Fells, wading through water as we tried to make sense of the incomprehensible, simply putting one foot in front of the other as we waited for the next email from Ray and I asked myself what kind of support I could possibly offer. Trudging around was a kind of distraction but did little to assuage the worst of my fears.

A week or so later, Lerxst and I flew from Toronto to LA. The three of us had not seen one another since the final show more than a year ago. Some reunion, eh? After some very long hugs, Neil shared what he knew: he had glioblastoma, the very same disease that our friend Gord Downey of the Tragically Hip was already suffering. The operation had gone well, the doctors had been able to remove most of the tumour, around 95 percent of it, but cutting all of it out would have risked total incapacitation. This meant that eventually and inexorably the cancer would return. He'd require radiation and chemo to beat it, but in the process, that would likely beat *him* into submission, which he said he was dreading. Still, he tried to remain positive, sticking to his old stoic mantra, "Mustn't grumble," and even began to refer to himself as "ChemoMan™."

In reality, there'd be no beating it. The doctors were giving him just eighteen months. The only cause for optimism was that some glioblastoma patients had survived for as long as ten years. We clung to that hope, but Pratt knew what kind of hell he was in for. As we now know, he outdid all the predictions. He was always a determined bull of a man, and that eighteen-month death sentence came and went and turned into three and a half years of ups and downs, sick spells, more treatments and unbearable stress on his wife, Carrie, and his daughter Olivia. They were lovingly supported by Neil's stalwart pals Michael Mosbach, Juan Lopez and the wonderful staff at his house, while Neil took regular visits from his siblings and his close circle of pals—Craig Renwick, Matt Scannell, Doane Perry, Chris Stankee, Stewart Copeland and Marjorie Wallace, widow of the drummer Ian Wallace, whom Neil had stood by throughout Ian's own battle with cancer. Ray Danniels and David Steinberg, meanwhile, were rock-solid throughout. Ray had lost one of his sons to brain cancer, and so Neil saw him as a brother-in-arms, while David was an invaluable advisor, helping to keep Neil's life in order however he could.

For those three years, Lerxst and I stayed in regular contact and visited whenever possible, sometimes on our own and sometimes together, the latter always the best option as the three of us automatically fell into our nonsensical ways. Our job was to tell Neil stories and make him laugh; that's all that mattered. Lerxst easily made him laugh as a matter of course, while I did the same by making fun of *Lerxst*, which always brought a devilish grin to Neil's face (*no one* made better fun of Lerxst than me; I had fifty years of Lerxst inanities to draw from), but with our own lives waiting for us back in Canada, those visits were always cut short, and saying goodbye without truly knowing when or if we'd ever see him again was brutal. We'd be totally drained after leaving him, always feeling that we hadn't done enough for him. What an unimaginably difficult time it had to have been for his wife and family to bear.

Pratt demanded that we keep his illness on the QT, and while we honoured that, keeping such a terrible secret was easier said than done. It required constant deception. There were people in our own organization as well as friends and families we could not tell. We lived in constant fear of the story breaking. Neil asked Ray to hire a PR person who was an expert in quashing these kinds of rumours. Every now and then something would leak out to other musicians, some of whom would ask me point blank if it was true that Neil was sick. To my dismay, I got very good at changing the subject or out-and-out lying about it. I felt terrible concealing it from certain people I felt should really know, but that call wasn't mine to make. I had to trust that in the end, true friends would understand that I had chosen loyalty to Neil over honesty with them.

In those few years, Neil and Alex and I did share some incredibly touching moments. I'll always remember the pride on Neil's face as he told us how he'd been giving Olivia drum lessons—and when she played for us on the drum kit in their living room, he could not have looked happier. Whenever Lerxst and I came to his house, he'd be waiting at his balcony with a big effin' smile, and, only after hailing us from above, descend to open the door for a firm hello hug and take us into the kitchen, where he'd set out three tumblers on the countertop. Then he'd pour us two fat fingers of the Macallan and clink glasses. At times, though—and for such a man of words this was particularly heartbreaking—his verbal acuity failed him, as when he meant to offer me an ice cube but said, "Bacon?" I laughed and put my arm around his shoulder and said, "Yes, please. Bacon"—to which he gave me a funny look, like *I* was the one who'd misspoken.

Lerxst and I would take turns playing with Olivia in the garden and spend time talking to Carrie, while Neil would disappear for a smoke on his balcony—a habit he refused to give up, right until the end. Early on, we'd go out for the occasional dinner, but supper at home soon became the norm.

This was our relationship on and off for more than three years, during which time I found it impossible to write music. At its best, rock and roll is a celebration, an expression of joy, but when your heart is empty, just try stirring up the molecules, it's almost impossible. At other moments of sadness and loss, I'd been able to dig deep and find an ember of hope to ignite me and send me to my instrument—after our friend Robbie Whelan died in a car accident, for instance, we'd turned around and written "Afterimage"; when my old pal Oscar passed away, I lost myself in our gigs and when Selena and Jackie passed away I found solace in working on *My Favourite Headache*. But this was different. It was simply too grave. The best I could do was bury myself in my latest project, the *Big Beautiful Book of Bass*. Perhaps because it was at times a more strictly technical exercise than a creative one—a historical, factual and anecdotal account of the instrument—it offered a decent enough distraction.

When it was published, I naturally sent a copy to my partners. Lerxst was effusive, and Pratt immediately sent me a note that, considering how rare and brief his emails had forcibly become during that period, meant a helluva lot to me.

> *Hey Deke—Just a M. Joe-style of saying "Excellente!" with the book. I've already spent more time reading it than I could have ever ee-magined—but of course 'tis a far, far bigger book on bass guitar than the world ever thought they wanted!*

Just lovely.

One visit Lerxst and I paid him, in October 2019, stands out in my mind. We'd been to the Bubba Cave earlier in the day, telling war stories and laughing, but Pratt tired easily and after lunch we could see he'd needed a rest, so we agreed to meet up again later at his house. After dinner, I kept him company on his balcony, where he enjoyed his smoke outside in the beautiful evening air. He had been going through a bad patch, but at that moment was finding his words with relative ease. We talked about how lovely the spot was, in view of the parakeets squawking in the nearby trees (we'd always shared a love of birds), and he expressed how lucky he felt to be alive, and then the subject turned to music. I was surprised to learn that every day over the past few months, as he was driven to his cave by his friend Juan Lopez, he'd passed the time by listening to each and every one of our albums in order, taking in different songs on every trip. He told me how surprised and happy he'd been to hear how well the interplay of bass and drums stood up after all these years. He'd re-analysed the songs' structure and listened closely to our individual parts and remarked on how our ambitious and quirky style of play had "filled each other's gaps," making us both sound better in the bargain. As he impressed upon me just how proud he was of all we'd accomplished, I was blown away by how closely he'd been listening. As I write this now, I find myself overwhelmed with emotion to think how he was reviewing his life, knowing he was at the end of it, and talking about how much our working relationship meant to him, wanting me to hear it from his lips.

Then he told me that he'd recently been listening to Gene Pitney's "A Town Without Pity," and how shocking it was to him that in the early sixties a song with that kind of lyrical content (essentially about a woman having to prove on trial that she'd been raped) had become such a success—a Top 20 hit, in fact. It was a remarkable monologue from someone who was so ill, showing me that despite his outward limitations, his mind was very much alive and working in all the ways I'd come to expect from him. Right until the end, he was still engaged and edified by music in all its expressions.

Soon Alex and Carrie came out to the balcony to join us. We had a few laughs, and then it was time to go. At the door he gave us each a bear hug and told us how sad he was to say goodbye. It was the last time I ever saw him.

Over the next two months he progressively deteriorated, but still insisted on visiting his beloved Bubba Cave every day, even if only for a couple of hours. It made him so happy that I thought as long as he could get there, he'd be okay. But the decline continued as Carrie, their staff and his inner circle gave him as much comfort as they could. Finally, early in the New Year—on January 7, 2020—as I was grocery shopping, my phone rang. It was David, who told me that Neil had slipped away.

It was the one day he hadn't had the strength to go to the cave.

# CHAPTER 28

SO MANY ENDINGS. TOO MANY PEOPLE
departed. A band ended, and a friendship, in tragedy. Two
phrases ring in my head: Pete Seeger's "To everything there is a
season," and Tolkien's "The road goes ever on . . ." With or
without our permission, in life and in death, those two things are
immutable. The band has run its course, but the music remains.

As I've described earlier, in the Jewish faith there is a process
called shiva that allows you to do your grief work for a limited period of
time and then requires you to give it up, but for one day a year on the
anniversary of your loved one's passing. I know it only too well from
when I was twelve. As I've said more than once, I'm not a religious
man, but I do like this idea. It's dogmatic and imperfect but also makes

practical sense. After a profound loss, one needs structure, and shiva provides a semblance of it. After Neil passed away, however, there was no funeral, just a private cremation, so most of us had no occasion, no ritual to process our grief, no place to put it. In hopes of comforting one another and finding some measure of closure, those of us in his Toronto circle went to Los Angeles to grieve with Carrie, Olivia, Neil's parents, his siblings and close friends—a shiva of sorts, but not the same. It was as tough, as quiet and mournful, as you could imagine. It was eerie to be in the house for the first time without him. I kept expecting him to come lumbering down the stairs and greet us at the door with big hugs—hugs that became longer and stronger once we knew he was living on bonus time. Carrie had arranged for his dressing room case to be brought from his Bubba Cave and placed in the entranceway to the living room. There it was as we walked in, the case I'd known for almost forty years. For others it might have been just another dressing case, but for the Guys at Work (as we'd once been), with all the miles we knew were on it, the hundreds and hundreds of gigs, it was a heavy moment. Still, I liked that it was there. His spirit was in that case. He kept his sticks there, his smokes, his pot, his stage clothes . . . It was his moveable office, his little bit of home on the road. It was the embodiment of him.

In the kitchen I noticed that one of their staff, Jody, must have felt that way too, because he had placed a glass of Neil's usual on the counter, on top of it a folded napkin written with Neil's name. That was so lovely, echoing what I was thinking all the while, that the man we'd known for so long would have wanted us to send him off more raucously. Alex and I agreed that what he'd have loved most was to see his pals gather, each holding two fat fingers of the Macallan, recounting his exploits and all the things that we'd loved about him. A real wake. Something he'd have attended for anyone else.

So we booked out a low-key bar he used to frequent and, in the evening of the second day with his family, slipped away to meet a clutch of his drinking buddies, to toast him and tell stories about the impact he'd had on all our lives. Man, there was laughter, but at the same time it was impossible to speak about Pratt in the past tense without choking up. We hugged it out, cried into our scotch and imbibed far too much of it. I'm sure he would have approved.

THERE WAS A surreal lull to the few days we spent in LA after he died, with his illness still a secret to the wider world. That, we knew, was to change fast, and we braced ourselves. When the story broke out of the blue, it must have felt like a gut punch to those friends outside the inner circle and to our fans, and suddenly we had no lack of company in our mourning. We were deluged with emails and phone calls, all full of sympathy and kindness but hard for us to read in our own still-tender state. The magazines and radio programs started to fill the air with respectful articles, some quoting the very few friends who'd suspected he was ill or in fact known what he was going through, but there were some interviews with those who couldn't wait to ingratiate and puff themselves up by telling the supposed "real behind the scenes" story of his struggles—names that I added to my memory's special blacklist. (Yes, I *am* a motherfucker who bears a grudge.) At first, we were concerned that fans might disturb the family by coming to Neil's home, but true to form, they knew better and remained incredibly respectful. All the while Lerxst and I remained silent. We took no calls. We couldn't bring ourselves to talk publicly for many months.

Ten days later, Nancy and I boarded a flight to peaceful New Zealand, a good place to still the soul and attempt to process what had transpired over the last few years. It helped a little, but easier said than done. The serenity of that natural wonderland made life feel no less surreal than La-La Land had been; if anything, the Crankbunny-like phantasmagoria intensified the unreality. There would be a lot more grief work to do when we got home.

When we did, it was to the news that Carrie had organized a memorial in LA for his family and many of his friends, so we packed yet again and returned to an emotionally charged event as his nearest and dearest eulogized him and photos of his life flashed by on the screen behind. Then, as Alex and I were in the process of organizing a similar event for the Canadian contingent of his family and friends who'd not been able to say goodbye, this thing called Covid-19 happened. The limbo that the goddamn pandemic thrust us all into amounted, you might say, to a kind of imposed shiva, but solitary, not communal as it should be, keeping us locked down for not one but two years with little to do beyond thinking about stuff. Stuff like the loss of loved ones.

During the first strict lockdown in Canada, like so many other people, my siblings and I were prohibited from seeing our mother. The rollout of vaccinations was painfully slow, and she was highly vulnerable. By that time she was battling dementia, which the isolation made much worse. When the harshest restrictions were lifted, we started to see her again in small doses, but the damage was done. By then, more often than not, she was trapped in another time and place; on some visits, I was sure that she had travelled back to the war and that frightening time in Starachowice-Wierzbnik. My sister, my brother and I would try to gently coax her back to the here and now, but she suddenly took seriously ill and passed away in July 2021. My god, what a painful loss that was for us—and even for those who knew her less well but respected her so much. She had touched a lot of people. You know, it doesn't matter how old the person is—my mom was ninety-five— you brace yourself for their demise but never really think it's going to come. And then it comes, and you can't fucking believe it.

What can I tell you? We had a bad pandemic.

My mother's dementia was a painful reminder of how fragile our memory banks are, but I had already been in a reflective mood before she died and decided that while I still had enough functioning grey matter, I should spend some time jotting down my own life story. If nothing else, it was a way to pass the time at home. At first it was a tremendous challenge. A lot of sleuthing was involved in putting together the puzzle pieces of my life and my parents' before me. It was painful to relive the more difficult events, but also fun to review the happier ones (sometimes through the rose-tinted glasses of retrospect). All told it was, as Pratt would have called it, a "healing road," an exercise in looking back in order to move forward; perhaps it's true, as he also said, that the way out is the way in . . . I've learned a lot about myself—most obviously that I talk too effin' much—but now that I've spent almost three years on the damn thing and life is returning to a new normal, I have to ask myself, has it been helpful in helping me determine what lies in store?

When I put my mind to a thing, whether a song, a tour, a collection, a journey or a book, it ruthlessly occupies my brain. For years, I'd wake in the middle of the night, thinking of a piece of music that wasn't working, fucking with it in my head until it was fixed and I could fall back asleep, telling myself that if I couldn't remember it in the morning, then it mustn't be any damn good in the first place. Regardless of who I'm with or what I'm doing, a part of my mind obsessively grinds away, preventing me from fully engaging in what's at hand. (It's what Mendelson Joe, Ben Mink and I called being "a mental Jew.") I always thought that over the years I'd gotten pretty good at faking it in social circumstances, covering up the fact that I'm really not all there, but Nancy seems to know. She'll look at me and say, "You're distracted." Shit. Busted!

This book has been an odyssey I never expected to embark upon— one that's required me to delve deeper into my gray matter than ever before, at times taking delight in my youthful escapades, at others cringing at my mistakes and indiscretions. Walking gingerly across a minefield of difficulties, scraping away to reveal some kind of truth, has been all-consuming, exhausting and at times distressing, but now that I'm nearing the end, I can already feel a weight lift off my shoulders. I feel like I can breathe fresh air through these cavernous nostrils for the first time in ages. And I can think about the future—about returning to the instrument that has powered me through my wonderful journey and rewarded me so well. I used to advise my kids or my pals whenever they were at a crossroads to just keep moving forward with positive energy; either you will find the answer or it will find you. Hmm . . . Note to self.

There has been an understandable expectation of me to carry on making music, either with Lerxst at my side or on my own. I would never discount it and frankly the thought of never stepping on a stage again seems, well, incorrect! I love Lerxstie to pieces and have no doubt that we would have some big fun writing and playing together again. In the abstract I could easily say that perhaps I'll do one or the other or both, but now I really do have to take the bull by the horns. I mean, *don't* I?

Regardless of where I end up, I won't be using the "R" word. No, my attitude about that hasn't changed a bit. (Wouldn't *that* be ironic or even hypocritical, after all my ranting?) So, no need for me to make cataclysmic pronouncements, but I have come to understand a little about why *Pratt* did it the way he did . . .

I now believe that he embraced (go on, say it) *retirement* because he didn't want to face waking up to find, say, an email from Ray wondering if he was ready to go back to work. Or from other players asking him to do this gig or that. Or to be incessantly wondering whether or not it was time to make a new musical statement. He wanted none of that. He was satisfied that he'd already done what he'd done to the best of his ability. He chose not to be driven crazy by questions from without *and* within. He wanted the freedom to enjoy life without the noise of some inner voice constantly second-guessing his decision—to walk away "unfettered and alive," as Joni Mitchell so poetically put it. He had been a drummer, the most physically demanding musical job on the planet, and his body had been sending warning shots across his bow, but he was still intact enough to attend to all the other things he cared about. Once again, Neil was ahead of the curve. I wasn't able to see that in 2015, when I was still in musical heat and entertaining further ambitions, but I get it now, my friend, and I'm sorry it took me so long.

NOW, JUST AS I finished recounting that episode, news broke about the sudden death of Taylor Hawkins in Bogotá. At *fifty*. Tragic and truly heartbreaking. He had reached out to me by email only a few weeks earlier for no reason other than to check in and see if I was okay. That's the kind of guy he was. The last time I'd seen him was at Neil's memorial, when he said to me in my grief, "I'm hip to you. You sit there very quietly, but every now and then you say something that tells me you're a *badass*." He cared about people—and, of course, about music—nudging me a few months later to "get that Lamborghini out of the garage!" Above all else he loved to play and was an effin' *monster* of a drummer. "Exuberant" doesn't do justice to his nature. How about "euphoric"? How about "explosive"? I've rarely met anyone so full of energy. There's barely a photo of him in which he's not wearing that megawatt smile. It's hard to accept that someone who was so vivacious, so full of life, has died. A rock and roller to his core, right to the end.

In September 2022, Alex and I participated in two extravagant tributes that Dave Grohl organized for Taylor—the first at London's Wembley Arena and the second at the Forum in LA. Both shows were hugely emotional experiences. I was surrounded by many fantastic musicians and friends sharing an abundance of love and talent, but the entire day in Los Angeles I was not myself.

It was, of course, on that very stage that Lerxst, Pratt and I had played our final show. But after I returned home, I began to understand that there was something eating at me even deeper down . . . After I lost my father when I was twelve, I was trained to mourn. The dogma and rituals of the Jewish faith taught me that when you lose someone close you don't simply move on. It's a matter of showing proper respect both for the dead and for your own feelings. Neil was more than a friend to me; he was a mentor, a partner, a *brother*, and as such I had lost yet another family member. Considering him in that light, I was suddenly able to see why I had reacted to his passing so . . . well . . . *gravely*, and why I felt entirely unable to so much as think about making music. My training had forbidden it. So for me that gig in LA also marked, at long last, the end of my shiva both for Neil and for my band. As a wise rabbi once told me, it was time to turn from grief to remembrance.

So, on to the future! I still have ants in my pants, and so does my lovely partner, Nancy, and there remain so many places on the face of the earth to wander. If I've learned anything from these last two years, it's the value of time, and that before I commit to *any* project, I have to consider her life as well as mine. She spent too many years being my plus-one and letting me put the band first. That's over now. We decide what we want to do together, and whatever big idea I come up with will just have to fit into *her* schedule too. Thankfully, she's still a woman who enjoys her independence and is happy to be rid of me from time to time — I say "happy," but that woman knows me well enough to understand that, however she feels, there will *always* be something lurking around the corner to whisk me away.

It bothers me that writing this book has meant spending so much time living in the past. I've never lived my life looking anywhere but forward, which is why I resisted doing this kind of thing for so long. Being in a band all those years was reassuring because it was an ongoing thing. It felt like it was forever. There was always unfinished business: the next record, the next set design, the next tour. I learned long ago that it's best to stop work when you know where you're going to pick up from the following day. It's been the theme of my life. But you need a lot more determination to proceed in the world of music without the comfort of your bandmates, and I can only hope that finishing this book will release me to return to what I do and love best.

Having said that, at my tender age my "extracurricular" creative interests — writing books, travelling, bird photography, collecting baseball memorabilia, oh, and drinking good wine — have become almost as important to me as writing music. Of course these things do not inspire the same visceral reaction and ego-feeding aggrandizement as a roaring live audience does, but in many ways they're as satisfying to the soul. There's a more contemplative creative pleasure to working alone. Photography is by necessity a more singular and solitary expression, not "art by committee" the way making a record is, and it's profoundly nourishing for me at this stage in life to be able to have that kind of creative conversation with myself. And if I really like the resulting work, well, that's an awesome bonus, ain't it!

Regardless, I confess that I could not imagine my life without the sweaty interaction and joy I get from writing a good piece of music or performing it well live, especially alongside people I love and respect. Some musicians like to write and record alone and have actually thrived during the pandemic, receiving files by email, adding their own ideas to songs and sending them back down the cyber pipe, but for me the chemistry of working with another human—face-to-face, side by side, laugh by laugh, watching the sparks fly—is what I dig the most and what I think captures the real spirit of rock and roll. The idea of me never doing that again is just plain wrong! Nothing replaces that feeling of being mid-song pumping out a complex series of riffs, lost in the moment, while trying to sing in tune. You can't effin' beat it!

ONE OF COVID'S few silver linings has been the time it's given me to spend with my grandson. Finnian's a remarkable little soul, oblivious to what I've done with my life but whose presence instantly pumps me up with optimism and hope for the future. There's nothing like a grandchild to make you aware of life's full circle. I recently took him to the Toronto cemetery where much of my family is buried. Near the plots that hold my parents is a large monument dedicated to the Jews from my mom's town of Wierzbnik, who were killed during its liquidation in 1942. I showed it to Finnian so he could see one name etched there: that of my namesake and his great-great-grandfather Gershon Eliezer. He was puzzled by the Hebrew version, so I told him it translates to Gary

Lee, my birth name before I changed it to Geddy. His eyes widened, then he smiled and said cheekily, "Hi, *Gary.*" He saw straight through all my alter egos, alternate names and nicknames, right to my essence. Can't fool him!

What an amazing character he is. For one thing, from his earliest days, he's seemed to understand irony, which I think is unusual for a child. He always gets my jokes and bats them back at me, as together we perfect the Art of Being Silly. He's eight now and loves to read; his parents—who are both educators—instilled a great love of books in him, largely by strictly limiting his screen time. He loves science. When the adults all gathered at his birthday party recently and called out to him to play with us, he was like, "Nah . . . Got new books." When I started giving him books on birds, he'd devour them in bed at night. One featured buttons you'd press to hear the birdsongs, and he's memorized them all. We were walking in the woods at the cottage together recently when I said, "Stop! Listen, Finn . . . What do you think that is?"

He rolled his eyes and said, "Zaidy, that's just a *robin.*"

"Are you sure?" I said. "I don't *think* so . . ." and insisted we go in search of it. Sure enough, as we snuck up to a tree, there it was, the robin sitting on the branch. He's infuriatingly correct.

Then one lazy afternoon during the first lockdown, we were whiling away the time reading and got to talking about outer space and galaxies. I mentioned that there was a small star, very far away, that was actually named after me.[*]

Of course he didn't believe me, so I googled it to show him.

He looked at me in wonder and said, "Wow, Zaidy. One day you're gonna be *famous.*"

---

[*] The Royal Astronomical Society of Canada also named one for Lerxst and one for Pratt; mine is Asteroid 12272 Geddylee.

# ACKNOWLEDGMENTS

---

*For the Holocaust chapter, I would like to thank:*

My siblings, Susie and Allan, and my brother-in-law Arthur Gitajn for their unwavering support and contributions.

Christopher R. Browning for his well-researched and well-reasoned book *Remembering Survival: Inside a Nazi Slave-Labor Camp*, which brought to light the lives and deaths of so many, including members of my own family, who would otherwise have remained in shadow.

The extensive, illuminating, heartbreaking and invaluable collection of personal stories compiled in *Wierzbnik-Starachowitz; a memorial book (Wierzbnik, Poland)*.

Abe Glowinsky for the introduction to Matan Shefi with the Muzeum Historii ydów Polskich POLIN, and Maciej Wzorek (researcher at the POLIN museum Resource Center Warsaw) for providing invaluable information and documents outlining my family history.

The Shoah Foundation for helping to ensure that the voices of the past are not forgotten.

Daniel Patt and his incredible project "Numbers-to-Names" for using AI technology to track down photographic evidence of my family's post-WWII experiences.

---

# *Acknowledgments*

---

*And for this book as a whole:*

As ever, Nancy Young, my magnanimous, vivacious and long-suffering companion for the last thousand years, for making our life together anything but dull, and then letting me write about it! And, of course, my wonderful, not-quite-as-long-suffering children.

The dozens of crew members, assistants, management personnel, technicians and professionals so essential to me getting on with my effin' life but whose names have barely graced the pages of this book . . . You all deserve so much more space than I was able to give you.

The Above and Beyond department: the indefatigable Richard Sibbald. Noah Eaker, Lynne Yeamans, and the good folks at HarperCollins. Paul Kepple at Headcase. Ron Eckel at Cooke International, Meghan Symsyk and Sheila Posner, and my archivist, Veronica Sinnaeve.

My friend, cowriter, editor, grammar instructor, literary mentor and unwitting instigator of this memoir: Daniel Richler. This book would simply not exist without his "evocations" and would not be what it is without his good humour and ever-watchful eye.

And last but not least, my soul brothers Alex and Neil for being such bloody good and hilarious partners, and for putting up with a half-century of Mr. Bossypants.

---

# PHOTOGRAPHIC CREDITS

**Ace Frehley:** color insert #2/page 4 (top right)

**Alex Lifeson:** color insert #2/ page 8 (left), color insert #3/page 6 (top), 329 (left, middle, right), 363 (left, right), 366, 472, color insert #4/page 1 (bottom middle)

**Allan Weinrib:** 80 (right)

**Andrew MacNaughtan:** 278, 315 (bottom right), color insert #3/page 6 (bottom), color insert #3/page 7 (top), 355, 361, 368, 375, 379 (top left, top right, bottom left, bottom right), 412, 413, 450 (left, right), 498

**Anthony Brown, Susie Brown:** color insert #1/page 1 (top, bottom)

**Arnold Bauer Barach—United States Holocaust Memorial Museum:** 77 (left)

**Barry Philp / Getty Images:** 26

**Bill Hawryschuk:** 208

**Copyright Patrick Harbron/ rockandrollicons.com:** 219, 226 (bottom)

**Courtesy of Anthem Core Music Publishing:** 196 (top left, top right, bottom left)

**Courtesy of SRO/YYZ Entertainment Group Inc.:** 196 (bottom right)

**Craig M. Renwick:** 470 (top right, middle right, bottom), color insert #4/page 1 (top)

**Dale Heslip:** color insert #4/page 3 (top)

**David Gahr Archive/Rock Negatives:** 159, 174 (top, middle, bottom)

**Deborah Samuel:** 307 (top, middle, bottom), color insert #3/page 4 (bottom)

**Dimo Safari:** 308 (top), color insert #3/page 5 (top left, top right, bottom)

**Donovan Lundstrom:** color insert #4/page 4 (top left), 482 (top left, top right, middle), 482 (bottom right)

**Ed Rottinger:** color insert #2/page 5 (middle, bottom)

**Everett Collection Inc / Alamy Stock Photo:** 315 (bottom left)

**Fin Costello / Getty Images:** 238 (top, bottom), 260 (left), 290 (top left, top right, middle, bottom left), 314, 315 (top left)

**Geddy Lee:** 41, 76 (left, right), 77 (right), 80 (left), 81 (top left, top right, middle left, bottom left, bottom right, 134 (bottom left, bottom middle), 156 (left), 165, 170 (top left, top right, middle, bottom left, bottom right), 178, 184 (left, right), 190 (left), 203, color insert #2/page 1 (top left, top right, middle, bottom left, bottom right), color insert #2/page 2 (middle left, middle middle, middle right, bottom left, bottom right), color insert #2/ page 3 (middle left, middle middle, middle right), color insert #2/page 4 (top left), color insert #2/page 6 (top right, middle left, bottom right), color insert #2/page 7 (middle left, middle right, bottom left, bottom right), color insert #2/page 8 (top right, upper middle right, lower middle right, bottom right), 228 (left, right), 245, 290 (bottom right), 298 (left), 304, 306 (top left), 316, color insert #3/page 1 (top left, top right, middle left, middle right), color insert #3/page 2 (top left, middle left, middle right, bottom, top left), color insert #3/page 3 (middle right), color insert #3/page 8 (top middle, top right, middle middle, middle right), 323, 335 (top, middle left, middle right, bottom left, bottom right), 341 (right), 354, 367, 384 (top), 386, 408 (bottom), 445, 457 (left), 462 (top, middle, bottom), color insert #4/page 1 (bottom left, bottom right), 497

**Geddy Lee Archive:** 8, 10, 12, 14, 16, 18, 22 (bottom), 33, 37, 56, 69, 72 (left, right), 74 (top left, top right, bottom), 83, 90, 96, 101, 103, 108 (bottom), 113, 121, 122, color insert #1/page 2 (top left, top right, bottom left, bottom right), color insert #1/page 3 (top left, top right, middle left, middle right, bottom left, bottom middle, bottom right), color insert #1/ page 4 (top, middle, bottom), color insert #1/ page 5 (middle), 133 (top, middle, bottom), 134 (bottom right), 142 (top left, top right, bottom left, bottom right), 172, 180, color insert #2/ page 2 (top left, top right), color insert #2/ page 3, bottom right, color insert #2/page 4 (middle, bottom right), color insert #2/page 5 (top), color insert #2/page 6 (top left, middle right), color insert #2/page 7 (top left, top right), 233, 236 (top, middle, bottom), 248 (top left), 262 (top, middle, bottom), 281, 283, 292, 294, 300, color insert #3/page 1 (bottom), color insert #3/page 3 (bottom), color insert #3/page 8 (middle left, bottom middle, bottom right), 341 (left), 343, 384 (bottom), 389 (left, right), 403, 408 (top), 427 (bottom), color insert #4/page 2 (top right, middle right)

**Hugh Syme:** 446

**Jeff Ervin:** 192 (top, bottom)

**John Arrowsmith:** 356, 427 (top, middle), 466 (top) , color insert #4/page 1 (middle), color insert #4/page 8 (top, bottom), 482 (bottom left)

**John Catto:** 151 (top, middle right)

**Larry Back:** color insert #1/page 5 (top)

**"Map: Wierzbnik-Starachowice: Ghetto, Factories and Camps,"** from REMEMBERING SURVIVAL: INSIDE A NAZI SLAVE-LABOR CAMP by Christopher Browning. Copyright © 2010 by Christopher R. Browning. Used by permission of W. W. Norton & Company, Inc.: 52

**Melody Maker:** 248 (top right)

**Michael Capotosto:** 179 (top, middle, bottom)

**Michael Mosbach:** 428 (bottom)

**Mike Curran:** color insert #3/page 8 (top left, bottom left), 436

**MRossi:** 423 (bottom)

**Muzeum Historii żydów Polskich POLIN:** (top, middle, bottom)

**Nancy Crompton / Gaby Landry:** color insert #1/page 5 (bottom)

**Nancy Young:** 3, 123, 126 (top left, bottom left, bottom right), 128, color insert #1/ page 8 (top), 298 (right), 486

**Neil Peart:** 303 (top right, middle left, middle right, bottom left), color insert #3/page 3 (middle left), 485 (top, middle, bottom)

**Nick Raskulinecz:** color insert #4/page 2 (top left, middle left, bottom)

**Nigel Scott:** 22 (top)

**Norma V. Toraya / Crankbunny:** color insert #4/page 3 (middle, bottom)

**Ossie Parsons:** 134 (top left, top right, middle left, middle right)

**Oscar Peterson Jr.:** 126 (top right)

**Paolo Rizzo:** color insert #3/page 7 (bottom)

**Photo by Joyce True, used courtesy of Fender:** 226 (top)

**Pinkpop Festival:** color insert #3/page 4 (top left)

**Randy Johnson:** 466 (bottom)

**REUTERS / Alamy Stock Photo:** 423, 470 (top left)

**Richard Sibbald:** color insert #1/page 6 (top), 303 (bottom left), 371, 392, 401, 473, color insert #4/page 4 (top middle, middle right), color insert #4/page 5 (top, bottom), color insert #4/page 6/7, 512 (final image)

**Richard Sibbald, Veronica Sinnaeve:** endpapers

**Roger Stowell:** 261

**Shawn O'Hearn:** 457 (right)

**Sheila Posner:** color insert #1/page 8 (bottom)

**Sounds Magazine:** 248 (bottom left, bottom right)

**SRO / Rush Archive:** 1, 98, 108 (top), color insert #1/page 6 (bottom), color insert #1/ page 7, 136, 137, 139, 141 (top, middle, bottom), 146, 148, 150, 151 (bottom), 156 (right), 162, 181, 190 (right), color insert #2/page 3 (bottom left), color insert #2/page 6 (bottom left), 229 (top, bottom), 260 (right), 308 (bottom), 315 (top right), color insert #3/page 4 (top right), 321, 337, 374, 428 (top), 470 (middle left), color insert #4/page 4 (middle left, bottom)

**Sulfiati Magnuson / Getty Images:** 87

**Terrance Bert:** 193, 206 (top left, top right, bottom)

**Town of Cochrane:** color insert #2/page 3 (top left)

**Yaël Brandeis Perry:** 301, 306 (top right, middle, bottom), 318